# MARKETING PLANNING

## Where Strategy Meets Action

Stephan Sorger
*University of California*

Boston   Columbus   Indianapolis   New York   San Francisco   Upper Saddle River
Amsterdam   Cape Town   Dubai   London   Madrid   Milan   Munich   Paris   Montreal   Toronto
Delhi   Mexico City   Sao Paulo   Sydney   Hong Kong   Seoul   Singapore   Taipei   Tokyo

Editorial Director: Sally Yagan
Editor-in-Chief: Eric Svendsen
Director of Editorial Services: Ashley Santora
Editorial Project Manager: Kierra Bloom
Director of Marketing: Patrice Jones
Marketing Manager: Anne Fahlgren
Production Project Manager: Renata Butera
Creative Art Director: Jayne Conte
Image Permission Coordinator: Karen Sanatar

Cover Designer: Suzanne Behnke
Cover Art: ©ImageZoo/Alamy
Full-Service Project Management: Shiny Rajesh,
    Integra Software Services, Pvt. Ltd.
Composition: Integra Software Services, Pvt. Ltd.
Printer/Binder: R.R. Donnelley/Crawfordsville
Cover Printer: Lehigh-Phoenix Color
Text Font: 10/12, Times

Credits and acknowledgments borrowed from other sources and reproduced, with permission, in this textbook appear on appropriate page within text.

**Library of Congress Cataloging-in-Publication Data**
Sorger, Stephan.
    Marketing planning: where strategy meets action/Stephan Sorger.—1st ed.
        p. cm.
    ISBN-13: 978-0-13-254470-2 (alk. paper)
    ISBN-10: 0-13-254470-9 (alk. paper)
    1. Marketing—Management. 2. Strategic planning. I. Title.
    HF5415.13.S637 2012
    658.8'02—dc23

                                        2011019814

10 9 8 7 6 5 4 3 2 1

**PEARSON**

ISBN 10:      0-13-254470-9
ISBN 13: 978-0-13-254470-2

## Dedication

*This book is dedicated to the memory of my father, Dr. Gunther U. Sorger*

# BRIEF CONTENTS

# Contents

# CONTENTS

# CHAPTER 6: Strategy 104

# CHAPTER 7: Products and Services 130

# PREFACE

## Purpose

The purpose of this book is to give marketing students and professionals a practical, step-by-step guide to creating marketing plans that deliver results. Using this book, you will learn how to develop strategic marketing plans twice as good as typical plans, in half the time.

## Marketing Planning

Marketing planning is the process of developing documents that propose concrete, measurable actions to accomplish specific marketing objectives. Marketing plans are the means by which organizational strategies are translated into actions that deliver results.

Yet many organizations rely solely on fill-in-the-blanks marketing plan templates or type-in-the-fields marketing plan software, which can lead to overly simplistic plans that are not perceived as credible. Alternatively, companies can build high quality plans from scratch with no tools to guide them except for basic marketing theories, but such an approach can consume large amounts of time that today's busy executives just do not have. In a world where marketing professionals are being asked to do more with less, neither alternative is acceptable.

This book fills the gap between theory-based and template-based methods by introducing a new, more effective approach to strategic marketing planning.

## A New Approach to Marketing Planning

This book differentiates itself from other books on the topic in its unique new approach to marketing planning:

**Easy to Use.** The book includes clear, step-by-step instructions, with helpful examples throughout.

**Practical.** The book is organized in the same order as the marketing plan, allowing readers to develop each section of the plan as they progress through the book.

**Insightful.** The book interprets proven marketing information in an insightful way to provide guidance to readers on the planning process and help them see the whole picture.

**Current.** The book is packed with current examples, demonstrating how the topics discussed in the book relate to the real-life situations faced by many different types of organizations.

**Comprehensive.** The book covers planning for both products and services, with examples and sample plans for each. In addition, the book addresses both B2C (business to consumer) and B2B (business to business) scenarios for maximum versatility.

**Effective.** The book leverages solid marketing theory and sound organizational practice in a new way to produce effective plans that transform strategy into actions that deliver results.

## Intended Audiences

This book is intended for three markets:

**Undergraduate courses involving marketing planning.**   This book is ideal as the principal textbook for courses dedicated to marketing planning. Alternatively, this book can be used as a supplementary textbook for courses which include a marketing plan as part of the course, such as Strategic Marketing. This book is relevant for the following courses:

- **Business Planning**
- **Capstone Marketing Course**
- **Entrepreneurship**
- **Marketing Management**
- **Marketing Planning**
- **Marketing Strategy and Planning**
- **New Product Development**
- **Strategic Marketing**
- **Services Management**
- **Strategic Planning**

**Graduate courses involving marketing planning.**   The book can also be used in graduate course programs that include marketing planning in their curricula. For example, many master of business administration (MBA) programs feature introductory marketing courses that assign marketing plans as the final project.

**Business professionals involved in marketing planning.**   Business professionals seeking a competitive edge in the speed and quality of their marketing planning will benefit from the techniques shown in this book. Virtually anyone involved in planning will find this book indispensable, such as:

- **Chief Executive Officers**
- **Chief Marketing Officers**
- **Chief Operating Officers**
- **Entrepreneurs**
- **Marketing Managers**
- **Product Managers**
- **Strategic Planning Managers**
- **Vice Presidents of Marketing**
- **Vice Presidents of Sales**

## Learning Features

The book employs several features to enhance learning:

**Chapter Checklist.**  Each chapter starts with a checklist of topics to be covered.

**Decision Charts.**  Chapter figures include decision charts showing recommended ways to apply different marketing techniques based on different situations.

**Examples.** Current examples are presented to contextualize learning.

**Exercises.** Discussion questions and problems are included to assess understanding.

**Key Terms.** Principal marketing terms are listed at the end of each chapter.

**Practical Planning.** Each chapter shows how its concepts are applied to a marketing plan.

**Marketing Plan Samples.** In addition to the Practical Planning marketing planning samples in each chapter, the book culminates with two versions of a complete sample marketing plan.

**Summaries.** Each chapter ends with a summary to help digest the chapter's topics.

## Instructor Supplements

**Instructor Manual:** This instructor's manual includes chapter outlines, answers to all end-of-chapter questions, and additional activities and assignments for your students. This manual can be downloaded from www.pearsonhighered.com/irc

**Test Item File:** This Test Item File contains multiple-choice, true/false, and essay questions. Each question is followed by the correct answer, page reference, AACSB category, question type (concept, application, critical thinking, or synthesis), and difficulty rating. It has been thoroughly reviewed by an assessment experts. The Test Item File is available for download at www.pearsonhighered.com/irc

**TestGen**: Pearson Education's test-generating software is available at www.pearsonhighered.com/irc. The software is PC/MAC compatible and preloaded with all of the Test Item File questions. You can manually or randomly view test questions and drag and drop to create a test. You can add or modify test-bank questions as needed. Our TestGens are converted for use in BlackBoard, WebCT, Angel, D2L, and Moodle. All conversions are available on the IRC.

**PowerPoint Presentation:** This presentation includes basic outlines and key points from each chapter and figures from the text.

# ACKNOWLEDGMENTS

The author is indebted to many people for the successful creation of this book. The book started out as a draft textbook for the author's course in Strategic Marketing Planning at the University of California, Berkeley Extension, and was forged into the book you read today as a result of the feedback of many impressive individuals.

Jim Prost, adjunct professor of the University of San Francisco, provided insightful feedback on the initial manuscript and championed the book's publishing. University of California, Berkeley Extension program director Tom McGuire inspired me in the way he skillfully administers the many departments under his leadership—business, management, marketing, entrepreneurship, and more. Of course, I want to thank the students in my Strategic Marketing Planning courses for their comments on the early drafts of the book and their feedback on the effectiveness of the planning process as applied in their own organizations.

In addition to the world of academia, I wish to thank the organizations with which I have been involved, such as Oracle, 3Com (now part of Hewlett-Packard), and NASA (National Aeronautics and Space Administration), where I implemented many of the methods outlined in this book to develop successful plans. The book's approach thus combines the rigor of academia with real-world experience gained from actual practice in professional organizations.

The author and the publisher would also like to thank the following reviewers for their time and valuable feedback:

Valerie Ellis, Santa Barbara City College
Dan Pyle Millar, University of Indianapolis
Talai Osmonbekov, Northern Arizona University
Rodney Oudan, Worcester State College
J. Alexander Smith, Oklahoma City University
Heather Weubker, Adams State College

The talented staff at Pearson Prentice Hall deserves praise for their role in shaping the book. In particular, I wish to thank Melissa Sabella, executive editor; Eric Svendsen, editor-in-chief; Laura Fischer, editor; Kierra Bloom, project manager; and, last but certainly not least, Gina Gimelli, evangelist of the Pearson brand to many of the top universities in the land.

# ABOUT THE AUTHOR

**Stephan Sorger**, M.S., M.B.A., became one of the leading authorities in marketing planning by combining expertise from three disciplines. First, he honed his skills as a strategic planning practitioner in leadership roles at some of the world's most innovative organizations such as Oracle, 3Com (now part of Hewlett-Packard), and NASA. Second, he develops marketing planning and strategy for companies seeking to accelerate revenue in his role as partner at strategic consulting firm On Demand Advisors (OnDemandAdvisors.com). And third, he has been teaching marketing planning courses, as well as courses in marketing analytics, marketing research, brand management, and new product development since 2003 at the University of California, Berkeley Extension. His educational background includes a bachelor's degree in engineering from California Polytechnic State University and master's degrees in electrical engineering, aerospace engineering, and business administration from the University of Southern California. For more information, please visit his website at StephanSorger.com.

# MARKETING PLANNING

# 1

# The Planning Process

## INTRODUCTION

Marketing plans translate organizational strategy into actions that deliver business results.

## CHAPTER CHECKLIST

We cover the following marketing plan section in this chapter:

❏ **Outline**: Structure of the marketing plan, which we use to build the plan

# What is a Marketing Plan?

A **marketing plan** is a written document that covers the situation, strategy, and tactics to accomplish a specified set of objectives within the time period covered by the plan. The plan can be seen as a blueprint for a marketing project, with objectives, tactics, and implementation details to ensure a successful outcome.[1]

---

**Effective marketing plans act as a blueprint for success**
*Source:* iStockphoto

---

Marketing plans are in written format, instead of verbal, because when marketers develop ideas on paper it is easier to circulate the plan among cross-functional group members, aiding collaboration.

In the definition, the term "organization" can be viewed in different ways, depending on what is to be accomplished with the plan.

- **Small Companies (like start-ups)**: Marketing plan for the entire firm
- **Large Companies (like IBM)**: Marketing plan for a strategic business unit (SBU)
- **Product/Service Companies**: Marketing plan for specific products or services

---

### Key Terms

**Marketing planning**   Process of creating written documents covering the situation, objectives, and actions for an organization for time period covered by the plan.

The time period covered by the plan depends on the volatility of that organization's market:

- **Annual Planning Cycle**: Sufficient for stable, well-established markets like industrial products
- **Quarterly Planning Cycle**: Recommended for dynamic markets, such as high technology
- **Ad hoc Marketing Plans**: Recommended to take advantage of market opportunities

Marketing plans can be written by different people in the organization, depending on the situation:

- **Small Companies:** Marketing plans are often written by the chief executive officer (CEO) or the vice-president of marketing.
- **Large Companies**: Often product managers or product marketing managers write marketing plans. In some companies, planning is performed by a dedicated planning department.
- **All Companies**: The best person to write the plan is the person who will lead the marketing effort once the plan has been completed and approved. This person is often referred to as the owner of the plan.

Marketing plans are similar to business plans in that they both map out the strategy to achieve a productive end. Unlike business plans, marketing plans do not include details on non-marketing-related activities such as operations and human resources.

## Marketing Planning in Action

**Nintendo Wii: Game Changer**. Nintendo observed a market opportunity and took advantage of it. At the time, console makers focused on killer processing power, high definition graphics, and Wi-Fi connectivity to win in the console wars. But Nintendo planned a different approach—target the casual gamer with an easy-to-play, interactive experience. In fact, Nintendo's development team concluded that "while we needed adequate processing power, there was a threshold beyond which customers didn't really need more"—heresy to the competitor's focus on speed and power. Another recommendation was the focus on non-hardcore gamers. As Nintendo president Satoru Iwata said, the Wii was "designed to appeal even to people who aren't interested in games." Time has shown that Nintendo's recommendations were sound, emphasizing ease of use over processor muscle and high-end graphics. The Wii turned out to be a game changer in the industry.[2]

## Advantages of Effective Planning

Figure 1.1 shows several advantages of effective planning. For example, the marketing planning process can identify potential new opportunities or threats that may adjust the organization's strategies to the market. In addition, it encourages active collaboration among groups, a topic we discuss further in the next section.[3]

**Figure 1.1** Advantages of Good Marketing Planning

| Advantage | Description |
| --- | --- |
| Discipline | Forces a disciplined approach to a market; can avoid the omission of a key aspect of the market and ensure a consistent approach across the organization when multiple groups participate in the planning process. |
| New Opportunities | Identifies potential new opportunities |
| New Competitors | Identifies potential new competitors |
| Clear Objectives | Establishes specific objectives and targets, laying the foundation to successful execution of the plan |
| Clear Programs | Lays out specific programs that contribute to the execution of the plan |
| Clear Responsibilities | Identifies specific responsibilities throughout the organization, ensuring that everyone knows what their role is and reducing potential conflicts |
| Clear Metrics | Quantifies success/ failure metrics |
| Customer Focus | Provides new information on customers, ways to segment them, and different approaches to serve their needs |
| Cross-Functional | Identifies involvement by other departments |

## Marketing Planning in Action

**Nintendo Wii: Battling the Market Leaders**. A well-conceived marketing plan was vital for Nintendo for its new Wii product, because of the competitive nature of the market. Microsoft (Xbox), Sony (PlayStation), and Nintendo (Wii) are all strong competitors with substantial experience in the industry. Each has its own competitive advantage—Microsoft with its strong selection of game titles, Sony with its realistic graphics system, and Nintendo with its emphasis on interactive motion control. Blogs covering the video game market reported that Nintendo's intent with the Wii was to create a unit that was family-friendly, where the fun factor of an interactive experience was more important than stellar graphics. As a result, Nintendo's main target customers were adults. Eighty percent of Nintendo's marketing budget was allocated toward convincing adults to purchase the system, shaking off Nintendo's traditional consumer perception of being for children and teens.[4, 5]

# Cross-functional Collaboration

Effective marketing planning demands **collaboration** across departments or groups within the organization throughout the entire planning process to gain buy-in on the plan. As Figure 1.2 shows, cross-functional collaboration is a vital element of modern organizations. Without buy-in from key stakeholders, even the most carefully prepared plan is doomed to failure.

**Figure 1.2** Cross-functional Collaboration

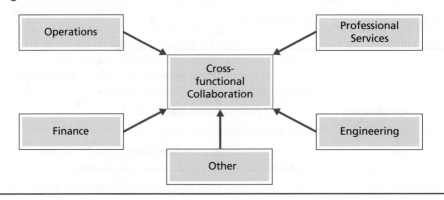

Figure 1.3 shows the inputs the stakeholder groups can provide to the plan, as well as how the output from the plan can affect the groups. For example, a marketing plan for a hotel chain requires collaboration with the hotel operations group. The input to the plan would be the group's cost structure of operations (costs to manage lobby areas, housekeeping, and so on). As an output from the plan, the operations group might be required to hire and train additional staff to support a recommended hotel expansion.

**Figure 1.3** Impact of Organizational Functions on Marketing Plan

| Group | Input into Marketing Plan | Output from Marketing Plan |
| --- | --- | --- |
| Operations | Cost structure for operations | Marketing plan sales forecast, which will drive the operations schedule |
| Finance | Required return on investment for new projects (sometimes called hurdle rate) | Financial break-even for new projects; Cost of goods sold; Funding required to develop new products and services |
| Professional Services | Implementation capabilities | New services and products to implement |
| Engineering | Customer feedback on services or products delivered to customers; Technological expertise | Specific services or product features demanded by market and overall plan for coming planning period |
| Other | Marketing staff and CEO/COO office could have specific requirements to support company-wide objectives | Marketing plan can impact HR hiring requirements and other groups |

## Marketing Planning in Action

**Nintendo Wii: Collaboration Leads to Cash**. Thanks to cross-functional collaboration and careful design, Nintendo's Wii can be produced at a relatively low cost. Because of its low costs, Nintendo makes profit on every Wii console sold, unlike Sony, which loses money on its Playstation console, hoping to make up the loss on sales of PlayStation video games. Because of its high popularity, Nintendo sold nearly 35 million Wii consoles by the end of 2008, including 12.6 million in the United States, Nintendo's biggest market. Nintendo also makes money from its games. Its three top-selling games—"Wii Play," "Super Smash Brothers Brawl," and "Super Mario Galaxy"—are all Nintendo's own titles. Compare that with the top three PlayStation games—"Grand Theft Auto IV," "Call of Duty 4," and "Assassin's Creed," which are all from outside developers, not from Sony.[6]

Cross-functional collaboration is vital to achieving buy-in for marketing plans
*Source:* Shutterstock

# The Marketing Planning Process

As Figure 1.4 shows, the marketing planning process used in this book consists of several steps, as described below. For an alternative approach to the marketing planning process, see Tim Calkins's book, *Breakthrough Marketing Plans*, for his GOST (goals and objectives, strategic initiatives, and tactics) framework.[7]

**Objectives**: First, we set objectives for the plan's project, based on the organization's mission and competitive advantage.

**Figure 1.4** The Marketing Planning Process

**Market Opportunities**: Next, we determine potentially profitable opportunities in the market, based on a review of market overview data, targeted market segments, and competitive landscape.

**Strategy**: We select our strategy, considering the objectives we want to achieve and the market opportunities available to us.

**Marketing Mix**: The **marketing mix** is the combination of elements we will use to execute the plan's strategy. The marketing mix is also called the 4Ps: product (or service), price, place (distribution), and promotion.

**Finance and Implementation**: We execute on the plan, allocating financial resources to it, controlling it by monitoring key marketing metrics, and enabling contingency plans if (or when!) things go wrong.

## Marketing Planning in Action

**Nintendo Wii: Success Step by Step**: Nintendo addressed multiple marketing planning steps in the development of its Wii video game console. The first step was developing the Wii's objective, which was to increase sales through a unique differentiator—its unique interactive controller. The second step was determining the strategies, in this case targeting casual gamers with its new offering, avoiding the graphics war between Microsoft and Sony. As Reginald Fils-Aime, president and chief operating officer (COO) of Nintendo of America, stated, "I think our two competitors will trade share between them, while we go off and grab share in a completely different way." The third step was developing the marketing mix, with a compelling product, a user-friendly price, familiar distribution channels, and promotion programs that highlighted its new Wii controller. The fourth step was implementation, where video game industry blogs estimate that Nintendo budgeted over $200 million in marketing costs to make its Wii a success.[8, 9]

# Marketing Plan Outline

The **marketing plan outline** follows the marketing planning process. Throughout the planning process, the marketer must make many decisions about how the organization's offerings will be marketed. The following sections make up the plan:

**Executive Summary**: This section gives the reader a quick overview of the plan. It should only be one or two pages in length. Although it appears first, it is written last, after all the other sections have been prepared and the writer is in a good position to summarize the plan.

**Objectives**:  This section covers the goals of the marketing plan project, reflecting the mission and competitive advantages of the organization.

**Market Overview**:  This section provides a sketch of the market in which the plan is to be implemented. We establish market characteristics such as size, growth rate, and trends.

**Market Segments**:  This section examines the separate groups that make up the market, and addresses positioning approaches for the segments.

**Competitive Landscape**:  This section surveys the organization's competition, and addresses strategies to take advantage of market opportunities.

**Strategy:**  This section leverages the market opportunities discovered in the previous section to determine a general approach to accomplishing the plan's objectives.

**Products/Services**:  With this section, we begin our focus on the marketing mix, starting with the tactics the organization will use to develop products and services for the market. [10]

**Price**:  The second portion of the marketing mix covers the tactics to establish pricing objectives and set the price.

**Place (Distribution)**:  With this section, we begin our focus on the marketing mix, starting with the tactics on how the organization will communicate the benefits of its products or services.

**Promotion:**  The final portion of the marketing mix covers the tactics on how the organization will communicate the benefits of its products or services.

**Finance**:  This section develops a financial analysis, including break-even, pro forma income statement, and budget.

**Implementation**:  This section discusses tools to ensure successful implementation of the plan, including schedules, control metrics, and contingency plans.

**Recommendations**:  This section is optional. It provides any additional information deemed vital by the plan's writer to include, such as prioritization of effort and/or sense of urgency.

Figure 1.5 summarizes the outline of the marketing plan. The remainder of the book will cover each one of the marketing plan sections in detail. In general, each chapter will be dedicated to a specific section or subsection. In this way, you can develop your own marketing plan section-by-section as you read this book.

## Key Terms

**Collaboration**   Working with key stakeholders in different departments in the organization, which can help gain buy-in for the marketing plan.

**Marketing mix**   Mix of controllable marketing variables to implement marketing strategy. Most common classification is called the four Ps: product, price, place, and promotion.

**Marketing plan outline**   The structure of a marketing plan, generally beginning with the executive summary, then describing the market and the strategy used to take advantages within it, followed by the marketing tactics and other tools to implement the strategy.

**Figure 1.5** Marketing Plan Outline

| Section | Description |
|---|---|
| Executive Summary | Encapsulates plan, emphasizing objectives (project objectives and fit with company's objectives), financials (budget requirements and projected revenue), and logistics (project staffing and duration) |
| Objectives | States goal of marketing plan project. |
| Market Overview | Determines market characteristics such as size, growth rate, and trends. |
| Market Segments | Covers market segmentation, targeting, and positioning. |
| Competitive Landscape | Gathers information about the company and its competitors, with the objective of completing a competitive comparison framework. |
| Strategy | Establishes strategy to accomplish the plan's objectives, while taking advantage of potentially profitable market opportunities. |
| Products/ Services | Covers tactics to develop products and services for the market |
| Price | Addresses tactics to establish pricing objectives, approaches, and set price |
| Place (Distribution) | Covers tactics to distribute organization's products or services to the customer |
| Promotion | Determines how to convey product or service's benefits to the market |
| Finance | Covers financial analysis, including break-even, pro forma income statement, and budget |
| Implementation | Discusses tools to ensure successful implementation of plan |
| Recommendations | (Optional section) Includes any specific recommendations, such as top three most important actions to take, implementation suggestions, and sense of urgency |

## Book Organization

The book follows the marketing plan outline. After covering the outline of the plan in this chapter, the remaining chapters cover the major sections of the plan:

**Chapter 1: The Planning Process** The first chapter introduces marketing planning and outlines the steps to complete the plan.

**Chapter 2: Objectives** The second chapter covers how to develop actionable objectives for the plan.

**Chapters 3–5: Market Overview, Market Segments, and Competitive Landscape** Together, these chapters make up a streamlined version of the situation analysis. The **situation analysis** covers the external and internal situations facing the company. It describes the market and the forces shaping it, the customer segments, and the competitive landscape (an analysis of the company and its competitors). The analysis will help us find opportunities in the market.

**Figure 1.6** Book Organization around the Marketing Planning Process

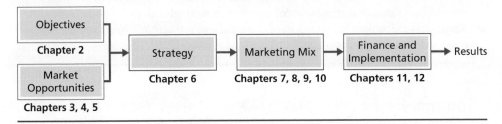

**Chapter 6: Strategy** This chapter shows how to establish strategy for the plan's project that will achieve the plan's objectives while taking advantage of potentially profitable market opportunities uncovered in the situation analysis.

**Chapters 7–10: Products and Services, Pricing, Distribution, and Promotion** These chapters cover the marketing mix elements for the plan.

**Chapters 11 and 12: Finance and Implementation** These two chapters discuss financial and control tools to ensure successful execution of marketing plans.

**Chapter 13: Sample Marketing Plans** The final chapter demonstrates the techniques shown in this book using two formats: a longer, traditional format, and a shorter, 10-slide format.

Figure 1.6 shows how the book allocates chapters to the major segments of the planning process.

## Marketing Planning in Action

**Nintendo Wii: Many Marketing Decisions**. The Nintendo Wii required many marketing decisions during its development, and even after launch. One decision was the name—the device, originally designated the Nintendo Revolution (used as the code name for the project) was re-named the Wii. Nintendo reported that the "ii" spelling is intended to represent both the unique controllers and the image of people gathering to play. As Nintendo stated at the time, "it's really not about you or me. It's about Wii." Once the product was launched, Nintendo had to decide on the ongoing price to charge for the unit—Nintendo believes the value proposition of the device is strong enough to justify its long-standing price of $249 despite drops in price by its competitors. In terms of distribution channels, Nintendo decided to launch a new

### Key Terms

**Situation analysis**   An evaluation of the external and internal situations facing the company. The analysis helps describes the market and the forces shaping it, the customer segments, and the competitive landscape.

channel, WiiWare, to download games over the Internet by redeeming WiiPoints. The new channel gives smaller game developers an alternative mechanism to sell their wares (other than the expensive retail distribution methods). Says Cammie Dunaway, Nintendo's executive vice-president of sales and marketing, "WiiWare is to the video game industry what independent films are to Hollywood."[11, 12, 13]

## Summary

As Louis Pasteur once said, "chance favors only the prepared mind."

Marketing success is rarely based on chance. It is often the result of a carefully prepared and executed marketing plan. A marketing plan is a written plan that covers the situation, objectives, and actions for an organization for the time period covered by the plan, generally one year.

An effective marketing plan is based on a strong outline, like the one used in this book, deep market knowledge, and enterprise-wide collaboration. Effective marketing planning brings with it many advantages, such as forcing a disciplined approach to the market, ensuring that no key aspect of the market is overlooked.

The approach used in this book makes the planning process easy and effective by following the outline of the marketing plan. Each chapter of the book corresponds to a section of the plan. That way, all the information needed for a particular section is available, and the plan can be built as the book progresses.

In the next chapter, we begin the planning process by identifying objectives for the plan.

 ## Key Terms

**Collaboration** Working with key stakeholders in different departments in the organization, which can help gain buy-in for the marketing plan. (p. 9)

**Marketing mix** Mix of controllable marketing variables to implement marketing strategy. Most common classification is called the four Ps: product, price, place, and promotion. (p. 9)

**Marketing plan** Document covering the situation, strategy, and tactics to accomplish specified objectives within the time period of the plan (p. 3)

**Marketing plan outline** The structure of a marketing plan, generally beginning with the executive summary, then describing the market and the strategy used to take advantages within it, followed by the marketing tactics and other tools to implement the strategy. (p. 9)

**Situation analysis** An evaluation of the external and internal situations facing the company. The analysis helps describes the market and the forces shaping it, the customer segments, and the competitive landscape. (p. 11)

 ## Discussion Questions

1. How well does your existing organization collaborate among its various groups? When new services and products are developed, does each group provide input into the plan?

2. What problems could have been avoided in your existing organization if a more rigorous planning process had been used? What opportunities could have been seized?

3. The marketing planning process diagram includes a feedback loop. What type of information would be useful for such feedback? How would it change future plans?

 Exercises

1. Develop an outline for your own marketing plan using the marketing plan outline given in this chapter. Enter brief answers for the questions raised in the marketing plan outline figures. For example, in the market overview section, the value proposition topic asks the question: "What benefit does the company bring to the market?" Answer the question with a statement such as, "We provide a near-luxury hotel stay at chain hotel prices."

2. Think about your current marketing plan project. Identify your top three concerns with the project. Common concerns for marketing plan projects include areas such as gathering market data, estimating market demand, developing pricing, and getting buy-in on your plan. Of course, many other concerns are also possible, but this short list should get you started.

3. Contact a representative within each major department, such as operations and finance, in your organization. Ask them how they would like to see the marketing planning process change.

## CHAPTER 2

# Objectives

## INTRODUCTION

We begin the marketing plan by declaring our objectives. Clear, actionable objectives are vital to the successful execution of the marketing plan. Murky objectives lead to indecisive strategy, which in turn will be difficult (and frustrating) to implement through the tactics of the marketing mix.

## CHAPTER CHECKLIST

We cover the following marketing plan section in this chapter:

❑ **Objectives**: Declare objectives based on organization's mission and competitive advantages

## Marketing Planning in Action

**Hilton: Global Growth Objective**. Hilton's objective of growth, especially in emerging markets, teamed with sound strategies to accomplish the objective, resulting in significant expansion for the organization. According to a 2008 Forbes Market Scan, the hotel chain reported that it is expanding at an average rate of five hotels per week. Hilton opened 241 hotels with 31,521 rooms in 2007, increasing its total number of hotels to 3,000 with 500,000 rooms. "We are focusing on accelerating the growth of our international management and franchise business," said Christopher Nassetta, CEO of Hilton Hotels. He continued, "In the last year, Hilton has secured eight strategic agreements representing 200 hotels in international markets. These significant developments are indicative of how we want to grow globally." Continuing on its objective of growth in international markets, the company has plans to expand further into Russia, Turkey, and China. The plans include a new Doubletree hotel in Beijing, opening in time for the 2008 Olympic Games.[1]

Hilton's growth objective drove impressive global expansion, like this property in Antwerp, Belgium

*Source*: Shutterstock

# Organizational Mission and Competitive Advantage

The mission and competitive advantage provide a sense of where the organization is going and the fundamental strengths it will use to get there. As such, they provide excellent starting points in determining the plan's objectives.

## Mission

The **mission** is the overall purpose of the organization. It describes the general scope of activities for the firm, and often includes fundamental principles of the manner in which the organization intends to do business. Many companies use mission statements to define their overall purpose. For example, Hilton's Hampton Inn franchise declares its mission statement as follows: "To create rewarding customer experiences that build long term loyalty to Hilton Worldwide, drive business to our hotels, and spread the warmth of Hilton hospitality worldwide."[2, 3]

## Competitive Advantage

The **competitive advantage** of an organization is its set of distinctive capabilities that give it a cost advantage or a differentiation advantage over the competition. For example, Hilton claims that its proprietary check-in computer system gives it a competitive advantage. The system improves guest recognition during check-in and provides more enhanced levels of service through real-time computer access to guest preferences.[4, 5]

Companies leverage their competitive advantage to succeed against other competitors in the market. Several different types of competitive advantages are available. This book introduces a new methodology to categorize competitive advantages, by extending Michael Porter's value chain model to show how each value chain element can be transformed into a competitive advantage. The value chain model asserts that companies can deliver customer value throughout the chain of activities that are used to create products and services and deliver them to market.

Hilton's proprietary check-in system gives the company a competitive advantage

*Source*: Shutterstock

In his book, *Competitive Advantage*, Michael Porter identified five primary activities (inbound logistics, operations, outbound logistics, marketing and sales, and service) and four support activities (infrastructure, human resource management, technological development, and procurement). For example, Steinway pianos leverage their inbound logistics value chain element to give them competitive advantage. By importing a special type of high-quality wood for the sounding boards of their pianos, they achieve a sound distinct from that of any other piano. Figure 2.1 demonstrates the process for all of the value chain elements.[6]

**Figure 2.1** Competitive Advantages: Typical Categories

| Competitive Advantage | Description | Example |
|---|---|---|
| Inbound Logistics | Access to unique production materials | Steinway pianos: Imports a special type of high quality wood for the sounding boards of their pianos, which Steinway credits for the pianos' unique sound |
| Operations | Unique manufacturing process; Unique service delivery process | McDonald's: Creates and enforces specific operating guidelines to ensure that their products always taste the same, whether in Tulsa or Tokyo |
| Outbound Logistics | Shipping products out of organization | WalMart: Uses advanced logistics processes to reduce inventory costs, identify top sellers, and maximize profit |
| Marketing and Sales | Marketing and selling products | Apple: Ensures consistency of brand, from its user-friendly design to its luxurious packaging |
| Service | Providing service before, during and after the sale | Nordstrom: Delivers on its reputation for helpful and friendly customer service |
| Infrastructure of Firm | Managing organization, including planning, finance, and legal affairs | Google: Leverages its considerable company assets, such as its strong cash position, to grow the company |
| Human Resources | Recruiting and training managerial talent | General Electric: Grooms some of the world's leading management talent |
| Technological Development | Leveraging technical expertise to develop innovative products | 3M: Develops culture of innovation and encourages employees to experiment with radical new ideas |
| Procurement | Purchasing materials | Toyota: Manages advanced procurement and inventory system to reduce costs and respond quickly to market demands |

## Key Terms

**Mission**   The overall purpose of an organization, the general scope of activities.

**Competitive Advantage**   Distinctive capabilities that give the organization a cost or differentiation advantage over its competition.

## Setting Objectives

The next step is to develop the objectives, based on the organization's mission and competitive advantage. **Objectives** are items that focus organizational effort toward improving the organization's competitive strength and its long-term market position. Limiting the number of objectives to only one will definitely improve the plan's focus. Trying to implement more than three objectives at once can be counterproductive, because the organization's efforts gets scattered in too many directions. For example, Hilton's 2006 general annual report states three primary objectives: to grow the hotel business, especially in emerging markets such as China and India; to further increase the strength of the Hilton brand; and to further improve customer service.[7]

Different types of missions and competitive advantages will dictate different types of objectives:

- A large organization with a mission emphasizing growth in new markets will often focus on increasing its market share by expanding geographically.
- A small organization with a mission to be an expert in its narrow category will often focus on increasing its market share within its current market, with the intent on dominating a particular niche.
- An organization with a mission focused on luxury services will often target an objective based on increasing its brand reputation, or improving its customer service for high-end customers.
- A company driven by innovation with a competitive advantage in technology will often try to leverage its advantage through new innovative products, or improving its responsiveness to dynamic market conditions by shortening its product development cycle time.

As shown in Figure 2.2, organizations generally have five types of objectives:

**Financially Related Objectives**:  Addressing monetary results

**Market Share-related Objectives**:  Focusing on the organization's size of the market

**Product or Service-related Objectives**:  Concentrating on the organization's offering to the market

**Figure 2.2** Types of Organizational Objectives

**Figure 2.3** Categories of Objectives and Examples for Each

| Objective Category | Examples |
| --- | --- |
| Financial | Revenue: Increase organization-wide sales by 12% by end of calendar year<br>Profitability: Achieve 20% rate of return by end of year<br>Survival: Maintain positive cash flow to survive double-dip recession |
| Market Share | Market Share, Existing Markets: Increase market share in existing market X from 23% to 29% within one year<br>Market Share, New Markets: Develop market share in new market Y from 0% to 5% within one year |
| Product/ Service | New Products/ Services: Increase sales of new services from 10% of total sales to 15% of total sales within one year<br>Market Responsiveness: Decrease development cycle time (inception to launch) from 18 months to 12 months<br>Perceived Quality: Improve perceived quality, as evidenced by third party analyst rating increasing from ranking #5 to ranking #2 in analyst report X<br>Product Line: Broaden product line to exceed that of competitors'<br>New Trial: Increase trial of product X from 2% to 5% of target group Y in one year |
| Brand | Brand Awareness: Increase brand awareness in market X by 25% within one year, as measured by survey Y<br>Brand Extension: Add new luxury brand to target high-end customer<br>Brand Preference: Increase preference of our brand over brand Z, for target market X, from 22% to 33% by end of calendar year |
| Customer Focus | Customer Service: Improve customer service, as measured by 15% reduction in customer complaints about service, by end of year<br>Customer Recommendations: Improve recommendations rate from 50% to 80% of customers surveyed, by end of year |

**Brand-related Objectives:**  Devoting effort to the brand of the organization or its offerings

**Customer-related Objectives:**  Engaging in customer-related issues

As an aid to declaring objectives, Figure 2.3 shows several typical examples of each type of objective.

## Clear Objectives

Objectives should be clear to ensure their success. Murky objectives invite confusion. For example, one of the Hilton objectives discussed earlier states that the hotel business should target emerging markets for growth, but how is growth defined? Number of rooms? Number of hotel properties? And when is the growth to be completed? How do we know we have completed the objective without knowing the specifics?

**Figure 2.4** S.M.A.R.T. Method of Declaring Objectives

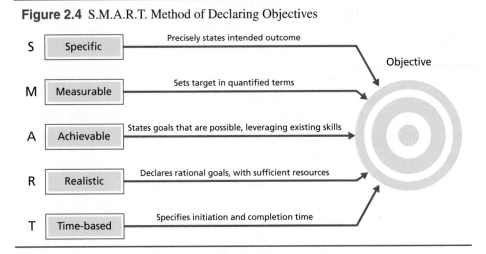

To ensure clarity, marketing plans should include specific objectives with which to manage the plan's proposed project (sometimes called management by objectives, or MBO). Objectives should follow the **S.M.A.R.T. objective framework**: specific, measurable, achievable, realistic, and time-based. Let us see how Hilton's growth objective might change using the S.M.A.R.T. method:[8]

**Specific**: Specific objectives are precise about what they intend to achieve (answering who, what, when, where, and why). For example, Hilton's growth objective could be made more specific by stating: "Increase the number of hotels in emerging markets..."

**Measurable**: Measurable objectives are quantified. For example, Hilton could state: "...by 200 hotels with a sum of 10,000 rooms..."

**Achievable**: Achievable objectives are possible and leverage existing abilities and skills (or abilities and skills that could be easily learned). For example, Hilton could mention that the objective leverages its current skill base.

**Realistic**: Realistic objectives are rational and allocate an adequate amount of resources to support their completion. For example, the Hilton objective could add the following phrase: "...leveraging a dedicated team and sufficient capital..."

**Time-based**: Time-based objectives state when the objective will be completed. Hilton could make the objective time-based by adding: "...to be completed by the end of the calendar year."

Figure 2.4 summarizes the S.M.A.R.T. method.

## Practical Planning

The Practical Planning sections in this book guide you through the planning process step-by-step. The sections apply decision charts and targeted information to guide you through the many decisions facing the marketing planner. As we continue through the chapters, the

Practical Planning sections will allow you to build the plan one portion at a time. By the time you have completed the book, you will have a solid draft of the entire plan.

As an aid to understanding the marketing plan process, we will demonstrate the preparation of a typical plan by creating a marketing plan for Expedia, Inc., an organization that provides online travel agency (OTA) services. To avoid confidentiality issues, the plan presented in this book uses only publicly available data. While we will be applying the process to a service-based organization, the book's approach works equally well for product-based organizations. For example, the sample plan shown in chapter 13 applies the book's approach to a product, the 2011 Ford Fiesta automobile.

Expedia started in 1996 as a small division in Microsoft to give consumers a new way to research, plan, and book their comprehensive travel needs. In 1999, Microsoft spun off Expedia, and it became a publicly traded company on the NASDAQ exchange under the symbol EXPE. Over time, Expedia added capabilities by acquiring travel-related firms, and now Expedia-branded websites feature airline tickets, hotel reservations, car rental, cruises, and many other in-destination services from a broad selection of partners.[9]

**Expedia helps consumers research, plan, and book trips to destinations like Paris**

*Source*: Fotolia, LLC–Royalty Free

## Key Terms

**Objective**   Goals of the marketing plan, in clear and specific language.

**S.M.A.R.T. Objective Framework**   Objectives should be specific, measurable, achievable, realistic, and time-based.

**Figure 2.5** Expedia: Organization Mission and Competitive Advantages

| Category | Expedia Example |
| --- | --- |
| Mission | "Expedia's mission is to become the largest seller of travel in the world, by helping everyone everywhere plan and purchase everything in travel." |
| Competitive Advantages | Portfolio of travel brands; Technology and content innovation; Global reach; Breadth of service offerings |

**Figure 2.6** Expedia: Marketing Plan Objective

| Category | Expedia Example |
| --- | --- |
| Objective | Increase sales of new travel services, such as new vacation packages (where new services are defined as those introduced within past 3 years), from 10% of total revenue to 15%, to be completed by end of calendar year 2012 |

Expedia's mission is shown on their investor relations page: "Our mission is to become the largest seller of travel in the world, by helping everyone everywhere plan and purchase everything in travel."[10]

Expedia's competitive advantage, as explained in its annual report, is the power of its four critical assets: its portfolio of travel brands, technology and content innovation, global reach, and breadth of service offerings.[11]

Figure 2.5 summarizes the information.

In order to remain true to Expedia's mission as "helping everyone everywhere plan and purchase everything in travel," and to leverage Expedia's competitive advantage in "breadth of service offerings," we will declare the objective shown in Figure 2.6.

The objective reflects Expedia's mission and competitive advantage. The new vacation packages will also aid in maintaining Expedia's focus on innovation and differentiating Expedia from other online travel agencies. The objective meets the S.M.A.R.T. framework, in that it is specific, measurable (10 percent to 15 percent), achievable (leverages existing skill sets), realistic (we will identify a marketing budget to implement the new line of vacation packages), and time-based ("by the end of 2012").

## Summary

Zig Ziglar can attest to the value of objectives and goals when he says: "Unless you have definite, precise, clearly set goals, you are not going to realize the maximum potential that lies within you."

Clear objectives and goals are vital to organizations, just as they are for people. Most organizations have a flow-down of objectives, from mission statements, covering the long-term direction of the company, to detailed product/service objectives, covering short-term tactics. Whether short-term or long-term, objectives should always be specific, measurable, achievable, realistic, and time-based.

In this chapter, we have covered a four-step process on how to set objectives that deliver results. The first step is to state the organization's mission and competitive advantage. Based on those two items, we can determine the types of objectives that align with the intended future of the organization. The objectives can be of various types. We can establish objectives that emphasize finance, service/product, brand, or customer focus, depending on the needs of the organization and the market.

The next step is to determine the appropriate strategy. The strategy will depend on the objectives selected. For example, an objective that called for increased market share in existing markets will benefit from a market penetration strategy. Alternatively, an objective that specifies faster market responsiveness should adopt a strategy to improve the organization's product/service development process.

The strategies get implemented using the four elements of the marketing mix—product/ service, price, place (distribution), and promotion.

## Key Terms

**Competitive Advantage** Distinctive capabilities that give the organization a cost or differentiation advantage over its competition. (p. 17)

**Mission** The overall purpose of an organization, the general scope of activities. (p. 17)

**Objective** Goals of the marketing plan, in clear and specific language. (p. 21)

**S.M.A.R.T. Objective Framework** Objectives should be specific, measurable, achievable, realistic, and time-based. (p. 21)

## Discussion Questions

1. Who should set the marketing objectives for the organization? Should that task be left exclusively to the marketing department?

2. How should the confidentiality of marketing objectives be treated? How do we weigh the advantages of having the entire team working together when they all know the objectives versus the disadvantage of having the objectives leak to competitors?

3. What are the consequences for incorrect objectives? For example, if we had specified an objective to grow market share, but in hindsight realize we should have devoted our efforts to developing a new service instead, how does that impact the organization?

## Exercises

1. Develop a set of objectives, strategy, and (draft) marketing mix tables for the marketing plan you are currently developing. Follow the model shown in the Practical Planning section.

2. Repeat Exercise 1 for a different set of objectives, strategies, and marketing mix elements that could also be relevant to the organization.

3. State the advantages and disadvantages of the two sets of objectives, strategies, and marketing mix elements. Which set comes closer to the organization's stated mission and competitive advantages?

## CHAPTER 3

# Market Overview

## INTRODUCTION

In this section, we cover how to develop a brief overview of the market for the marketing plan. The overview includes a description of the market based on customer need, an estimate of the size and growth rate of the market, and identification of market trends. The brief overview will help us detect any detrimental (or beneficial!) trends in the market while we can still do something about them. The chapter also covers tips on gathering market data.

## CHAPTER CHECKLIST

We cover the following marketing plan sections in this chapter:

❏ **Market Description**: Define the market based on customer need

❏ **Market Sizing**: Estimate the size and growth rate of the market

❏ **Market Trends and Forces**: Predict the future state of the market

While market needs persist, like that for portable computing power, the physical products fulfilling those needs can change over time, from abacus to calculator to laptop to smartphones and beyond
*Source*: Shutterstock

# Market Description

We can use several tools to describe the market accurately. First, we look at describing the market by customer need (instead of describing it by its physical products). Next, we review another tool to describe a market, the North American Industrial Classification System (NAICS) code, which will help us as we gather information through government sources. We start off by reviewing a few basic definitions.

## Industry, Category, Customer Need

Marketers use the term **market** to describe the collective set of customers buying products or services from sellers; the sellers making products or services that are substitutes for each other constitute the **industry**. A subset of an industry is a **category**, which is a group of competing firms in a segment of an industry. For example, Sub Zero is a company making luxury built-in refrigerators and other appliances. Sub Zero is in the high-end appliances category, which is part of the white goods (appliances) industry, selling to a market of affluent, discriminating customers.[1]

Beware of describing the market too narrowly. Focus on the need that the product or service fulfills, instead of any particular product or service that might exist today. We focus

---

### Key Terms

**Market**  Collective set of customers purchasing products or services from sellers.

**Industry**  Group of sellers making products or delivering products that are substitutes for each other.

**Category**  Group of competing firms in a segment of an industry.

on the **customer need** rather than on the physical format because formats can become obsolete. Wang was once the dominant force in computer-based documents, but it saw itself as a word processing company, not as a company dedicated to making it easier for users to create and edit documents. The overly narrow market focus contributed to tumbling profits.[2]

---

## Marketing Planning in Action

**Portable Computing Evolves.** Consumers have a continuing basic need for solving complex problems, and have developed a variety of devices over the ages to satisfy that need. Years ago, this need was met with an abacus. Currently, the need is met with a laptop computer and can be augmented with a portable computing device like a smartphone. In the future, the design of the device could look completely different. For example, Apple's introduction of the iPad in 2010 revolutionized the personal computer (PC) industry with its tablet format and intuitive user interface. Other manufacturers are experimenting with new designs as well. V12Design developed the Canova concept notebook, which features two touch-sensitive displays hinged together. The displays can be oriented as a traditional laptop for typing or writing, laid flat as a large sketchpad, or turned on its side as an e-reader.[3]

---

## NAICS Code

The **North American Industrial Classification System (NAICS) code** is a classification system used by the U.S. Census Bureau to organize industries. The NAICS system starts out with 20 industry groups and appends digits on to those codes as the industries become more specific, resulting in a six-digit hierarchical structure that covers (virtually) every industry. Industry data, as collected by the U.S. Census Bureau, are categorized by NAICS code and is available free at http://www.census.gov/eos/www/naics/.

The NAICS system replaces the older standard industrial classification (SIC) codes developed in 1987 for a similar purpose. The newer NAICS system permits more specific categories (NAICS codes can contain six digits, whereas SIC codes only contain four), it recognizes more service categories, and it facilitates international use because it was developed jointly by the United States, Canada, and Mexico.

In addition to the information that the U.S. government provides, private-sector firms have sprouted up which provide a wealth of different information about various industries, all indexed by NAICS code. Unlike the U.S. government information, however, this information is not free.

## Market Sizing

**Market sizing** is the process of estimating the total amount of potential sales to all customers within a given market (for dynamic markets, we could also include "within a given timeframe"). In established industries, market size is often expressed as the total annual revenue of all suppliers in that industry.

In general, large, growing markets are considered desirable for three reasons:

**Consumer Demand Validation**—stagnant or declining markets (like printed newspapers, thanks to declining readership) are not seen as a good place to invest scarce company resources.

**Larger Upside Potential**—capturing 50 percent of a $1 billion market produces more revenue than 50 percent of a $1 million market.

**More Available Segments**—markets with more segments often generate more revenue, because each segment can be targeted with different types of products and services. For example, the multibillion dollar video game market boasts six major segments, from heavy gamers to portable gamers.[4]

Data for market sizing can be obtained in a number of different ways. Figure 3.1 shows several popular data sources. The author recommends gathering data from several different sources, then comparing the results to converge on a final value.

## Available Published Reports

The most common approach, often viewed as the most reliable, is to obtain available published market reports written by industry analysts and market research services. Industry research firms cover a wide variety of markets and publish reports on them on a regular basis, knowing that a demand for such information exists. Industry analyst reports often cover many other market characteristics, including market size forecasts and trends. In addition, discipline-specific academic journals can be useful, especially for specific market areas.

Figure 3.2 shows samples of industry analysts for business to consumer (B2C) and business to business (B2B) markets. The advantages of this approach are speed

**Figure 3.1** Some Popular Market Sizing Data Sources

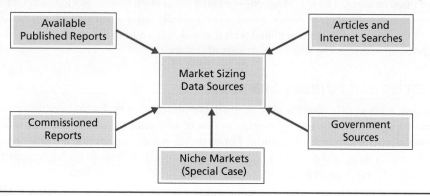

### Key Terms

**Customer need**   Enduring desire from customers to satisfy physical, emotional, or intellectual requisites.

**NAICS code**   North American Industrial Classification System, a classification system developed by the U.S. Census Bureau to organize industries.

**Market sizing**   Process of estimating the total amount of potential sales to all customers within a given market, within a given timeframe.

**Figure 3.2** Industry Analysts for Consumer and Business Markets

| Market Type | Typical Markets Covered | Sample Analysts |
|---|---|---|
| B2C: Consumer | Haircare Products | Arbitron (www.arbitron.com) |
| | Small Appliances | Dun & Bradstreet (www.dnb.com) |
| | Apparel and Footwear | Nielsen (www.nielsen.com) |
| B2B: Business | Welding Machinery | Forrester (www.forrester.com) |
| | Management Consulting Services | Gartner (www.gartner.com) |
| | Enterprise Software | IDC (www.idc.com) |

and convenience. To get the reports, the user simply goes to the industry analyst's website, searches for one of the many available reports on their industry, and purchases it. The disadvantage to this approach is the price—the reports are expensive, often costing thousands of dollars. Many research firms offer annual subscription services, which can prove cost-effective in the long run if the organization requires many reports.

## Commissioned Reports

If a market is unusual and the information is not available using the techniques discussed in this chapter, then a custom market research study can be commissioned from a specialty market research company. Such specialty research companies often focus on one particular industry, or industry niche, and can be very knowledgeable about their area.

The advantage of this approach is that the data is highly relevant. The approach has two disadvantages. The first is speed—research firms often take weeks to collect data. The other disadvantage is cost. Custom reports usually require research on a niche topic. With the significant labor associated with that task, such a bespoke report can be very expensive, often costing tens of thousands of dollars.

## Articles and Internet Searches

To save money, a thorough search of available literature over the Internet using search engines such as Bing, Google, or Yahoo! will often reveal satisfactory results without having to purchase a report. For example, press releases and advertisements with "teaser data," published by some marketing research firms to entice readers to purchase research reports, can reveal the desired information for free.

Market data are also available from industry associations, which operate websites that aggregate articles relating to the industry. Searching the organization's database can often lead to high-quality market data at bargain prices (members often get data for free). For example, the Automotive Service Association website (www.asashop.org), representing the automotive repair services industry, includes articles dealing with market trends and proposed legislation in the automotive repair industry.

One should consider the source of the data when searching. An established market research firm or industry association is likely to be more reputable than an individual's blog.

## Marketing Planning in Action

**Gartner**: **B2B Industry Analyst**. Business to business (B2B) industry analysts, such as Gartner, frequently publish press releases to showcase their work and advertise their expertise. The press releases can contain a wealth of valuable information, all for free. For example, a recent Gartner press release on smartphones revealed vital market data: sales of all mobile phones by year worldwide; sales of smartphones by year worldwide; growth rate of the market; and even market share for the major manufacturers, such as Nokia, Research in Motion, Apple, and others. The press release even included the analyst's evaluation of the market. A few minutes searching on the Internet can often lead to valuable finds like this one.[5]

## Government Sources

The U.S. government publishes volumes of industry data, accessed through the industry NAICS code. For example, NAICS codes are used to access data from the U.S. Census Bureau such as its Industry Statistics Samplers, which show total value of shipments (revenue) from all companies in an industry. The advantage with government data is that they are free. The data have several disadvantages: They are often several years old, and are not broken down finely enough to be useful for smaller industry segments.

## Niche Markets

**Niche markets** are a special case for market sizing. Niche market vendors sell highly specialized services and products, generally to a small set of customers. In such markets, marketers can employ a bottom–up approach, adding up the number of customers who would have the need, income, and access for the particular equipment being sold.

### Key Terms

**Niche markets**   Markets (generally small in size) for highly specialized services and products.

For example, companies providing restoration services for antique Chris-Craft boats (high-quality mahogany-hulled powerboats made in the 1920s through the 1950s) employ niche marketing techniques, posting ads on Chris-Craft boat club websites, knowing that only a limited number of these fine boats still exist.

## Marketing Planning in Action

**PET-CT: Niche Market**. PET-CT (positron emission tomography-computed tomography) scanning machines can more accurately detect cancer in patients with certain neurological symptoms, according to U.S. researchers. The neurological symptoms can occur in people with lung, breast, ovarian, and other types of cancer when cancer-fighting antibodies mistakenly attack nervous system cells. While PET-CT machines are likely accurate, they can cost millions of dollars, so their use would be limited to a selected group of medical facilities. Marketers can estimate the size of the market by counting up the medical facilities they believe would have the interest and funds for such devices.[6]

Services for classic Chris-Craft wooden speedboats represent a niche market due to the rarity of these admirable vessels

*Source*: Shutterstock

**Figure 3.3** P.E.S.T. Environmental Analysis Overview

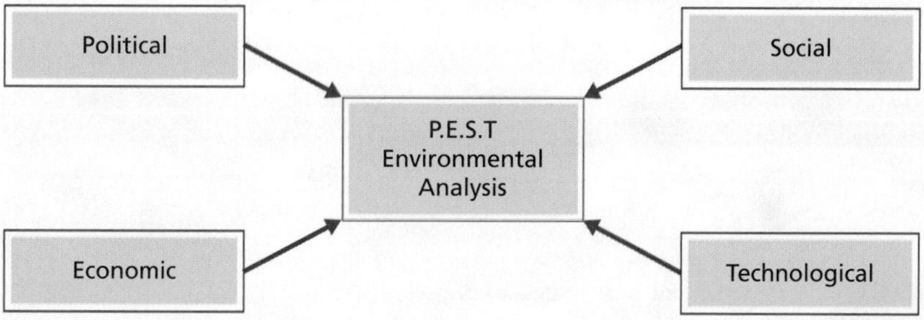

# Market Trends and Forces

We can examine market trends and forces to predict the future state of markets. For example, substantial new taxes levied on goods or services will likely cause demand to shrink.

## Market Trends

**Market trends** are long-term behaviors that provide clues about the future state of markets. To help identify the impact of market trends, we can conduct a **P.E.S.T. analysis** (i.e., political, economic, social, and technological analysis), which studies the effect of environmental forces on the market. Figure 3.3 provides an overview of the analysis.[7]

**Political** The impact of political legislation, taxes, governmental agencies, and special interest groups can dramatically affect markets. Here are a few examples:

- **New Taxes**: The U.S. Congress enacted a 10 percent excise tax on luxury pleasure boats (defined as boats over $100,000) in the middle of a recession in the early 1990s, resulting in a 33 percent decline in sales for the industry overall.[8]
- **Import Tariffs**: Brussels considered enacting a carbon tariff on all imported goods into Europe in an effort to counteract the carbon dioxide emissions created during production.[9]
- **Political Parties**: Changes in political parties, such as changes in the constituency of the U.S. Senate from a majority of Republicans to a majority of Democrats, can cause changes in markets such as defense and health care.

### Key Terms

**Market trends** Ongoing behaviors in a market that suggest its future state.

**P.E.S.T. analysis** Study of political, economic, social, and technological trends to gauge the effects of environmental forces on the market.

The 2009 Cash for Clunkers program drove new-car sales by providing incentives to trade in older, less fuel-efficient models
*Source*: Shutterstock

## Marketing Planning in Action

**Political Impact: Cash for Clunkers**. In 2009, the U.S. government enacted its Cash for Clunkers program in an effort to boost lagging new-car sales and increase automotive fuel efficiency nationwide. The program offered Americans up to $4,500 if they traded in their older-model cars and purchased more efficient new cars. The $1 billion in government grants was followed by another $2 billion in funding, as the popularity of the program soared. By the end of the program, about 625,000 autos sold through the program, accounting for nearly $18.2 billion in retail automotive sales.[10]

**Economic** Economic forces affect markets by changes in employment income, savings amounts, debt levels, interest rates, and availability of credit. Interest rates have a significant impact on investment, because cost of investment rises with interest rates. Here are a few examples:

- **Interest Rates**: A study of mortgage interest rate increases found that an increase from 5 percent to 5.79 percent could cut the potential market of borrowers with an incentive to refinance by 50 percent.[11]

## Marketing Planning in Action

**Economic Impact: Small-Business Credit Card Use.** According to a study conducted for the American Bankers Association by Keybridge Research, the increase in small-business credit card use from 2003 to 2008 "contributed directly to the creation of 592,000 small business jobs and an additional one million direct or induced jobs throughout the U.S. economy." In addition, the available credit gives small businesses a financial cushion against cash shortages. Mike Nagle, general manager of Chase's Ink credit card, said that the company saw "great opportunity" in small business. According to Mr. Nagle, "It's a large market. There are 27 million small businesses with up to $5 trillion a year in spending. The majority of that spending still happens on a check. There's a great opportunity to provide innovation."[13]

- **Exchange Rates**: Foreign currency exchange rates can affect companies that do business internationally. For example, restaurant chain McDonald's reported that same-store sales rose in May 2009, but total sales fell slightly during the same period because of fluctuating currency exchange rates.[12]

**Social** Social attitudes can affect markets because society's beliefs, values, and norms largely define consumer tastes and preferences. Here are a few examples:

- **Environmental Responsibility**: People's concerns about the environment are influencing sustainability efforts by companies. Hilton Hotels announced that they intend to reduce energy consumption from direct operations as part of "building sustainability into the core fabric of its businesses worldwide."[14]

- **Health**: Social attitudes toward health and wellness are spurring sales of organic foods. For example, marketers are watching baby boomer eating trends. Boomers represent 78 million people and as such can have a big impact on the market for healthy foods.[15]

- **Marriage**: Social attitudes toward marriage might affect wedding-related industries. Marriage rates in general are declining, and those who do marry now stay together for longer, causing lower divorce rates, especially in the United Kingdom.[16]

## Marketing Planning in Action

**Social Impact: The End of Overindulgence**. Some people feel that the devastating economic recession of 2007–2010 was not just an economic event, it was a social one, indicating a social trend toward the end of excess in America. Social trends like this can impact marketing plans. For example, if people feel guilty about spending, virtually all markets could be affected, especially those associated with luxury. The markets for high-end items such as fine clothing, watches, and automobiles could shrink.[17]

Mini-mansions like this one could become less popular if the social trend away from overindulgence continues
*Source*: Shutterstock

**Technological** Technological trends can devastate markets. The invention of the transistor virtually annihilated the vacuum tube market. The popularity of the automobile almost ended passenger transport on trains. Here are a few more examples:

- **Portable Computing**: Portability of computing is a growing technological trend. Laptop personal computers outsold desktop-based PCs for the first time in history in 2008.[18]
- **Alternative Fuels**: The use of alternative fuels, such as hydrogen fuel cells to power automobiles instead of gasoline, would affect many markets.

## Marketing Planning in Action

**Technological Impact: Virtualization**. Virtualization, which allows one computer to host multiple devices, is a strong technological trend. Using virtualization, a large corporation can cut costs by serving the programs used by employee personal computers from a central computer server. To update computer programs, the corporation just changes the program in the central server, instead of demanding that all employees turn in their computers to perform the change. Virtualization can also result in reduced energy usage. One VMworld virtualization conference consumed only 2 percent of the typical power required by similar events, because its 32,248 virtual machines were packed onto only 776 physical servers.[19]

**Figure 3.4** P.E.S.T. Analysis: Political, Economic, Social, and Technological Trends

| Trend Category | Description | Examples |
|---|---|---|
| Political | Impact of political legislation, taxes, government agencies, and special interest groups | New taxes Import tariffs Political parties |
| Economic | Impact of changes in employment income, savings amounts, debt levels, and availability of credit | Interest rates Exchange rates |
| Social | Impact from society's beliefs, values, and norms | Environmental responsibility Health Marriage |
| Technological | Impact from changes in technology | Portable computing Alternative fuels Cloud-based computing |

Figure 3.4 summarizes the P.E.S.T analysis process.

## Market Forces

Harvard professor Michael Porter developed an industry analysis framework, called the **Five Forces model**, which categorizes five different types of forces acting on industries. The Five Forces model can be used as an adjunct to the P.E.S.T. analysis to study how various forces are shaping the market, what changes one can anticipate as a result, and what strategies can be used to mitigate (or take advantage of!) the forces: [20]

**Threat of Entry**:  New entrants into an industry can decrease profitability for incumbent firms due to increased competition. For example, multiple entrants in the extra-large (over 70 inches) liquid crystal display (LCD) television industry caused prices (and profits) to drop. Companies can reduce the threat of incoming firms by erecting **barriers to entry**, such as by establishing a strong brand or controlling access to distribution channels. For example, Samsung invests heavily in its brand, so it will be perceived as an industry leader and attract buyers away from competitors.[21]

---

**Key Terms**

**Five Forces model**   Analysis of five different forces acting on industries, and countermeasures against those forces.

**Intensity of Rivalry**: Profits can drop if industry members engage in price competition, especially if the companies are perceived as near-equals. For example, home improvement leaders Home Depot and Lowe's fight for customers through aggressive low pricing. Intensity can be reduced by various means such as introducing new kinds of products and services. For example, Home Depot introduced its Kids Workshops, where parents can bring their children to stores to build their choice of a window birdhouse or Declaration of Independence frame kit.[22]

**Pressure from Substitute Products**: Industry profits can decrease if new products or services delivering the same function are introduced to the industry, especially if they cost less than existing offerings. For example, the sugar industry saw a drop in sales with the introduction of high fructose corn syrup as a substitute sweetener. Incumbent companies can reduce the pressure by showing how their product or service is superior to those of substitutes. For example, fans of natural foods perceived high fructose corn syrup so negatively that the Corn Refiners Association petitioned the U.S. Food and Drug Administration to change the name to "corn sugar" to reduce the negative connotation.[23]

**Bargaining Power of Buyers**: Powerful buyers (such as organizations that purchase much of the industry's capacity) can drive down profits by demanding lower prices on products and services, especially those that buyers see as undifferentiated, commodity items. Industry firms can counter the bargaining power of buyers through various means such as showing that the product or service is essential to successful operation. For example, Intel introduced its "Intel Inside" campaign to showcase the importance of its microprocessor chips.

**Bargaining Power of Suppliers**: Powerful suppliers (such as companies with controlling interests in vital resources necessary for production) can reduce profitability by charging more for their products and services. For example, 70 percent of the world's low-cost lithium (required for lithium-ion batteries in hybrid and electric automobiles) comes from a salt flat in Chile's Atacama Desert, controlled by Soquimich, based in Santiago, Chile, and Rockwood Holdings, based in Princeton, New Jersey. One means of countering supplier power is by locating substitutes for scarce supplies. For example, Toyota is conducting research in magnesium-sulfate batteries as a replacement for lithium-ion technology.[24]

## Marketing Planning in Action

### Radiohead: No Pot of Gold at the End of the Rainbow for Record Companies.
British band Radiohead released its album *In Rainbows* over the Internet, bypassing traditional record labels such as Warner Music Group. Other suppliers of music, such as Nine Inch Nails and Madonna, are considering switching to an Internet-based distribution model or have already done so. Meanwhile, the three major music labels—Universal Music Group, Sony BMG Music Entertainment, and EMI Group—are suffering reductions in their stock price valuations due to slipping compact disc (CD) sales.[25]

**Figure 3.5** Market Description: Online Travel Agent Services

| Market Factor | Description |
|---|---|
| Industry | Travel agencies. Category: Online travel agent (OTA) |
| NAICS/ SIC code | NAICS 561510 Travel Agencies<br>SIC 4724 Travel Agencies |
| Customer Needs | Research travel accommodations according to customer's own criteria<br>Book accommodations<br>Obtain feeling of empowerment by doing it oneself |
| Size | $200 Billion worldwide online travel agency market in 2010 |
| Growth Rate | 3.5% growth rate of number of U.S. customers booking trips online in 2010 |

## Practical Planning

In this section, we will continue demonstrating the planning process using our ongoing example, online travel agency (OTA) Expedia.

We start this portion of the plan with a summary of Expedia's market, summarized in Figure 3.5.

**Industry**: Travel agencies. The category is online travel agents.

**NAICS/ SIC Code**: The U.S. Census Bureau categories travel agencies using NAICS 561510 and SIC 4724. The Bureau does not break the industry down further into the OTA category.

**Customer Needs**: Several customer needs are met with this service. The first customer need is the researching of various accommodations (airlines, hotels, etc.) according to specific customer criteria. The second need is the actual booking of the accommodations. The third need is the sense of empowerment that a customer gets when one does it oneself—some people might feel a sense of power, freedom, or economy (money saved) by establishing their own travel accommodations.

**Market Size**: According to PhoCusWright, a leading travel research company, the market size of the online travel agency market worldwide in 2010 is about $200 billion.[26]

**Market Growth Rate**: According to a Forrester Research report, the number of U.S. customers booking trips online will increase by only 3.5 percent, a substantially lower growth rate than years before.[27]

The second step in our market overview is to conduct a P.E.S.T. analysis, summarized in Figure 3.6. In practice, the market description table is often combined with the P.E.S.T. analysis table for one overall market overview table. Political, economic, social, and technological trends can shape the OTA market:

**Political**: First, some governmental bodies restricted travel during health epidemics, such as the severe acute respiratory syndrome (SARS)/bird flu and H1N1

**Figure 3.6** P.E.S.T. Analysis: Political, Economic, Social, and Technological Trends in Travel

| Trend Category | Description |
| --- | --- |
| Political | Reductions in permitted travel due to SARS/ bird flu and H1N1 health concerns |
| | Political turmoil in some countries |
| | Improved train, auto, and rail infrastructure reduces number of short-haul flights |
| Economic | General reduction in travel due to 2001–2002 and 2007–2010 recessions |
| | Super-budget travel, aka "No-Star" hotels |
| | Luxury travel: Customized, unique experiences to exciting new destinations |
| Social | Potential rise in retiree travel as more baby boomers leave the workforce |
| | Growing interest in unique travel ideas, especially adventure travel |
| | Environmentalists reluctant to travel by air because of airplane carbon footprint |
| Technology | Maturity of online booking technology; increased usage by late adopters |
| | Increasing popularity of web conferencing in lieu of physical travel |
| | Advanced smartphones driving growth of mobile travel applications |

epidemics. Second, many travelers delayed or canceled their travel plans due to political turmoil in certain areas. Third, improved train, auto, and rail infrastructure can reduce the number of short-haul flights, such as the reduction in flights within Europe due to the Chunnel and the Gotthard pass tunnel.[28]

**Economic**: First, the general recessions of 2001–2002 and 2007–2010 reduced travel in general. Second, the tight economic condition led to the advent of super-budget travel, featuring the newly coined "no-star" hotels, such as the Tune Hotel located near Kuala Lumpur's airport, offering rooms at $0.20 per night. Third, high-worth individuals sought luxury travel, with customized, unique experiences in exciting, new destinations.[29]

**Social**: First, retiree travel is likely to increase as baby boomers leave the workforce and want to remain socially active. Second, interest in unique travel ideas, especially adventure travel (heli-skiing, safari tours, and so on) is increasing. Third, the social trend of environmental sustainability might impact travel, where some environmentalists might be reluctant to travel by air because of the carbon footprint that airliners make.[30]

**Technology**: First, online booking technology is now considered mature, which could cause increased usage in late adopters. Second, Web conferencing technology is improving (and dropping in cost), making it more appealing. Third, increasing smartphone functionality is driving growth of mobile travel applications.[31]

We can also examine the market forces acting on the online travel agency industry by using Porter's Five Forces industry analysis framework.

**Threat of Entry**: High. Software development firms could create the needed technology or acquire it from another party. For example, Google purchased travel software developer ITA Software to acquire its innovative travel pricing, shopping, and availability technology.[32]

**Intensity of Rivalry**: High. The major OTAs differ little in their services, and price drops from one OTA (such as the elimination of airline booking fees) are quickly copied by the other OTAs.

**Pressure from Substitute Products**: Medium. While it is unlikely we will return to traditional travel agents, other substitutes could appear. For example, multi-OTA search firms such as Kayak (which searches multiple OTA databases such as those of Expedia and Hotwire) could become more prevalent.

**Bargaining Power of Buyers**: Medium. Some corporate buyers bypass OTAs, believing they can find lower prices with their corporate buying power. For example, executive assistants and event planners often negotiate directly with hotel management for lower pricing when booking large blocks of rooms.

**Bargaining Power of Suppliers**: Medium. Some travel providers, such as high-end luxury hotels, might refuse to provide low prices to OTAs, fearing that the practice could damage their brands.

We will be leveraging the market summary data from this section as we continue our ongoing Expedia marketing plan example in subsequent chapters.

## Summary

Thomas Watson, chairman of IBM in 1943, said, "I think there is a world market for about four or five electronic computers."

Marketers often make the mistake of focusing too hard on trying to sell a physical item, rather than on focusing on solving a market need. What if Apple simply made Macintosh computers and never invented new ways of satisfying the market need for portable computing devices, such as the iPhone or the iPad?

This chapter also covered NAICS/SIC codes, which are a handy way to describe an industry using a standardized industrial classification system.

The next step is to estimate the total size and growth rate of the market. To determine the market's size and growth rate, we have a number of potential sources. Often, the fastest, easiest, and most credible source is a purchased industry analyst report. This can be very expensive, though, running into thousands of dollars, which can be prohibitive for small businesses. To address the cost issue, we can gather data from industry associations, available articles, and government data.

Market trends and forces can provide insight on the future of the market. A quick, effective way to gather data is with the P.E.S.T. analysis. The P.E.S.T. analysis considers the political, economic, social, and technological trends shaping the market. The Five Force industry analysis framework by Michael Porter can offer further insight by examining industry impacts due to new entrants, rivaling firms, substitute products, and the bargaining power of buyers and suppliers. Often, the insights help us uncover new opportunities and threats with the analysis.

In the next chapter, we study how to segment the market, and how to position our services and products to those segments.

## Key Terms

**Category** Group of competing firms in a segment of an industry. (p. 25)

**Customer need** Enduring desire from customers to satisfy physical, emotional, or intellectual requisites.(p. 27)

**Five Forces model** Analysis of five different forces acting on industries, and countermeasures against those forces. (p. 35)

**Industry** Group of sellers making products or delivering products that are substitutes for each other. (p. 25)

**Market** Collective set of customers purchasing products or services from sellers. (p. 25)

**Market sizing** Process of estimating the total amount of potential sales to all customers within a given market, within a given timeframe. (p. 27)

**Market trends** Ongoing behaviors in a market that suggest its future state. (p. 31)

**NAICS code** North American Industrial Classification System, a classification system developed by the U.S. Census Bureau to organize industries. (p. 27)

**Niche markets** Markets (generally small in size) for highly specialized services and products. (p. 29)

**P.E.S.T. analysis** Study of political, economic, social, and technological trends to gauge the effects of environmental forces on the market. (p. 31)

## Discussion Questions

1. Think of a company that is viewing its market too narrowly. What will be the consequences if it does not begin to view the market more broadly?

2. What are some other resources for market data not listed in this chapter?

3. Blogs are pervasive on the Web, and some cover niche markets in which we are interested. How can we assess the reputation and reliability of the information we find in blogs?

Exercises

1. Describe your organization's market, using industry, category, customer needs, and NAICS/ SIC code. Did the uncovering of customer needs suggest new ways of satisfying them in the market, perhaps with new products or services?

2. Estimate the market size and growth rate for your marketing plan. Are you considering the total market size, or a narrower market, such as the geographic area or niche your organization specializes in?

3. Conduct a P.E.S.T analysis for your marketing plan. Which trends show possible opportunities for the organization? Which trends threaten the organization's success? How do the trends impact the objectives you set forth in the previous chapter?

# CHAPTER 4

# Market Segments

## INTRODUCTION

This chapter discusses market segmentation, targeting, and positioning (STP). Sound STP strategy can give a competitive advantage to organizations, just like it did for General Motors long ago when it offered different models to cater to different markets, instead of the mass market approach pursued by Ford with its Model T. By identifying market segments, deciding which to target, then positioning our services and products toward those segments, we can concentrate our marketing energy to win against competition in the marketplace.

## CHAPTER CHECKLIST:

We cover the following marketing plan sections in this chapter:

❏ **Segmentation**: Identifying groups of customers within the overall market

❏ **Targeting**: Selecting segments on which to focus the organization's efforts

❏ **Positioning**: Occupying a distinct place in the target market's mind with our offerings

To increase the versatility of this book, it address planning aspects of both consumer markets (such as selling tourist travel services to consumers) and business markets (such as selling industrial forklifts to businesses).

## Market Segmentation: Consumer Markets

Through market **segmentation,** companies divide large markets into smaller segments. The smaller segments can be reached more efficiently and effectively with services and products that meet their unique needs. For example, Hilton Hotels knows better than to offer a "one-size-fits-all" hotel to accommodate every type of traveler. Instead, it offers several different types of hotel experiences, such as the Waldorf Astoria for the affluent, Hampton Inn for value-conscious travelers, and Homewood Suites for extended stays.

The Waldorf Astoria hotel targets affluent travelers in New York City.
Source: Alamy

Organizations providing services and products to consumer markets can use a variety of different segmentation techniques. As shown in Figure 4.1, the most popular consumer segmentation methods include demographic, geographic, psychographic, behavioral, and other approaches (for special situations). The most appropriate technique will depend on the particular characteristics of the service or product offering. For example, an organization selling geography-specific products, like surfboards, should use geographic segmentation. After we review the popular segmentation methods, we provide decision criteria to guide the selection of the appropriate method, and suggest market research tips to get the data needed to execute the segmentation process.[1]

**Figure 4.1** Consumer Market Segmentation Approaches

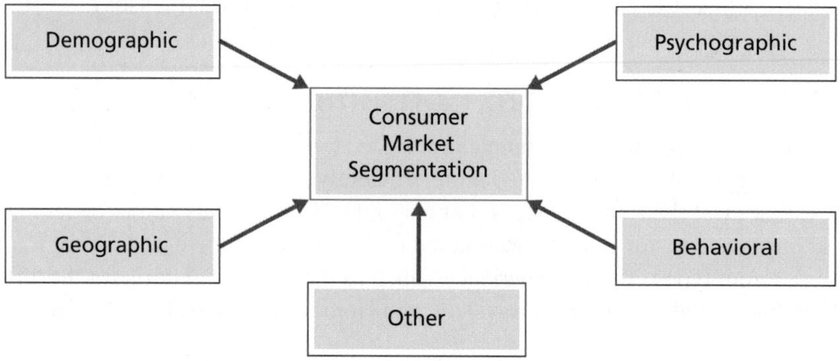

## Consumer Market Segmentation: Demographic

**Demographic segmentation** techniques segment the population using personal attributes such as age, income, sex, occupation, and education. Demographic segmentation is very popular, especially for mature markets. Here are several demographic segmentation categories and examples:

**Age:**  Companies can group the population into age segments. For example, hearing aids are typically marketed to the elderly.

**Income**:  Organizations can segment the population by levels of personal income. For example, financial planning services often target high-income, high-worth individuals.

**Sex**:  Organizations can segment based on the gender of an individual. For example, many fashion brands are targeted to women.

**Household Type**:  Organizations can segment the population by the type of household. For example, amusement theme parks target families with children.

**Occupation**:  A company's products or services can be directed toward a particular occupation. For example, rugged clothing apparel manufacturer Dickies targets individuals in blue-collar jobs, such as construction and manufacturing.

### Marketing Planning in Action

**U.S. Census Bureau Demographic Data**. The U.S. Census Bureau data is a popular source for demographic data. For example, the bureau recently reported that Lincoln County, South Dakota, is one of the top twenty fastest growing midsized counties. In addition, Lincoln County residents appear to be getting more educated—the number of people aged 25 or older with a bachelor's degree increased 25 percent. On the other hand, the City of Muskegon, Michigan, led the entire nation in unemployment during the period from 2005 through 2007, where they suffered an unemployment rate of 22.1 percent. Nearby Detroit did not fare much better—their jobless rate was 21.6 percent.[2]

# Consumer Market Segmentation: Geographic

**Geographic segmentation**, where companies segment the market according to physical location characteristics, is another popular segmentation technique. The technique works well when geographic areas possess unique traits that are relevant to the service or product offering that the company provides, such as surfboards or food seasoned to satisfy local tastes. Here are several geographic segmentation examples:

**International**:  Companies can choose to market their brands in certain countries, but not others. For example, Nike improved its brand associations around soccer when it chose to market its shoes to the European market.

**Geographic Feature**:  Distinctive features of a geographical area can influence the types of services or products to market there. For example, Southern California boasts long stretches of coastline, making it ideal for the sales of personal watercraft and surfboards, and providing boating repair services.

**Climate**:  Typical climates of a geographical area can also be used to the company's advantage. For example, the cold climate of the Rocky Mountains makes the area well suited for skiing and snowboarding.

**Metro Size**:  The size of a particular region can impact marketing. For example, some businesses select larger cities because of greater available market sizes. A concept often used in metro size geographic segmentation is the **Metropolitan Statistical Area (MSA)**, defined by the U.S. Census Bureau as a concentrated core area (like a major city) surrounded by adjacent communities tightly integrated socially and economically with that core. For example, MSA #16980, the Chicago-Joliet-Naperville MSA (sometimes called Chicagoland) centers on Chicago, Illinois, with 9.5 million people in 14 counties over three states.[3]

**Density**:  The density of an area, or the number of people packed into the area, can also aid marketing. For example, dog walking services are popular in large cities like New York because so many people with dogs live fairly close together, making it relatively easy for a dog walking service to prosper there.

**Local Area**:  Companies can choose to only serve restricted areas within a community. For example, a pizzeria offering delivery services might choose to specialize in a specific area to keep delivery times low.

## Key Terms

**Segmentation**   Identifying distinct groups of customers with different needs within an overall market.

**Demographic segmentation**   Type of segmentation approach used in consumer and business markets. Uses attributes like age, income, and occupation to segment consumer markets, and physical attributes, such as such as company size and industries, to segment business markets.

**Geographic segmentation**   Type of consumer market segmentation. Uses physical location characteristics, such as metro size and density, to segment consumer markets.

**Metropolitan Statistical Area (MSA)**   Standard term used by the U.S. Census Bureau to denote a concentrated core area, like a major city, surrounded by tightly integrated adjacent communities.

**PRIZM** (Potential Rating Index by ZIP Markets), developed by Claritas, is an example of a commercial segmentation tool that combines geographic data with demographic data to provide richer descriptions of consumer segments. The tool considers multiple factors, such as education, income, urbanization, mobility, and family life cycle, and then breaks down the data by ZIP code. Segments have their own demographic traits, lifestyle preferences, and consumer behaviors—as well as catchy names. For example, the segment "Country Squires" is described as "the wealthiest residents in exurban America." The segment falls in the "Landed Gentry" social group and the "Accumulated Wealth" lifestage group.[4]

---

## Marketing Planning in Action

**Yelp Can Make or Break Small Businesses**. *Inc.* magazine noted that the online review service Yelp plays a large role in the success (or failure) of local small businesses. Yelp offers customers the chance to review the quality of services and products offered by local businesses, and many potential customers read Yelp reviews to decide if they want to patronize a local business. Before Yelp, dissatisfied customers might have complained to the owner or simply walked away. With Yelp, they now seek relief by detailing their negative experiences over the Web for all to see. As such, Yelp ratings can literally make or break a small company, and many small business owners check their Yelp pages often to monitor their ratings.[5]

---

## Consumer Market Segmentation: Psychographic

**Psychographic, or lifestyle, segmentation** uses psychological traits, lifestyles, and personal values to group customers into segments. Psychographic segmentation works well for markets with many niche segments, such as magazines (both print and online) and markets that are too complex to be modeled with geographic or demographic variables alone. Here are a few examples:

**Lifestyle**:  Marketers can segment the market based on the lifestyle of individuals. For example, urban-lifestyle magazines emphasize the pre-family lifestyle segment (people owning or renting their own home that enjoy partying with friends at nightclubs in the evening) over the family lifestyle segment (people with children who enjoy child-oriented activities).

**Interests and Opinions**:  Marketers can target the segment of individuals who are interested in organic foods and believe that such foods are healthier.

**Activities**:  Some magazines cater to segments that enjoy particular activities or hobbies, such as gardening, bicycling, or motor racing.

The Strategic Business Insights' VALS™ (values, attitudes, and lifestyles) framework is an example of a commercially available psychographic segmentation tool. The VALS framework segments U.S. adult consumers into one of eight segments (called "mindsets") based on their responses to the VALS questionnaire. The framework segments consumers in two dimensions: their degree of resources and innovation (the vertical dimension) and their primary motivations (the horizontal dimension). The combination of resources and motivations predicts how a consumer will behave in the marketplace. For example, VALS defines Innovators as "successful, sophisticated, take-charge people with high self-esteem."[6]

## Marketing Planning in Action

**Hallmark: Boomer Cards Meet with Cold Greeting.** Hallmark, the famous maker of greeting cards, should have considered psychographics, instead of only demographics, when developing its new line of cards for aging baby boomers. It carefully considered demographic data, determining that 78 million baby boomers would soon hit age 50, and developed cards to meet that market. The new line of cards, called The Time of Your Life, aimed to incorporate boomers in the cards. The cards featured active midlifers looking youthful as they frolicked on beaches and dived into swimming pools. One problem: Baby boomers strongly believed that they were not, in fact, aging, let alone old. No self-respecting boomer wants to be seen shopping in the "old person's cards" section. As a result, the Time of Your Life line of cards was dropped shortly after its launch.[7]

## Consumer Market Segmentation: Behavioral

**Behavioral segmentation** can be considered a subset of psychographic segmentation. It segments consumers based on their knowledge of a brand, their attitude toward it, their use of the brand, and their response to it. Behavioral segmentation works well when the services or products have strong associations with behaviors, such as eating hot dogs at baseball stadiums. The segmentation technique also works well when heavy users account for much of the market, such as teenagers accounting for the vast majority of text messages sent on mobile devices. Here are some examples of behavioral segmentation:

**Occasions:** Some consumers purchase higher-quality coffee (and liquor) when entertaining than for everyday use.

**Benefits**: Different people perceive different benefits from the same product. For example, some consumers may purchase a large sports utility vehicle (SUV) for its

## Key Terms

**PRIZM** (Potential Rating Index by ZIP Markets). Commercial segmentation tool combining geographic data with demographic data.

**Psychographic segmentation** Type of consumer market segmentation. Uses psychological traits, lifestyles, and personal values, such as interests in organic foods, to segment consumer markets.

**Behavioral segmentation** Type of consumer market segmentation. Uses brand knowledge, attitudes, and usage, such as heavy usage of a brand, to segment consumer markets.

cavernous capacity. Others may purchase it for its perceived safety, even if they never intend to carry big loads.

**Usage Rate**:  Heavy users are often a small percentage of the market but account for most of the consumption. For example, heavy beer drinkers account for 80 percent of all beer sold.

**Readiness to Buy**:  Marketers can segment the market based on a consumer's readiness to buy. Consumers are in one of four stages: unaware, aware, interested, and intending to buy. Each segment requires a different marketing communications program.

**Loyalty**:  Some companies group markets into four segments: Faithfully loyal (would never switch brands), losable (generally loyal to the brand, but might switch), winnable (generally loyal to a competitor's brand, but might switch to your brand), and lost (faithfully loyal to another brand).

## Consumer Market Segmentation: Other Approaches

Marketers can also use other approaches to segment the market, such as price segmentation, time segmentation, and distribution channel segmentation. The approaches work well to address the specific situations of unique markets.

**Price Segmentation**:  Marketers have long used **price segmentation** as a way to segment the market. For example, General Motors won market share over its rivals in the early days of automotive history by offering Chevrolet, Pontiac, Oldsmobile, Buick, and Cadillac brands that varied in price (and status) along a clearly defined spectrum to appeal to successively higher-income groups.

**Occasion Segmentation (also called time segmentation)**:  We can **segmentation** market our services and products to certain times. For example, we market turkeys and cranberry sauce for Thanksgiving, toys for Christmas, and fireworks for Independence Day.

**Distribution Channel Segmentation**:  We can also use **distribution channel segmentation** to target our product or service to selected markets. For example, Apple originally sold its popular iPhone smartphone only through AT&T's cellular phone service.

Figure 4.2 summarizes the types of consumer market segmentation approaches, sample categories within the segmentation types, and typical situations where particular segmentation approaches should be used.

## Market Research for Consumer Markets

This section discusses useful data sources to gather market research for consumer markets, including finding data for segmentation.

As Figure 4.3 shows, we have three goals in our market research efforts.

**Segmentation Data**:  Understand the market well enough so that we can segment the market into groups

**Targeting Data**:  Understand the potential profitability of the segment and the alignment with our capabilities

**Positioning Data**:  Understand the segments' needs and motivations for purchase so we can position our products and services to them

**Figure 4.2** Decision Chart: Consumer Segmentation Approaches

*Source:* Adapted with permission from Kotler and Keller, *Marketing Management*, 13th ed. (Upper Saddle River, NJ: Pearson Prentice-Hall, 2009). Table 8.1, p. 214.

| Segmentation Type | Sample Categories | Decision Guidelines:Best used for following situations: |
| --- | --- | --- |
| Demographic | Age<br>Income<br>Sex<br>Occupation | Mature markets |
| Geographic | International<br>Feature<br>Climate<br>Metro Size<br>Density | Geography-specific services or products |
| Psychographic | Lifestyles<br>Interests and Opinions<br>Activities | Niche segments |
| Behavioral | Occasions<br>Benefits<br>Usage Rate<br>Readiness to Buy<br>Loyalty | Heavy users account for 80% of sales |
| Other Approaches | Price<br>Occasion<br>Distribution Channel | Address specific markets |

**Figure 4.3** Market Research Goals

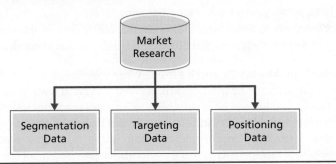

## Key Terms

**Price Segmentation** Type of consumer market segmentation. Uses differing price points to sell to different markets.

**Time Segmentation** Type of consumer market segmentation. Sometimes also called occasion segmentation. Segments the market by using specific times during the year, such as marketing turkeys and cranberry sauce for Thanksgiving, and fireworks for Independence Day.

**Figure 4.4** Consumer Market Research Data Sources

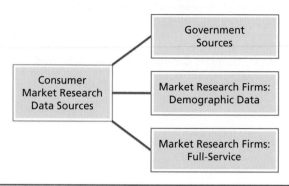

To achieve these goals, we show several categories of sources, examples of each, and suggest the data sources to use for each type of segmentation approach. As Figure 4.4 shows, some useful consumer market research data sources include government sources, market research firms specializing in demographic data, and full-service market research firms. While every market is different, the sources listed here are a good place to start.

**Government Sources.**  The U.S. government as well as state and local municipalities publish a wealth of data, often broken down to the neighborhood level. The data are all free and easily available online. Here are a few examples:

- **U.S. Census Bureau**: The United States offers detailed demographic data through its U.S. Census Bureau (*census.gov*). For example, marketers starting a line of baby clothing will certainly benefit from knowing census bureau data such as recent birth rates.
- **Statistics Portal**: The U.S. government operates a statistics portal called usa.gov that provides links to census, labor, and economic information.
- **FactFinder**: The FactFinder tool (factfinder.census.gov) is available to look up population, housing, economic, and geographic data.
- **Local Chambers of Commerce**: Many municipalities eagerly want to help small businesses located there, and will offer relevant information about that area.

**Demographic Data Market Research Firms.**  When government sources do not offer the detail needed, private firms are available to drill down to the next level. Some firms, such as GeoLytics (geolytics.com) and ESRI (esri.com), offer census and demographic data to study thousands of variables on a large- and small-scale basis. The services are especially useful for areas where it is more difficult to find information, such as international markets. The disadvantage of this approach is that the information provided is not free.

**Full-Service Market Research Firms.**  As shown in Figure 4.5, some popular market research techniques include focus groups, observational research, ethnographic research, and surveys. In-depth, qualitative research techniques such as focus groups, observational research, and ethnographic research work well for psychographic segmentation. Qualitative research provides the insight, the conceptual knowledge, and

Government sources, like the Library of Congress in Washington, D.C., can provide a wealth of market data.

*Source*: Shutterstock

**Figure 4.5** Sample Market Research Techniques

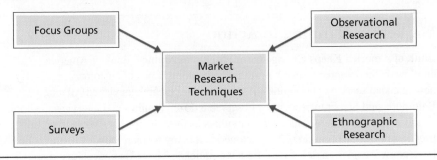

## Key Terms

**Distribution channel segmentation**   Type of consumer market segmentation. Uses different distribution channels to target certain markets. For example, Apple originally only sold its popular iPhone smartphone through AT&T's cellular phone service.

the consumer's exact language necessary to understand the market. Often, marketers will augment their initial qualitative research with a detailed survey over a large representative sample of consumers.

- **Focus Groups**: **Focus groups** are a traditional approach to primary research. In focus groups, a professional moderator asks a group of carefully chosen individuals about a topic. The goal is to understand consumers' motives behind their behaviors— why they do what they do. Many see focus groups as artificial, however, and they are not as popular now as they were in the past.[8]
- **Observational Research**: The goal behind **observational research** is to watch what people actually do with products in the context of their natural environment. By watching behaviors and listening, researchers can get unique insights on how to solve their problems.

## Marketing Planning in Action

**Intuit Success Follows Observational Techniques**. Intuit used observational research techniques in its "Follow Me Home" program to watch how people actually use their tax preparation and accounting products. For example, Intuit learned that accountants spend a lot of time creating statements for clients. Consequently, Intuit launched a product called Financial Statement Reporter that can easily create documents like balance sheets and income statements to streamline the statement creation process.[9]

- **Ethnographic Research**: **Ethnographic research** is similar to anthropological research in that the researchers immerse themselves into consumers' lives to understand them better.

## Marketing Planning in Action

**Bank of America Keeps Change through Ethnographics**. Bank of America employed ethnographic research to study the banking habits of customers to identify new financial service opportunities. A team of nine researchers visited Atlanta, Baltimore, and San Francisco. They observed a dozen families and interviewed people on the streets. They tagged along with mothers as they shopped at Costco, paid bills, and tried to save for their children. They learned that many women rounded up their checkbook entries to an even dollar because it was quicker. They also noticed that many boomer mothers had difficulty saving for their children. As a result of the research, Bank of America launched their "Keep the Change" program, where transactions are rounded up, and the extra amount transferred to the customer's savings account.[10]

- **Surveys**: Marketers will often supplement the initial qualitative research techniques, previously discussed, with a detailed **survey** over a large representative sample of consumers. For example, in designing a market segmentation questionnaire for a hotel, a series of in-depth interviews could be conducted to help create the survey instrument. The instrument would likely have a values section (What is the most important attribute for a hotel?), an attitudes section (What do you enjoy about hotel stays?), and a perceptions section (How does the Hilton brand compare to the Hyatt brand?).

## Marketing Planning in Action

**Hilton Travel Survey**. *Inc.* magazine reported on a Hilton Garden Inn telephone survey of 1,020 travelers. Contrary to the popular notion that most people dislike business travel, many female travelers responded that they secretly enjoy business travel. The survey results suggested something about the attitudes and values that drove their enjoyment. Nearly 75 percent of female business travelers enjoy having someone else clean up after them, whereas only 58 percent of men felt this way. Sixty-two percent of women said they also appreciated having someone else make breakfast for them, and over 50 percent said that having the bed to themselves was another big travel perk. The Hilton Garden Inn can use this type of survey feedback to tailor their marketing messages to the attitudes and values of female travelers.[11]

Figure 4.6 summarizes several market research sources, examples of each, and segmentation approaches suited for the sources.

**Figure 4.6** Decision Chart: Consumer Market Segmentation Market Research Sources

| Source | Examples | Decision Guidelines: Best Used for Following Situations: |
| --- | --- | --- |
| Government Sources | U.S. Census Bureau Statistics Portal Fact Finder Local Chamber of Commerce | Demographic Geographic |
| Market Research Firms, Demographic Data | Geolytics ESRI | Demographic Geographic |
| Market Research Firms, Full Service | Focus Groups Observational Research Ethnographic Research Surveys | Psychographic Behavioral |

# Market Segmentation: Business Markets

Just as with consumer markets, the goal of segmentation, targeting, and positioning for business markets is to identify clusters of prospective customers that have consistent patterns of behavior and preferences (segmentation), select several segments on which to focus (targeting), then develop communications to those segments using associations relevant to those segments (positioning).

## Business Market Differences from Consumer Markets

Business markets consist of companies involved in business-to-business (B2B) transactions. In business markets, businesses sell products and services to other businesses, instead of consumers. As a result, business markets differ from consumer markets in several important areas: [12]

**Fewer Buyers**: Business-to-business companies sell their products to fewer buyers than their business-to-consumer (B2C) counterparts. In fact, some B2B companies target their sales to only one, large buyer, like General Motors or the U.S. government.

**Larger Orders**: B2B orders are generally larger, and worth more than B2C orders. For example, a medical supply company selling to a hospital might process orders worth hundreds of thousands of dollars, much more than consumers would spend on such supplies.

**Multiple Sales Calls**: B2B salespeople often visit prospects ten times or more to close a major sale. It is rare to find such a large number of visits for consumer items.

**Longer Sales Cycles**: Sales cycles for complex B2B products can take six months or more to close. Sales cycles for consumer items, even big-ticket items like houses, are rarely longer than 30 days.

**Close Seller–Buyer Relationship**: B2B companies that sell to other businesses form a close relationship with their buyers over many years. Consumers, on the other hand, have a limited involvement with sellers.

**Professional Purchasing Role**: Most B2B companies appoint a purchasing agent to manage purchase negotiations and contracts for the firm. Consumers typically represent themselves.

**Multiple Buying Roles**: B2B companies involve multiple people, with multiple roles, in the buying process. Except for some major decisions, like buying a house, most consumer buying decisions are made alone.

Figure 4.7 summarizes the differences between business markets and consumer markets.

**Figure 4.7** Comparison of Business and Consumer Markets

| Business Market Characteristic | Business Markets | Consumer Markets |
|---|---|---|
| Fewer Buyers | Typical businesses sell to only hundreds of buyers. Some businesses sell to only a few huge buyers like GM or the U.S. government | Typical consumer-based companies sell to thousands, perhaps millions of consumers. |
| Larger Orders | An order from a hospital to a medical supply company might be worth hundreds of thousands of dollars | A purchase by a consumer for adhesive bandages might be worth less than $10 |
| Multiple Sales Calls | Salespeople for complex products and services might visit a prospect 10 times or more before closing a sale | Consumers are rarely visited by sales people, and even those that are, like remodeling contractors, rarely make more than 1–2 visits to close the sale |
| Longer Sales Cycles | Sales cycles for complex products and services might take 6–9 months, or longer, before the sale is closed | Sales cycles for consumer goods are rarely longer than 30 days even for complex items like houses and cars |
| Close Seller–Buyer Relationship | Many businesses have known their customers for many, many years. They value their long-term relationship. | Most consumers have a limited involvement with sellers. Once the deal is done, it is rare to see that seller again. |
| Professional Purchasing Role | Most organizations dedicate a special person, or even a department, to the purchasing role | Consumers rarely have a professional background in the negotiation and execution of purchase contracts. |
| Multiple Buying Roles | Most organizations have multiple people, with multiple roles, in the buying process | Except for some decisions made with two or more people, like the purchase of a house, most decisions are made alone |

## Key Terms

**Focus groups**   Research technique to gather opinions of carefully chosen individuals about a topic.

**Observational research**   Research technique to watch people's actual behaviors in the context of their natural environment.

**Ethnographic research**   Research technique where researchers immerse themselves into consumers' lives to understand them better.

**Surveys**   Research instruments to gather data (generally quantitative) over a large population of potential customers.

## Marketing Planning in Action

**Timken: Bearing down on the Energy Market**. Timken, known best for their ball bearings, sells their products to businesses. To prevent overexposure to any individual business sector, it has embarked on a diversification strategy. It purchased six new businesses while reducing its sales to the auto industry from 40 percent of revenues to less than 20 percent. The company's goal is to demand a premium price for its products by shifting its focus from commodity products, such as the bearings it sells to Detroit, to high-margin niche markets, such as aerospace. One potentially lucrative new market for Timken is supplying parts for windmills, which use turbines "the size and weight of a school bus" to generate electricity.[13]

Now that we understand the differences between business and consumer markets, we will cover different approaches to identifying segments within business markets. Sometimes we can use the same segmentation techniques as we covered for consumer segmentation (and indeed, demographic segmentation is often used in business market segmentation). Usually, though, more specific tools are required. As shown in Figure 4.8, the most popular business segmentation methods include demographic, operating variables, purchasing approaches, situational factors, and personal characteristics. In addition, we suggest several sources with which to start the market research process for each segmentation approach.[14]

## Business Market Segmentation: Demographic

Similar to demographic segmentation on the consumer side, business market **demographic segmentation** divides the market into groups based on physical attributes. Businesses can use demographic data to describe the customer segments (other businesses) to which they can sell. As with consumer-based demographic segmentation, this approach works well with mature, easily identifiable markets. Here are a few typical demographic segmentation categories:

**Customer Industries**:  Businesses can segment the market by industry. For example, a ball bearing company can sell its bearings to the automotive industry, the aerospace industry, or to the energy industry to make wind turbines.

**Customer Company Sizes**:  Businesses can sell to small-, medium-, or large-sized companies. For example, a company selling multi-million-dollar enterprise software packages might sell only to large businesses, whereas another software provider might sell smaller, less expensive programs to small- and medium-sized businesses.

**Customer Location**:  Businesses can segment by location. For example, businesses wanting to sell automotive parts will likely have to sell to Detroit, Michigan, where many U.S. automotive manufacturers are located.

**Figure 4.8** Business Market Segmentation Approaches

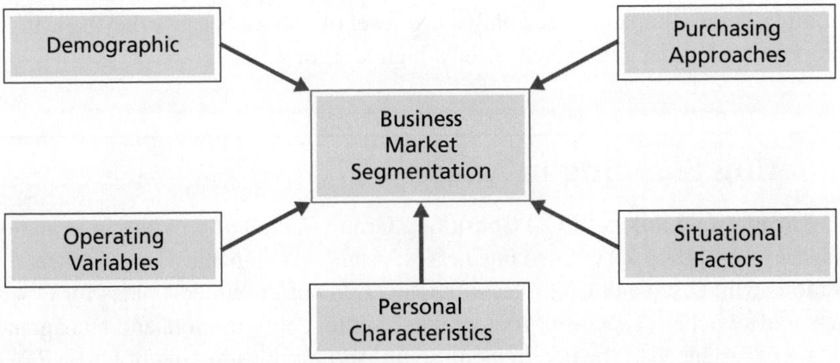

Marketing Planning in Action

**Chicago Nut and Bolt: Large Orders for Large Companies**. Chicago Nut and Bolt (*chicagonutandbolt.com*) manufactures custom nuts, bolts, screws, clips, and other types of fasteners. They target large company sizes by specializing in large orders, up to 1,000,000 pieces. The company maintains a massive inventory of fastener blanks for quick responsiveness to customer needs. Chicago Nut and Bolt can also warehouse a year's worth of product for their customers, for businesses which demand large orders, but have no place to store the fasteners before use.[15]

## Business Market Segmentation: Operating Variables

Business markets can be segmented using the **operating variables** approach, which segments markets according to the way that customers run their organizations. The operating variables approach is useful when the business sells tools to increase operational efficiencies of companies. Here are a few typical operating variable categories:

**Customer Technology:** We can segment the market based on the technologies that prospective customers use to run their operations. For example, if target customers run their operations using Cisco networking technology, then our solution must be compatible with that technology. Colloquially this is referred to as "running a Cisco shop."

**User or Nonuser**: We can target customers that are light users of a product, or heavy users. For example, Software as a Service (SaaS) software systems typically have small

### Key Terms

**Operating variables segmentation** Type of business market segmentation. Uses the different ways businesses operate their organizations, like the technology they use, to segment business markets.

feature sets, so are suited for light users, whereas enterprise software systems have rich functionality, so are better suited for heavy users.

**Customer Capabilities**: We can consider companies needing different levels of service. For example, some companies need only a low level of service because they have in-house support personnel; other departments need a high level of service.

---

## Marketing Planning in Action

**LOD Targets Technology**. LOD Consulting Group (*lod.com*) provides information technology consulting services to businesses. It targets companies running their operations with Cisco and UNIX technologies. LOD offers support plans for Cisco routers and switches. They offer router/switch setup, configuration, and management. They are experienced in the deployment, setup, and troubleshooting of Cisco PIX firewalls, as well as Cisco VPN network installations and management.[16]

---

## Business Market Segmentation: Purchasing Approaches

Business markets can be segmented according to the **purchasing approaches** of the company buying the product or service. This type of segmentation is useful for companies that sell services or products that are not highly differentiated from those of competitors. Instead of differentiating on services or products, these businesses can differentiate them selves in being easy to do business with, like working well with the target company's purchasing department. Here are a few typical purchasing segmentation categories:

**Purchasing Organization**: Type:  Companies can target centralized purchasing organizations, like those of Walmart, or decentralized purchasing organizations, like those of large multinational firms that have several autonomous divisions.

**Power Structure**:  Businesses can also segment the market based on the power structure of the target companies. For example, they can pursue engineering-driven organizations, such as those in high technology, or financially driven organizations, such as many industrial products companies.

**Existing Relationship**:  Companies can segment based on the type of existing relationship they have with their customers. For example, they can focus on companies with long existing relationships with the firm, or emphasize new business to companies that have never done business with the firm.

**Purchasing Policies**:  Businesses can segment the market based on purchasing policies. For example, it can cater to companies employing leasing arrangements, like automotive dealerships; it can emphasize service contracts, like consumer electronics stores; or it can emphasize bidding situations, like contracting with the U.S. government.

**Purchasing Criteria**:  Companies can segment based on purchasing criteria, and cater to companies seeking quality (like large industrial companies), cater to companies emphasizing service (like those in construction), or cater to companies demanding the lowest price (like government organizations).

Heavy equipment manufacturer Caterpillar is renowned for its outstanding customer service for business markets.

*Source*: Shutterstock

## Marketing Planning in Action

**Caterpillar: Moving Mountains for Its Customers**. Caterpillar (*cat.com*) is the world's leading manufacturer of construction equipment. One key to its success is that it targets companies that place service high on their list of purchasing criteria. For example, a construction company might be contracted to build structures in remote locations under tight deadlines. Caterpillar understands that companies such as this can not afford long delays due to broken construction equipment, so it provides real-time access to over 800,000 Caterpillar parts and operates an extensive network of dealers all around the world.[17]

## Business Market Segmentation: Situational Factors

Business markets can be segmented according to the **situational factors** facing the company buying the product or service. This segmentation approach is useful for businesses that sell to companies that regularly experience special situations. For example, businesses in the third-party logistics industry often cater to companies needing to expedite orders by providing rapid shipping services (at an additional fee). Here are a few typical categories:

**Sense of Urgency:** Businesses can segment based on the customer's sense of urgency. For example, it can target companies needing immediate response to service requests because they can not afford to be shut down a single minute.

**Specific Applications**: Companies can also segment the market based on customers' specific applications. For example, the business can manufacture unique products designed for special-purpose applications, or perform niche services for businesses.

**Order Size**: Businesses can segment on order size. For example, they can focus on organizations placing large orders like hospitals and government agencies.

---

## Marketing Planning in Action

**Aisle-Master: Narrow Niche for Narrow Aisles**. Aisle-Master (*aisle-master.com*) is a business-to-business company that manufactures forklifts. They employ the situational factors segmentation method by manufacturing unique forklifts specifically designed for warehouse operations. Their forklifts articulate to fit in the very narrow aisles of crowded warehouses. The articulated design permits the forklift to approach storage racks at an angle, avoiding the problem of swinging the back of the forklift around in tight spaces. The company offers their special forklifts in different capacities and different fuels (liquid petroleum gas or electric) to suit different applications.[18]

---

## Business Market Segmentation: Personal Characteristics

Business markets can be segmented according to the degree to which the seller's **personal characteristics** match those of the buyer's. This approach to segmentation is useful for businesses with a strong sense of values or a distinct "personality." For example, many businesses have adopted a "green" philosophy and prefer to do business with companies which feel the same way. Here are a few typical categories:

**Buyer–Seller Similarity**: Businesses can segment the market based on the similarity of the buyer with the seller. They can emphasize selling to companies with personal values similar to their own.

**Attitude to Risk:** Companies can also segment based on attitude to risk, catering to companies with either very low or very high tolerances to risk.

**Supplier Loyalty**: Businesses can segment on supplier loyalty, by emphasizing sales efforts primarily toward buyers that have shown a high degree of supplier loyalty in the past.

Solar panel manufacturer DM Solar targets companies that share the company's "green" values.
*Source*: Shutterstock

## Marketing Planning in Action

**DM Solar Seeing the Light**. DM Solar (*dmsolar.com*) designs and builds photovoltaic arrays for the solar panel industry. The company targets companies that value environmental responsibility by communicating its own "green" values. To demonstrate its commitment to renewable energy, it states that it is a global leader in the renewable energy industry. It is also a member of the Green Building Council. In its blog, the company features several "green" posts, such as an article discussing how Silicon Valley will face stiff Chinese competition in the growing "cleantech" environmental products market.[19]

## Key Terms

**Purchasing approaches segmentation**   Type of business market segmentation. Uses the different ways businesses purchase products and services, like policies, to segment business markets.

**Situational factors segmentation**   Type of business market segmentation. Uses unique situations businesses find themselves in, such as having to frequently expedite orders, to segment business markets.

**Personal characteristics**   Type of business market segmentation. Uses matches between personal characteristics of the seller and the buyer, such as adoption of a "green" philosophy, to segment business markets.

**Figure 4.9** Summary of Business Segmentation Approaches
*Source:* Adapted with permission from Kotler and Keller, *Marketing Management*, 13th ed. (Upper Saddle: NJ: Pearson Prentice-Hall, 2009). Table 8.2, p. 227.

| Segmentation Type | Sample Categories | Decision Guidelines:Best Used for Following Situations: |
|---|---|---|
| Demographic | Customer Industries Customer Sizes Customer Locations | Businesses in stable, mature markets |
| Operating Variables | Customer Technology User or Non-User Customer Capabilities | Businesses selling tools to increase operational efficiencies |
| Purchasing Approaches | Purchasing Organization Type Power Structure Existing Relationship Purchasing Policies Purchasing Criteria | Businesses wanting to differentiate themselves by being easy to do business with |
| Situational Factors | Sense of Urgency Specific Applications Order Size | Businesses with flexible operations or development processes that can respond to unique customer requests |
| Personal Characteristics | Buyer-Seller Similarity Attitude to Risk Supplier Loyalty | Businesses with a strong sense of values or distinct personality |

Figure 4.9 summarizes the types of business market segmentation approaches, sample categories within the segmentation types, and typical situations to select particular segmentation approaches.

## Market Research for Business Markets

Similar to the section on market research sources for consumer market segmentation, this section discusses useful data sources to gather market research for business markets, summarized in Figure 4.10.[20]

**Government Sources**.  As we saw earlier with consumer markets, the U.S. government collects and publishes a wealth of data, often useful for demographic and geographic segmentation of markets. The data are all free and easily available online. Examples of government sources include Industry Samplers accessed through industry North

**Figure 4.10** Business Market Research Data Sources

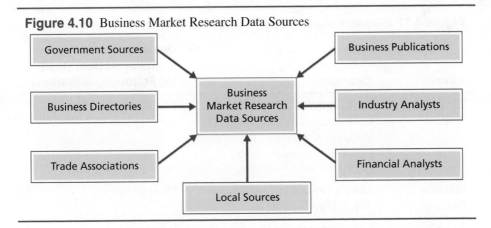

American Industry Classification System (NAICS) code (*census.gov/naics*), business and industry statistics (*census.gov/econ*), and the U.S. Government Printing Office (*gpo.gov*).

**Business Directories**. Online directories can be useful to gain an overview of the categories of particular industries and the companies which serve them. The data are useful for demographic segmentation of markets. Like government sources, the data are free and available online. Examples include the Google Business Directory and the Yahoo! Business Directory.

**Trade Associations**. Virtually every industry is represented by some type of trade association. Often, the association publishes studies of that industry's market characteristics. The data published are useful for demographic segmentation, but can be used for a host of other research activities as well. Some sources are free and available online. Thousands of trade associations exist. They can be found by accessing association directories, such as the Gale Encyclopedia of Associations, the Google Directory of Industry Associations, and the Yahoo! Business Trade Associations index.

**Business Publications**. Business publications cover general trends in business markets. They cater to their readership (businesses) by publishing articles discussing productivity-enhancing tools and capabilities, which are useful for finding data to support operating variables segmentation. Business publications for particular industries can be found through magazine indexes such as the Google Business Magazines Index, the TradePub Index, and the Yahoo! Trade Magazines Index.

**Industry Analysts**. Industry analysts specialize in analyzing industries (like those dealing in enterprise software and manufacturing equipment) that sell to businesses. Examples include analysts such as Forrester Research (*forrester.com*) and Gartner, Inc. (*gartner.com*).

**Financial Analysts**. Financial analyst firms publish finance-oriented data for companies in their focus industries. Examples include companies such as Goldman Sachs (*golmansachs.com*), Hoovers (*hoovers.com*), and Morgan Stanley (*morganstanley.com*).

**Figure 4.11** Consumer Market Segmentation: Market Research Sources

| Source | Examples | Decision Guidelines: Best Used for Following Situations: |
|---|---|---|
| Government Sources | North American Industry Classification System (NAICS) Business & Industry Statistics U.S. Government Printing Office | Demographics Geographics |
| Business Directories | Google Directory: Business Yahoo Directory: B2B | Demographics |
| Trade Associations | Gale Encyclopedia of Associations Google Directory of Industry Associations Yahoo Business Trade Associations | Demographic Purchasing Many other uses |
| Business Publications | Google Business Magazines Index TradePub Index Yahoo Trade Publications Index | Operating Variables Purchasing Many other uses |
| Industry Analysts | Forrester Research Gartner | Operating Variables Many other uses |
| Financial Analysts | Goldman Sachs Hoovers Morgan Stanley | Financial Data |
| Local Sources | Local chambers of commerce Local colleges or universities Vocational schools | Operating variables Small business data Many other uses |

**Local Sources.** For businesses catering to other local businesses, getting information from local sources is recommended. This is especially relevant for small businesses. Examples include sources such as local chambers of commerce, local colleges and universities, and local vocational schools.

Figure 4.11 summarizes several market research sources, examples of each, and segmentation approaches suited for the sources.

## Targeting: Consumer Markets

Once the segments have been identified, the next step is to decide which of the segments the company should target. Targeting every segment is generally not profitable. As shown in Figure 4.12, we cover a three-factor approach to determining which segments

**Figure 4.12** Three Factors to Consider When Selecting Segments to Target

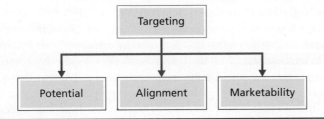

to target, studying each segment's market potential, its alignment with the organization, and its marketability.[21]

**Potential**: To extract financial benefit from a segment, it should be large, growing, and profitable to serve. We discussed assessing size and growth earlier in the book. We must also consider profitability. Even if the planet Mars had a large and growing market segment, we still would not target it because the cost to serve that segment would be "astronomical."

**Patrons are raving about the environmental responsibility of the Greenhouse Nightclub in New York City.**
*Source*: Shutterstock

## Marketing Planning in Action

**Greenhouse Nightclub Goes Green**. Manhattan nightclub Greenhouse took advantage of the large and growing market segment for environmental responsibility. At Greenhouse, environmentalists and eco-friendly consumers can celebrate knowing their revelries are consistent with their environmentally responsible lifestyle. These new clubs emphasize renewable, natural resources such as bamboo floors. Greenhouse also found a way to make the segment profitable, by emphasizing the inherent savings of conservation measures. They use low-flow sink faucets and waterless urinals, saving over 28,000 gallons per year compared to regular clubs. The bartenders sport uniforms made from organic cotton. The nightclubs are illuminated using LED (light emitting diode) light fixtures, which cuts energy use by 20 percent.[22]

**Alignment**: The segment should align with the mission, resources, and competitive advantages of the organization. We need to determine if consumers perceive a fit between the technological capabilities of the company and the needs of the segment. For example, a new line of haute couture clothing would be a better fit at Bloomingdales than at Home Depot.

## Marketing Planning in Action

**Canon: Picture Perfect Digital Imagery**. Canon developed a core competency in digital imagery. It leverages this advantage to develop a variety of products that rely on image technology. The products range from printers for home and office use to cameras for amateurs and professionals. Its excellence in image technology has catapulted its market share of single lens reflex (SLR) cameras beyond that of Nikon, once king of cameras. Newer Canon cameras can shoot high-definition (HD) video and capture photographs in low-light situations bordering on night-vision territory.[23]

**Marketability**: Segments should also have certain characteristics to facilitate **marketability**, the ability to market effectively to that segment. We need to consider **accessibility**—the ease of reaching our target market. A segment described as "sports enthusiasts" will be much easier to reach than one described as "people who like the color blue." We also need to ensure that the segments are distinct from each other. If teenagers and retirees respond similarly to the introduction of a new smartphone, they will not work well as separate segments. Another characteristic is the ease of creating a value proposition that clearly differentiates our service or product from others in that segment. We cover value propositions further in the *Products and Services* chapter in this book.

## Marketing Planning in Action

**Boy Scouts of America Apply Diversity Marketing to Reach Target Market**. The nonprofit Boy Scouts of America organization uses diversity marketing to reach the Hispanic community, a growing segment of its membership. The Boy Scouts discovered that Hispanics account for more than 20 percent of children under the age of five and are projected to make up one-quarter of the nation's population by the year 2050. At first, the Boy Scouts attempted to target the segment by simply translating its existing materials into Spanish. Because the directly translated materials were neither culturally resonant nor especially rousing, the first effort failed. In response, the Boy Scouts created a national office for the Hispanic initiative, began hiring local Latino staff, and started crafting a national ad campaign directed only at Hispanics.[24]

## Targeting: Business Markets

The targeting process for business markets is similar to that of consumer markets. Once the segments have been identified, the next step is to decide which of the segments the company should target. As we did with consumer markets, we consider three factors when targeting: potential, alignment, and marketability.[25]

**Potential**: Just as with consumer markets, we should select market segments that are large, growing, and profitable to serve in order to extract financial benefit from that segment.

## Marketing Planning in Action

**E-A-R Hears the Cha-Ching of Profit in the Military Market**. E-A-R manufactures hearing protection devices such as earplugs for its traditional markets: construction, industrial manufacturing, automotive, and law enforcement. Due to the demand for hearing protection for the military, it sells its E-A-R Combat Arms earplugs to the large military market segment. Hearing loss due to excessive noise is a significant problem, and is the number one disability from the Afghan and Iraq wars of the 2000s: 58,000 soldiers were disabled due to hearing loss. Many experts agree that properly fitting earplugs worn during periods of high noise, such as firearm discharge, can help prevent hearing loss. Awareness of the effectiveness of hearing protection continues to develop, leading to growing market demand and profitability for E-A-R's offerings.[26]

---

### Key Terms

**Accessibility**   Ease of reaching target market through marketing campaigns.

**Marketability**   Characteristics of a given segment that govern the ease of marketing effectively to that segment.

**Alignment**: Just as it is with consumer markets, the market segment we target should align with the mission and resources of the organization. We need to ensure there is a good fit between the company's capabilities and resources and the market segment.

## Marketing Planning in Action

**EnGarde: A Bulletproof Approach to Targeting New Markets**. EnGarde is a Dutch company specializing in the manufacture of bullet-resistant body armor. What once started as a product strictly for the military has expanded to include body armor for civilians, a trend made popular by the Jack Bauer character of the television program *24*. EnGarde is able to successfully target this new market segment because it aligns so closely with its existing mission and capabilities. EnGarde claims that it produces the ultimate bulletproof vests, combining comfort, durability, and maximum protection. EnGarde vests use Dyneema and Spectra fibers, which are claimed to be 40 percent stronger than Aramid fibers such as Kevlar. Jack Bauer never looked so good, or felt so safe.[27, 28]

**Marketability**: Just as with consumer market segment targeting, segments should be accessible, distinct, and have a clear value proposition that differentiates the business's service or product from others in that segment.

## Marketing Planning in Action

**JIMS USA Targets Pro Motorcycle Mechanic Market**. JIMS, a specialty tool manufacturer, leverages the marketability of its target market segment (professional mechanics of Harley-Davidson motorcycles) to succeed. The market segment is accessible—locations of Harley-Davidson dealerships are easy to find. The market segment is distinct—nonprofessional "shade-tree" mechanics do not buy their products at the same rate as professionals, because the high cost of JIMS's tools can only be justified if used frequently. And the value proposition is clear—professionals need a wide variety of tools to save them time, and JIMS delivers. Their tool catalog spans 209 pages and includes such niche items as "H-D Cruise Drive 6-Speed Main Drive Gear Installer Tool."[29]

# Positioning: Consumer Markets

**Positioning** a product or service is more than just differentiating it from other offerings. It is ensuring that the differences occupy a distinct position in the minds of consumers. For example, "FedEx" occupies the position of "overnight delivery" even though many other companies also offer overnight delivery. In this section, we discuss different approaches to positioning within consumer markets.

**Figure 4.13** Consumer Market Positioning Approaches: Pizza Example

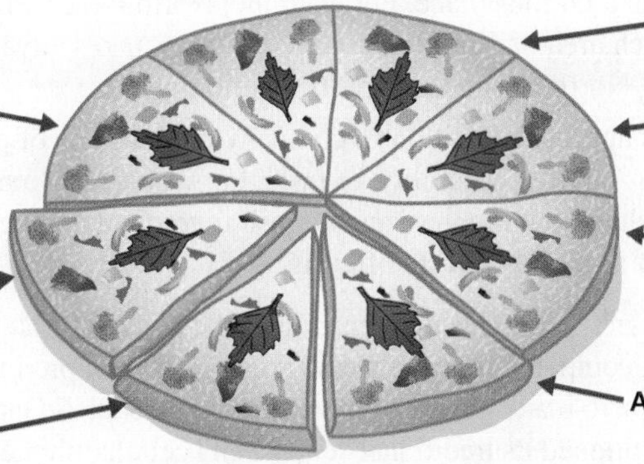

**Pizza**
**Positioning Approaches**

**Benefits**
Great Taste:
Round Table

**Geography**
San Francisco: North
Beach Pizza

**Niche**
Unusual: California
Pizza Kitchen

**Usage**
Delivery: Domino's

**Attributes**
Low Price: Pizza Hut

**Classes of Users**
Self-Baker: DiGiorno

**Away from Competitors**
Antichain: Pizza
My Heart

## Positioning Approaches

Companies can use a variety of positioning approaches, even within a single market. Figure 4.13 summarizes several approaches, all within the pizza industry.[30]

Several different positioning approaches are available to consumer marketers:

**Usage**: This approach positions a company on the basis of the way the product or service is used or consumed. For example, Domino's Pizza guarantees quick, reliable delivery.

**Attributes**: Here, the company is positioned on the basis of a key attribute, such as speed, size, or price. For example, PizzaHut is positioned as a low-cost pizza with its relatively low price and fastfood associations, such as locations in malls, its ready availability, and its close association with Taco Bell.

**Classes of Users**: In this approach, the company is positioned on the basis of the classes of people who will be using the product or service. For example, DiGiorno's is positioned to people who like to bake their own pizza.

**Away from Competitors**: This approach positions a company as being distinct from the leading competitors in the market. For example, PizzaMyHeart, a San Francisco Bay Area chain of restaurants, positions itself away from its competitors through its tagline "Not Your Typical Pizza Place."

### Key Terms

**Positioning**   Ensuring that differences of a company's offering occupy a distinct position in the minds of customers.

**Niche**: Here, the company is positioned on the basis of offering highly unusual varieties of products and services. California Pizza Kitchen, a nationwide chain of restaurants serving specialty menu items such as Cheeseburger pizza, positions itself as a niche vendor.

**Geography**: In this approach, the company is positioned on the basis of being associated with a famous place. For example, North Beach Pizza, a pizzeria located in the North Beach area of San Francisco, California, takes advantage of the Italian heritage of the North Beach area for its positioning.

**Benefits**: This approach positions a company on the basis of providing a distinct benefit, such as quality, reliability, or taste. For example, Round Table Pizza, a nationwide chain that emphasizes its fresh ingredients and great tasting pizza, positions itself as a high-quality offering.

Faded brands with a solid history can at times be revived through repositioning. In **repositioning**, companies change messaging (along with product/service enhancements in some instances), to make the brand more relevant to specific target markets. For example, Samsung repositioned its traditional "clamshell" cellular phone as a simple alternative to complicated smartphones, renaming it the Jitterbug and targeting it to the elderly. Arm & Hammer repositioned its baking soda from a baking ingredient targeted to serious bakers to a refrigerator deodorizer targeted to the homemaker, and has expanded its line from simple boxes of soda to dedicated sanitizer products, such as the Fridge Fresh™ Refrigerator Air Filter. Adidas repositioned its older tennis court shoes from the 1970s, renaming them Adidas Originals and targeting them to the urban youth market.

## Points of Difference and Parity

To help position a brand for competitive advantage, it is useful to establish points of difference and points of parity.[31]

**Points of Difference.** **Points of difference** (PODs) are attributes or benefits that consumers strongly associate with the brand, that they feel are favorable, and that make the brand unique or special. PODs help set the brand apart from others in its category.

---

### Marketing Planning in Action

**Select Comfort: Sleep Number System to Dial in a Difference**. Select Comfort leverages its Sleep Number system to differentiate its mattresses from the many competitors in the market. The system allows users to adjust the mattress's firmness for their own comfort level. Each side of the bed adjusts independently, allowing couples who share a bed to sleep more harmoniously.[32]

---

**Points of Parity.** **Points of parity** (POPs) are attributes or benefits that the brand shares with other brands in the category. POPs help the brand claim membership in a particular category. While points of parity might not be the reason for consumers to choose a brand, the absence of important POPs can cause consumers not to consider the brand when making a choice.

## Marketing Planning in Action

**Friendster.com: Friend or Foe**? Social networking site Friendster.com does not appear to have a strong set of points of parity, because it is not clearly a member of any distinct social networking category. It does not appear to be a business social networking site, such as LinkedIn.com, because it is too informal for that purpose. At the same time, it does not appear to have distinct membership in any other category, such as personal social networking (*Facebook.com*), finding old friends (*Classmates.com*), or dating (*eHarmony.com*).[33]

# Positioning: Business Markets

As we showed for consumer products, positioning a service or product for business markets is more than just differentiating it from other offerings. It is ensuring that the differences occupy a distinct position in the minds of consumers. For example, "Caterpillar" occupies the position of "outstanding service" in the heavy equipment category even though many other companies also provide service for their equipment.

## Positioning Approaches

Figure 4.14 demonstrates the use of a variety of different positioning approaches, all within the market for forklifts.[34]

Several different positioning approaches are available to business-to-business marketers:

**Usage**: This approach positions a company on the basis of the way the product or service is used or consumed. For example, Komatsu's network of dealers can provide short- and long-term rentals and leases to accommodate businesses who use forklifts part-time.[35]

**Figure 4.14** Business Market Positioning Approaches: Forklift Example

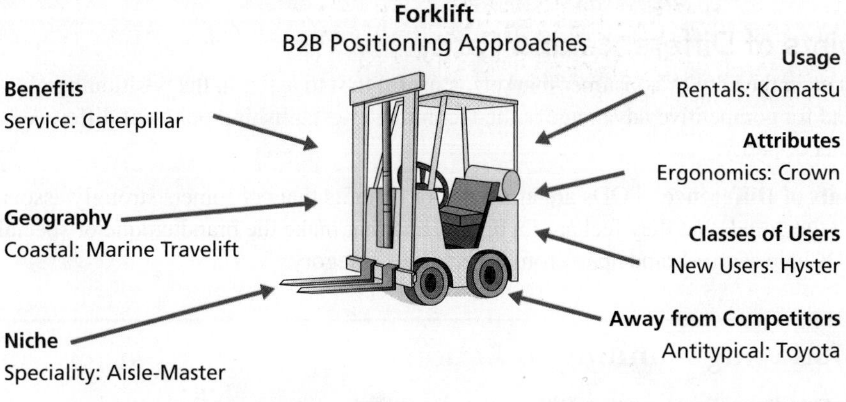

**Forklift**
B2B Positioning Approaches

**Benefits**
Service: Caterpillar

**Geography**
Coastal: Marine Travelift

**Niche**
Speciality: Aisle-Master

**Usage**
Rentals: Komatsu

**Attributes**
Ergonomics: Crown

**Classes of Users**
New Users: Hyster

**Away from Competitors**
Antitypical: Toyota

## Key Terms

**Points of difference (PODs)** Attributes or benefits that customers strongly associate with a brand, that they feel are favorable, and that make the brand unique or special.

**Repositioning** Changing messaging (sometimes along with product/ service enhancements) to enhance the relevance of a faded brand to a particular market segment.

**Points of parity (POPs)** Attributes or benefits that a brand shares with other brands in the category.

**Attributes**:  Here, the company is positioned on the basis of a key attribute, such as speed, size, or price. For example, Crown positions its forklift using the attribute of ergonomics, citing a number of industrial design awards for human design innovations that can reduce operator fatigue.[36]

**Classes of Users**:  In this approach, the company is positioned on the basis of the classes of people who will be using the product or service. For example, Hyster positions itself toward new users, emphasizing its forklift operator education programs.[37]

**Away from Competitors**:  This approach positions a company as being distinct from the leading competitors in the market. For example, Toyota positions its forklifts away from its competitors by promoting them differently from the rest. Where most companies' websites show forklifts at work, Toyota's website shows a beehive, implying that its forklifts are busy as bees.[38]

**Niche**:  Here, the company is positioned on the basis of offering highly unusual varieties of products and services. For example, Aisle-Master positions itself as a niche vendor by offering just one product, its articulating forklift for very narrow aisles, to just one industry, warehouse operations.[39]

**Geography**:  In this approach, the company is positioned on the basis of being associated with a certain place. For example, Marine Lift Systems sells forklifts to lift boats out of the water onto dry docks. It positions itself geographically, basing its operations out of Tampa, Florida, one of the busiest marinas on the U.S. eastern seaboard.[40]

**Benefits**:  This approach positions a company on the basis of providing a distinct benefit, such as quality, reliability, or service. For example, Caterpillar positions itself as a leader in after-sales service, with a network of thousands of service dealers all over the world. It also started the unique S.O.S. Fluid Analysis program, where Caterpillar analyzes the oil and coolant from forklifts to monitor the health of the equipment and prevent unanticipated downtime.[41]

## Points of Difference and Parity

Just as in the case of consumer markets, a useful tool to assist in the positioning of a brand for competitive advantage is the technique of establishing points of difference and points of parity.[42]

**Points of Difference**.  PODs are attributes or benefits that consumers strongly associate with the brand, that they feel are favorable, and that make the brand unique or special. PODs help set the brand apart from others in its category.

### Marketing Planning in Action

**Caterpillar: Diesels with a Difference**. In addition to its emphasis on service, Caterpillar sets itself apart from other heavy equipment manufacturers by emphasizing its environmental sustainability efforts, such as its development of clean-burning diesel engines. As emission controls become ever stricter, this point of difference could become very important to potential customers.[43]

**Points of Parity**. POPs are attributes or benefits that the brand shares with other brands in the category. POPS help the brand claim membership in a particular category. For business-to-business products, an important point of parity is the availability of dealers for parts and service.

---

## Marketing Planning in Action

**Komatsu: Worldwide Dealer Network**. Komatsu is less well known in the United States than it is in Japan, where its headquarters are located. Because it is less well known, potential U.S. buyers might be concerned about the availability of parts and service for Komatsu's products. To allay these fears, and affirm an important point of parity, the Komatsu-USA website emphasizes that Komatsu Forklift has over 195 dealer locations throughout the United States, Canada, Mexico, the Caribbean, and Central and South America.[44]

---

# Practical Planning

In this section, we will continue demonstrating the planning process using our ongoing example, Expedia online travel agent services.

We begin by considering the various ways that Expedia could segment the vast travel market. It is often helpful to fill out a segmentation overview chart like the one in Figure 4.15 to consider different segmentation possibilities. This chart would not generally be included in the marketing report—it is best viewed as a tool to help identify compelling segments.

As shown in the figure, many different segments are possible. It would not be profitable to target every segment, even if it were possible to do so. If we researched the various segmentation options, we would find that a few segments are worthy of consideration for targeting because their segment sizes are large and growing (finance), they fit with Expedia's mission (alignment), and are easy to reach (marketability). We might decide to study the following segments further, based on our target criteria:

**Demographic**:  Continue to attract traditional market of 35 to 55-year-olds (Age), and consider targeting the families with children segment (household type), which can result in more revenue per trip.

**Geographic**:  Continue to offer travel within the United States (domestic segment), and consider targeting the European market segment (international), where profit margins are often higher.

**Psychographic**:  Continue to offer travel to the jet-setter segment (lifestyle), and consider targeting the adventure travel and luxury travel segments, where profits are often higher.

**Behavioral**:  Continue to offer travel for traditionally travel-intensive occasions, such as Thanksgiving (occasions), and consider targeting the information-seekers

**Figure 4.15** Segmentation Overview Chart: Expedia

| Segmentation Type | Categories | Sample Segments |
|---|---|---|
| Demographic | Age: | Under 18; 18–30; 30–40; etc. |
| | Income | Below $50K/yr; Above $100K/yr |
| | Sex | Male; Female |
| | Household Type | Single; Family with Children |
| | Occupation | Professional; Blue Collar; Student |
| Geographic | International | United States; Europe; Asia Pacific |
| | Feature | Shoreline travel; Mountain travel |
| | Climate | Summer trips; Winter trips |
| Psychographic | Lifestyles | Jet-Setter; Stay-at-Home |
| | Interests and Opinions | Family Gatherings |
| | | Adventure Travel; Luxury Travel |
| | Activities | |
| Behavioral | Occasions | Thanksgiving; Other Holidays |
| | Benefits | Leisure travel; Business travel |
| | Usage Rate | Infrequent Travel; Heavy Travel |
| | Readiness to Buy | Need ticket immediately |
| | Loyalty | Loyal to certain airline |
| Other Approaches | Price | Price-conscious travelers |
| | Time | Peak season trips; Off-season trips |
| | Distribution Channel | Purchase through agent; Online |

segment (readiness to buy), to increase the conversion rate on the websites, aiding individuals to advance from prospects to revenue-paying customers.

**Other Approaches**: Continue to offer travel to the peak-season segment (time), where prices are generally higher than off-peak, and consider targeting the price-conscious travelers segment (price), which can improve our market penetration.

Marketing plans should include a segmentation target chart that shows the segments to target, the advantages those segments give to the organization, and the method for targeting them. Figure 4.16 shows such a chart. For example, if we decided to target price-conscious travelers, we would identify our target segment as price-conscious

**Figure 4.16** Targeting Chart: Expedia

| Market Segment | Potential | Alignment | Marketability |
|---|---|---|---|
| Adventure Travel | $89 billion spent | Expedia offers exotic travel options to satisfy adventurers | Distinct values, like to read adventure oriented magazines |

travelers, and the segment advantage as "gain market penetration." Expedia targets the price-conscious travelers segment through its Hotwire.com website. Hotwire.com's approach matches flexible, price-sensitive travelers with suppliers who have excess seats, rooms, and cars they wish to fill without affecting the public's perception of their brands by lowering their prices overall.

One particularly attractive segment is the adventure travel segment. According to a George Washington University study, consumers spent $89 billion in 2009 on adventure tourism, making it a lucrative segment. Adventure travelers are affluent and educated, as well as environmentally and culturally aware, according to the study. Because of the segment's large size, high-profit potential, fit within the organization, and easy marketability, we will select it for the new service to achieve the Expedia objective introduced in Chapter 2. Figure 4.16 summarizes the targeting process.[45]

With our segments identified, we move on to positioning. We do this by creating a positioning chart, shown in Figure 4.17, for the marketing plan. The chart shows the positioning approach, points of difference, and points of parity for our target segment, adventure travel.

Expedia's general positioning approach is that of market leader because of "more choices" and "more savings." The approach relies on the so-called network effect. The network effect states that a service, like online travel agency services, becomes more valuable as more people use it. eBay dominates the online auction market because it has the largest network of buyers and sellers. Job seekers and employers select Monster.com because both groups know it's where the largest audience lies. Expedia, with its reputation of having the greatest selection and widest network of all the online travel agencies, benefits from the network effect.[46]

**Figure 4.17** Positioning Chart: Expedia

| Market Segment | Positioning Approach | Points of Difference | Points of Parity |
|---|---|---|---|
| Adventure Travel | Niche: Unique, distinctive travel packages for the discerning traveler | Widest span of available activities and destinations (Network Effect) | Easy online access, 24x7 customer service |

The adventure travel market segment size is large and climbing.

*Source*: Shutterstock

## Summary

As Donald Norman, an advocate of human-centered design, says, "Market segmentation is a natural result of the vast differences among people."

The chapter discussed market segmentation, targeting, and positioning (STP). Just as military strategists use "concentration of force" to overwhelm their enemy by focusing their resources, marketers can capture market segments with STP strategy.

The STP process consists of three steps:

- **Segmentation**: Identifying segments within the market, then developing profiles for each
- **Targeting**: Selecting one or more target markets on which to focus our attention, based on an evaluation of the attractiveness of each segment
- **Positioning**: Designing the company's offering and image to occupy a distinct place in the target market's mind

The chapter covered different segmentation methods for consumer and business markets.

In consumer markets, we considered demographic, geographic, psychographic, and behavioral segmentation methods. In addition, we covered other approaches, such as price, time, and distribution channel segmentation methods.

Demographic and geographic methods use physical characteristics, such as a person's age, income, or location to segment the market. Psychographic techniques segment the market based on a person's lifestyle, interests and opinions, and activities. Behavioral techniques segment the market based on the behaviors a person has toward the brand, such as their usage rate.

Psychographic and behavioral approaches work well for complex markets, where demographic and geographic methods might be too simplistic to work. In our Expedia example, psychographic techniques segment the luxury travel market more effectively than demographics, because some lower-income individuals might want to treat themselves to luxury travel, even though demographics would suggest we consider only people with high income.

In business markets, we considered demographic, operating, purchasing, situational, and personal characteristics approaches to segment the market. As with consumer markets, demographic segmentation considers physical characteristics, such as customer business size and location. The use of the other approaches depends on the situation facing the business. For example, businesses selling tools (like software, machinery, and training services) to improve productivity would do well to segment the market using operating variables.

To gather the market data required for segmentation, and for other areas of the marketing plan, we reviewed some effective avenues for gathering market data. We showed how to get data from government sources, market research firms specializing in demographic data, full-service market research firms, industry analysts, and other sources.

Once we have identified the segments, we need to select a segment to pursue. This process is called targeting. In targeting, we examine the segment's financial potential, the alignment between the segment and organization's mission and capabilities, and the ease of marketing into that segment.

With the next step, positioning, our goal is to ensure that the product is perceived as different, and that the differences occupy a distinct position in the minds of consumers. Two tools to help with the process are points of difference, which demonstrate to consumers how the brand is different, and points of parity, which demonstrate to consumers why the brand has the necessary requirements to belong to the product category.

Now that we have a clear idea on how to segment the market, which segments to target, and how to position the product, we will examine the competitive landscape to help us succeed against other businesses in the industry.

### Key Terms

**Targeting**   Selecting segments on which to focus the organization's efforts

## Key Terms

**Accessibility** Ease of reaching target market through marketing campaigns. (p. 67)

**Behavioral segmentation** Type of consumer market segmentation. Uses brand knowledge, attitudes, and usage, such as heavy usage of a brand, to segment consumer markets. (p. 47)

**Demographic segmentation** Type of segmentation approach used in consumer and business markets. Uses attributes like age, income, and occupation to segment consumer markets, and physical attributes, such as such as company size and industries, to segment business markets. (p. 45)

**Distribution channel segmentation** Type of consumer market segmentation. Uses different distribution channels to target certain markets. For example, Apple originally only sold its popular iPhone smartphone through AT&T's cellular phone service. (p. 51)

**Ethnographic research** Research technique where researchers immerse themselves into consumers' lives to understand them better. (p. 55)

**Focus groups** Research technique to gather opinions of carefully chosen individuals about a topic. (p. 55)

**Geographic segmentation** Type of consumer market segmentation. Uses physical location characteristics, such as metro size and density, to segment consumer markets. (p. 45)

**Marketability** Characteristics of a given segment that govern the ease of marketing effectively to that segment. (p. 67)

**Metropolitan Statistical Area (MSA)** Standard term used by the U.S. Census Bureau to denote a concentrated core area, like a major city, surrounded by tightly integrated adjacent communities. (p. 45)

**Observational research** Research technique to watch people's actual behaviors in the context of their natural environment. (p. 55)

**Operating variables segmentation** Type of business market segmentation. Uses the different ways businesses operate their organizations, like the technology they use, to segment business markets. (p. 57)

**Personal characteristics** Type of business market segmentation. Uses matches between personal characteristics of the seller and the buyer, such as adoption of a "green" philosophy, to segment business markets. (p. 61)

**Points of difference (PODs)** Attributes or benefits that customers strongly associate with a brand, that they feel are favorable, and that make the brand unique or special. (p. 71)

**Points of parity (POPs)** Attributes or benefits that a brand shares with other brands in the category. (p. 71)

**Positioning** Ensuring that differences of a company's offering occupy a distinct position in the minds of customers. (p. 69)

**Price Segmentation** Type of consumer market segmentation. Uses differing price points to sell to different markets. (p. 49)

**PRIZM** (Potential Rating Index by ZIP Markets). Commercial segmentation tool combining geographic data with demographic data. (p. 47)

**Psychographic segmentation** Type of consumer market segmentation. Uses psychological traits, lifestyles, and personal values, such as interests in organic foods, to segment consumer markets. (p. 47)

**Purchasing approaches segmentation** Type of business market segmentation. Uses the different ways businesses purchase products and services, like policies, to segment business markets. (p. 61)

**Repositioning** Changing messaging (sometimes along with product/service enhancements) to enhance the relevance of a faded brand to a particular market segment. (p. 71)

**Segmentation** Identifying distinct groups of customers with different needs within an overall market. (p. 45)

**Situational factors segmentation** Type of business market segmentation. Uses unique situations businesses find themselves in, such as having to frequently expedite orders, to segment business markets. (p. 61)

**Surveys** Research instruments to gather data (generally quantitative) over a large population of potential customers. (p. 55)

**Targeting** Selecting segments on which to focus the organization's efforts. (p. 77)

**Time Segmentation** Type of consumer market segmentation. Sometimes also called occasion segmentation. Segments the market by using specific times during the year, such as marketing turkeys and cranberry sauce for Thanksgiving, and fireworks for Independence Day. (p. 49)

Discussion Questions

1. When would psychographic and behavioral segmentation techniques work better than traditional techniques, like those using demographic data, to identify segments?

2. What type of segmentation approach do you believe will work best for your market? How would you define "works best"?

3. If you work in an organization selling to business markets, what type of segmentation approach are you currently using? Would another approach be more effective?

 Exercises

1. Prepare a segmentation overview chart, similar to what we developed for the Expedia example, for your marketing plan. Show sample segments for the various segmentation approaches (using either consumer or business segmentation techniques, depending on your market).

2. Create a segmentation target chart, like we developed for the Expedia example, for your marketing plan. Show the segments you plan to target, the advantages those segments give to your organization, and how you plan to target them.

3. Prepare a positioning chart, similar to the Expedia example, for your marketing plan. Include the positioning approach for each segment, the points of difference, and the points of parity for each of the target segments.

*Chapter 4*
*2 + 3*

# 5

# Competitive Landscape

## INTRODUCTION

The chapter provides a competitive framework and a section on competitive research to gather competitive data, and then assess it to understand the competitive landscape. Understanding the landscape will help us uncover market opportunities not already dominated by competitors, a topic we will explore further in the next chapter.

## CHAPTER CHECKLIST

We cover the following marketing plan sections in this chapter:

❑ **Competitive Framework:** Determining characteristics of principal competitors

❑ **Competitive Research:** Gathering information about competitors

Target is a fierce competitor, both on and off the track
*Source:* Shutterstock

## Competitive Framework

In this section, we create a framework with which to compare our principal competitors. We start by identifying the company's competitors. Next, we gather selected information about each of them. Then, we enter the information into the framework so we can easily compare them.

## Competitor Identification

The first step in building the profiles is to identify the top three or four competitors to study. Of course, the number of competitors varies by industry, but many organizations find it useful to have a limited set of competitors on which to focus. To aid in uncovering the most relevant competitors, we cover two competition identifications methods: the market structure method and the levels of competition method.

The **market structure method** of competition identification acknowledges that most markets have a familiar structure. The method is useful for finding direct competitors. While some fragmented markets do not follow the structure, many do, especially in consumer markets. The structure is shown in Figure 5.1:[1]

**Market Leader**:  Most markets have a market leader on top with a large amount of market share, often about 40 percent (the exact amount varies from market to market). The market leader often dictates the tempo and pricing of the market. For example, Hertz is the acknowledged market leader of the rental car market.

**Market Challenger**:  Just below the market leader is the **market challenger**. The challenger is the established number two in the market, often with about 30 percent of the market share. For example, Avis is the acknowledged market challenger of the rental car market.

**Market Follower**:  Following behind the market challenger is the **market follower**, a company that basically follows the lead of the market leader and challenger. For example, companies like Dollar Rent a Car could be viewed as market followers, because they generally follow the lead of Hertz and Avis.

**Market Niche Firms**:  At the bottom is a wide variety of **market niche firms** that fulfill market needs of specialty areas within the market, often with only a few share points each. For example, niche firms in the rental car market include a wide spectrum of offerings to accommodate different tastes, from exotic car rentals to Rent-A-Wreck.

An easy way to use this method to spot direct competitors is to determine the market share for each competitor regularly seen in the primary distribution channel. (We will cover tips on determining market share in the Competitive Research section later in this chapter). In consumer markets, one would study the competitors regularly seen in the

**Figure 5.1** Competition Identification: Market Structure Method

| Market Role | Market Share (%) | Example in Breakfast Cereal Market |
| --- | --- | --- |
| Market Leader | 40 (varies) | Kellogg's (Frosted Flakes, Corn Flakes, etc.) |
| Market Challenger | 30 (varies) | General Mills (Cheerios, Wheaties, etc.) |
| Market Follower | 20 (varies) | Malt-O-Meal and others (Puffed Rice, Puffed Wheat, etc.) |
| Market Niche Firms | 10 (varies) | Many companies with small market shares: Organic cereals, granolas, etc. |

stores or other locations where the organization's products or services are offered. In business markets, one would study the competitors regularly seen in deals with potential customers. For example, most supermarket breakfast cereal aisles sell offerings from each competitor type: Kellogg's (market leader), General Mills (market challenger), Malt-O-Meal (market follower), and various granolas and specialty cereals (market niches).

## Marketing Planning in Action

**Breakfast Cereal Market Structure**. The breakfast cereal market demonstrates the typical structure present in most markets. The market leader is Kellogg's (Frosted Flakes, Corn Flakes, etc.), with nearly 40 percent share of the market. The market challenger is General Mills (Cheerios, Wheaties, etc.), with about 25 percent. The breakfast cereal has several firms below Kellogg's and General Mills, including Post (Grape Nuts, etc.) and Quaker (Cap'n Crunch). One company exhibiting classic market follower behavior is Malt-O-Meal, which makes imitations of brand-name cereals, including Puffed Rice and Puffed Wheat.[2]

To get a more comprehensive view of the competitive landscape, we can consider both direct competitors and indirect competitors.[3]

**Direct Competitor**: A **direct competitor** is an organization offering nearly identical products or services to the same market. Often, the competitors are archrivals. In the breakfast cereal example cited earlier, all the companies listed are direct competitors.

**Indirect Competitor**: An **indirect competitor** is an organization offering similar, but not identical products or services. In the breakfast cereal example, we could consider other breakfast foods, such as waffles and pancakes, as indirect competitors.

As shown in Figure 5.2, we examine three factors to identify our principal competitors, those that pose the most credible threat to the organization in the near term.

### Key Terms

**Market Structure Method** Competitor identification method. Helps identify competitors by fitting companies into common market structure: market leader on top, followed by market challenger, then market follower, and then market niche firms.

**Market leader** Competitor that is leader in the market, often dictating the tempo and pricing of the market.

**Market challenger** Competitor that is number two company in market, behind market leader.

**Market follower** Competitor that follows the lead of the market leader and challenger.

**Market niche firms** Companies that fulfill market needs of specialty areas within the market.

**Direct competitor** Organization offering nearly identical products or services to the same market.

**Indirect competitor** Organization offering similar, but not identical products or services.

**Figure 5.2** Principal Competitor Identification Factors

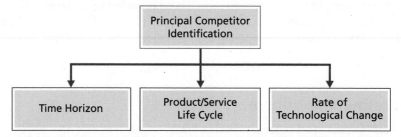

**Time Horizon**: Narrow down the list of competitors to those posing a threat in the time horizon of the marketing plan, typically one year. The list will generally contain direct competitors, with the occasional indirect competitor added to the list to reflect current trends. For example, breakfast cereal manufacturers in the 1990s could include protein-rich foods as a result of the Atkins diet. In this case, the Atkins diet could be considered an indirect competitor for the time horizon of their marketing plan. The Atkins diet, which claimed to achieve weight reduction by replacing carbohydrate-rich foods with proteins, recommended eating bacon and eggs instead of cereal for breakfast.

**Product/Service Life Cycle**: Reduce the number of competitors to those relevant for the product or service's stage in its product life cycle. In the early stages of the product life cycle, indirect competition is more of a threat. Direct competition is more relevant once the product matures. For example, in the early stages of the product life cycle for cellular telephones, manufacturers had to consider both direct competitors, such as Motorola and Nokia, and indirect competitors, such as pay phones.

**Rate of Technological Change**: Markets with rapid rates of technological change should consider indirect competitors as well as direct ones. The consumer electronics industry, with its high rate of change, should consider competition more broadly than say, the food industry, with slower rates of change. For example, Xerox lost sales in its stand-alone fax machine business both by direct competitors, such as Canon, and also by indirect substitutes, such as all-in-one printers (with built-in fax functionality) and scanners.

## Competitive Comparison Framework

With our principal competitors identified, our next step is to develop a **competitive comparison framework** chart that compares key criteria for each. Figure 5.3 provides an overview of the chart. Our goal is to compare our competition using the criteria listed below.

**Market Share**. In an earlier chapter, we discussed determining the total size of the market. As we discovered, industry analyst reports that estimate the size of the market are frequently available. Those same industry analyst reports often also state the market shares for each main competitor. If not, then dividing the revenue of each competitor by the total market size will calculate the **market share**.

**Figure 5.3** Competitive Comparison Framework Overview

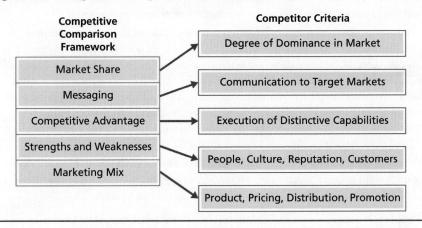

**Messaging.** External messaging can indicate the types of individuals the competitor is targeting, as well as the features or benefits used to target them. For example, Apple emphasizes the design of its iPhone smartphone to attract style-conscious individuals, whereas Motorola focuses the messaging of its Droid unit toward technically savvy people, mentioning its advanced capabilities.

## Marketing Planning in Action

**Nokia: Losing Share in the United States Due to Unclear Messaging?** Nokia, the number one mobile handset maker in the world, is losing market share in the smartphone category to rivals Research in Motion, Apple, and HTC. Nokia faces several problems, including savvy competitors, low brand recognition in North America (the area of fastest market growth), and software usability issues. But perhaps its biggest problem is its lack of clear messaging. Apple is the leader in stylish, full-featured phones with its iPhone. HTC, leveraging the Google Android operating system, is positioned as the "Anti-iPhone" with a nod to business users, thanks to its pull-out keyboard. RIM's BlackBerry is positioned as a basic, business-oriented device. But Nokia has no clear message, which could be the reason for its low brand recognition.[4]

**Competitive Advantage.** As covered in Chapter 2, Objectives, the competitive advantage of an organization is its set of distinctive capabilities that give it a cost advantage or a differentiation advantage over its competitors.

## Key Terms

**Competitive comparison framework** Model to compare characteristics of principal competitors.

**Market share** Company sales compared to total sales within relevant industry.

**Strengths and Weaknesses**. The popular **SWOT analysis** (strengths, weaknesses, opportunities, and threats) interprets the internal (company strengths and weaknesses) and external (market opportunities and strengths) marketing environment.

The competitive comparison framework used in this book compares the strengths and weaknesses of principal competitors. The framework does not compare opportunities and threats directly, because these are often very similar across the principal competitors, resulting in little additional insight. If the marketing plan format of the organization demands a typical SWOT four quadrant diagram, it is a simple matter to append market opportunities and threats (covered in the PEST analysis and Five Forces industry analysis sections in Chapter 2) to the strengths and weaknesses developed below.

An organization's strengths and weaknesses, as the names imply, are areas where it is superior or inferior, respectively, to its competitors. As shown in Figure 5.4, one can gain insight into competitors by evaluating strengths and weaknesses in four primary areas: people, culture, company reputation, and customers.[5]

- **People**: Dynamic, visionary leaders can be an overwhelming strength for an organization. Not only does their superior strategy lead the company in the right direction, their charisma can propagate throughout the organization, resulting in the entire company pulling together. For example, witness the impressive performance by Apple under the leadership of CEO Steve Jobs.

## Marketing Planning in Action

**Steve Jobs: Visionary or Tyrant?** *Wired* magazine interviewed Apple CEO Steve Jobs, and found that he appears to take pride in bucking current management trends. Hewlett-Packard encouraged executives to communicate informally with employees in their "management by walking around" approach. In contrast, Steve Jobs rules with an "iron hand," attending to minute product details, and keeping employees on a roller coaster of praise and fear. Despite Jobs's tirades, Apple employees are devoted. According to Apple lead designer Andy Hertzfeld, the approach works because "his autocracy is balanced with his famous charisma—he can make the task of designing a power supply feel like a mission from God."[6]

**Figure 5.4** Competitive Comparison Framework: Strengths and Weaknesses

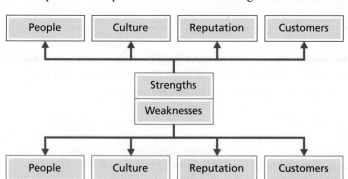

- **Culture**: A company's culture is defined as the set of shared experiences, beliefs, and norms that characterize an organization. Organizations with achievement-oriented cultures, where optimism and "can-do" attitudes rule, are generally much better set up for success than those with pessimistic or indifferent cultures.

## Marketing Planning in Action

**Best Buy: Culture of Optimism** Consumer retailer giant Best Buy believes that their culture of optimism sets them apart from other similar firms. But unlike some companies, they do more than just talk about the power of optimism. They consider it a strength. As such, they have developed a metric around it: employee engagement. Employee engagement measures workplace optimism. It is measured by outside consultants who survey the staff with questions such as: Does your boss support you in getting your job done? Do you have a best friend at work? Best Buy has calculated that a 2 percent increase in employee engagement at one of their stores translates to a $100,000 increase in sales there.[7]

- **Company Reputation**: Positive reputations are earned by doing the right thing over extended periods of time. Reputations set companies apart from their competitors. Companies with reputations for high levels of expertise, like L.L. Bean, or treating the customer right, like Amazon.com, triumph over companies with reputations of greed, like Enron.

## Marketing Planning in Action

**Amazon.com: Five-Star Reputation for Customer Service**. In a world where bad service seems to be the norm (try asking a cellular phone customer what she thinks about her phone company!), Amazon.com wins in the marketplace through its well-deserved reputation. Amazon.com goes to great lengths to make customers feel at home. Its easy website navigation is remarkable, considering the vast array of available products. Its user rating system, Listmania lists, and customer forums lend a sense of community to the site. Its checkout system makes it easy to get what you want, and uses advanced technology to recommend other items you might find useful. Its generous and flexible return policy seems designed to make it easy to return unwanted items, as compared to the onerous policies of most e-commerce sites. Amazon.com earns five stars for its reputation.[8]

## Key Terms

**SWOT (strengths, weaknesses, opportunities, and threats) analysis** A popular analysis tool to interpret the internal (company strengths and weaknesses) and external (market opportunities and strengths) marketing environment.

- **Customers**: Loyal, happy customers are a source of strength for a company. Their loyalty ensures a steady income stream as they purchase new products and services from the company. They share their happiness with word of mouth recommendations to others, boosting sales from nonusers of the brand. Some customers, like those of Harley-Davidson and Apple, even tattoo the brand's logo on their arms.

## Marketing Planning in Action

**Apple Customers: Loyal to the Core.** Apple's customers love the brand. They tattoo the logo on their arms. They start their day reading Apple blogs. They go to Apple stores to find dates. In fact, the Apple Store in Manhattan's SoHo neighborhood is a "singles hotspot," according to the *New York Post*. And they believe that Apple cofounder and CEO Steve Jobs is their god. They lovingly document the unboxing of new Apple products with YouTube videos, carefully unwrapping their treasures as if they were the finest jewelry. Apple customers are a worthwhile group to court, as well. According to MetaFacts, Apple users are more likely than PC users to have a higher household income, have a graduate degree, and live in trend-setting places such as San Francisco and New York. Most importantly, their loyalty is remarkable: 50 percent of Apple customers plan to buy another Apple, a far greater percentage than for any other personal computer, according to MetaFacts.[9]

**Figure 5.5** Examples of Strengths Used for Completing SWOT Analysis

| Strengths | Descriptions |
| --- | --- |
| People | Leadership ability, skill, knowledge, background, character, passion Example: Steve Jobs as CEO of Apple |
| Culture | Positive, winning attitude Example: Best Buy |
| Company Reputation | Reputation for category knowledge: L.L. Bean Reputation for customer service: Amazon.com |
| Customers | Loyal, happy, committed customer base: Buick |

**Figure 5.6** Examples of Weaknesses Used for Completing SWOT Analysis

| Weaknesses | Descriptions |
| --- | --- |
| People | Inexperience, poor judgment, unethical Example: Bernard Madoff as head of investment fund |
| Culture | Pessimistic, indifferent attitude Example: Initech company in the movie *Office Space* |
| Company Reputation | Reputation for greed: Enron |
| Customers | Unhappy customers: Cell phone carrier customers, many others |

Figure 5.5 summarizes categories for strengths and includes examples for each. Figure 5.6 does the same for weaknesses.

**Marketing Mix: Products/Service, Price, Place, and Promotion.** Competitors execute their strategies through their marketing mix, so we need to examine the products/services, pricing, place (distribution), and promotion tactics of competing firms.

---

**Whole Foods attained market leadership through its mastery of the marketing mix**
*Source:* istockphoto

---

> ## Marketing Planning in Action
>
> **Whole Foods Marketing Mix**. Whole Foods Market, the world's largest retailer of natural and organic foods, executes its strategies consistently through each marketing mix element. For products, it emphasizes its selection of certified organic foods. The premium nature of the products is matched with a premium price—prices of organic foods run 20 percent higher than food not so certified. For place (distribution), Whole Foods operates its line of well-stocked, high-end retail stores in upscale neighborhoods across North America and the United Kingdom. For promotion, it advocates the benefits of healthy foods with its website, featuring items such as grass-fed beef, bean sprouts, and baked tempeh. Whole Foods also promotes its brand through cause-related marketing, using its Whole Planet Foundation to provide microloans to developing-world communities.[10]

Once we have the data collected for each competitor, we compile the data in a competitive comparison framework chart, with one column for each major competitor. Figure 5.7 shows such an example chart for the smartphone market, based on market data from a 2009 Gartner report.[11]

## Competitive Research

**Competitive research** is information gathered about competitors, with the intent of discovering market opportunities (which we will exploit in the next chapter, Strategy). As Figure 5.8 shows, we gather competitive research by leveraging primary and secondary data sources.

In the previous chapter, we sought out information for the market at large. In this chapter, we need much more specific information, focused on individual companies. While general sources like government census figures might help, company-specific resources, like company websites, will be of more value.

Organizations can save time and money in their research efforts by leveraging research done by others (secondary research) before embarking on creating the information on their own (primary research). It is often surprising how much relevant data already exists about competitors, if one takes the time to look.

While every market is different, and often requires unique approaches to competitive research, the sources listed here are a good place to start.[12]

## Secondary Data

**Secondary data** are information created by others. The data usually already exist somewhere—it is just a question of finding them. Here are some secondary data sources, and how they can be useful in analyzing competitors.

**Industry Analysts**. We used industry analyst reports earlier to determine the overall market size and trends. In addition to reports covering the state of the overall market, industry analysts also publish reports comparing companies within a given market, and

**Figure 5.7** Competitive Comparison Framework Chart: Smartphone Market

| Criteria | Nokia | Research in Motion | Apple | HTC |
|---|---|---|---|---|
| Market Share (units) | 45.0% | 18.7% | 13.3% | 6.0% |
| Messaging | Enabling mobility by offering a range of phones for different stakeholders | Focus on e-mail for enterprise | The cool phone, for style-conscious consumers | Rapid evolution of advanced functionality, for an "anti-iPhone" |
| Competitive Advantage | World leader; Many devices cover many market segments | Optimized for e-mail; government approved security | Stunning style and design; iPhone Apps; Steve Jobs | Leverage power of Google Android operating system |
| Strengths | Large scale, good design, and tight operations | Focus on enterprise core business; strong security | Outstanding brand. Stylish design. Profitable retail operations. | Solid hardware. Partnerships with Google Android and Palm webOS. |
| Weaknesses | Exclusive focus on hardware (vs. software) led to losing share in smart phones | Low levels of resources; slow traction in consumer market | No clear succession plan once Steve Jobs leaves | Being sued by Apple for patent infringement |
| Product (Flagship) | Nokia N97 | BlackBerry 9700 | Apple iPhone 3GS | Droid |
| Pricing | Moderate; subsidized by cell phone carriers | Premium; subsidized by cell phone carriers | Premium; subsidized by cell phone carriers | Premium; subsidized by cell phone carriers |
| Place (distribution) | Selective distribution through T-Mobile, Verizon, and AT&T. Also can purchase unlocked mobile phones online. | Wide distribution through Alltel, AT&T, BestBuy, MetroPCS, Sprint, T-Mobile, U.S. Cellular, Verizon, Virgin, and Walmart, among others. | Exclusive distribution via AT&T Wireless Services | Wide distribution through Alltel, AT&T, Qwest, Sprint, T-Mobile, U.S. Cellular, and Verizon. Also can purchase at HTC online store. |
| Promotion | Advertise online at nokia.com and on carrier's websites. | Promotions through cellular carriers | AT&T website; Apple website; Steve Jobs keynote speeches | Social media, such as HTC Wildfire Friend Stream promotion |

**Figure 5.8** Competitive Research Sources

even create reports profiling individual companies. Such reports can be highly useful for competitive research.

- **Consumer Markets**: Arbitron (arbitron.com) and Nielsen (nielsen.com), among others, publish a variety of reports covering companies in consumer markets.
- **Business Markets**: Forrester Research: (forrester.com) and Gartner (gartner.com), among others, publish reports on companies in business markets. Some of their most popular offerings are reports comparing the competitors in a market, highlighting the strengths and weaknesses of each company, like the Forrester Wave and the Gartner Magic Quadrant.

**Financial Analysts**. Financial analyst firms provide financially oriented information on competitors. Fairly detailed information is available for public firms. Data on private firms are often limited.

- **General Financial Information**: Hoovers, a Dunn and Bradstreet company (hoovers.com), among others, provides financial data on millions of companies, searchable by NAICS code and industry name.
- **Investment Bankers**: Companies like Goldman Sachs (goldmansachs.com) provide detailed financial information about companies, geared for investors.

**Annual Reports/ 10-Ks**. Public companies must issue financial reports, such as annual reports and 10-K forms, to the Securities and Exchange Commission (SEC) on a regular basis. As a result, it is easier to find financial data on public companies than it is for private ones. Annual reports can aid competitive analysis through their financial information, of course, and also with their introductory letters from the CEO, which can offer insights into future directions for the company.

- **Public Companies**: In the past, one had to be a company stockholder to obtain annual reports. Now, financial reports are routinely available on the company's website, generally filed under "investor relations."
- **Private Companies**: Private firms, which do not issue publicly traded stock, do not have the obligation to publicly release the same kind of information as publicly held companies. As a result, gathering data for privately held firms is often more difficult. Use some of the other research resources listed in this section to gain this type of information.

**Trade Publications**. Print publications and online articles exist for many industries. The publications often profile individual companies, and sometimes feature interviews with company CEOs, which offer considerable insight into the company.

- **Consumer Markets**: An example is *Advertising Age* (adage.com), which concentrates on the marketing and media trades.
- **Business Markets**: An example is Rubber News (rubbernews.com), which covers rubber and plastic products, especially automotive tires.

**General Business Publications.** Occasionally general business publications will publish fairly detailed articles about a company, especially public interest stories showing how the company benefited the community. The publications can include traditional print magazines, online articles, or content for portable device reader applications, such as Apple iPad Apps.

- **Small Businesses**: Some examples include *Inc.* (inc.com) and *Entrepreneur* (entrepreneur.com) publications, which profile small businesses.
- **Large Businesses**: Some examples include *Wired* (wired.com) and *Fast Company* (fastcompany.com) publications for the high-technology market, and *The Economist* (economist.com) for political and societal news affecting business and finance.

**Company Websites.** Competitor's websites, especially those of larger companies, provide financial information (under Investor Relations), information about their go-to-market strategy (under Partners & Suppliers), and insight into future strategies (by studying job descriptions to support future plans, under the Careers section).

- **Consumer Markets**: Websites like that for consumer packaged goods giant Procter & Gamble (pg.com) provide an overview of the company.
- **Business Markets**: An example of a business market website is that of IBM (ibm.com), which lists the various services it provides, along with detailed explanations of each.

**Social Media Content.** Weblogs (blogs) and other social networking tools (like Twitter streams) are used by many companies to share their opinions on the market. Competitors' social media can give insight into their support issues and often hint at future service and product releases. *Caution:* Just like with any other nonverified source of information (professional journalists typically insist on multiple sources to verify their sources; bloggers do not), execute due diligence and check the source before using the information. Many blogs are reputable, but many others are not.

- **Consumer Markets**: Some companies, like Dell (dell.com), are famous for their community-oriented blogs, providing support and hinting at new products and services.
- **Business Markets**: Many analyst firms, like Gartner (blogs.gartner.com), use blogs as a mechanism for analysts to discuss current events in their respective markets that would not warrant a dedicated report.

---

## Key Terms

**Competitive research**   Gathering data around primary and secondary competitors, with the intent of discovering market opportunities.

**Secondary data**   Information created by others, often published in print or on the Web.

Social media content, such as blogs, Facebook postings, or Twitter streams, can be useful sources of competitive information
*Source:* Shutterstock

**Company Collateral**. Many companies offer company collateral, such as brochures that highlight their service offerings. From a competitive research standpoint, collateral can give detailed service or product information, and hint at the company's positioning strategy by explaining how their offering compares to others.

- **Consumer Markets**: Many consumer companies offer brochures which detail their offerings.
- **Business Markets**: Aramark (aramark.com), which delivers cleaning, lodging, and food services for many industries, offers downloadable case studies and white papers on its website.

**Press Releases**. Public relations departments issue press releases on a regular basis. The releases can be valuable competitive tools, because they cover information like company-specific news and management changes before it is covered in other sources.

- **Consumer Markets**: Releases such as Procter & Gamble's August 2010 release, "P&G Announces Plan to Use Innovative Sustainable Packaging," suggests P&G's stance on community concerns, such as environmental sustainability.

- **Business Markets**: Press releases in business markets sometimes announce new customers. Such releases often include a quote from the new customer. Note the title of the person being quoted to gain insight into how the business positions their offerings to companies. If the person being quoted is the vice-president of sales, it suggests a different kind of positioning than a quote coming from the vice-president of customer support.

Figure 5.9 summarizes secondary research sources and the competitive insights they can bring.

**Figure 5.9** Competitive Research: Secondary Sources

| Source | Examples | Competitive Research Insight |
|---|---|---|
| Industry Analysts | Consumer markets: Arbitron, Nielsen <br> Business markets: Forrester, Gartner | Company comparisons Individual company profiles |
| Financial Analysts | General information: Hoovers <br> Investment bankers: Goldman Sachs | Revenue Funding |
| Annual Reports/10Ks | Public companies: Available <br> Private companies: Not available | Business operations Financial summary |
| Trade Publications | Consumer markets: *Advertising Age* <br> Business markets: Rubber News | Company profiles CEO Interviews |
| Business Publications | Small businesses: *Inc.* <br> Large businesses: *The Economist* | Company news Management changes |
| Company Websites | Consumer markets: P&G <br> Business markets: IBM | Product/Service details Executive teams |
| Social Media Content | Consumer markets: Dell <br> Business markets: Gartner | Support issues New products/services |
| Collateral | Consumer markets: Brochures <br> Business markets: Data Sheets | Detailed service/ product data Positioning |
| Press Releases | Consumer markets: Community <br> Business markets: New customers | Company news Management changes |

## Primary Data

**Primary data** is created by the researcher herself, often by contacting people associated with a project or company. The researcher has several different types of people she can contact:

**Customers**: In consumer markets, direct research with customers who purchased products from competitors can be useful to learn why they did so. Apply the focus group, ethnographic, or observational techniques covered earlier in this book. In business markets, many companies require customers to sign NDAs (nondisclosure agreements), barring customers from speaking with competitors about the company's products, thus making this type of research more difficult.

**Distribution Channels**: In consumer markets, retailers work with customers every day and can provide useful feedback as to why customers select competitors' products. In business markets, this method is not as fruitful because many channel members have NDAs with competitors as part of the distribution agreement. If the organization employs a salesforce to sell into major accounts, interviews with them can provide insight into the market.

**After-sales Service personnel**: In consumer markets, complex services and products often demand service after the initial sale. People providing this service can give valuable feedback, based on the contact they have with customers and their likes and dislikes about the product or service. For example, automobile manufacturers gather feedback from automotive service personnel to understand their customers better. In business markets, after-sales service personnel (called field service representatives) are routinely asked to provide feedback.

Figure 5.10 shows examples of primary data sources and the insight they can provide to competitive research.

**Figure 5.10** Competitive Research: Primary Sources

| Source | Examples | Competitive Research Insight |
| --- | --- | --- |
| Customers | Consumer markets: Ask directly<br>Business markets: Blocked by NDAs | Product/service evaluation criteria<br>Competitor evaluation |
| Distribution Channels | Consumer markets: Ask retailers<br>Business markets: Ask sales force | Aggregated customer feedback<br>Evaluations of competitive products |
| After-Sales Service | Consumer markets: Ask repairmen<br>Business markets: Ask field service | Product/service evaluation criteria<br>Long-term usage feedback |

Casual conversations about confidential information in public places can have disastrous consequences
*Source:* Alamy

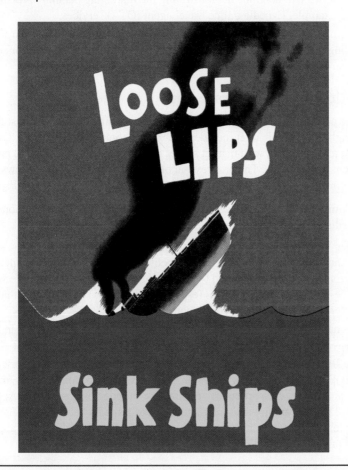

## Marketing Planning in Action

**Loose Lips Sink Ships**. *Inc.* magazine urges caution when speaking with fellow employees in public places. Even casual conversations might divulge important competitive information. The *Inc.* article tells of a shuttle bus ride the article's author (a management consultant specializing in competitive intelligence) took from Tokyo's airport to its downtown area. He overheard two gentlemen sitting in the seat in front of him. "I'm telling you, we need to refine our distribution strategy," one of them said. "OK. And what do you suggest?," enquired the other. They proceeded to divulge confidential marketing plans and distribution strategies in explicit detail. Luckily, the consultant was not a competitor of theirs. As a stunt, he wrote down what they said, and then presented them with the information when the bus stopped. The gentlemen were embarrassed, but the situation could have been much worse.[13]

## Practical Planning

In this section, we will continue demonstrating the marketing planning process using our ongoing example, Expedia online travel agent (OTA) services.

We begin by identifying the competitors on which to focus. For the purpose of demonstrating the methods used in this chapter, we will identify competitors using both the market structure and the direct/indirect competitors approaches.

### Competitor Identification

**Direct Competitors**.  According to a 2009 report by airline industry analyst firm PhoCusWright, the OTA market includes four direct competitors: Expedia, Orbitz, Travelocity, and Priceline, with market shares of 43 percent, 26 percent, 22 percent, and 9 percent, respectively. The progression of share amounts closely follows the prototypical market share structure found in many industries, as we see in Figure 5.11.[14]

**Indirect Competitors**.  We can identify several indirect competitors, but none appear to be an immediate threat to Expedia:

- **Supplier Websites**: Booking directly through travel supplier's websites, such as airline and hotel sites, is an indirect competitor to OTAs, but not a compelling one. Supplier's choices are too limited (forcing consumers to contact multiple suppliers), and prices obtained through OTAs (especially for hotels) can be lower than the rates offered by suppliers directly to consumers.
- **Traditional Travel Agents**: Human travel agents, once the mainstay of the industry, are now decreasing in popularity as a result of the low prices and convenience of OTAs.
- **Mobile Device Travel Apps**: Software developers are creating travel-oriented software applications to research and book travel options. The applications, or "apps," as they are known, are particularly popular for mobile devices like the Apple iPhone. The apps are not an immediate threat to Expedia because the OTA companies themselves have created their own apps, including Expedia.com's apps at the Apple Online Store and Priceline.com's Hotel Negotiator.[15]

### Competitive Comparison Framework

With the primary competitors identified, we now build the competitive comparison framework chart.

**Market Share**.  We determined the market share earlier, as part of the market structure exercise.

---

**Figure 5.11** Competition Identification: Market Structure Method: Expedia and Competitors

| Competitor | Market Share (%) | Market Structure: Typical (%) |
|---|---|---|
| Expedia | 43 | Market leader: 40 |
| Orbitz | 26 | Market challenger: 30 |
| Travelocity | 22 | Market follower: 20 |
| Priceline | 9 | Market niches: 10 |

**Messaging**.  Referencing competitors' websites, we obtain messaging for each firm.

- **Expedia**: For variety-seeking travelers, who want to save money on many different choices of travel, our service provides with easy, flexible booking options that save time and money. Unlike our competitors, our research website, TripAdvisor, provides vast research on thousands of travel options, all at a competitive price.
- **Orbitz**: For value-conscious travelers, who value money and convenience, our service provides with a variety of travel accommodations and packages. Unlike our competitors, we refund the difference if someone else books the same itinerary for less.
- **Travelocity**: For travelers who value deep travel expertise, our service provides travelers with a wide array of travel options. Unlike our competitors, we leverage our competitive advantage of the technology and expertise behind the SABRE airline reservations system at a competitive price.
- **Priceline**: For aggressively budget-oriented travelers, who want to save the maximum amount of money and are flexible with accommodations, our service provides travelers with the potential of greatly reduced prices. Unlike our competitors, we do the negotiation for you, resulting in prices that can be significantly less than those of competitive travel services.

**Competitive Advantage**.  Next, we determine the competitive advantages of each competitor, as discussed by industry analysts and claimed in competitors' annual reports.

- **Expedia**: Expedia's TripAdvisor travel research website is a competitive advantage for the company. The competitive advantage benefits both the customer (customers can search for a wide variety of accommodation options) and the company (TripAdvisor generates significant advertising and media business, in addition to being a differentiator for the company).[16]
- **Orbitz**: Its associations with the large airlines that created it (American, Continental, Delta, Northwest, and United) give it the potential for a sustainable competitive advantage in pricing.[17]
- **Travelocity**: Travelocity has a competitive advantage in electronic ticketing (an important aspect of online travel booking) because it is majority-owned by SABRE Holdings, which has the largest electronic ticketing system in the world.[18]
- **Priceline**:Priceline.com's principal competitive advantage is the perception that it negotiates hard for its customers, delivering rock-bottom pricing. It offers two proof points to validate the perception: its "Name Your Own Price" tagline and its "Best-Price Guarantee."[19]

**Strengths and Weaknesses**.  We now consider the principal strengths and weaknesses for each of the competitors:

- **Expedia**: Strengths include first mover advantage (it was the first to enter the market), strong brand recognition, and a successful business model with good profitability. Weaknesses include lack of train reservations, an overemphasis to date on the U.S. market, and seasonality of business.

---

**Key Terms**

**Primary data**    Data created by the researchers themselves, generally for a specific purpose.

- **Orbitz**: Strengths include its relationships with the major airlines (collectively, the five airlines that teamed to create Orbitz own 90 percent of seats on domestic commercial flights), its corporate travel focus, and a fast website (claimed to be the world's fastest OTA website). Weaknesses include poor relationships with airlines not associated with Orbitz (Orbitz was sued by Southwest Airlines in 2002).

- **Travelocity**: Strengths include strong execution of travel booking (not surprising, considering its relation to travel reservation system behemoth SABRE), and a good focus on corporate travel through its Travelocity Business unit. Weaknesses include limited search capability for leisure travel (one user indicated that it was not the best place to discover a new Caribbean hideaway) and exposure to changing costs (not unique to Travelocity).

- **Priceline**: Strengths include its famous "name your own price" bidding model, quick and easy airline comparisons, and low-price guarantees. Weaknesses include the uncertainty of not knowing the exact airline or hotel using the process and the waiting time to process requests using the bidding model.

**Marketing Mix**. We move on now to the marketing mix: the product (in this case, service), price, place, and promotion of the four competitors:

- **Services**: All four companies offer the ability to research thousands of available accommodations all over the world, book itineraries, and obtain travel insurance. Travelocity offers premium customer service through its "Travelocity Customer Bill of Rights." Priceline offers both auction ("name your own price") and nonauction booking services.

- **Pricing**: All four companies offer low prices on travel arrangements, having eliminated most, if not all, booking fees to stay competitive. Expedia also offers its best price guarantee, where prices are matched on trips booked within the past 24 hours. Expedia will refund the difference and provide a travel coupon worth $50. Orbitz and Travelocity offer similar guarantees. Priceline, of course, emphasizes its "name your own price" pricing policy.

- **Place**: All four companies distribute their offerings through a variety of online channels, including mobile phone apps, to target different market segments. Expedia differentiates itself through its large number of different websites to cater to different demographic and psychographic segments, as well as both consumer markets (leisure and business travelers) and business markets (travel agents). In addition, Expedia operates its TripAdvisor website, featuring a staggering amount of accommodation possibilities all over the world.

- **Promotion**: All four companies offer a variety of promotions for vacation packages and other deals. Each company uses traditional media, like contacting previous customers via e-mail, as well as nontraditional media such as social networking. Each runs its own blogs covering travel-related topics, such as Expedia's Trip Advisor blog, Orbitz's blog with posts tailored to the season, the Window Seat Blog operated by Travelocity, and the Travel Ekspert blog by Priceline.

In Figure 5.12, we summarize the competitive information in our competitive comparison framework chart.

**Figure 5.12** Competitive Comparison Framework Chart: Expedia and Direct Competitors

| Criteria | Expedia | Orbitz | Travelocity | Priceline |
|---|---|---|---|---|
| Market Share (units) | 43% | 26% | 22% | 9% |
| Messaging | Unmatched variety of travel possibilities | Refund the difference to you if someone else books for less | Technology and expertise behind SABRE | Name your own price |
| Competitive Advantage | TripAdvisor, research tool exposing thousands of accommodation possibilities | Ties with several large airlines, giving it sustainable competitive advantage in price | Deep understanding of airline reservation system due to link to SABRE reservation system | Perception of aggressive negotiation on customer's behalf |
| Strengths | First mover advantage<br>Brand recognition<br>Profitable business model | Good relationships with airlines that founded it<br>Corporate travel<br>Fast website | Good reservation execution<br>Travelocity Business Unit | Famous bidding model<br>Easy airline price comparisons<br>Low price guarantees |
| Weaknesses | No train reservations<br>Overemphasis on U.S. market<br>Seasonality | Poor relationships with some airlines | Limited leisure travel search capabilities<br>Exposure to changing costs. | Uncertainty of not knowing actual hotel or airline before booking<br>Waiting time |
| Service (Product) | Research trips<br>Book trips<br>Travel insurance | Research trips<br>Book trips<br>Travel insurance | Research trips<br>Book trips<br>Travel insurance<br>Premium customer service | Auction service<br>Nonauction services<br>Travel insurance |
| Pricing | Expedia Best Price Guarantee | Orbitz Price Assurance | Travelocity Price Guarantee | Auction-style: "Name Your Own Price" |
| Place (distribution) | expedia.com<br>Other sites<br>tripadvisor.com<br>B2B sites<br>iPhone App | orbitz.com<br>Other sites<br>Orbitz mobile access | travelocity.com<br>Other sites<br>iPhone App | priceline.com<br>Other sites<br>Hotel Negotiator<br>iPhone App |
| Promotion | Television<br>Other traditional media<br>Social media | Television<br>Other traditional media<br>Social media | Television<br>Other traditional media<br>Social media | Television<br>Other traditional media<br>Social media |

## Summary

As co-founder and CEO of Oracle Larry Ellison said, "You can't win without being completely different. When everyone else says we are crazy, I say, gee we really must be on to something."

The chapter covered how to understand the competitive landscape with the objective of finding market opportunities not already dominated by competitors, a topic we will pursue further in the next chapter.

We covered using a competitive comparison framework to compare key characteristics of principal competitors in the market, including market share, external messaging, competitive advantage, strengths, weaknesses, and the marketing mix. We addressed different research tools to gather the data used in the Framework.

We closed the chapter by demonstrating the competitive landscape approach using our ongoing example of online travel agent services.

In the next chapter, we will show how to leverage the information from the competitive comparison framework to find profitable market opportunities and then develop strategies to capitalize on them.

## Key Terms

**Competitive comparison framework** Model to compare characteristics of principal competitors. (p. 84)

**Competitive research** Gathering data around primary and secondary competitors, with the intent of discovering market opportunities. (p. 90)

**Direct competitor** Organization offering nearly identical products or services to the same market. (p. 83)

**Indirect competitor** Organization offering similar, but not identical products or services. (p. 83)

**Market challenger** Competitor that is number two company in market, behind market leader. (p. 82)

**Market follower** Competitor that follows the lead of the market leader and challenger. (p. 82)

**Market leader** Competitor that is leader in the market, often dictating the tempo and pricing of the market. (p. 82)

**Market niche firms** Companies that fulfill market needs of specialty areas within the market. (p. 82)

**Market share** Company sales compared to total sales within relevant industry. (p. 84)

**Market Structure Method** Competitor identification method. Helps identify competitors by fitting companies into common market structure: market leader on top, followed by market challenger, then market follower, and then market niche firms. (p. 82)

**Primary data** Data created by the researchers themselves, generally for a specific purpose. (p. 96)

**Secondary data** Information created by others, often published in print or on the Web. (p. 90)

**SWOT (strengths, weaknesses, opportunities, and threats) analysis** A popular analysis tool to interpret the internal (company strengths and weaknesses) and external (market opportunities and strengths) marketing environment. (p. 86)

## Discussion Questions

1. How should we be on the lookout for potential new competitors for our market?

2. Many entrepreneurs claim, "My new product is so unique that it has no competition!" How would you respond to such a claim?

3. What are some ways that you find helpful in gathering information about privately-owned competitors?

## Exercises

1. Identify the direct and indirect competitors for your industry. Which competitors do you need to focus on, considering the time horizon of the marketing plan?

2. Develop a competitive comparison framework chart for your marketing plan. How did you gather the data to complete the chart?

3. Develop a list of "go-to" resources that you found particularly helpful when researching competitive data. Ask colleagues if they can identify any other useful sources.

Exercise 1

# CHAPTER 6

# Strategy

## INTRODUCTION

Congratulations! We now have all the ingredients we need (objectives, market data, market segments, and competitive data) to develop the strategy for the plan. In this chapter, we introduce a simplified approach to establishing strategy based on organizational objectives and market opportunities.

## CHAPTER CHECKLIST:

We cover the following marketing plan sections in this chapter:

❏ **Market Opportunities**: Identifying promising market areas not dominated by competitors

❏ **Strategy**: Selecting strategies based on the objectives and market opportunities

❏ **Marketing Mix**: Introduction to implementing strategies using marketing mix tactics

Figure 6.1 summarizes the strategy process. Back in Chapter 2, we determined our objectives, based on the organization's mission and competitive advantages. In the past few chapters, we gathered valuable market data: market overview, market segments, and competitive landscape. We will now leverage the data to uncover potential market opportunities. The opportunities will be combined with the objectives to guide us in selecting appropriate strategies. The strategies will be implemented using tactics from the marketing mix (product/service, price, distribution, and promotion).

Starbucks brewed success with its strategy of reinventing the coffee experience and expanding it across the globe
*Source*: Alamy

**Figure 6.1** Strategy Formulation Based on Objectives and Marketing Opportunities

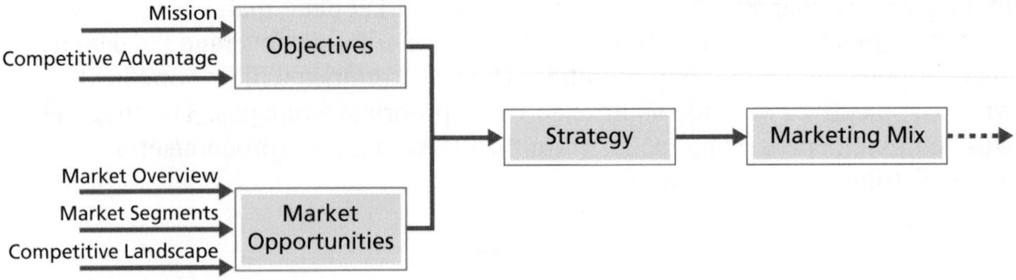

# Market Opportunities

Now that we have a good overview of the market and the competitive landscape, the next step is to take advantage of the knowledge. To do this, we use the data to find **market opportunities**, here defined as market segments that offer potential profit opportunities. The goal is to find an area to exploit that is not already targeted by our competitors. We can then leverage our market opportunities to transform our objectives into strategies.

As shown in Figure 6.2, market opportunities generally fall into one of three categories:

- **New Market Segments**: Discover a portion of the market not targeted by competitors
- **Go-to-Market Approach**: Establish a mechanism to reach a new class of customers
- **Differentiating Functionality**: Develop unique products and services to attract niche markets

Let us consider the three categories of market opportunities, using the smartphone market to demonstrate each type of market opportunity.

## New Market Segments

In this first approach, we apply competitive information to target a new market segment that the other competitors are not currently targeting (also called a "**whitespace**"). The market segment might be a geographical area (like expanding into a new country), or a

**Figure 6.2** Market Opportunity Categories

unique psychographic (see the Prada Phone example). For example, Prego created extra chunky tomato sauce when market research discovered that no major food manufacturer made a chunky style, although about 33 percent of the population wanted it. The discovery was a revelation, and generated $600 million for the firm.[1]

To execute a strategy to capture a new market segment, companies must check to see if they have the competitive advantages required to maintain leadership in their newly chosen market segment. Similarly, marketers should ensure that other companies do not possess a competitive advantage that might jeopardize the business's leadership in the market. For example, given the design prowess of Apple, one wonders if Prada's strategy of introducing an ultra-stylish phone to the "fashion elite" market segment will work, or if Apple will simply come out with an even more stylish version of the iPhone that the fashion elite will prefer over the Prada Phone.

## Marketing Planning in Action

**Prada Phone: Calling the Ultra-Fashion Cell phone Market**. The success of Apple's elegant iPhone validated the market of people who valued style in their cell phones. Not to be outdone, cellular phone manufacturer LG discovered a niche market within that larger "style-conscious" market. LG partnered with fashion icon Prada to introduce a new ultra-premium phone for the fashion elite. The Prada Phone, as it is called, sells at the premium price of $780, and that is with a two-year service contract. According to Giacomo Ovidi, head of new business development at Prada Group, "This is the result of almost one year of collaboration between Prada and LG to present a touch-screen phone with a particularly large screen, in association with a style of advertising and packaging that represent something never seen before for the industry."[2]

## Go-to-Market Approach

A company's **go-to-market approach** is the mechanism the company uses to deliver its products and services to customers. For example, high-technology company Hewlett-Packard sells its laptop computers in standardized versions (for instance, offering two versions of its 17" model) to consumers through its corporate website, other online resellers, and retail stores like Best Buy. By contrast, Dell's traditional go-to-market approach has been to let consumers configure their laptop computer to their own personal taste (offering potentially thousands of different configurations), then selling directly to consumers, bypassing retail channels (although Dell has recently added new distribution channels, such as Best Buy, to bolster sales).

## Key Terms

**Market opportunities**    Market segments that could be targeted by the firm for potential profit.

**Whitespace**    Market segments not currently targeted by other competitors.

**Go-to-market approach**    Mechanism used by company to deliver its products and services to customers.

To use this approach to create new market opportunities, we develop a different way to deliver our products and services. Often, the products or services the company delivers are similar (or identical!) to those of competitors; we are only changing the way we deliver them. The competitive comparison framework data from Chapter 5, Competitive Landscape, enables us to assess competitor go-to-market strategies and determine if a different type of go-to-market approach would give us an advantage in the market.

For example, the major cellular phone service carriers employ similar go-to-market strategies to deliver their service to customers. They charge up front for a cellular phone (often subsidizing its price), then lock customers in to a two-year contract. The price of the service during the contract's term greatly exceeds the subsidy for the phone, which boosts profitability for the carrier. The contract also reduces customer defections to other carriers. Customers wanting to break the contract are forced to pay early termination fees, often exceeding $300.

BoostMobile is an example of a carrier that sought to "be where the others are not" by adopting a new go-to-market approach. Instead of locking customers into a two-year contract, customers just pay month to month. Alternatively, customers can also adopt prepaid plans (also called pay-as-you-go or gas tank plans), where one makes payments in advance, replenishing the account by topping off as needed, like filling up a gas tank in a car. BoostMobile's different go-to-market approach gives it a chance to participate in the lucrative cellular phone carrier market once only available to the major carriers.

## Marketing Planning in Action

**BoostMobile: No-Contract Go-to-Market Approach**. Boost Mobile shuns the traditional go-to-market approach of the major cellular phone carriers (like AT&T and Verizon) with its no-contract plans. Just like the major carriers, BoostMobile offers a dependable nationwide network and technology savvy phones from Samsung, Motorola, and RIM's BlackBerry. The difference is that BoostMobile avoids the commitment of signing a long-term contract. Customers can choose among three plans: the monthly unlimited plan, at $50 per month with unlimited talk, text, e-mail, and Web; the BlackBerry monthly unlimited plan, at $60 per month. If even a month sounds like too big a commitment for you, BoostMobile offers the daily unlimited plan at $2 a day.[3]

## Differentiating Functionality

The third approach to finding new opportunities in the market is to develop services and products with **differentiating functionality**, features that distinguish the product or service from similar ones in the market. The new functionality is intended to attract a new class of users that value the specific new functionality. As shown in Figure 6.3, for the differentiating functionality approach to be successful, customers must recognize the difference, value the difference, and constitute a large enough market to justify the difference.

Apple's iPhone is a good example of the power of the differentiating functionality approach. Its emphasis on style and ease of use set it apart from other phones at the time of its launch. Customers valued the difference, and it soon became the "cool" phone to

**Figure 6.3** Differentiating Functionality Approach: Requirements for Successful Usage

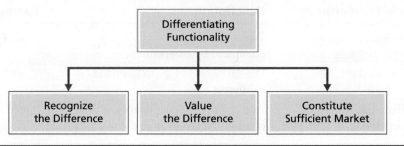

own. In addition, millions of the devices have been sold, providing substantial profits for Apple and transforming it into one of the industry leaders.

The approach is not without its disadvantages. Many companies, especially those in high technology, develop products and services they feel are "better" than existing ones, only to find that consumers either find little difference in the products and services from competing offerings, or do not value the difference. For instance, in the cellular phone service carrier example discussed earlier, the major carriers would argue that their service is unique, but most customers would disagree, stating that they are all virtually identical as far as they are concerned.

As we see in the cell phone microscope example in the box "CellScope: Dial 'M' for Microscope," even if a product or service is acknowledged to be different, and those differences are valued, the market may be too small to justify the differentiating functionality.

## Marketing Planning in Action

**CellScope: Dial "M" for Microscope**. The World Health Organization estimated that the world suffered from 247 million cases of malaria in 2006, most of which occurred in African nations. U.C. Berkeley engineers have invented a new technology that can help diagnose infectious diseases of this type, helping to avoid their spread. The device is called the CellScope, which transforms an ordinary camera phone into a portable microscope—perfect for spotting malaria parasites in the field. Enterprising (and altruistic) cellular phone manufacturers might consider building this functionality into existing cell phones. The functionality certainly differentiates it from other cell phones. And some people might value it as well, especially those involved in disease prevention in developing countries. But one must ask, will the relatively small market potential of a CellScope-equipped phone be enough to catapult the manufacturer to the status of an industry leader? [4]

## Key Terms

**Differentiating functionality**   Unusual features that set products and services apart from existing offerings.

**Figure 6.4** Summary: Types of Market Opportunities

| Market Opportunity | Description | Example |
| --- | --- | --- |
| New Market Segment | Target new segment not already dominated by competitors | Prada Phone |
| Go-to-Market Approach | Deliver our offerings to customers in a different way | BoostMobile |
| Differentiating Functionality | Add distinctive functionality to make offerings stand out from the rest | Apple iPhone |

Figure 6.4 summarizes the different types of market opportunities. In the next section, we will show how market opportunities can be teamed with objectives to develop strategies.

# Strategy

Having identified advantageous market opportunities, our next step is to develop strategies that specifically target those opportunities, while still reflecting the objectives of the plan.

Selecting appropriate strategies for an organization can be an intimidating task. To help guide the process, this chapter introduces a streamlined method to select relevant strategies. Figure 6.5 illustrates the process, where each type of objective maps to a corresponding strategy. Though the strategies discussed here can be used in a wide variety of situations, we will focus our discussion to show how the strategies can be applied to our marketing objectives, while taking advantage of the marketing opportunities we discovered in the previous chapter.

We review several types of popular strategies, as they pertain to different objectives.[5]

**Figure 6.5** Selecting Strategies based on Corresponding Objectives

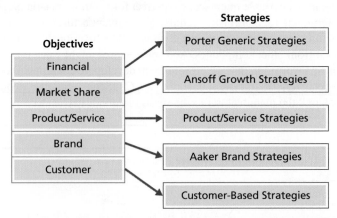

# Strategies for Financially Based Objectives

Financial objectives can be quite general, simply stating that a certain revenue or profit target be met by a certain date. Because of the general nature of the objectives, we will use Porter's generic strategies to address them.[6]

Michael Porter proposed three generic strategies that provide a good starting point for a company's overall strategic approach to the market: overall cost leadership, differentiation, and focus.

**Cost leadership**: In the **cost leadership generic strategy**, companies leverage their competitive advantages in low-cost production or lean supply chains (or low-cost service delivery) to price their products lower than those of their competitors, in an effort to boost volume and increase profit. Companies can take advantage of **economies of scale** (companies reduce their per-unit cost through large-scale operations, like enormous automotive assembly plants) and **experience curve** effects (companies become more efficient at building products and delivering services as they gain experience) to reduce manufacturing and service delivery costs. For example, Walmart employs its sophisticated inventory system to keep prices low and profits high.

**Differentiation**: In the **differentiation generic strategy**, companies with competitive advantages in design can create products or services clearly superior and different to those of competitors to differentiate their firm from others. Customers must be able to acknowledge the difference and pay a premium for it. For example, Apple's unique products combine style, luxury, and a compelling user experience (with a premium price tag to match) to drive profit.

**Focus**: In the **focus generic strategy**, organizations target a particular market segment or niche using either the cost or differentiation method. For example, The Cupcakery (thecupcakery.com) focuses on retail sales of cupcakes. The narrow focus differentiates the company from general bakeries and provides potential economies of scale (infrastructure set up exclusively for cupcakes) to give it cost advantages as well.

We will now apply Porter's generic strategies to financial objectives:

**New Market Segment**: Organizations can use either cost leadership or differentiation to drive profits in new market segments, depending on the company's competitive advantages (a focus approach could also be used for smaller niche markets). For example, in the cosmetics market, some companies want to enter the new market segment of

---

## Key Terms

**Cost leadership generic strategy**   Leveraging competitive advantages in low-cost production or service delivery to price products and services lower than competitors.

**Economies of scale**   Reduction of per-unit cost through large-scale operations.

**Experience curve**   Reduction of cost through higher productivity gained by learning knowledge around production and delivery operations.

**Differentiation generic strategy**   Setting company apart from its competitors through developing different products and services acknowledged to be superior by customers

**Focus generic strategy**   Targeting a small segment with a cost leadership or differentiation strategy.

---

The Cupcakery's focus on premium cupcakes differentiates it from general bakeries
*Source:* Shutterstock

---

mass-market antiaging creams. In the new segment, the Dr. Perricone brand developed its new product line and positioned it using a differentiated approach, touting that the line was formulated by a top-tier team of dermatologists, and emphasizing antiaging articles on the company's website. Its Neuropeptide Facial Conformer 2 ounce product retails for $495. By contrast, Olay's Professional Pro-X product retails for $42, leveraging its cost advantage due to economies of scale and widespread distribution channels.[7]

**Go-to-Market Approach**:  Again, organizations can use either cost leadership or differentiation approaches to drive revenue or profit (focus approaches can be used for niche markets). Here, though, we improve financial results by changing the way we deliver our products and services to customers. For example, we can examine different go-to-market strategies in the computer market. For cost leadership, Dell traditionally has delivered desktop and laptop computers to its customers at relatively low prices, thanks to its efficient manufacturing systems and its direct sales that bypass retailers (though Dell made recent changes to the model, as mentioned earlier). For differentiation, Google delivers computing power in an entirely different way. Instead of relying on a locally located device for computing power (like a high-powered desktop computer), a simple terminal can connect to Google applications (Apps) to deliver computing power to individuals using so-called cloud computing methods.[8]

**Differentiating Functionality**:  As the name implies, this approach is best employed using the differentiation and focus generic strategies. In the differentiation approach, the company sets itself apart from the competition through unique offerings the competition can not (or will not) match. For example, the Earthwatch Institute sets itself apart by providing cause-based vacations for the traveler looking for something truly different in travel. Focus takes differentiation to the extreme, targeting on an extremely narrow segment. For example, Light Bulbs Unlimited (bulbs.com) sells only light bulbs—thousands of different styles and types.

## Marketing Planning in Action

**Earthwatch: A Different Path to Travel**. The Earthwatch Institute (*earthwatch.org*) is a nonprofit organization applying a differentiated type of generic strategy to the travel industry. Earthwatch provides a new alternative to vacation plans. Instead of lounging by a pool or visiting museums, travelers join Earthwatch expeditions to help solve the earth's environmental problems. While Earthwatch's mission is more about finding creative ways to respond to environmental threats, and less about being a travel agency, Earthwatch offers a unique choice for travelers weary of commodity holidays. In addition to the unique activities, Earthwatch participants get a rigorous sense of purpose. Traveling volunteers head to Greece to count dolphins for a population census, or go to the Amazon to conduct spotlight surveys of caimans.[9]

Figure 6.6 summarizes how to apply the generic strategy approaches for financially based objectives.

**Figure 6.6** Porter Generic Strategies for Financially Based Objectives

| Market Opportunity | Strategies: Financial (Generic) | Example |
|---|---|---|
| New Market Segment | **Cost Leadership**: Profit in new markets by leverage competitive advantages in costs | Olay |
| | **Differentiation**: Profit in new markets with high-priced, differentiated products | Dr. Perricone |
| Go-to-Market Approach | **Cost Leadership**: Profit by delivering products and services at lower cost | Dell |
| | **Differentiation**: Profit by delivering value in new ways that customers will pay for | Google Cloud Computing |
| Differentiating Functionality | **Differentiation**: Profit by selling unique offerings competitors can't match | Earthwatch |
| | **Focus**: Profit by catering to unique niche | Light Bulbs Unlimited |

## Strategies for Market Share-Based Objectives

Market share objectives target growth. Often, growth comes from increasing market share at the expense of competitors. Other times, growth techniques can increase total market size. For example, analysts estimate that the Apple iPhone not only stole market share from its competitors, it grew interest in (and sales of) smartphones in general. To target growth, we can consider Ansoff's growth strategies from his Harvard Business Review paper, *Strategies for Diversification*. In his paper, Ansoff proposed four different approaches to growth.[10]

**Market Penetration**: In the **market penetration growth strategy**, companies grow market share by marketing existing products and services to existing customers in new ways. Three typical ways include targeting competitor's customers (such as Ford ads comparing its cars to those of Toyota), increasing purchase frequency (such as Oral B toothbrushes, whose bristles change color to remind you to replace worn-out brushes), and increasing purchase amount (such as fast-food restaurants encouraging customers to "super-size" their order at checkout).

**Market Development**: In the **market development growth strategy**, companies grow by selling their existing products and services into new markets. Two typical approaches include expanding geographically into new areas (such as selling internationally) and expanding to a new class of buyers (such as targeting different demographic segments).

**Product/Service Development**: In the **new product/service development growth strategy**, companies grow market share by marketing new products and services to existing groups of buyers. For example, Victorinox developed its Swiss Army brand of watches to complement its ubiquitous Swiss Army knife. Both items are sold to the same market, and are often sold together in gift packs.

**Diversification**: In the **diversification growth strategy**, companies grow by marketing new products and services to new groups of customers. For example, Toys "R" Us, which sells toys and games to children of varying ages, diversified into Babies "R" Us , which sells clothing to infants.

Ansoff's growth strategies can be applied to market share objectives:

**New Market Segments**: Organizations can grow market share over competitors (and further grow revenue by expanding the total size of the market) by expanding into new market segments, such as new geographical areas. For example, coffee powerhouse Starbucks has grown its market share through aggressive geographic expansion (indeed, in the 1999 comedy *Austin Powers: The Spy Who Shagged Me*, Dr. Evil's organization takes advantage of Starbucks' rapid expansion to achieve world domination!).

**Go-to-Market Approach**: Companies can capture market share from competitors by marketing their products and services in ways that competitors cannot match. For example, the cellular phone service carrier market suffers from slow growth overall (few net new customers per year; most customers are defectors from other carriers). To gain market share away from its competitors, AT&T leveraged its exclusive relationship with the Apple iPhone.

**Differentiating Functionality**: Organizations can grow market share by developing new products and services with differentiating functionality for existing markets (product/service development) or for new markets (diversification). For example, the

BMW MINI subcompact automobile has grown its market share, first by developing differentiating features that its target segment values (small size, high performance, luxury amenities), and then expanded its market by offering new models to new segments (the MINI Clubman to small families and the MINI Countryman to those who need the versatility of all-wheel drive).

## Marketing Planning in Action

**Zara: Fashioning Joint Ventures to Expand into New Markets**. Zara, a fashion retailer, is targeting a market development growth strategy to expand into Asia. Zara and other business units owned by parent Inditex have grown to 150 stores since opening its first store in Tokyo in 1998. Joint ventures with local companies, like the venture with Korean conglomerate Lotte Group, have helped it penetrate into Asian markets. Inditex joined up with Tata group to aid its entry into the Indian market.[11]

Figure 6.7 summarizes how to apply Ansoff growth strategies for market share-based objectives.

**Figure 6.7**  Ansoff Growth Strategies for Market Share-Based Objectives

| Market Opportunity | Strategies: Market Share (Growth) | Example |
|---|---|---|
| New Market Segment | **Market Development**: Grow market share by selling existing products and services into new markets, such as new geographies | Starbucks: Grow share through aggressive geographic expansion |
| Go-to-Market Approach | **Market Penetration**: Grow market share by marketing existing products and services to existing customers in new ways | AT&T: Capture share from competitors using Apple iPhone |
| Differentiating Functionality | **Product/ Service Development** (Existing markets); **Diversification** (New markets): Grow market share by marketing new products and services | MINI: Grow share by offering multiple models to multiple segments |

## Key Terms

**Market penetration growth strategy**   Gaining market share (or total market size) by marketing existing products and services to existing customers in new ways.

**Market development growth strategy**   Growing market share (or total market size) by marketing existing products and services to new market segments.

**New product/service development growth strategy**   Growing market share (or total market size) by marketing new products and services to existing customers.

**Diversification growth strategy**   Growing market share (or total market size) by marketing new products and services to new customers.

The Zara fashion brand deployed a market development growth strategy, expanding quickly into new markets
*Source*: Shutterstock

## Strategies for Product and Service-Based Objectives

Product and service objectives often involve the entire organization, not just the product development department, because of the importance of products and services in the market. As shown in Figure 6.8, most organizations use one of five approaches to developing products and services.

**Innovation Focus**: Organizations can use an **innovation product/service strategy**, emphasizing strong research and development capabilities, fostered in a culture of innovation. The organization is often "first to market" with its innovations, gaining a head start over its competitors, which are forced to imitate the first-mover to stay competitive. Organizations with innovation focus encourage risk-taking by rewarding employees for new ideas, and understanding that failure is an inevitable part of deve-loping cutting-edge services and products. For example, one of 3M's most popular products, Post-it notes, was bred from the "failure" of glue that did not stick well.

**Responsiveness**: Alternatively, organizations can use a **responsive product/service strategy**, which still leverages strong research and development capabilities, but emphasizes speed over innovation for its own sake. Here, products and services are constantly in development to adapt to dynamic market demands. For example, social gaming software developer Zynga updates its online multiplayer game FarmVille frequently to keep the game fresh and relevant for its user base. And the approach works—in February 2010, its total user count surpassed 80 million active users, with almost 30 million people playing FarmVille every day![12]

**Low Cost**: Companies using a **low-cost product/service strategy** specialize in delivering products and services at low cost. Such an approach emphasizes

**Figure 6.8** Strategies for Product- and Service-Based Objectives

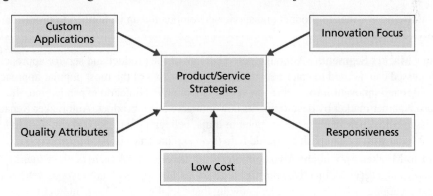

### Key Terms

**Innovation product/service strategy**  Emphasizing research and development capabilities to develop distinctively new offerings to the market.

**Responsiveness product/service strategy**  Emphasizing speed of development to respond to dynamic market demands.

**Low-cost product/service strategy**  Emphasizing low-cost production and distribution techniques to deliver products and services at low cost.

competitive advantages in low-cost production and distribution techniques to achieve profitability. The approach requires little in the way of research and development (and its costs), resulting in potentially higher profits. Such companies are limited to fairly generic products, however. For example, PNY Technologies manufactures USB flash drives, flash memory cards, and other standard computer peripherals, and sells them at low prices.

**Quality Attributes: Reliability, Durability, and Safety**: Organizations specializing in selling to demanding customers often use a **quality attributes product/service strategy**. Needs can include demand for extremely high reliability (or risk a failed mission, as in the aerospace industry), extremely high quality (or face severe injuries to patients, as in the medical device industry), extreme durability (or face expensive downtime, as in the heavy construction equipment industry), or be extremely focused on safety (or risk death, as in the hazardous materials safety equipment industry). For example, Panasonic manufactures its rugged Toughbook line of portable computers to address the rigorous needs of the military and law enforcement markets.

**Custom Applications**:  Some organizations use a **custom applications product/service strategy**, targeting customers needing unique applications. In consumer markets, Dell provides an online configurator (Web-based application assisting the user in specifying parts of a system) for customers to build their own custom personal computer, enabling them to select the processor speed, memory size, and so on. In business markets, Grainger and other industrial parts suppliers have applications engineers on staff to modify existing components for customer applications, such as modifications and adjustments to basic electric motors to meet specific requirements. Sometimes this type of operation is called BTO (build to order). Such organizations excel in low-cost and rapid development work (although here, "development" often involves minor modifications to existing platforms). Organizations must also have adaptive production capabilities.

The five approaches to product and service development can be applied to product and service objectives:

**New Market Segments**:  Although potentially all of the product and service approaches discussed can be used to enter new market segments, two of the most popular approaches are through innovation focus and low cost. For example, Nintendo expanded into the casual gamer market by developing its new interactive Wii product. Automaker Renault-Nissan built a new manufacturing plant in India, believing that a $3,000 car, built in low-cost India with a local partner, would help them capture sales in Asian markets.[13]

**Go-to-Market Approach**:  Two common ways for organizations to achieve their product and service objectives through a go-to-market approach are responsiveness and custom applications. For example, knowing that social gamers crave interactivity, Zynga delivers its FarmVille game using social media sites like Facebook, rather than sending the gamer a traditional CD-ROM in a box. The BMW MINI allows customers to "build" their cars on its configurator-equipped website (selecting from 10 million option and accessory combinations)...

**Differentiating Functionality**:  While an innovation focus is an obvious way to acquire differentiating functionality, employing an approach using quality attributes can also prove effective. For example, consumer electronics giant Samsung was one of the first companies to innovate three-dimension (3D) television technology. The Panasonic Toughbook personal computer employs differentiating functionality, such as gel-mounted hard drives (for shock resistance) and a magnesium chassis (for ruggedness and light weight), that gives it the durability soldiers and police officers respect.

---

## Marketing Planning in Action

**3M: Posting High Profits with Post-its**. 3M, widely known for its emphasis on innovation, struggled between efficiency and creativity in the early 2000s. In the 1990s, 3M innovated well, but its stock price struggled. In 2000, 3M hired James McNerney, a former contender for the CEO spot at General Electric (GE). McNerney got to work, slashing 8,000 jobs, sharpening the performance review process, and implementing GE's Six Sigma quality process. A few years later, he left for a better position, CEO at Boeing. His successors wondered if all the emphasis on efficiency made 3M less creative. 3M built its reputation as an invention machine—the creator of masking tape, Thinsulate, and Post-it notes. But those were all in the past. With McNerney gone, new CEO George Buckley increased 3M's emphasis on research and development, and some say that he has "brought back a spark around creativity."[14]

---

Figure 6.9 summarizes how to apply different development approaches to product and service-based objectives.

## Strategies for Brand-Based Objectives

Many objectives involve improvements to one of the organization's core assets—its brands. The Aaker Brand Equity model presents a set of five effective strategies to address brand objectives: [15]

**Brand Loyalty**: Aaker defines **brand loyalty** as the degree to which customers are satisfied, have some degree of switching costs (time and money required to change brands, which can discourage some customers from changing brands), like the brand, and are committed to it. Brand loyalty is important for three reasons. First, it reduces the cost of sales because the cost of acquiring new customers is higher than that of keeping existing ones. Second, existing customers can create brand awareness and give assurance to potential new customers. Third, brand loyalty reduces vulnerability to competitors. For example, Apple loyalists remained true to their brand even when Microsoft introduced its new Windows 7 operating system, acknowledged to be superior to its lackluster predecessor, Vista.

---

### Key Terms

**Quality attributes product/ service strategy**   Emphasizing high degrees of reliability, durability, or safety to markets that value those attributes.

**Custom applications product/service strategy**   Emphasizing build to order (BTO) capabilities to deliver products and services modified for customer's unique needs.

**Brand loyalty**   The degree to which customers are satisfied with a particular brand, have some degree of switching costs to discourage changing from that brand to another, and are committed to the brand.

**Figure 6.9** Product and Service Development Strategies for Product and Service-Based Objectives

| Market Opportunity | Strategies: Product/ Service | Example |
|---|---|---|
| New Market Segment | **Innovation Focus**: Emphasize strong R&D to capture new market segment | Nintendo Wii |
| | **Low Cost**: Leverage low-cost production advantages to target price-sensitive segment | Renault-Nissan |
| Go-to-Market Approach | **Responsiveness**: Continually innovate to keep product or service fresh and engaging | Zynga |
| | **Custom Applications**: Build products or service to order to cater to customer preferences | BMW MINI |
| Differentiating Functionality | **Innovation Focus**: Emphasize strong R&D to target early adopters of new technologies | Samsung 3D TV |
| | **Quality Attributes**: Target users who demand extreme quality, reliability, or durability | Panasonic Toughbook |

**Brand Awareness**: **Brand awareness** consists of brand recognition (confirming prior exposure to a brand, like seeing it before in a TV ad) and brand recall (retrieving the brand from memory, given the product category or some other cue). Recognized and recalled brands are often selected over unknown brands, because many people assume that familiar brands are likely to be more reliable, have solid financial strength, and are of reasonable quality. For example, many people trust Sears DieHard batteries, because they are familiar with the brand.

**Perceived Quality**: **Perceived quality** is the customers' opinion of the brand's ability to fulfill their expectations. High perceived quality of a brand is important for three reasons. First, it can directly influence purchase decisions and brand loyalty, especially when buyers are not motivated or able to conduct a detailed analysis (such as consumer packaged goods like toothpaste and breakfast cereal). Second, it can support a premium price ("expensive but worth it"). Third, it can support a brand extension because it is assumed that the quality will carry over to the new extension. For example, Toyota's reputation for high-quality automobiles helped it extend the brand to luxury automobiles bearing the Lexus name.

**Brand Associations**: According to Aaker, **brand associations** (anything mentally linked to brands) can affect the processing and recall of information (like linking Volvo with safety), provide points of differentiation ("Volvo is different from other brands because it values safety"), provide a reason to buy ("I bought a Volvo for my daughter because I wanted her to be safe"), create positive attitudes and feelings ("I feel relieved knowing my daughter is driving her Volvo"), and aid brand extensions (Volvo expanded from its traditional sedans to include coupes and crossover vehicles).

**Other Proprietary Brand Assets**:  **Proprietary brand assets**, company assets associated with the brand, like patents, trademarks, and distribution channel relationships, can help protect brand equity. Patents related to the brand help to prevent competitors from stealing the intellectual property (ideas, inventions, and other "creations of the mind") that support the brand. Brand trademarks give a legal recourse to prevent competitors from seeking to confuse consumers by using a similar name (like introducing a new line of soft drinks called "Coco-Cola"). Distribution channels controlled by the brand can be lucrative assets because of historical brand performance (Lay's potato chips have a long history of strong sales, so competitors are not likely to get into the supermarket shelf space occupied by Lay's).

The five brand strategies can be applied to brand-related objectives:

**New Market Segment**:  Although potentially all of the brand strategies discussed can be used to enter new market segments, two of the most popular approaches are brand awareness and perceived quality. For example, mineral-based cosmetics maker Bare Escentuals used aggressive brand awareness programs as part of their successful expansion into the European cosmetics market despite stiff competition there. As we saw earlier, Toyota leveraged its reputation for high perceived quality to target luxury car buyers with its Lexus brand.

**Go-to-Market Approach**:  Two common ways for organizations to achieve their brand objectives through a go-to-market approach are through brand associations and leveraging brand assets. For example, motorcycle manufacturer Harley-Davidson's marketing approach emphasizes "biker lifestyle" associations to build the brand and promote sales. Fashion clothier Rent the Runway leverages its relationships with clothing designers to let customers rent designer fashions like Dolce & Gabbana, Diane von Furstenberg, and Vera Wang for only 10 percent of the retail price of the garment. As the company website states, "It's high fashion with the hassle."

**Differentiating Functionality**:  Two ways for organizations to achieve their objectives through a differentiating functionality approach are through brand loyalty strategies and leveraging proprietary brand assets. For example, the Doubletree hotel employs a variety of techniques to differentiate itself from competing hotels, but what every guest remembers is the fresh, warm chocolate chip cookies they receive upon arrival. Breakfast cereal manufacturer Kellogg's exploits its long-standing relations with top-tier supermarkets to get prime shelf space, making its cereals stand out from a sea of seemingly identical boxes.

---

## Key Terms

**Brand awareness**    Brand recognition (confirming prior exposure to a brand) and brand recall (retrieving the brand from memory).

**Perceived quality**    Customers' opinion of the brand's ability to fulfill their expectations.

**Brand associations**    Thoughts or beliefs mentally linked to a brand.

**Proprietary brand assets**    Company assets associated with the brand, like patents, trademarks, and distribution channel relationships.

## Marketing Plannning in Action

**Doubletree: Delicious Differentiation**. Doubletree, like any other hotel chain, focuses on making its guests comfortable—and standing out in the increasingly competitive hotel market. But many guest services, such as curbside valet service, are easily copied by other hotels, thus failing to provide a sustainable competitive advantage. Doubletree hit upon its differentiating strategy long ago. For over 20 years, it has been giving away its trademark chocolate chip cookies to guests upon their arrival. According to Doubletree, it has baked over 200 million of the delicious treats. Ask the average business traveler what differentiates most hotels and you will likely get an array of answers. Ask them what differentiates Doubletree and you will get a smile.[16]

**Figure 6.10** Brand Strategies for Brand-Based Objectives

| Market Opportunity | Strategies: Brand | Example |
|---|---|---|
| New Market Segment | **Brand Awareness**: Build brand by increasing awareness | Bare Escentuals |
| | **Perceived Quality**: Build brand by increasing perceived quality | Lexus |
| Go-to-Market Approach | **Brand Associations**: Build brand by reinforcing positive associations | Harley-Davidson |
| | **Other Proprietary Brand Assets**: Build brand by leveraging distribution channel relationships | Rent The Runway |
| Differentiating Functionality | **Brand Loyalty**: Build brand by reinforcing elements responsible for brand loyalty | Doubletree |
| | **Other Proprietary Brand Assets**: Build brand by leveraging assets to make it stand out from pack | Kellogg's |

Figure 6.10 summarizes how to apply different brand strategies to brand-based objectives.

## Strategies for Customer-Based Objectives

As shown in Figure 6.11, organizations employ three basic customer strategies: customer acquisition (getting customers), customer retention (keeping customers), and customer revenue growth (increasing revenue per customer).[17]

**Figure 6.11**  Strategies for Customer-Based Objectives

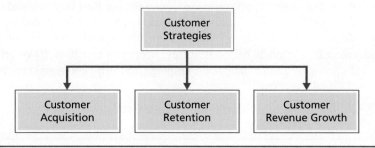

**Customer Acquisition (Getting Customers):**  Different types of companies adopt different types of **customer acquisition strategies** to adapt to the needs of their particular market. Whether the company acquires new customers using market penetration methods (like capturing competitors' customers) or market development methods (like selling existing services to a new group of customers), companies must ensure that customers value their offering, or they will not be successful. For example, the customers of women's clothing company Lane Bryant appreciate the variety and quality of plus-size fashion apparel the company offers.

**Customer Retention (Keeping Customers):**  Having acquired the customer, companies use **customer retention strategies** to keep them. Retention is not just a question of keeping customers; it is of keeping the *right* customers. Spending large amounts to keep unprofitable customers rarely makes sense. To increase customer focus while still maintaining profitability, companies must realize that different customers have different customer lifetime values (the total profit resulting from the business relationship with the customer over their lifetime). As a result, many companies employ customer tiering to rank their customers according to their customer lifetime value. For example, brokerage firm Schwab assigns special service teams to affluent clients, while those less wealthy must suffice with self-service websites.[18]

**Customer Revenue Growth (Growing Customers):**  Retaining customers helps keep customer lifetime value; growing customers increases it. **Customer revenue growth strategies** typically involve increasing their lifetime (introducing them to the product or service earlier to extend the relationship), increasing the amount of revenue generated from every customer interaction (like super-sizing), or extending the company's value proposition to provide an array of products and services that customers appreciate.

## Key Terms

**Customer acquisition strategy**  Method for gaining sales from new customers.

**Customer retention strategy**  Method for keeping customers (especially profitable ones).

**Customer revenue growth strategy**  Method for increasing amount of revenue generated per customer.

Customer relationship management (CRM) software helps grow customer value by capturing customer preferences so companies can tailor value-added products and services to them. For example, consumer electronics retailer Best Buy acquired electronics assistance services company Geek Squad to provide value-added services for Best Buy customers, from simple mobile phone e-mail setups to computer virus removal. The arrangement has definitely helped Best Buy. According to a 2008 *ZDNet* article, Geek Squad's services "are the thing that's keeping [Best Buy] going amid pricing pressure and a weak economy."[19]

**The Geek Squad provides value-added services, increasing Best Buy's revenue per customer**
*Source*: Alamy

The three broad customer strategies can be applied to customer-related objectives:

**New Market Segment**: As mentioned earlier, companies can pursue customer acquisition methods to target new market segments, like the approach used by Lane Bryant. Companies can also target new market segments using "share of wallet" techniques. For example, after Best Buy acquired high-end electronics retailer Magnolia (which now sells products in many Best Buy retail stores), it entered the high-end home theater installation market by expanding Geek Squad services to include sophisticated electronics installation services.

**Go-to-Market Approach**: Focusing on the customer means that customers can deliver their offerings in different ways, as long as customer needs are met. As we discussed earlier, Best Buy grew revenue per customer by delivering value-added services through its Geek Squad team, in addition to Best Buy's traditional product business. In addition, companies can take advantage of market opportunities suggesting new go-to-market strategies by employing CRM technology. For example, luxury hotel chain Ritz-Carlton is able to deliver its services differently, thanks to its CRM database it calls "Mystique." Using Mystique, the Ritz-Carlton can track information such as guest preferences, frequency of visits, and issues from previous stays to provide a fundamentally more personal experience.[20]

**Differentiating Functionality**: Companies can take advantage of market opportunities suggesting the use of differentiating functionality by employing a customer retention strategy. Market studies have found that discount broker Schwab ranks higher in serving the affluent market than many of its rivals (such as online brokerage services provider E-Trade) by providing superior functionality, such as its keen market research and sophisticated investment portfolio management tools. Its customer tiering approach should help it retain its affluent clients, who represent high profit potential for the firm.[21]

## Marketing Planning in Action

**Marni: Catering to Customers by Using Convenience and Confidence**. Customers have spoken. They want convenience—but don't want to give up knowledgeable sales advice and terrific customer service to get it. In the past, customers had to choose between boutiques (providing better service, but lower convenience) or the Web (more convenient, but not very engaging). Marni and other online boutiques have changed that model by revising their websites to be more interactive and offer personal styling advice. For example, Marni offers customers the option of sorting its merchandise by look, from "modern muse" to "macramé pop." Thanks to Marni's different delivery model, customers can easily coordinate the perfect ensemble—even if it involves finding the perfect patterned scarf to go with that herringbone jacket.[22]

Figure 6.12 summarizes how to apply different customer strategies to customer-based objectives.

**Figure 6.12** Customer Strategies for Customer-Based Objectives

| Market Opportunity | Strategies: Customer | Example |
|---|---|---|
| New Market Segment | **Acquisition**: Acquire customers from new markets with unmet needs | Lane Bryant |
| | **Revenue per Customer**: Grow revenue per customer by expanding into new areas | Magnolia-based services |
| Go-to-Market Approach | **Revenue per Customer**: Grow revenue per customer by adding value-added services | Geek Squad |
| | **Retention**: Retain customers by leveraging CRM to capture preferences | Ritz-Carlton |
| Differentiating Functionality | **Retention**: Retain customers by providing top service to top customers | Schwab |

## The Marketing Mix

With the strategy selected, the next step is to decide how to implement it. The strategy is implemented with the tactics of the marketing mix: product/service, price, distribution, and promotion. Each strategy can involve multiple elements in the marketing mix. For example, a strategy to launch a new service would require product/service tactics (to develop the new service), price tactics (to set pricing for the new service), distribution tactics (to decide how to deliver the service), and promotion tactics (to encourage trial of new service).[23]

Over the next four chapters, we will address each of the four marketing mix elements. The chapters will show how to decide on specific tactics, given a product/service's stage in its product life cycle.

## Practical Planning

In this section, we will continue demonstrating the marketing planning process using our ongoing example, Expedia online travel agent (OTA) services.

The first step is to determine our market opportunities. We desire to find opportunities that are not already dominated by our competitors, that expand our business, and that align with the current direction of the company. Most companies do not have the resources to go after every identified market opportunity, and we can use our objectives (already identified earlier in the marketing plan) to prioritize which market opportunities to target. The market opportunities can also help us transform the objectives into specific strategies.

As you recall, we have the following objective for the Expedia example:

**Objective**. Increase sales of new travel services, such as new vacation packages (where new services are defined as those introduced within past three years), from 10 percent of total revenue to 15 percent, to be completed by the end of calendar year 2012.

**Figure 6.13** Market Opportunity and Strategy: Expedia

| Objective | Market Opportunity Identification | Strategy |
|---|---|---|
| Increase sales of new travel services | Adventure Travel | Differentiate by developing new services: Adventure travel packages |

To identify the market opportunity, we consider the market segment analysis from Chapter 4 (where we learned that the adventure travel segment is strong and profitable) along with the competitive research of Chapter 5 (where our research shows us that other OTAs offer few adventure travel packages). The result is the following market opportunity:

**Market Opportunity**. We have identified a potentially profitable market opportunity not already dominated by competitors: Adventure travel services.

We select our strategy by determining the course of action that would enable us to take advantage of the market opportunity we have identified. Because our objective is primarily financially oriented (to increase sales), we will select from the generic strategies (cost leadership, differentiation, and focus). We select a differentiation approach to correspond with our choice of market opportunity type and strategy type. The result is the following strategy:

**Strategy**. We will create a new line of adventure travel packages. We will use a differentiation approach, developing a unique set of services to differentiate the offerings and attract this niche market.

Figure 6.13 summarizes how we exploited market opportunities to transform our objectives into strategies.

## Summary

As an old German proverb warns, "What's the use of running if you are not on the right road?" Without the right strategy in place, organizations risk ineffective use of resources and ultimate failure.

The chapter covered how to identify market opportunities based on the results of the market analysis and competitive comparison framework done earlier. Most market opportunities fall into one of three categories: new market segments, go-to-market approaches, and differentiating functionality. New market segments are portions of the market not targeted by competitors, such as new geographic areas or unique psychographic segments. Unique go-to-market approaches, which are the mechanisms by which companies reach their customers, can be used to differentiate companies from its competitors. Differentiating functionality can be used to develop unique products or services to attract niche markets.

We covered how to select our strategy for the marketing plan's project, based on the market opportunity and the plan's objective. We covered five types of strategic approaches, each corresponding to different types of objectives. The first strategy approach applies Porter's generic strategies to financially oriented objectives. The second approach employs Ansoff's growth strategies for market share growth-based objectives. The third approach uses product and service strategies to achieve product/service-related objectives. The fourth approach applies Aaker's Brand Equity model to brand-based objectives. The final approach engages customer-based strategies to achieve customer-based objectives.

In the next chapter, we will show how our strategies are implemented using marketing mix tactics, starting with products and services. While strategy is a vital part of any marketing plan, it must be set into action to deliver results.

 ## Key Terms

**Brand associations** Thoughts or beliefs mentally linked to a brand. (p. 120)

**Brand awareness** Brand recognition (confirming prior exposure to a brand) and brand recall (retrieving the brand from memory). (p. 120)

**Brand loyalty** The degree to which customers are satisfied with a particular brand, have some degree of switching costs to discourage changing from that brand to another, and are committed to the brand. (p. 119)

**Cost leadership generic strategy** Leveraging competitive advantages in low-cost production or service delivery to price products and services lower than competitors. (p. 111)

**Custom applications product/service strategy** Emphasizing build to order (BTO) capabilities to deliver products and services modified for customer's unique needs. (p. 118)

**Customer acquisition strategy** Method for gaining sales from new customers. (p. 123)

**Customer retention strategy** Method for keeping customers (especially profitable ones). (p. 123)

**Customer revenue growth strategy** Method for increasing amount of revenue generated per customer. (p. 123)

**Differentiating functionality** Unusual features that set products and services apart from existing offerings. (p. 108)

**Differentiation generic strategy** Setting company apart from its competitors through developing different products and services acknowledged to be superior by customers. (p. 111)

**Diversification growth strategy** Growing market share (or total market size) by marketing new products and services to new customers. (p. 114)

**Economies of scale** Reduction of per-unit cost through large-scale operations. (p. 111)

**Experience curve** Reduction of cost through higher productivity gained by learning knowledge around production and delivery operations. (p. 111)

**Focus generic strategy** Targeting a small segment with a cost leadership or differentiation strategy. (p. 111)

**Go-to-market approach** Mechanism used by company to deliver its products and services to customers. (p. 107)

**Innovation product/service strategy** Emphasizing research and development capabilities to develop distinctively new offerings to the market. (p. 117)

**Low-cost product/service strategy** Emphasizing low-cost production and distribution techniques to deliver products and services at low cost. (p. 117)

**Market development growth strategy** Growing market share (or total market size) by marketing existing products and services to new market segments. (p. 114)

**Market opportunities** Market segments that could be targeted by the firm for potential profit. (p. 106)

**Market penetration growth strategy** Gaining market share (or total market size) by marketing existing products and services to existing customers in new ways. (p. 114)

**New product/service development growth strategy** Growing market share (or total market size) by marketing new products and services to existing customers. (p. 114)

**Perceived quality** Customers' opinion of the brand's ability to fulfill their expectations. (p. 120)

**Proprietary brand assets** Company assets associated with the brand, like patents, trademarks, and distribution channel relationships. (p. 121)

**Quality attributes product/service strategy** Emphasizing high degrees of reliability, durability, or safety to markets that value those attributes. (p. 118)

**Responsiveness product/service strategy** Emphasizing speed of development to respond to dynamic market demands. (p. 117)

**Whitespace** Market segments not currently targeted by other competitors. (p. 106)

Discussion Questions

1. Some people say, "Companies have become so globally-oriented, and create so many products and services, that there are no new markets or products left to develop." How would you respond to such a claim?

2. How would you adapt some of the strategies discussed in this chapter for Internet-based campaigns, especially those involving social media?

3. English statesman Sir Winston Churchill is quoted as saying, "However beautiful the strategy, you should occasionally look at the results." What did he mean by the statement?

 Exercises

1. Identify market opportunities for your project. What type are they—new market segments, go-to-market approaches, or differentiating functionality?

2. Select a strategy for your project based on market opportunities and objectives. Identify an example company that executed a similar strategy.

3. Identify which marketing mix elements (product/service, price, distribution, and promotion) will likely be most affected by the strategy.

Exercise 1

## CHAPTER 7

# Products and Services

## INTRODUCTION

Now that we have completed our objectives, market opportunities, and strategies, our next step is to select the appropriate marketing mix tactics (the four Ps: product, price, place, and promotion) to execute on them. This and the following three chapters of the book will guide us in our marketing mix decisions, with one chapter for each of the four Ps, starting with this chapter on products and services.[1]

## CHAPTER CHECKLIST:

We cover the following marketing plan sections in this chapter:

❏ **Product/Service Tactics:** Determining target customers, features, quality, packaging, and brand attributes, based on the offering's stage in the product/service life cycle

❏ **Value Proposition:** Clarifying the unique value a product or service provides to its customers

❏ **Differentiation:** Showing how the product or service is distinct from others

Services, like the ones FedEx provides, are a large and growing segment of the world economy
*Source:* Shutterstock

Effective product and service development can propel companies to greatness. For example, shipping services leader FedEx is one of the great service success stories. Frederick W. Smith realized his vision of an overnight-delivery service, even though he only earned a C on the college term paper that proposed the idea. FedEx's commitment to outstanding service generated significant profits—and earned the company a place in entrepreneurial legend.[2]

## Marketing Planning in Action

**Sony Network Walkman: A Missed Opportunity**. Sony launched its S2 Sports Network Walkman NW-S23 several years after the successful launch of Apple iPod MP3 player. Sony was in a good position to leverage the knowledge gained by Apple's success, as well as Sony's own success when it introduced its Walkman cassette player line back in the 1980s. Nevertheless, the S2 failed in the market. Users complained of confusing controls, small displays, and cumbersome proprietary software. Early models would not support native MP3 playback, the most popular standard for digital music encoding. With Sony's excellent record of accomplishment in this category, the Network Walkman represented a missed opportunity to capture market share away from Apple.[3]

# Product and Service Tactics

In this section, we apply the familiar **product/service life cycle model** to guide us in deciding on the tactics to use to improve the marketability of our product or service.

## Product/Service Life Cycle Model

Figure 7.1 shows a typical life cycle for a product or service. Much like the human life cycle, the cycle is divided into four stages: introduction, growth, maturity, and decline. During the introduction stage, sales are slow as the product or service is introduced to the market. At the growth stage, sales expand rapidly as the market adopts the product or service. At the maturity stage, sales growth slows down because the product or service has been adopted by most potential buyers. During the decline stage, sales drift downward, unless the product or service's life is extended through new features, new uses, repositioning, or brand extensions, shown as a life extension in the figure.[4]

Product/service tactics will vary based on the life cycle stage of the market for the product or service. For example, product and service decisions for smartphones (a growing market) will differ from those for VCRs (a declining market). Five product and service characteristics need to be addressed.

**Customers to Target**: The type of customer we target varies depending on the life cycle stage, because different individuals show different adoption characteristics. The introduction stage attracts **innovators** (the very first to try the product or service, often pioneering types who relish innovation) and **early adopters** (among the earliest to try the new product or service). The growth stage transitions from the early adopters to the **early majority** (people who value the product or service's benefits, but are unwilling to suffer the defects often inherent in early models). The maturity stage corresponds to **late majority** customers (conservative individuals who wait for products to reach full maturity before purchasing). The decline stage is characterized by a transition from late majority customers to **laggards**, who are highly conservative and risk-averse, and are often niche markets who perceive that no substitute exists.[5]

**Figure 7.1**  Product/Service Life Cycle
*Source:* Adapted with permission from Kotler, Philip, *Marketing Management*, 6th ed. (Upper Saddle River, NJ: Prentice-Hall, 1988). Figure 12-2, p. 349

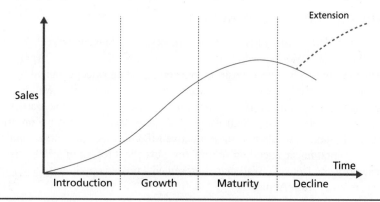

## Marketing Planning in Action

**Video Game Market: Targeting Heavy Gamers**. The multi-billion-dollar video game market boasts six major segments, according to a survey done by market research firm NPD Group. The segments include Heavy Gamers, Avid Console Gamers, Mass Market Gamers, Prefer Portable Gamers, Secondary Gamers, and Infrequent Gamers. The Heavy Gamer segment represents the early adopters in the category, and comprises only 3 percent of the total game-playing population. Nevertheless, the early-adopting segment is targeted for new games, because the segment's opinion on new games influences the other segments, and is therefore critical to the games' success.[6]

**Features**:  Different life cycle stages demand differing levels of attention to features. Early adopters are more concerned with key functionality than complete feature sets, whereas mature markets demand fully featured products and services.

## Marketing Planning in Action

**Zune: Feature-rich, But Still No iPod**. The Microsoft Zune MP3 player included features the Apple iPod did not have, but the iPod still won in the market. Why? Because the features customers truly wanted, such as intuitive user interfaces and system compatibility, were designed into the iPod from the start. Microsoft, on the other hand, added extra features like wireless Internet access and radio functionality, which consumers did not value highly when selecting a portable MP3 player. Instead of offering superfluous features, many users wish the Zune had improved compatibility—in fact, early versions of the Microsoft Zune were not even compatible with Microsoft's own operating system, Vista.[7]

### Key Terms

**Product/service life cycle model**   Model showing sales levels over time, passing through four distinct "life" stages: introduction, growth, maturity, and decline.

**Innovator**   Customers associated with the earliest part of the introduction phase of the product/service life cycle. Innovators are generally pioneering types who tolerate minor defects for the thrill of being the first.

**Early adopter**   Customers associated with the introduction phase of the product/service life cycle (though after the Innovators). Early adopters are generally risk takers who place a high value on the offering's benefits.

**Early majority**   Customers associated with the growth phase of the product/service life cycle. Early majority customers value the offering's benefits, but are unwilling to suffer the defects commonly found in the earliest versions of a product or service.

**Late majority**   Customers associated with the maturity stage of the product/service life cycle. Late majority customers are generally conservative individuals who wait for products to reach full maturity before purchasing.

**Laggards**   Customers associated with the late maturity and decline phases of the product/service life cycle. Laggards are highly conservative and risk-averse. They are the last ones to adopt a product or service.

**Quality**: Required quality by the market will vary during the life cycle. Early adopters will accept minor faults, whereas high quality is expected in mature markets. High quality is a must in a world where dissatisfied customers can express their anger online with a click of a mouse.

---

## Marketing Planning in Action

**YouTube: Wielding an Ax against Poor Quality**. Some consumers are sick of poor-quality products and services and are just not going to take it any more. In the past, consumers would just grumble to themselves, or mention it to anyone within earshot. Not anymore. Thanks to online reviews, dissatisfied customers can complain to the world—and have people read it. Witness how many people read Amazon review before buying a book. But mere reviews are sometimes just not enough. Some consumers take it to the next level. Welcome to the world of the consumer vigilante. After Apple refused to fix Michael Whitford's ailing Macbook, he took a golf club, an ax, a sword, and finally a sledgehammer to smash his Macbook to bits. He captured the carnage on YouTube. More than 340,000 people watched the mayhem.[8]

---

**Packaging**: In the larger sense, packaging consists of more than just a cardboard box. It is the way the product or service is presented to the customer. For products, this can mean the number of sizes, colors, and flavors available. For services, this can mean the range of service options available, such as different types of hotel rooms to accommodate different types of travelers.

The focus on the packaging of products and services will change during the life cycle. In the introduction stage, companies will often provide a limited number of variants (partially because many companies do not know which specific variants customers prefer when the offering is first launched), whereas later stages warrant more choices. For example, a company starting a new travel service to Antarctica (introductory stage of the life cycle) might only offer a few departure times, while a travel service providing tours to Europe (mature stage) would offer dozens of different trips to suit multiple types of travelers.

---

## Marketing Planning in Action

**Apple: Elegance in Packaging**. Apple delights its buyers with its "packaging experience." Many users feel that the elegance of the user interface begins with the bold graphics and sleek texture of the box in which the new device is enshrined. Users are treated to a luxurious experience as each layer of the packaging reveals new components, wrapped in elegant trappings. Some users, called Apple Pack Rats, keep the packaging as a testament to the experience, and cannot even imagine throwing the boxes away. Some even display the boxes in their homes, illuminating them with strategically placed lights. For many, the box is more than a record of a serial number, "it's a record of a good event that happened in my life."[9]

**Brand**:  Brands help make products and services distinct and relevant to the buyer. In essence, the brand is a trustworthy, relevant, distinctive promise to customers. Our branding efforts will vary during the life cycle.

## Marketing Planning in Action

**Perez Hilton: Building Brands through Blogs**: Perez Hilton built his personal brand by covering the celebrity scene with his blog. Hilton (his real name is Mario Armando Lavandeira) realized that he was passionate about many interests, not just celebrity gossip, so he extended his brand from perezhilton.com to books, a clothing line, and a VH1 series. His next brand extension is his new music label, Perezcious, with his first artist, Sliimy. Perez ensures that his brand remains consistent over his many ventures by leveraging common brand associations across them. His goal is to have each of his ventures complement each other, taking advantage of his massive online platform and brand equity to express his passion over his many interests.[10]

## Product/Service Tactics during Life Cycle Stages

We will now cover the life cycle in more detail, determining the relevant types of product and service tactics to execute during each of the four stages. We demonstrate the tactics using examples from the cellular telephone market as it existed in the year 2010.[11]

**Introduction**:  During the introduction stage, the focus should be on the development of new products and services, as well as supporting marketing tactics, to ensure that those products and services succeed. For example, applications ("apps") that ran on the Android cellular phone-based operating system were largely in the introduction stage in the early part of 2010. Apps were often limited in functionality and plagued with problems ("buggy"), but early adopters still greeted them with enthusiasm because they were optimistic about the potential the new technology would deliver.

- **Customers to Target**: Innovators and early adopters should be targeted during the introductory stage. These adventurous customers enjoy cutting-edge products or services, and perceive a fundamental advantage in them that no existing offering delivers.
- **Features**: The product or service must have at least one blockbuster feature that defines why this new offering is worthy of consideration and makes it stand out from offerings from competitors. The unique feature will be an important part of the nascent product or service's branding efforts.
- **Quality**: The refinement of features is not critical at this stage. In fact, secondary-level features can be imperfect (or even be missing!), but the primary features must work well.
- **Packaging**: Early adopters are tolerant of offering the product or service in only one or two varieties.
- **Brand**: Category awareness must be built if no similar products or services exist. Brand awareness can be developed by creating strong, favorable, and unique associations with the product or service. The intellectual property should be protected with copyrights and patents.

**Growth**: In the growth stage, competitors are attracted to the growing market, so the focus should be on building brand preference, differentiating the product or service from others in a quickly crowding field, and gaining market share. For example, competing cellular phone manufacturers witnessed the success of the early Apple iPhone smartphones and decided to enter the market with their own smartphone variants, forcing Apple to emphasize the unique styling and user interface that set its phones apart.

- **Customers to Target**: At the growth stage, we transition from targeting early adopters to targeting the early majority. The early majority tend to be pragmatists, people who value the benefits that the product or service offers but do not want to be "guinea pigs" like the early adopters. Often, the market will become segmented into different customer groups at this stage.

- **Features**: The emphasis at this stage is to develop additional features desired by customers, thus "filling out" the product or service to be competitive with other companies. It is helpful to group features into four categories: blockbuster features (the product/service must be a clear leader in one important aspect), technology features (advanced capabilities to target sophisticated markets), premium features (luxury materials to target status-seeking markets), and parity features (features expected for products in that category, such as the inclusion of a remote control when purchasing a new HDTV set).

- **Quality**: All features, including secondary ones, are refined. Support services might be added.

- **Packaging**: Products are offered in different sizes and shapes. Different service packages are offered for different needs.

- **Brand**: At this stage, efforts should be made to increase brand preference. Market communications should demonstrate how the product or service has features, advantages, and benefits over competing brands.

**Maturity**: During the maturity stage, the focus should be on defending market share while maximizing profit. For example, in early 2010, "talk and text" cell phones (capable of voice calls and text messaging) were in the mature stage. Cell phone manufacturers attempted to maintain and grow market share by emphasizing their unique approach, such as ruggedized design, "skins" to change the color of the phone, and different keyboard layouts (slide out, swing out, or fixed on the front of the phone).

- **Customers to Target**: Here, we transition away from the early majority and move toward the late majority. Many of the sales will be to conservatives, people who will be one of the last people to purchase a product because of their cautious nature. The end of the maturity cycle will see sales transition to laggards, who are even more cautious than the late majority. The market should continue to be segmented into different customer types, as well as expanded geographically.

- **Features**: Features should be added to the product or service to differentiate it from that of competitors and "freshen" the offering.

- **Quality**: Quality levels must be high. Some companies might use exceptional levels of quality to stand out from the pack. For example, Southwest Airlines stresses the high quality of its customer service (in addition to its low price) to differentiate it from other airline services.

- **Packaging**: At this stage, a fairly wide range of products and services should be offered to accommodate the needs of different market segments.
- **Brand**: Organizations must define and refine the unique aspects of the product or service. Organizations selling to large, multi-segment markets might adopt a range of brands to reflect various quality levels. For example, Hilton Hotels offers multiple quality levels, such as its economy brand Hampton Inn, and its premium brand Conrad Hotels.

**Decline**:  The market should be researched to determine if the sales decline is a short-term phenomenon or signs of a dying market. As shown in Figure 7.2, the marketer has three options: maintain the product or service, harvest it, or discontinue it. Marketing mix tactics will depend on the option chosen,

- **Maintain the Product or Service**: Sometimes, faded brands can be revitalized through repositioning, introducing a brand extension, or finding new uses for the brand.
  - **Repositioning**: As we discussed earlier in the book, we can reposition existing products or services to new segments.
  - **Brand extensions**: Alternatively, we can introduce brand extensions, where we market similar products or services to existing segments. Generally, messaging is maintained throughout the extensions to help consumers associate them as related entities. For example, Hollywood is famous for extending the life cycle of its movies by introducing brand extensions (sequels), such as the popular *Matrix* series.
  - **New uses**: The final revitalization technique is to suggest new uses for the product or service. The messaging is often changed from a product or service focus (such as an emphasis on speed or reliability) to an application focus (such as its ability to solve problems experienced by the target market). Kraft found new uses for its Cheez Whiz brand of processed cheese, reinvigorating the brand by suggesting a new use as a perfect complement for microwave-prepared dishes, because it maintains its consistency while traditional cheese becomes rubbery.

**Figure 7.2**  Options for Decline Phase of Life Cycle

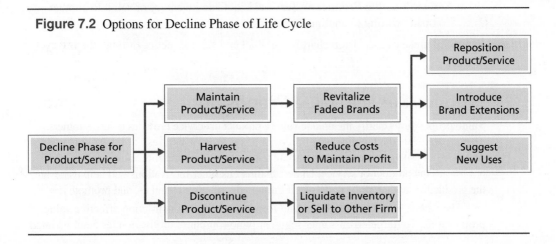

**Figure 7.3** Decision Chart: Product/Service Tactics during Life Cycle Stages

| Criteria | Introduction | Growth | Maturity | Decline |
|---|---|---|---|---|
| Target Customers | Early adopters | Pragmatists | Conservatives | Niche markets |
| Features | At least one block-buster feature to gain attention of market | Fill out feature list to be competitive | Add features to differentiate product or service and keep it "fresh" in market | If harvesting, adjust features to match demand of niche markets |
| Quality | Must function, but early adopters are tolerant of minor glitches | Refine features for problem-free functionality | Must be of high quality | If harvesting, cut costs to boost prof-itability |
| Packaging | Offered in only a few variants | Offer several variants | Offer a wide variety of variants to cater to different segments | If harvesting, cut number of variants to reduce costs |
| Brand | Build category and brand awareness | Increase brand preference by differentiating product or service | Define and refine what makes brand unique | If harvesting, reposition to niche market with new brand |

- **Harvest the Product or Service**: Reduce costs and continue to offer it, possibly to a loyal niche segment. For example, blank VHS (video home system) tape cartridges are still sold for the niche segment still using VCRs (video cassette recorders), but are only available in limited lengths and are rarely, if ever, advertised (to reduce costs).
- **Discontinue the Product or Service**: Liquidate inventory or sell it to another company willing to continue the product.

Figure 7.3 presents a decision chart for product and service tactics through the life cycle stages.

## Product/Service Value Proposition

**Value propositions** clarify the unique value a product or service provides to its customers. They clearly state the tangible benefits customers will enjoy as a result of using the product or service. As such, value propositions can tell us the underlying motivations a customer has toward the product or service. Understanding customer motivations will help us design the product or service, price it, deliver it through distribution channels, and promote it.

The author has found the following format useful for constructing effective value propositions: To (targeted customer segment) who (purchase motivation, as demonstrated

**Figure 7.4**  Product/Service Value Proposition Format

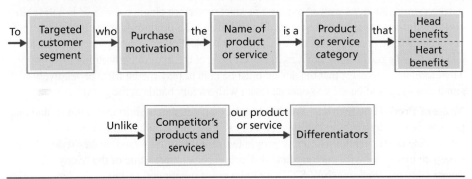

by use cases) the (name of product or service) is a (product or service category) that (head and heart benefits). Unlike (competitor's products and services), our product or service (differentiators).[12]

Figure 7.4 shows the value proposition development approach in a graphical format.

Here is how the format would be applied to Molly Maid house cleaning services (from mollymaid.com).

"To (busy people) who (appreciate a clean house but have no time to clean), the (maid service) is a (professional cleaning service) that (keeps a clean house and keeps you proud of your house). Unlike (amateur services), our company (provides bonded, insured residential maids and a satisfaction guarantee)."

To complete the value proposition for our product or service, we need to determine the value proposition elements—targeted buyer, customer's purchase motivation and use cases, and so forth. We define each element in turn, using the Apple iPod as an illustrative example.

**Targeted Customer Segment**:  We identify the targeted segment using the standard customer characteristics reviewed earlier (demographics, psychographics, etc.). Next, we create several buyer descriptions, also called **buyer personas**, to describe the type of buyer intended for this product. To be certain that the product or service is properly focused, we can create a persona about a buyer whose needs will *not* be satisfied. For example, the Apple iPod is not targeted for people who do not go online frequently (because users with little or no Web access would find it difficult to purchase new music through Apple iTunes). In fact, a recent study of owners of digital music players like the iPod found that 94 percent of them reported they shopped (i.e., researched and/or purchased) online in the past six months.[13]

---

## Key Terms

**Value proposition**    Clear statement of the tangible benefits a customer will enjoy by using the product or service.

**Buyer personas**    Descriptions of the type of buyer intended for a particular product or service. Buyer personas are useful when constructing value propositions.

**Customer Purchase Motivation and Use Cases**:  The next step is to state why customers purchase this type of product or service (their purchase motivation). To understand the purchase motivation, as well as required product or service characteristics, it is helpful to consider the usage scenarios the customer intends for the product or service. For example, people could use portable media players like the Apple iPod to be entertained with music and video while performing activities like exercising at the gym or commuting to work. Therefore, we can assert that the device must be able to play media files, be relatively small and light, and be easy to operate (even with sweaty hands at the gym).

**Name of Product or Service**:  We should select a name that is short, memorable, and has positive associations within its category. For example, the Apple iPod is a short and memorable name. In addition, many people feel that the Apple brand evokes style. Compare that name with the long (and difficult to remember) name of the "Sony S2 Sports Network Walkman NW-S23" MP3 player we mentioned earlier.

**Category of Product or Service**: Next, we state the category of the product or service in terms that the targeted segment would use. For example, instead of Apple describing its iPod product as a "network-ready multi-format-capable high definition multimedia device" or some other description that might be technically accurate but not familiar to customers, Apple describes it simply as a "portable media player."

**Benefits**:  We then state the benefits that customers will get from the product or service. To help describe benefits in a customer-oriented way, it is worthwhile to separate benefits into two categories: head and heart. **Head benefits** are rational reasons for buying a product or service, such as saving time or money. **Heart benefits** are emotional reasons for buying a product or service, such as feelings of self-esteem when using it. For example, the Apple iPod appealed to the head because it was a conveniently sized unit that performed all the functions it needed, using an easy-to-use interface. Emotionally, it was a winner as well, giving even social outcasts a possibility of being perceived as cool.

**Competitors**:  Next, we list the competitors, both direct and indirect, for the product or service. As we discussed in chapter 5, direct competitors offer products and services nearly identical to ours, whereas indirect competitors offer products and services in different categories, but still address the problem that the customer is trying to solve. For example, the Apple iPod faced other MP3 players as direct competitors. Indirect competition came from devices like smartphones that, while not in the MP3 player category, can still play media (even if they do not sound as good as the iPod).

**Differentiation**:  The next step is to state the characteristics that make this product or service distinct from similar versions in the market. For example, at the time of the Apple iPod's introduction, many media players were bulky (one popular music player category, portable CD units, had devices that measured over half-a-foot square in size, making them virtually impossible to stow in a jacket) and difficult to operate (some required two hands even for basic functions like powering up the unit). Apple succeeded in the market by solving these two problems with its small size and intuitive user interface. But it set itself apart in another important way: style. Nothing looked like an iPod. In a world of plastic boxes with tiny buttons, the simple, elegant style of the iPod differentiated it from everything else.

Figure 7.5 summarizes the process, showing entries for each value proposition element.

**Figure 7.5** Decision Chart: Product/Service Value Proposition Elements

| Element | Description | Apple iPod Example |
|---|---|---|
| Targeted Customer Segment | Segments, as defined using personas describing different sets of customer characteristics | Apple iPod likely not intended for people rarely using Internet |
| Customer Purchase Motivation and Use Cases | Scenarios under which buyers use the product; problems they are solving with it | To be entertained while working out at gym; while walking; while at office. (And look cool doing it) |
| Name of Product or Service | Short and memorable name, with positive associations in its category | Apple iPod: Short and memorable name (compare with Sony S2 Sports Network Walkman NW-S23) |
| Category of Product or Service | Category as customers describe it | Portable media player |
| Benefits | Head: Rational reason for purchasing, such as saving money<br>Heart: Emotional reason for purchasing, such as status or self-esteem | Head: Convenience of portability<br><br>Heart: Being considered cool |
| Competitors | Direct competitors: Providing near identical products & services.<br>Indirect competitors: Product or service different, but still addresses problem | Direct competitors: Other MP3 players.<br>Indirect competitors: Smartphones |
| Differentiation | Characteristics that make product or service distinct from others in market | Intuitive user interface |

## Marketing Planning in Action

**Tune Hotels: Hitting the Right Notes**. Tune Hotels, a chain of hotels in the United Kingdom, Indonesia, and Malaysia, offers a distinctive value proposition with their tagline, "5-Star Beds at 1-Star Prices." Tune skips the pools, spas, saunas, room service, and other premium services luxury hotels provide for what its target customer segment wants: budget-friendly room rates. Tune offers many features beyond price, though. Its hotels are strategically located close to major shopping, sightseeing, and business destinations. And its cheap price does not equate to the dirty and dangerous environments of other budget hotels. It provides its "5-Star Beds" with 250-thread count duvets, its high-pressure, heated "Power Showers," and 24-hour security. As Tune says, guests should not "risk robbery either by stepping out of the room, or by paying the bill at check-out."[14]

# Differentiation

Earlier in this chapter, we reviewed different types of product and service tactics to execute, given an offering's stage in the life cycle. One critical area that spanned every stage of the life cycle was the organization's need to differentiate its products and services from those of its competitors. Therefore, we dedicate the next section to differentiation.

## Differentiation Approaches: Products

As shown in Figure 7.6, we can select from several **product differentiation approaches**.[15]

**Form**: Products can be differentiated through their physical size or shape. This type of differentiation approach works well when consumers see the physical product during the purchase selection process, as in a supermarket or liquor store. For example, Absolut Vodka's unique shape is featured in many of its advertisements.

**Features**: Products can be differentiated if they have many useful features that similar products do not. This type of approach works well for products that are used to increase productivity, such as power tools and computer software. For example, Microsoft Office software has many features, helping it to maintain its lead in office productivity software.

**Ease of Use**: Products can be differentiated by being easy to use. This type of approach works for two categories of products. The first is safety-oriented products which are seldom used, but must be easy to use when the time comes, such as fire extinguishers. The second category is complex products that are often used, but need to hide their complexity to avoid confusion during operation, like home theatre systems or MP3 players. For example, the Apple iPod's simple, intuitive user interface and style revolutionized the MP3 market and made it a top seller.

**Quality**: Products can be differentiated on the quality of their craftsmanship. This type of approach works well for almost every category, and especially well for luxury and premium-priced goods. For example, Rolex wristwatches are renowned for their high level of fit and finish.

**Durability**: Products can be differentiated on the basis of their long operating life. This approach is suited for products for which customers expect to keep a long time, like

**Figure 7.6** Overview: Differentiation Approaches for Products

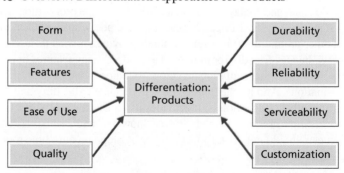

kitchen appliances, or wear out and are costly to replace, like automotive tires. Adidas understands that many tennis shoes wear out during grueling tennis matches on asphalt surfaces, so it differentiates itself by offering a six-month durability guarantee on its Barricade V tennis shoes.

Adidas differentiates its Barricade V tennis shoes by offering a six-month durability guarantee

*Source:* Fotolia

## Key Terms

**Head benefits**   Rational reasons for buying a product or service, such as saving time or money. Compare with heart benefits.

**Heart benefits**   Emotional reasons for buying a product or service, such as feelings of self-esteem when using it. Compare with head benefits.

**Reliability**: The ability for a product to avoid malfunctions is another basis for differentiation. As with ease of use, the approach benefits two types of goods: critical items that are not regularly used but cause physical hardship when they fail, like automotive airbags, and items that are costly to repair, like appliances. *Consumer Reports* magazine believes that reliability is so important in products that it conducts exhaustive tests and surveys to predict the likelihood of future problems. Top-rated appliances, such as Maytag washing machines, score well in reliability.

**Serviceability**: Products can be differentiated on how easy they are to repair. This differentiation approach works well for products where regular maintenance is required, such as automobiles and household appliances. For example, Bryant furnaces and air-conditioning systems are ranked highly for their serviceability.

**Customization**: In this approach, a product is tailored to the unique needs of the individual. This approach works well when customer needs in a category are diverse, such as with computers and automobiles. For example, Toyota's Scion xB is highly customizable, which helps it compete in the highly competitive compact automobile category.

---

## Marketing Planning in Action

**Scion: Customizing Cars in a Crowded Category**. Toyota's Scion brand targets its youthful market so successfully that its sales exceeded Toyota's expectations by 25 percent. Toyota differentiates the Scion in a crowded market of youth-oriented cars by allowing buyers to customize the car with thousands of different possibilities. For example, buyers can order different grilles, spoilers, ground effects kits, audio systems, exhaust tips, exterior and interior appliqués, shift knobs, brakes, performance shock absorbers, mufflers, sway bars, and wheels ranging from stock 16" rims to monster 19" high-performance units. Toyota consulted with hip-hop artists before building the car to ensure that the Scion line would target the youth culture accurately.[16]

---

Figure 7.7 presents a decision chart recommending certain differentiation approaches, given the application of the product.

## Differentiation Approaches: Product-Related Services

**Product-related services differentiation approaches**, such as installation and consulting, can make products stand out in crowded markets. The technique is especially effective for complex and expensive products. As shown in Figure 7.8, we can choose from several different approaches.[17]

**Ordering Ease**: One way to differentiate a company through value-added services is to make ordering through them easy, and perhaps even pleasurable. This type of

**Figure 7.7** Decision Chart: Differentiation Approaches for Products

| Differentiation Approach | Description | Decision Guidelines: Bestused for Following Situations: |
| --- | --- | --- |
| Form | Distinctive physical size or shape | Products seen during purchase selection process, such as consumer packaged goods |
| Features | Extra or unusual functionality | Products used to increase productivity, such as power tools or computer software |
| Ease of Use | Easy to understand and operate | Safety-oriented products, like fire extinguishers, and complex products, like consumer electronics |
| Quality | High level of fit and finish | Almost every product category; especially applicable to luxury goods |
| Durability | Long operating life | Durable goods, like kitchen appliances, and maintenance items, like tires |
| Reliability | Few malfunctions | Safety-oriented products, like automotive airbags, and products expensive to repair, like appliances |
| Serviceability | Ease of repair | Products requiring regular maintenance, like automobiles and appliances |
| Customization | Tailored to individual | Products where customer needs are diverse, like computers and automobiles |

**Figure 7.8** Overview: Differentiation through Product-Related Services

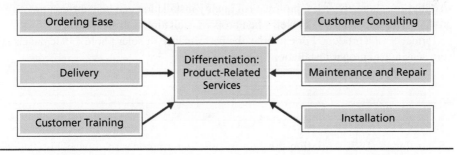

## Key Terms

**Product differentiation approaches**    Differentiation methods to show how the organization's product offering is distinct from similar versions on the market. Typical approaches include form, features, ease of use, quality, durability, reliability, serviceability, and customization.

**Product-related services differentiation approaches** Differentiation methods that use value-added services accompanying the product to make it stand out in the market. Typical approaches include ordering ease, delivery, customer training, customer consulting, maintenance and repair, and installation.

differentiation approach works well for products in categories with many choices, such as consumer electronics and books. Amazon.com is one such company, with one-click ordering and recommendations on additional items based on the products other customers have purchased.

**Delivery**: Another way to differentiate through value-added services is to provide hassle-free delivery. This type of approach works well for large, bulky, fragile items, like large-screen televisions. Crutchfield, for example, offers white glove delivery for its large television sets. For a nominal fee, the professional delivery crew will bring the television to the customer's home and carry it to any accessible room.

**Customer Training**: Here, companies differentiate themselves by training customers how to use the product. This type of differentiation approach works well for complex products where correct user operation is critical to the performance of the machine. For example, GE Medical trains technicians how to use their magnetic resonance imaging (MRI) machines to ensure the best possible care for the hospital's patients.

**Customer Consulting**: Companies can set themselves apart by providing consulting services for the products they sell, such as relevant products to use in certain applications. This type of approach works well for complex products where additional information is essential to proper selection. For example, industrial supply company Grainger advises customers on the application of their wide collection of industrial products.

**Maintenance and Repair**: Companies can differentiate themselves on their ability to keep the products they sell in working order. This differentiation approach works well for products that contribute to productivity, such as tools, and products requiring regular maintenance as part of their operation, like construction equipment. For example, large construction projects depend on Caterpillar heavy equipment to function well even in extreme conditions. And when a part does break, Caterpillar dispatches a crew immediately to repair it, minimizing expensive downtime.

**Installation**: In many cases, professional quality installation can help differentiate a product. This approach works well when proper installation is critical to the performance of a product. For example, the performance of solar photovoltaic panels is very sensitive to proper installation.

## Marketing Planning in Action

**Solar Panels: Differentiation through Installation**. Improper solar panel installation can reduce efficiency. And lower efficiency can result in customer dissatisfaction when they learn that the panels do not produce the amount of energy they had expected. Installation is such a critical issue with solar panels that new companies are sprouting up with new technologies that make the panels easier to install. One such technology is thin-film panels. Thin-film panels can decrease the effective cost of the solar panel module by almost 40 percent, from $4 per watt for existing crystalline-silicon units to around $2.40 per watt for thin-film units. In addition, thin-film technology results in thinner, lighter panels, which can make them easier to install.[18]

**Figure 7.9** Decision Chart: Differentiation through Product-Related Services

| Differentiation Approach | Description | Decision Guidelines: Best Used for Following Situations: |
|---|---|---|
| Ordering Ease | Ease of ordering | Products in categories with many choices, such as electronics and books |
| Delivery | Bringing product to customers | Large, bulky, fragile products, such as large-screen television sets |
| Customer Training | Training to use product | Complex products where correct operations are critical to performance, such as hospital MRI machines |
| Customer Consulting | Advising customers on products | Complex products requiring additional information to select correct version, such as industrial products |
| Maintenance and Repair | Keep product in working order | Productivity-oriented products, like tools, and maintenance-intensive products, such as construction equipment |
| Installation | Making product operational | Products where installation is critical to performance, such as solar panels |

Figure 7.9 presents a decision chart discussing differentiating products through the use of product-related services.

## Differentiation Approaches: Services

Many types of organizations such as government agencies (courts, hospitals, police, and fire departments), nonprofits (charities, museums, churches, and universities), and for-profit businesses (airlines, banks, hotels, and law firms) deliver services to their customers. Because of the unique demands of service-based organizations, the traditional marketing mix, or 4 Ps, can be supplemented to transform it to the **extended marketing mix**, or 7Ps. The three extra Ps include people (services are highly dependent on the people delivering them), processes (the flow of activities to execute the service), and physical evidence (tangible elements of the service, such as cleanliness of the area, neatness of dress, and quality of signage and equipment).[19]

---

### Key Terms

**Extended marketing mix**    Supplements the 4 Ps of traditional marketing mix (product, price, place, and promotion) with three more Ps (people, processes, and physical evidence) to adapt the mix for services.

**Figure 7.10** Overview: Differentiation Approaches for Services

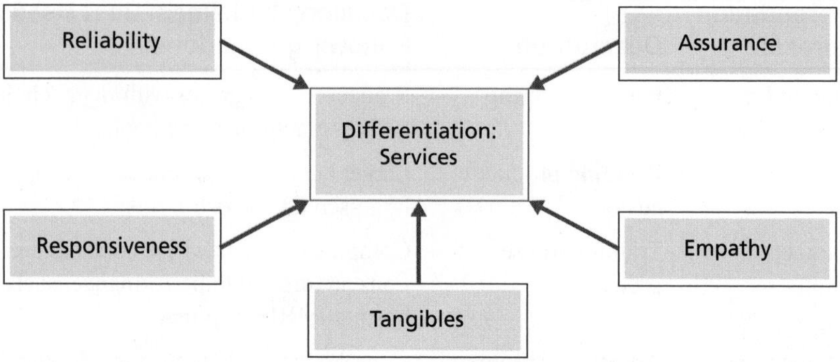

So far, we have focused on differentiation of products. But services are a growing area with high profit potential—often higher than that of products—and many would also benefit from a sound differentiation approach. As Figure 7.10 shows, we can select from several **service differentiation approaches**.[20]

**Reliability**: One way to differentiate services is by providing exceptional levels of reliability. Indeed, reliability is the number one determinant of service quality. Service reliability is defined as the ability to perform the promised service dependably and accurately. This type of differentiation approach works well for critical services, where customers will experience distress if the service is not executed correctly. For example, FedEx differentiates its shipping services using reliability, with its tagline, "When it absolutely, positively has to be there overnight."

## Marketing Planning in Action

**U.S. Post Office: Delivering Differentiation**. The U.S. Postal Service (USPS), once heralded for its commitment to reliably deliver the U.S. mail, where "neither rain nor sleet nor dark of night" would hinder its progress, now suffers a perception of low service reliability. Competitors such as FedEx, UPS, and email threaten to drive it out of business. The USPS faced a nearly $7 billion net loss at the end of 2009, causing it to be added to the government list of federal programs at "high risk" of collapse, along with the Medicare program. A commonly heard fix is to cut costs by reducing service to fewer days per week, eliminating postal delivery on Saturdays and perhaps other days as well. Perhaps a more effective approach would be to increase the service's reliability and availability by delivering the mail every day, which would be a clear differentiator for the USPS.[21]

**Responsiveness**: A second way to differentiate services is by high responsiveness to customer needs. Responsiveness is defined as the willingness to help customers and provide prompt service. This type of differentiation approach works well for process-driven services, such as dining services at restaurants and order fulfillment, where customers must endure long waits if the service provider is not responsive to their needs.

Restaurants rated as offering high-quality service maintained higher prices, higher margins, and higher sales growth than those rated as offering poor quality service

*Source:* Shutterstock

## Marketing Planning in Action

**Restaurants: Responsiveness = ROI**. *Entrepreneur* magazine noted that growing customer expectations of responsiveness from e-commerce are "raising the bar" on the service standards customers use to evaluate brick-and-mortar businesses like local restaurants. In addition, the Strategic Planning Institute found that quality service leads to financial and business success—businesses offering high-quality service maintained a price differential of 11 percent, a 9 percent higher return on sales, and 9 percent greater annual sales growth than businesses rated as offering lower-quality service. The study recommended improvements to service quality to increase service perception, such as setting customer-focused performance goals on responsiveness.[22]

### Key Terms

**Service differentiation approaches**    Differentiation methods to show how the organization's service offering is distinct from similar versions on the market. Typical approaches include assurance, empathy, reliability, responsiveness, and tangibles.

**Assurance**: A third way to differentiate services is by providing customers with assurance that the organization can provide quality service. Assurance is defined as the knowledge and courtesy of employees, and their ability to convey trust and confidence. Assurance is important for all services, but is especially applicable for medical procedures (patients want to be sure their doctor is knowledgeable and conveys trust and confidence) and luxury services, such as high-end hotels.

## Marketing Planning in Action

**Ritz-Carlton Hotels: The Right Staff**. Jeff Hargett, Ritz-Carlton's corporate director of learning, content, and delivery at the Ritz-Carlton Leadership Center, knows what customers want—personalized service, fast access to knowledge, and hassle-free interactions. Ritz-Carlton Hotels are so famous for their ability to cater to customers' unique wishes that other companies hire the training service for their own employees. The differentiation pays off, as well—the company repeatedly outperforms its competition, increasing its customer loyalty (the average guest spends $250,000 at a Ritz over his lifetime), and has won the Malcolm Baldridge National Quality Award twice.[23]

**Empathy**: A fourth way to differentiate services is by showing empathy to customers, that is, to "put yourself in their shoes." Empathy is defined as the degree of caring and individual attention provided to customers. This type of differentiation approach works well for services that deal with customers in a caring fashion, such as health-care procedures, as well as services that give customers a high degree of individual attention, such as financial organizations specializing in high net worth individuals.

## Marketing Planning in Action

**Taiwan Hotels: Not Empathetic to Service?** An article in *Entrepreneur* magazine recommended that the Taiwan Tourism Bureau incorporate empathy ratings in their hotel rating systems to improve customer service. According to the article, "In an international tourist hotel, considering the needs of every customer is important for maintaining service quality." In addition, China and Taiwan still inform hotels in advance of when their ratings will occur, throwing their ratings into question. In the United States and United Kingdom, evaluations are done anonymously—the hotel is not aware that the rating is taking place. As China and Taiwan increasingly open their doors to international tourists, perhaps they should consider modifying their rating systems to deliver world-class service standards.[24]

**Tangibles**:  A fifth way to differentiate services is by using tangible elements to denote quality of service. Tangibles are defined as the appearance of physical facilities, equipment, and personnel. Service marketers sometimes refer to this approach as "making the intangible tangible." This type of differentiation works for services with some type of physical presence, such as law offices (with luxurious surroundings), hospitals (with attentive doctors), and banks (with impressive safes). For example, Ferrari automotive service departments keep their floors spotless to emphasize the company's commitment to servicing these fine motor vehicles.

## Marketing Planning in Action

**Westin: Heavenly Service through Heavenly Tangibles**. The Westin chain of hotels differentiate their hospitality services using luxury-oriented tangibles like their Westin Heavenly Beds and Westin Heavenly Bath. The Heavenly Bed features 250-count sheets, five plush pillows, and Westin's exclusive pillow-top mattress. The Heavenly Bed includes Westin's exclusive dual-head shower, White Tea Aloe bath amenities, Brazilian-combed cotton bath sheets, and custom-designed velour bathrobes. The Heavenly experience provides the customer with an unexpected level of luxury. The Heavenly branded products allow Westin to leverage its "tangibles" differentiation approach across all its hotels.[25]

Westin hotels "make the intangible tangible" with their Heavenly Beds, featuring 250-count sheets, five plush pillows, and Westin's exclusive pillow-top mattress

*Source:* Shutterstock

**Figure 7.11** Decision Chart: Differentiation Approaches for Services

| Differentiation Approach | Description | Decision Guidelines: Best Used for Following Situations: |
|---|---|---|
| Reliability | Ability to perform the promised service dependably and accurately | Critical services where customer will experience distress if service is performed poorly, like delivery services |
| Responsiveness | Willingness to help customers and provide prompt service | Process-driven services, such as restaurants and order fulfillment |
| Assurance | Knowledge and courtesy of employees, and their ability to convey trust and confidence | Medical services (need knowledgeable, trustworthy doctors) and luxury services, such as high-end hotels |
| Empathy | Degree of caring and individual attention provided to customers | Services dealing with customers in a caring fashion, like healthcare, and services providing individual attention, such as personal banking services |
| Tangibles | Appearance of physical facilities, equipment, and personnel | Services with physical presence, such as law offices, hospitals, and banks |

Figure 7.11 presents a decision chart recommending service differentiation approaches to apply for certain application scenarios.

## Practical Planning

In this section, we continue demonstrating the marketing planning process using our ongoing example, Expedia online travel agent (OTA) services.

When we completed the previous chapter, we had determined that Expedia should pursue the strategy of differentiation by creating a new line of adventure travel packages. Here, we examine three areas: developing tactics based on the product/service life cycle, building the value proposition, and determining the differentiation approach.

### Product/Service Tactics

The introduction of the new service packages will cater to consumers' thirst for adventure.

**Customers to Target**:  We will target customers using demographic segmentation (targeting relatively high-income individuals) and psychographic segmentation, appealing to adventurous lifestyles (or their desire for adventure).

**Features**:  Packages will include a variety of exotic destinations not frequented in most vacation packages. In addition, adventurous activities will be offered, such as scuba diving, swimming with sharks in Bermuda, hiking in Alaskan wilderness, river rafting, and riding an ATV (all-terrain vehicle) in the backcountry.

**Quality**:  Expedia will use their deep knowledge of the travel market to ensure quality, by screening service providers for quality (and safety!).

**Packaging**: Expedia will begin with 10 pre-arranged vacation packages, from caving in the depths of Iceland to riding zip lines high above the ground in the forest canopy of Puerto Vallarta.

**Brand**: The packages will be referred to as "Expedia Adventure Vacations," to emphasize the competency and assurance of quality that Expedia brings.

Figure 7.12 presents the example decision chart for the tactics of Expedia Adventure Vacation packages.

The next step is to build the value proposition for the Expedia Adventure Vacations.

## Value Proposition

The value proposition should entice adventurous-minded consumers to book an adventure vacation.

**Targeted Customer Segment**: We will target high-income individuals with a thirst for adventure.

**Customer Purchase Motivation and Use Cases**: Several use cases could be envisioned. First, consumers might purchase a vacation package for themselves to reward themselves (or simply to get some adventure in their life!). Second, couples might purchase packages for themselves to celebrate an event, such as their honeymoon or anniversary. Third, companies might purchase packages for employees to reward them for achieving a significant goal.

**Name of Product or Service**: The name "Expedia Adventure Vacations" emphasizes the competency and assurance Expedia promises, as well as hinting at the adventure that awaits.

**Figure 7.12** Decision Chart: Product/Service Tactics during Life Cycle Stages: Expedia Adventure Vacations

| Criteria | Phase: Introduction (Typical) | Expedia Adventure Vacation Packages |
|---|---|---|
| Targeted Customer Segment | Early adopters | High-income individuals with a thirst for adventure |
| Features | At least one blockbuster feature to gain attention of market | Variety of exotic destinations and activities. Blockbuster feature: Swim with sharks in Bermuda |
| Quality | Must function, but early adopters are tolerant of minor glitches | Leverage Expedia's deep knowledge and competency in travel industry to ensure quality (and safety!) |
| Packaging | Offered in only a few variants | Offer 10 packages to start; will consider more as demand grows |
| Brand | Build category and brand awareness | Brand packages as "Expedia Adventure Vacations" to emphasize Expedia's competency and assurance of quality |

**Category of Product or Service**: Vacation packages.

**Benefits**: "Head," or rational, benefits: Savings in time and money over booking all the components individually. "Heart," or emotional, benefits: Make it easy to give someone the gift of the adventure of a lifetime!

**Competitors**: Direct competitors include somewhat similar (but not as exotic) packages from other OTAs, like Orbitz, Travelocity, and Priceline. Indirect competitors include travel to other (less exotic) destinations, as well as booking the trip directly through the travel suppliers (directly contacting and negotiating with each airline, each hotel, etc.)

**Differentiation**: The service will be differentiated through assurance, by emphasizing the vast array of exotic travel options available to a market leader like Expedia. Smaller, less capable companies might be limited only to popular destinations, like Disneyland and Hawaii, which do not offer the variety and excitement adventurous individuals seek.

**Figure 7.13** Decision Chart: Product/Service Value Proposition Elements: Expedia Adventure Vacations

| Element | Description | Expedia Easy Manage Service |
| --- | --- | --- |
| Targeted Customer Segment | Segments, as defined using personas describing different sets of customer characteristics | High-income individuals with a thirst for adventure |
| Customer Purchase Motivation and Use Cases | Scenarios under which buyers use the product; problems they are solving with it | Consumers purchasing for themselves; couples purchasing together to celebrate an event; companies purchasing for their employees |
| Name of Product or Service | Short and memorable name, with positive associations in its category | "Expedia Adventure Vacations" is short, memorable and has positive associations with the category |
| Category of Product or Service | Category as customers describe it | Vacation packages |
| Benefits | Head: Rational reason for purchasing, such as saving money Heart: Emotional reason for purchasing, such as status or self-esteem | Head: Savings in time and money over booking each component yourself Heart: Make it easy to give someone the gift of the adventure of a lifetime! |
| Competitors | Direct competitors: Providing near identical products & services. Indirect competitors: Product or service different, but still addresses problem | Direct competitors: Packages from other OTAs, like Orbitz, Travelocity, and Priceline Indirect competitors: Booking travel directly through suppliers |
| Differentiation | Characteristics that make product or service distinct from others in market | Assurance; market leader can bring you exotic choices no smaller provider could |

**Figure 7.14** Decision Chart: Differentiation Approaches for Services: Expedia Adventure Vacations

| Differentiation Approach | Description | Expedia Easy Manage Differentiation |
|---|---|---|
| Assurance | Knowledge and courtesy of employees, and their ability to convey trust and confidence | Emphasize the exotic choices and extreme activities only a market leader like Expedia, with its vast network of suppliers, could provide. |

The resulting value proposition is as follows:

To (high-income individuals with a thirst for adventure) who (want the vacation of a lifetime), the (Expedia Adventure Vacation) is a (vacation package) that (can save time and money over booking all the components individually). Unlike (other OTAs and travel suppliers like airlines), our service (provides an array of exotic destinations and heart-pounding activities).

Figure 7.13 presents the example decision chart for Expedia Adventure Vacations' value proposition.

## Differentiation

The third step is to develop our differentiation approach. Again, Expedia certainly intends to provide a reliable, responsive, assuring, and empathetic service with tangibles to demonstrate it, but it is more effective to emphasize only one area. Therefore, we emphasize an "assurance" differentiation approach to emphasize the exotic locales and activity choices a market leader like Expedia can deliver. The resulting decision chart is shown in Figure 7.14.

## Summary

As Henry Ford, the founder of the Ford Motor Company, once said, "A market is never saturated with a good product, but it is very quickly saturated with a bad one."

This chapter covered how to develop and market successful products and services by focusing on market needs. Products that incorporate market needs from the start are several steps ahead of those from the competition.

The chapter started with a decision chart showing relevant product/service tactics to execute depending on the product/service's stage in the product/service life cycle. For example, products that are new to the market (in the introductory stage) should target early adopters (who often crave novelty and adventure), whereas products in mature markets should target more conservatively minded individuals.

The second decision chart showed how to construct a product/service value proposition. Value propositions are vital to the development and marketing of a product or service, because they define the product or service's benefit from the customer's point of view.

The third decision chart showed how to select a differentiation approach for the product or service. In today's market where products and services appear increasingly similar, effective differentiation can be a powerful competitive advantage.

We concluded the chapter by demonstrating the application of all three decision charts with our ongoing example of Expedia online travel agency.

In the next chapter, we will cover pricing of products and services.

## Key Terms

**Buyer personas** Descriptions of the type of buyer intended for a particular product or service. Buyer personas are useful when constructing value propositions. (p. 139)

**Early adopter** Customers associated with the introduction phase of the product/service life cycle (though after the Innovators). Early adopters are generally risk takers who place a high value on the offering's benefits. (p. 132)

**Early majority** Customers associated with the growth phase of the product/service life cycle. Early majority customers value the offering's benefits, but are unwilling to suffer the defects commonly found in the earliest versions of a product or service. (p. 132)

**Extended marketing mix** Supplements the 4 Ps of traditional marketing mix (product, price, place, and promotion) with three more Ps (people, processes, and physical evidence) to adapt the mix for services. (p. 147)

**Head benefits** Rational reasons for buying a product or service, such as saving time or money. Compare with heart benefits. (p. 140)

**Heart benefits** Emotional reasons for buying a product or service, such as feelings of self-esteem when using it. Compare with head benefits. (p. 140)

**Innovator** Customers associated with the earliest part of the introduction phase of the product/service life cycle. Innovators are generally pioneering types who tolerate minor defects for the thrill of being the first. (p. 132)

**Laggards** Customers associated with the late maturity and decline phases of the product/service life cycle. Laggards are highly conservative and risk-averse. They are the last ones to adopt a product or service. (p. 132)

**Late majority** Customers associated with the maturity stage of the product/service life cycle. Late majority customers are generally conservative individuals who wait for products to reach full maturity before purchasing. (p. 132)

**Product differentiation approaches** Differentiation methods to show how the organization's product offering is distinct from similar versions on the market. Typical approaches include form, features, ease of use, quality, durability, reliability, serviceability, and customization. (p. 142)

**Product/service life cycle model** Model showing sales levels over time, passing through four distinct "life" stages: introduction, growth, maturity, and decline. (p. 132)

**Product-related services differentiation approaches** Differentiation methods that use value-added services accompanying the product to make it stand out in the market. Typical approaches include ordering ease, delivery, customer training, customer consulting, maintenance and repair, and installation. (p. 144)

**Service differentiation approaches** Differentiation methods to show how the organization's service offering is distinct from similar versions on the market. Typical approaches include assurance, empathy, reliability, responsiveness, and tangibles. (p. 148)

**Value proposition** Clear statement of the tangible benefits a customer will enjoy by using the product or service. (p. 138)

## Discussion Questions

1. How do the product/service features, quality, packaging, and brand vary between the competitors in your industry?

2. What types of value propositions are your competitors using to market their products or services? How effective do you think they are?

3. What differentiation approaches are your competitors using? What differentiation approaches (of the ones discussed in this chapter) have not been applied yet by your competitors?

# Exercises

1. Determine the set of tactics to execute on your product or service, based on its stage in the product/service life cycle. Use the decision chart.

2. Build the value proposition for your product/service using the decision chart shown in the chapter. Does your offering have a clear benefit for consumers? What insights can you draw from this exercise?

3. Select a differentiation approach for your product/service using the product (or service) differentiation approach decision tables. What type of differentiation approach is your organization currently pursuing and how does it compare with the approach you selected through the decision chart?

# CHAPTER 8

# Pricing

## INTRODUCTION

We continue our treatment of the marketing mix with the second element, pricing. Pricing affects several marketing aspects. It influences profitability. It serves as an indicator of quality to customers. It also has an effect on other marketing mix elements, such as product or service features, channel decisions, and promotion techniques. Pricing can even be used as a competitive advantage, as demonstrated by Walmart.

## CHAPTER CHECKLIST:

We cover the following marketing plan sections in this chapter:

❏ **Pricing Tactics**: Determine the pricing tactics to be executed based on the offering's stage in the product/service life cycle.

❏ **Pricing Objectives**: Assess the appropriate pricing objective for the situation

❏ **Pricing Approaches**: Review approaches to setting prices, based on the price objective

Walmart executes an everyday low pricing policy, avoiding deep discount sales, unlike many other retail stores
*Source:* Alamy

## Marketing Planning in Action

**Walmart: Proficiency in Pricing**. According to Mike Duke, CEO of Walmart, a fundamental aspect of Walmart's business model is its everyday low pricing (EDLP) policy. EDLP can create greater efficiencies and lower operating expenses by avoiding traditional short-term deep-discount sales. These types of sales can cause "ragged" customer demand, with high demand during the short-term sales period, then low demand after the sale, because customers have already stocked up when prices were low. Ragged demand curves cause havoc throughout the supply chain (the network of retailers, distributors, transporters, and other organizations involved in bringing good to customers) because quantities change so radically from one day to the next. EDLP smoothes out the demand curve, allowing for more efficient supply chain operations.[1]

## Pricing Tactics

In this section, we recommend specific pricing tactics for each stage in the life cycle. We start by reviewing several characteristics that can influence pricing, then show how those characteristics change pricing tactics during the stages of the product/service life cycle.

## Pricing Characteristics

We start by reviewing the characteristics that can influence pricing:[2]

**Objective**. Organizations can select from different **pricing objectives**, depending on the situation. Objectives include:

- **Survival pricing objective**: Setting price with the objective of maintaining positive cash flow for short-term survival during traumatic business situations.
- **Profit maximization pricing objective**: Setting prices with the objective of maximizing profitability, often using demand curves.
- **Market share maximization pricing objective**: Setting prices (generally low), with the objective of maximizing market share.
- **Market skimming pricing objective**: Setting prices high shortly after product launch with the objective of recouping development costs.
- **Product/service-quality leadership pricing objective**: Setting prices high with the objective of signaling high quality.

We cover pricing objectives in more detail later in this chapter.

## Marketing Planning in Action

**Apple: Premium Price for a Premium Product**. Apple employs a product-quality leadership pricing objective in the pricing of its computer and personal technology products. It strives to denote quality and style in everything it produces. Where many personal computers show indifferent design, Apple designs its products as luxury goods, crafting them from premium materials like aluminum and glass instead of cheap-feeling plastic. And its units are priced to match. Where many low-end personal computers are available for under $500, the iMac costs $1,999 for its 27-inch model, with no discounting permitted. As evidence of its high-end pricing objective, market researcher NPD Group reported that Apple iMac computers accounted for only 18.9 percent of all personal computers sold in U.S. retail outlets in 2009, but commanded a staggering 89 percent share in computers priced above $1,000.[3]

**Competitor Impact**. Just as Adam Smith (author of *The Wealth of Nations*) predicted, prices tend to fall as competitors enter the market. The success of a new product or service will attract new competitors to a market. The introductory phase will have little impact from direct competitors ( but should consider prices of indirect competitors' offerings). As more competitors enter the market, the organization will have to acknowledge the prices of competitive offerings. If prices are too high relative to the competition, the organization risks losing market share, unless those high prices are justified.

Strong consumer demand for extralarge (70"+) LCD TVs meant for robust growth, increased volumes, and lower unit costs
*Source:* Shutterstock

## Key Terms

**Pricing objective**    Organizational goal to be implemented via pricing.

**Survival pricing objective**    Pricing with the objective of maintaining positive cash flow for short-term survival

**Profit maximization pricing objective**    Setting prices with the objective of maximizing profit.

**Market share maximization pricing objective**    Setting prices (typically at very low levels) with the objective of capturing market share

**Market skimming pricing objective**    Recouping development costs by initially setting prices high

**Product/service quality leadership pricing objective**    Setting prices with the objective of signaling high quality to the market.

## Marketing Planning in Action

**Samsung: Entry into Extra-Large TV Segment Gets Strong Reception**. Korean consumer electronic giant Samsung Electronics, sensing the potential profits for extra-large (70″ and up) televisions, entered the market with its LCD (liquid crystal display) technology, even though plasma traditionally dominated this size category. Samsung's competitors, such as Sony, Sharp, and Panasonic, jumped in as well. In the past, competitors used price skimming (charging high prices during the introductory period) to recoup development costs of the XL TVs. For example, Matsushita (parent of the Panasonic brand) charged $51,000 for its early 103-inch plasma TVs. As competitors battle for market share by offering lower prices, cost reductions from manufacturing efficiencies contribute to profitability. The price reductions trickle down to the smaller sets as well. A 42″ LCD TV, once only available at prices of several thousand dollars, can now be purchased at Walmart for only a few hundred dollars.[4]

**Channel Impact**. Products employ distribution channels, such as distributors and retailers, to distribute their products to the end customer. Services can use distribution channels as well, such as Geek Squad services being distributed by Best Buy. The impact of distribution channels can change throughout the life cycle.

## Marketing Planning in Action

**Google Android: Calling All Cell Phone Carriers**! Google aims to maintain control of the customer relationship with the launch of its cellular phone Nexus One, which runs on the Android operating system. The industry norm is for the cellular phone service provider, such as AT&T, T-Mobile, or Verizon, to sell the phones exclusively, and own the relationship. But Google means to change that. During the introduction stage of the Nexus's product life cycle, Google believes it has a chance to deal with customers directly. Therefore, it sells both a traditional "locked" version (tied to T-Mobile only) for $179 (with a new two-year contract) and an "unlocked" version (no contract) for $529, which customers can run on different providers' networks.[5]

**Costs**. Costs, which can impact price, can vary considerably through the life cycle. Product costs in the introductory stage are high. Development costs, initial promotion costs, production costs, and other costs are often the highest at this stage.

We are especially interested in **unit cost** (the cost to produce each unit) because it will impact production costs during the entire lifetime of the product or service. Unit costs are made up of **fixed costs** (costs that do not vary with the quantity of products sold, such as overhead costs like rent and utilities) and **variable costs** (costs associated with the materials and labor required to make each unit of product).

Three factors can reduce unit cost over the life cycle. The first factor, known as economies of scale, reduces unit cost as quantities increase (especially during the growth phase) because manufacturers get quantity discounts for larger orders of materials.

The second factor is the use of specialized equipment to reduce long-term production costs. The third factor is the experience curve (also called the learning curve), which tends to reduce production cost over time as manufacturers gain accumulated production experience and learn what works and what does not. Service costs vary over the life cycle as well. Costs are often high during introduction due to heavy training and promotion efforts.

## Marketing Planning in Action

**Samsung: Taking the Lead in LED** Samsung has invested heavily in its AMOLED (active matrix organic light emitting diode) flat-panel display technology. The combination of brilliant colors and low energy consumption makes the display technology an ideal match for portable consumer devices like cell phones. Samsung's cell phones with AMOLED screens were well regarded when they were introduced to the market in 2010. The problem is the cost: AMOLED technology is complex, and had been very expensive to produce. To drop the cost per unit, Samsung invested in processes and equipment to increase its AMOLED mass production techniques. By 2010, it had increased its cumulative production to 30 million units, up from 20 million units only eight months earlier.[6]

**Environment**.  Economic constraints, legal situations, and other environmental factors can affect pricing throughout the life cycle. While environmental factors can sometimes have negative effects on the organization, they can also trigger the development of new products and services. For example, increased gasoline prices spurred the market introduction of hybrid and electric automobiles.

## Marketing Planning in Action

**Online Travel Agencies: Hotel Tax Rollback**. Expedia, Orbitz, and other online travel agencies (OTAs) rejoiced at a major change in tax legislation for hotels. A California court had formerly ruled that the agencies were liable for $21.3 million in back hotel taxes and penalties. The court complained that the OTAs had only paid taxes on the wholesale price they paid for the rooms, not the final price consumers paid. A Los Angeles Superior Court judge overturned the ruling, agreeing with the OTAs that the OTAs do not operate or manage hotels, so their fees cannot be considered taxable rent under the tax law.[7]

---

### Key Terms

**Unit cost**  Cost to produce each unit of manufacture, including material and labor as well as any allocated overhead costs.

**Fixed cost**  Costs that do not vary with production quantity, such as overhead costs like rent and utilities.

**Variable costs**  Costs associated with the materials and labor required to make each unit of product.

## Pricing Tactics during the Life Cycle

This section covers how pricing tactics change during each of the four stages in the product/service life cycle. The section ends with a decision chart on pricing tactic recommendations depending on the product/service's stage in the life cycle.[8]

**Introduction**. Pricing during the introduction stage can be especially challenging because the product/service is new, and customers often have no direct competitive offerings with which to assess the company's prices.

- **Objectives**: Two types of pricing objectives work well at this stage. For first-generation high-end technology products, such as the first plasma and LCD television sets, market skimming works well. Skimming charges high prices for initial units in an effort to recoup development costs. For lower-end products going to mass markets, such as food and household items, the market share maximization objective should be used. The market share maximization objective intends to capture market share by setting prices low.

- **Competitor Impact**: The product or service is new. Direct competitors (those with nearly identical offerings) have not entered the market yet. As a result, pricing should reflect prices of indirect competitors, not direct competitors. For example, a new type of non-laser high-quality computer printer must acknowledge the pricing of laser printers (an indirect competitor) when determining the price.

- **Channel Impact**: During the introduction stage, trade discounts (price discounts to distribution channel members) might be required in order for channels to stock the unknown new product.

- **Costs**: At this stage, costs are very high. For products, the low quantities being produced causes high material costs (material prices per unit generally drop as volume increases) and high labor costs (expensive machinery to replace manual labor cannot be justified at such low production volumes). For services, costs are also high because of the intensity of staff training in the new services.

- **Environment**: The environmental situation, such as recent legislation and technology advances, can benefit the new product/service.

**Growth**. During the growth stage, revenue increases rapidly as customers adopt the new product or service. The success of the new product or service (and its potential profits) attracts competitors. As more competitors enter the market, prices begin to drop. Advertising by multiple competitors can cause the total market size to grow as awareness increases. Growth might be further accelerated by targeting additional market segments.

- **Objectives**: During this stage, pricing objectives should focus on profit maximization (setting prices to maximize profit) in the early part of the growth stage, because demand is high and competition is still low. As competition intensifies, the firm must consider reducing prices to avoid losing market share. Alternatively, the firm can look to build share quickly using a market share maximization objective for near-commodity goods or a product/service quality leadership pricing objective for premium goods.

- **Competitor Impact**: During the growth stage, the competitor impact shifts from focusing on indirect competitors to direct ones. As more competitors enter, companies must ensure that the product or service has a distinct value proposition for the customer and that the proposition is clearly communicated, or else they risk losing market share to competitors.

- **Channel Impact**: Trade discounts to channel members to add new products or services to their system should be lower than in the introduction stage, because demand is stronger now.
- **Costs**: Material and labor costs should decrease at this stage due to increasing volumes. Service costs should also decrease due to reduced training costs. If forecasted demand is particularly strong, the organization should consider investing in areas that will reduce costs further, such as specialized machinery, process improvements, and (for services) training centers.
- **Environment**: The company should keep a watchful eye for environmental changes that could affect the success of its offering. New laws should be reviewed for their effect on the company. Technology and economic developments should also be surveyed for their impact.

**Maturity**.  Profit during the maturity life cycle stage can be maximized by pricing to maintain market share and introducing product/service variants to extend the life cycle. Price discounts should be used strategically, such as to encourage customers of competitors to switch to the company's brand.

- **Objectives**: The pricing objective should continue to be long-term profit maximization, although many short-term adjustments might need to be executed over time due to actions by competitors, channels, and the environment. Premium goods should use a product/service quality leadership pricing objective.
- **Competitor Impact**: Possible price reductions might be required in response to competitive price drops. Avoid a price "war" (where competitors quickly match each others' price cuts) by maintaining a clear value proposition, showing how the company's products or services are superior (and different!) in some important way over those of its competitors.
- **Channel Impact**: During the maturity stage, the company's distribution approach will move from selective (only a few channels) to intensive (many channels), and this move can require different trade discounts for different channels. Low value-added channels (like the Internet) that simply list the product or service for sale will require little, if any, trade discounts. High value-added channels (like premium retailers providing consulting with the sale) will likely require greater trade discounts.
- **Costs**: Costs are often at their lowest at this stage. Employ design for manufacturing techniques to reduce costs further for products with long design lives.
- **Environment**: The maturity stage is often the longest one in the life cycle. As such, it will be the one most susceptible to long-term changes in the environment, such as new legislation. Marketers must keep abreast of the changes and their impact on pricing.

**Decline**.  At this stage, sales begin to decrease as the market saturates, the product becomes technologically obsolete (like manual typewriters), and the service goes out of fashion (chauffeurs are rare now), or customer tastes change (no more tail fins on cars).

Assuming that we want to continue the product or service, we have the following pricing criteria:

- **Objectives**: For best success, target the product or service to loyal customers. Maintain pricing levels to prevent further erosion of profit. Consider raising prices if customers perceive no other acceptable substitute for it. Consider a survival pricing objective if sales continue to decline (alternatively, consider discontinuing the product or service).

- **Competitor Impact**: Declining markets rarely attract competitors. Markets for obsolete items such as cassette tapes and vacuum tubes target niche markets and are often supplied by a limited set of manufacturers (and sometimes only one).

- **Channel Impact**: Reduce the number of distribution channels to reduce cost. Often, the product will only be offered in low-cost, low value-added channels such as mail order, telephone, or Internet sales.

- **Costs**: Costs per unit are generally higher than during the maturity stage because volumes are lower. Costs should be cut wherever possible, such as limiting the number of colors, sizes, and styles.

- **Environment**: Declining products have little to lose with negative environmental impacts ("we were going to kill the product anyway"), and everything to gain. Sometimes, hopelessly obsolete products can resurge due to popular fads. For example, vinyl photograph albums, left for dead in the 1980s, suddenly became cool again in 2008, increasing their sales.

Vinyl records, once a declining market, are now booming due to an appreciation for their fine sound quality and cover art
*Source:* Shutterstock

## Marketing Planning in Action

**Declining Markets: Vinyl Records Get Their Groove Back**. Long-playing records (LPs), considered obsolete after the introduction of the compact disc player, have made a comeback. Some of its new fans are baby boomers, reminiscing about their youth. Surprisingly, though, the majority of vinyl's advocates are members of the iPod generation. These young fans appreciate the elaborate album covers, liner notes, and high-quality artwork that accompanied the records. Oh yes, the records. Many listeners report they enjoy the sound quality of LPs over compressed digital music, which they describe as "harsh." Sensing the popularity, some contemporary bands, like the Killers, issue their new releases on vinyl as well as on CD.[9]

Figure 8.1 presents a decision chart recommending pricing tactics through the life cycle stages.

**Figure 8.1** Decision Chart: Pricing Tactics during Life Cycle Stages

| Criteria | Introduction | Growth | Maturity | Decline |
|---|---|---|---|---|
| Objective | Market skimming to recover development costs, OR Market share maximization | Profit maximization objective, unless company wants to continue with market share maximization to grow share | Profit maximization for general goods; Product quality leadership pricing for premium goods | Profit maximization if possible. Use survival objective if needed |
| Competitor Impact | Indirect competition will place ceiling on price | Direct competition begins in earnest. Distinct value proposition critical. Otherwise, price might need to be lowered | Possible price reductions might be required to react to competitor actions. Avoid price war | Few competitors are attracted to declining markets. |
| Channel Impact | Moderate; possible trade discounts to get new offering in distribution channel | Moderate; some concessions might be required; not as severe as Introduction stage | Approach will move from selective to intensive. Expect different types of channels to demand different trade discounts | Reduce number of distribution channels. Change type of channel to low value-add, like direct sales |
| Costs | Highest of all stages | Still fairly high, but starting to reduce | At their lowest. Consider lowering if market cycle expected to be long | Fairly high due to low production volumes |
| Environment | Possibly beneficial to success of new product or service | Survey environment to watch for changes affecting product/ service | Longest of all cycle stages, so most prone to environmental affects on price | Fads and other short-term trends can have resurgence effects |

# Pricing Objectives: Determining the Role of Price

We expand our treatment of pricing objectives in this section due to their important role in pricing. As Figure 8.2 shows, companies can select from several pricing objectives.[10]

## Survival Pricing Objective

This objective sets pricing low with the objective of maintaining positive cash flow to get through a crisis situation. The objective is sometimes used if the company is plagued by overcapacity or intense competition. Survival mode should only be used in the short term. In the long term, the company must learn how to add value.

An example of this approach would be memory chip pricing in 2007, when industry oversupply of chips caused their price to plummet. Manufacturers had to slash prices just to stay alive. "Blood, blood, and more blood" is how one semiconductor analyst described the situation.11

## Profit Maximization Pricing Objective

Here, prices are set at specific levels with the objective of maximizing current profits. With this objective, the company must know its demand and cost curves.

For example, Walmart employs a sophisticated supply chain system that calculates demand and costs for their products, and adjusts their product mix and prices to maximize profit.

## Market Share Maximization Pricing Objective

Here, prices are set (generally fairly low) with the objective of maximizing market share. The idea behind this objective is that lower prices lead to higher sales volume, which lead to lower unit costs, which in turn leads to higher long-run profit. This objective is appropriate when demand is relatively elastic (customers are sensitive to price, so the quantity demanded will increase significantly as price decreases).

For example, manufacturers of digital versatile disc (DVD) players in the mid-2000s set prices low, which increased volume and lowered manufacturing costs. As a result, DVD players, which once retailed for $1,000, could be purchased at warehouse stores for under $40.

**Figure 8.2** Pricing Objectives Overview

## Market Skimming Pricing Objective

In this method, prices are set very high with the objective of skimming the upper 10 percent of the market. The objective is appropriate when demand is relatively inelastic (customers are not very sensitive to price). Companies often use this objective if they are unveiling a new technology that is unique to the industry.

For example, Sony set a price of $2,500 for its first 11" OLED (organic light emitting diode) television at a time when traditional Sony 40" LCD HDTVs (high-definition televisions) were priced under $500. The objective can backfire if competitors sell the same, or similar, technology for less.

## Product/Service-Quality Leadership Pricing Objective

Here, we set prices higher than those of competitors (but lower than skimming prices) with the objective of signaling high quality. The price helps position the product or service as an "affordable luxury," products or services of high quality, taste, or status, with a price tag just within the reach of affluent consumers.

An example of this approach would be Mercedes automobiles, perceived as high status and expensive, but not as expensive as supercars like Maserati and Lamborghini.

# Pricing Approaches

Having established the pricing objective, the marketer selects a **pricing approach** to accomplish that objective. We start by using standard pricing approaches to set the price, then use net pricing analysis to determine the final net price after discounts. We conclude by examining how different pricing approaches affect the product/service's profit contribution.

## Setting the Price

As Figure 8.3 shows, companies can select from several pricing approaches. In general, each approach is suited for a particular pricing objective. For example, a markup pricing

**Figure 8.3** Pricing Approaches Overview

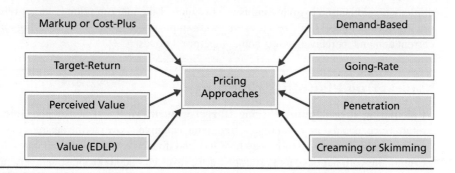

### Key Terms

**Pricing approach**   Particular tactic or method used to implement related pricing objective.

**Markup, or cost-plus pricing approach**   Adding standard amount, such as 20 percent, to the unit cost of products or services.

approach can be useful to implement a survival pricing objective, because the approach ensures that the "survival" price will maintain positive cash flow for the company by taking the company's costs into account.[12]

**Markup, or Cost-Plus, Pricing Approach**. In this method, a standard amount, such as 20 percent, is added to the unit cost of products or services. This approach is often used in retail, such as apparel sales, and professional services, such as attorney services. It is easy to implement, but rarely results in the highest profit for the firm because it does not take customer demand into account. This approach could be used to implement a survival pricing objective, for example, because it can help ensure that even a low "survival" price will at least cover the company's costs.

## Marketing Planning in Action

**Calculating Markup Pricing**: **Unit Cost**. Start by determining the product's unit cost, based on the variable cost (the materials and labor required to make each unit of product), the fixed cost (the overhead costs like rent and utilities that do not vary with the quantity of products sold), and the forecasted unit sales (the number of units we expect to sell). If we are making a desk light with a variable cost of $30, fixed costs of $200,000, and a sales forecast of 20,000 units, our unit cost would be calculated as follows:

$$\text{Unit Cost} = \text{Variable Cost} + (\text{Fixed Cost/Unit Sales}) = \$30 + (\$200,000/20,000)$$
$$= \$40$$

**Markup Price**. Next, calculate the markup price by dividing the unit cost by (1 − desired return on sales). If we want to make 20 percent markup, then our price would be calculated as follows:

$$\text{Markup Price} = \text{Unit Cos} / (1 - \text{Desired Markup}) = \$40/(1-0.20) = \$50$$

**Target-Return Pricing Approach**. In this approach, the company calculates the price required to achieve a target rate of return on investment (ROI). If the actual level of sales falls below the forecasted level, the ROI will not be met. This approach is easy to implement and is used by many industrial products. Like markup pricing, target-return pricing does not necessarily result in an optimum profit for the firm because it ignores current demand, perceived value, and competitor's prices.

## Marketing Planning in Action

**Calculating Target-Return Pricing: Target-Return Price**: To calculate the target-return price, add the unit cost (calculated in the example above) to the desired return, multiplied by the amount of money invested, and divided by the forecasted unit sales. Continuing with our desk light example, if we invested $600,000 and sought a return on investment (ROI) of 20 percent, then our target-return price would be calculated as follows:

$$\text{Target-Return Price} = \text{Unit Cost} + (\text{Target ROI}) \times (\text{Investment})/(\text{Unit Sales})$$
$$= \$40 + (0.20) \times (\$600,000/20,000) = \$46$$

**Break-even Quantity**: The target-return price depends on the accuracy of our sales forecast. If the forecast is wrong, the price will not deliver the ROI promised. With some algebra, we can rearrange the target-return price formula to solve for the actual ROI, as follows:

$$\text{Actual ROI} = \text{Unit Sales} \times (\text{Target-Return Price} - \text{Unit Cost})/\text{Investment}$$

For example, if we only sold 15,000 units, we would yield only 15 percent, not the 20 percent we had expected. We can compare the unit sales with the break-even quantity. At the break-even quantity, our total revenues (price $\times$ quantity) cover our total costs (fixed costs + variable costs). At any quantities above break-even, we are generating profit. We calculate break-even in our case as 12,500 units:

$$\text{Break-Even Quantity} = \text{Fixed Cost}/(\text{Price} - \text{Variable Cost})$$
$$= \$200,000/(\$46 - \$30) = 12,500$$

We cover break-even analysis in detail in the finance chapter later in this book.

**Perceived-Value Pricing Approach.** In this method, the company conducts market research to find out the perceived value of the product or service by consumers. Consumers might feel that a particular product is worth a higher price because they believe it to be superior to competitive products. Note that the price often has little to do with the actual cost to make the product or deliver the service. The approach is often used when the product or service's brand is seen as a status symbol, such as those of luxury watches, perfumes, and cars.

## Marketing Planning in Action

*Newsweek*: **Perceived Value Pricing for Premium Content**: *Newsweek* magazine plans to use a perceived-value pricing approach as part of its major magazine redesign. As costs escalate to capture additional news details of current events, *Newsweek* realizes it is currently losing money trying to serve a mass audience. As the demand for printed magazines shrinks, it must find a new approach. The new approach is to position *Newsweek* as a more premium brand, charging a higher price. Its premium brand will be supported by a more luxurious look, with thicker, high-quality paper and unique content. Editorially, the magazine will emphasize opinionated, offbeat takes on events, in addition to the traditional analysis and commentary.[13]

**Value Pricing Approach.** This approach, sometimes referred to as everyday low pricing (EDLP) at retailers, attracts customers by charging consistently low pricing and avoiding short-term discounts and other promotions. To execute value pricing, the company must engineer its operations to become a low-cost provider. Southwest employs this approach, offering low fares while still delivering strong customer service.

## Key Terms

**Target-return pricing approach** Setting price to achieve a particular target rate of return on investment

**Perceived-value pricing approach** Price is selected to reflect market demand, based on market research

**Value pricing approach** Also called everyday low pricing (EDLP); this approach uses low pricing to attract customers

Southwest Airlines delights its customers by keeping prices low and service high
*Source:* Shutterstock

## Marketing Planning in Action

**Southwest Airlines: Fun and Frugal**. Southwest Airlines operates as a low-cost, no-frills airline. It keeps cost low by sticking to its winning business model: short, quick trips into secondary airports of major markets. It also standardized on one type of aircraft, the Boeing 737, to reduce maintenance time and cost. Nevertheless, Southwest delivers service levels that satisfy customers. "Southwest treats customers much better than any other airline I fly and still manages to remain profitable without nickel-and-diming people to death," said frequent Southwest flier Margaret Bowles during a recent interview with *USA Today*.[14]

**Demand-based Pricing Approach**. This approach attempts to maximize profit by examining product/service demand curves (the change of sales quantity with price). The demand curves are generated by measuring consumer response to various price points over a range of prices. The approach is suited for situations where the same product can be purchased through multiple sources. For example, Amazon.com occasionally adjusts its prices on the books it sells online to generate demand curves in near real-time.

In industrial markets, a variation of this approach is called **value-in-use pricing**, where the price represents the value the product is worth in its likely usage scenario.

Here, higher-priced products can still be a good value if they result in a lower total cost of operations for the organization. For example, synthetic engine oils, such as those from Mobil 1, can justify higher prices than conventional petroleum-based oils because they can reduce the frequency of engine oil changes, resulting in lower total overall costs.[15]

---

## Marketing Planning in Action

**Chinese Car Dealers: Decreasing Prices due to Decreasing Demand**. Chinese automobile dealerships are finding that their cars (including those from General Motors), once in high demand, are now sitting unsold on car lots. Car dealers are offering incentives to sell the cars. Customers at a GM dealership in the central Chinese city of Zhengzhou get a 14 percent discount, a refund of sales tax, and a chance to win a free Apple iPod if they buy a Matiz compact car, priced at 41,800 yuan (about $6,170). Demand in the world's largest vehicle market has dropped from the previous years, triggering price wars as dealers compete to clear inventories.[16]

---

**Going-Rate Pricing Approach**. Here, the firm aligns its price with those of its competitors, believing that the prices reflect the collective wisdom of the industry. In this approach, market leaders set prices, which are then adopted by smaller firms in the industry. This approach is often used in concentrated industries (industries dominated by a few major players) like gasoline, airlines, and hotels. For example, in the home improvement warehouse market, prices at market follower Lowe's are often similar to market leader Home Depot.

---

## Marketing Planning in Action

**Price-Matching: Words of Warning**. When employing going-rate pricing, companies must be careful not to appear as if they are working together to establish a collective price. The U.S. Congress enacted the Sherman Act in 1890 with the intent of encouraging healthy competition and preventing such collusion. The Sherman Act prevents companies from entering "contracts, combinations, or conspiracies" in restraint of trade. Investigators do not need to find a written contract between businesses to convict them; simply having a pattern of ongoing conversations between competitors can sometimes be used as evidence against them, which means that weekly lunches to chat with people at competing firms could be used as evidence in a Sherman Act case.[17]

---

### Key Terms

**Value-in-use pricing approach** Setting price to represent value the product or service is worth in its likely usage scenario.

**Demand-based pricing approach** Maximizing profit by examining demand curves (changes of sales quantity with price)

**Going-rate pricing approach** Aligning price with that of competitors' products or services

**Penetration Pricing Approach**. Here, companies set a relatively low entry price, often lower than the eventual market price, to attract new customers. The approach can entice customers to switch to a new brand because of the lower price. Once accustomed to the new brand, customers are reluctant to switch even if the price is raised moderately. The approach is suited for a market share maximization objective and is often used for consumer packaged goods.

## Marketing Planning in Action

**The Brunch Bunch: Penetration Pricing in Restaurants**. Restaurants are applying penetration-pricing tactics to attract patrons into brunches at restaurants. Restaurants are dropping prices and adding incentives—like free liquor—to increase brunch traffic. Many restaurants offer a free mimosa or Bloody Mary as part of the deal, and several eateries offer unlimited cocktails (referred to as "boozy" brunches). As a result, brunch traffic was up 8 percent during the first eight months of 2009 compared to the same period in 2008, according to market research firm NPD Group.[18]

**Creaming or Skimming Pricing Approach**. This approach sets prices very high to help reimburse the organization for the high cost of developing the product. The approach targets early adopters, who perceive the value of innovation in the new product, or enjoy the prestige of owning such a new device, and are willing to pay for it. Companies must switch to another pricing approach once competitors introduce similar products. The approach is suited for glamorous consumer electronics products like high-end computers and home theater equipment.

## Marketing Planning in Action

**Playstation Price Skimming: Cream of the Crop**? The shiny black Sony Playstation 3 (PS3) was the long-awaited supercomputer sequel to the PS2. The PS2 sold more than 100 million units, so it was a tough act to follow. The PS3 built upon the successes of its predecessor, promising startling graphics resolution, blazing computer speeds, and multiplayer gaming. And the PS3 was priced to match—a whopping $600 for the deluxe model with 60-gigabyte hard drive and Wi-Fi connectivity. Sony limited production to only 400,000 units for North America, resulting in long lines at electronic retailer stores even at that high price.[19]

Figure 8.4 presents a decision chart recommending specific pricing approaches for different pricing objectives.

**Figure 8.4** Decision Chart: Pricing Approach for Different Price Objectives

| Pricing Objective | Sample Pricing Approach | Description |
| --- | --- | --- |
| Survival | Markup Pricing | Add a standard markup to product's cost |
| Profit Maximization | Demand-Based Pricing (Value Pricing in some cases) (Going-Rate Pricing in some cases) (Target-Return Pricing in some cases) | Adjust price to maximize profit based on measured consumer demand for product |
| Market Share Maximization | Penetration Pricing (Value Pricing in some cases) | Set price low to entice customers to switch to new brand |
| Market Skimming | Creaming/ Skimming Pricing | Set price very high to target early adopters of a new product or service |
| Product Quality Leadership | Perceived Value (Value-In-Use Pricing in some cases) | Set price relatively high to suggest high value to consumers |

## Net Pricing Analysis

No matter which pricing approach is used, planners should conduct a net pricing analysis to determine the final price, to determine the actual revenue the organization will receive. The final price is lower than the manufacturer's suggested retail price (MSRP) due to expenses like the following: [20]

**Price Discounts**:  Reductions in price paid by the end customer as part of a sale or other incentive.

**Trade Margins**:  **Trade margins** are price discounts given to distribution channel members like wholesalers and retailers to carry merchandise. Trade margins are generally calculated as a percentage of selling price and can run 30–60 percent.

### Key Terms

**Trade margins**    Price discounts given to distribution channel members like wholesalers and retailers to carry merchandise. Often accounts for a large portion of selling expenses, beyond 50% in some cases.

**Creaming/skimming pricing approach**    Setting prices very high during introductory stage of product or service with the objective of recouping development costs

**Penetration pricing approach**    Setting price low to gain market share

**Market Development Funds**: Payments given by manufacturers to distribution channel members to market the manufacturer's brand, generally as part of a specific plan ratified by the channel members and the manufacturer.

**Co-op (Cooperation) Advertising Money**: Funds given by manufacturers to retailers to feature their brand in advertisements, such as Heinz paying Safeway to include an ad for its ketchup in Safeway newspaper inserts.

For example, a bracelet priced at $100, on sale for $10 off, at a jewelry store with a 40 percent trade margin would provide only about $50 in revenue to the bracelet manufacturer.

## Pricing and Profit

The profit of a product or service is dependent on the product or service's unit contribution, which is the amount of money extracted from the market (the price) less the amount it cost to make (the cost). Chapter 11, Finance, will explore how pricing drives profit in further detail. For now, we want to see how different pricing approaches can impact the unit contribution. In addition, we are interested in how price and cost can vary during the product/service life cycle.

Figure 8.5 shows how a typical product or service's unit cost and price can change over the life cycle. The gap between the price curve and the unit cost curve represents the profit contribution. The figure emphasizes the differences between the pricing approaches. Actual pricing approaches would generally result in smaller differences

**Figure 8.5** Profit Impact of Pricing Approaches (Differences among Approaches Exaggerated)

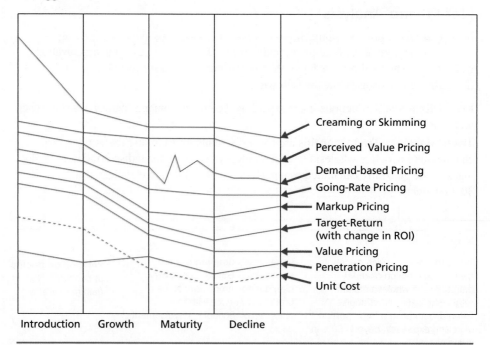

among the different techniques. In addition, the order of the different pricing approaches might be different for actual products and services—for example, a particular service might have a higher going-rate price than a perceived-value price.

**Unit Cost**: As we learned earlier in this chapter, the cost to make each unit tends to decrease over time due to three factors: economies of scale, specialized equipment, and the experience curve. In the figure, we can see that unit costs show a minor drop during the introduction phase, then decrease significantly during the growth phase (due to greatly increasing production quantities), and then reduce still further during the maturity cycle. In the decline phase, unit costs actually increase due to decreasing production quantities.

**Markup Pricing**: Because markup pricing is simply a percentage above the unit cost, the resulting pricing curve parallels the unit cost curve.

**Target-Return Pricing**: Similar to markup pricing, target-return pricing is based off the unit cost. In the figure, we show how the price would increase if the company were to arbitrarily increase its target-return rate at the end of the maturity cycle, perhaps due to rising interest rates.

**Perceived Value Pricing**: Because value pricing depends on customers' perception of value, not on unit cost, the price is generally more stable through the maturity phase. As the product or service drops in popularity during the decline phase, its price will often drop as well.

**Value Pricing**: Many products and services that use value pricing are in the consumer packaged goods industry (like frozen pizza). Because consumers would not tolerate premium prices on familiar items (few people would pay $100 for a frozen pizza at a grocery store), value pricing generally follows unit costs. Actual pricing might be influenced by consumer perception, though. In the figure, note how the value pricing curve nears the unit cost curve at the end of the life cycle.

**Demand-based Pricing**: This type of pricing is based on customer demand, which gives it two unique characteristics. First, the price might have little to do with unit cost. Second, pricing can be volatile as fickle customers change their demand for the product or service.

**Going-Rate Pricing**: Most organizations who use going-rate pricing either are commodity based (such as gasoline stations) or sell to business markets (such as industrial supplies). As such, prices generally follow unit cost, with some exceptions. Exceptions could include a sudden spike in prices due to perceived future cost increases (such as the impact of rising gasoline prices on shipping costs) or a long-term reaction to changing economic conditions (like general reductions in industrial supply prices during recessionary periods).

## Key Terms

**Market development funds (MDF)**   Payments given by manufacturers to distribution channel members to market the manufacturer's brand. Often used when launching new products and services.

**Penetration Pricing**:  Prices in this approach are set deliberately low, often just above the unit cost, in an effort to capture market share away from higher-priced competitors. Prices might be even lower than unit cost for a short period, as shown in the figure.

**Creaming or Skimming Pricing**:  In a completely opposite approach from penetration pricing, creaming or skimming pricing employs very high (sometimes exorbitant!) pricing in the introduction phase. It can be effective for companies with an effective monopoly, where consumers perceive no substitutes. Once competitors offer similar products/services during the growth and maturity phases, the company must reduce its prices or risk losing market share.

As the figure demonstrates, the pricing approach used can have a dramatic effect on a product or service's potential profit.

# Practical Planning

In this section, we continue demonstrating the marketing planning process using our ongoing example, Expedia online travel agent (OTA) services. From the previous chapter, we decided on product/service tactics for Expedia adventure travel vacation packages. We now continue the process of marketing mix decisions by focusing on the pricing of the new service.

## Pricing Tactics

The introduction of the new service packages will target growing demand for a potentially profitable demographic. As we learned earlier, adventure travelers tend to be both affluent and well educated. In addition, they spent $89 billion on adventure travel in 2009, according to a George Washington University report. Due to the segment's affluence and high spending to date, we will target a price skimming approach, focusing on vacation packages that deliver adventuresome activities in exotic locales at premium to super-premium price points.21

**Objective**:  Expedia should consider a market skimming objective for the adventure vacation packages, focusing on delivering exotic vacations at premium prices.

**Competitor Impact**:  Expedia can justify high pricing by emphasizing its ability to book exotic vacations easily, which addresses both direct competitors (other OTAs do not offer such exotic vacations) and indirect competitors (supplier sites make booking adventure travel difficult).

**Channel Impact**:  Expedia's marketing reach (its wide audience) should reduce the amount of trade discounts required to sign new channels to provide adventure services (like guides for kayaking and cave exploration).

**Costs**:  Costs should be moderate, including the cost of developing the packages and any contractual arrangements necessary to secure space with preferred providers, such as obtaining an exclusive contract for guide services in the Nepalese mountains.

**Environment**:  Poor economic climates could cause low demand for adventure travel vacation packages. Nevertheless, the adventure travel segment purchased $89 billion of adventure travel services in 2009, which was certainly not a period associated with strong economic growth.

**Figure 8.6** Decision Chart: Pricing Tactics during Life Cycle Stages: Expedia Adventure Vacations

| Criteria | Phase: Introduction (Typical) | Expedia Adventure Vacation Packages |
|---|---|---|
| Objective | Market skimming to recover development costs, OR market share maximization | Market skimming: Exotic vacations at premium prices |
| Competitor Impact | Indirect competition will place ceiling on price | Direct competitors: Adventure travel packages from other OTAs. Indirect competitors: Adventure travelers booking directly through travel suppliers |
| Channel Impact | Moderate; possible trade discounts to get new offering in distribution channel | Significant channel sign-on discounts not likely to be required due to Expedia's marketing reach |
| Costs | Highest of all stages | Costs include development costs of the service, plus any contractual arrangements to secure preferred providers |
| Environment | Possibly beneficial to success of new product or service | Lackluster economic environment could dampen demand. Position packages as "affordable luxuries" by emphasizing value of exotic experiences. |

Figure 8.6 presents the example decision chart for Expedia adventure travel vacation package pricing tactics.

## Pricing Approach

The next step is to decide on the pricing approach, given the objective of market skimming. Here, we will employ a creaming or skimming price approach, setting prices high to target early adopters, who crave innovation. The result is shown in Figure 8.7.

In the next chapter, we will discuss distribution tactics for Expedia's new services.

**Figure 8.7** Decision Chart: Pricing Approach for Different Price Objectives: Expedia Adventure Vacations

| Price Objective | Sample Pricing Approach | Description |
|---|---|---|
| Market Skimming | Creaming/ Skimming Pricing | Set price very high to target early adopters, those that value exoticness over frugality. |

## Summary

As renowned billionaire investor Warren Buffet said, "Price is what you pay. Value is what you get."

We covered three important aspects of pricing. The first was an overview of pricing tactics and how they can change during the product/service life cycle. We identified five characteristics which can influence pricing tactics during the life cycle: objectives, competitor impact, channel impact, cost, and the environment.

The second aspect of pricing was that of pricing objectives. We covered five different types of objectives, including survival (trying to keep the company afloat during extraordinary times), maximizing profit (adjusting our price to maximize the potential from current demand), maximizing profit share (pricing the product or service fairly low to gain as much market share as possible), skimming (temporarily setting prices very high during the introductory stage), and product-quality leadership (charging premium prices for premium quality products and services).

The third aspect of pricing was that of pricing approaches. We reviewed several different approaches to setting prices, based on the objective the organization is trying to fulfill with the price. We covered markup pricing (adding a standard percentage to the cost), target-return pricing (pricing the product or service to achieve a given ROI), perceived value pricing (reflecting the image of the product or service in its cost), value pricing (everyday low pricing), demand-based pricing (setting prices to keep pace with market demand), going rate pricing (aligning prices with those of competitors), penetration pricing (setting prices low to grab market share), and skimming pricing (setting premium pricing in the early stage of the life cycle).

We concluded the chapter with a Practical Planning section, showing how pricing tactics, objectives, and approaches can be applied to Expedia travel-related services.

The next chapter covers the third element of the marketing mix, distribution.

## Key Terms

**Creaming/skimming pricing approach** Setting prices very high during introductory stage of product or service with the objective of recouping development costs. (p.174)

**Demand-based pricing approach** Maximizing profit by examining demand curves (changes of sales quantity with price). (p.177)

**Fixed cost** Costs that do not vary with production quantity, such as overhead costs like rent and utilities. (p.162)

**Going-rate pricing approach** Aligning price with that of competitors' products or services. (p.173)

**Market development funds** Payments given by manufacturers to distribution channel members to market the manufacturer's brand. Often used when launching new products and services. (p.176)

**Market share maximization pricing objective** Setting prices (typically at very low levels) with the objective of capturing market share. (p.160)

**Market skimming pricing objective** Recouping development costs by initially setting prices high. (p.160)

**Markup, or cost-plus pricing approach** Adding standard amount, such as 20 percent, to the unit cost of products or services. (p.169)

**Penetration pricing approach** Setting price low to gain market share. (p.174)

**Perceived-value pricing approach** Price is selected to reflect market demand, based on market research. (p.171)

**Pricing approach** Particular tactic or method used to implement related pricing objective. (p.169)

**Pricing objective** Organizational goal to be implemented via pricing. (p.160)

**Product/service quality leadership pricing objective** Setting prices with the objective of signaling high quality to the market. (p.160)

**Profit maximization pricing objective** Setting prices with the objective of maximizing profit. (p.160)

**Survival pricing objective** Pricing with the objective of maintaining positive cash flow for short-term survival. (p.160)

**Target-return pricing approach** Setting price to achieve a particular target rate of return on investment. (p.170)

**Trade margins** Price discounts given to distribution channel members like wholesalers and retailers to carry merchandise. Often accounts for a large portion of selling expenses, beyond 50% in some cases. (p.175)

**Unit cost** Cost to produce each unit of manufacture, including material and labor as well as any allocated overhead costs. (p.162)

**Value-in-use pricing approach** Setting price to represent value the product or service is worth in its likely usage scenario. (p.172)

**Value pricing approach** Also called everyday low pricing (EDLP); this approach uses low pricing to attract customers. (p.171)

**Variable costs** Costs associated with the materials and labor required to make each unit of product. (p.162)

 ## Discussion Questions

1. How would you price a new product or service that has never before been offered to the market?

2. What would you do if the perceived value of your product by consumers was less than the cost required to manufacture it?

3. What are some pros and cons of increasing the price of products in declining markets?

 ## Exercises

1. Prepare a decision chart for your product or service, identifying its stage in the life cycle and the appropriate tactics for that stage. Cover the impact of all five influences on tactics (objectives, competitor impact, channel impact, cost, and the environment).

2. Identify the pricing objective to be used. How does it tie in to the overall objective of the marketing plan? How does it compare to other pricing objectives currently being implemented by the organization?

3. Based on the pricing objective, specify the pricing approach. How will the pricing approach impact profitability?

# CHAPTER 9

# Distribution

## INTRODUCTION

Products and services are distributed from manufacturers (in the case of products) or service providers (in the case of services) to buyers using **distribution channels** (also known as marketing channels). For example, Brooks Brothers retail locations sell apparel products to consumers, and Jiffy Lube retail locations provide automotive repair and maintenance services to consumers.

Distribution channels employ **distribution channel members**, such as wholesalers, distributors, and retailers. The channel members are interdependent—retailers cannot sell products unless wholesalers stock them, and wholesalers cannot stock products unless manufacturers make them.

In this chapter, we present a framework for quickly developing the distribution tactics for products and services. We also provide decision charts to adapt the tactics to correspond to the product or service's stage in its life cycle.

## CHAPTER CHECKLIST:

We cover the following marketing plan sections in this chapter:

❏ **Distribution Intensity**: Deciding on exclusive, selective, or intensive distribution

❏ **Distribution Levels**: Establishing the distribution structure to use for consumer and business markets

❏ **Logistics**: Planning, delivering, and controlling the flow of goods to customers

**Figure 9.1** Distribution Example: Traditional Book Distribution versus Distribution in the Digital Era

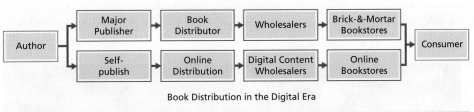

Consider the case of book distribution. Figure 9.1 shows a simplified version of the traditional book distribution process, starting with the author. The author in this case is the "manufacturer" of the manuscript. The author brings the manuscript to a major publisher like HarperCollins, Pearson, or Random House. The publisher performs many tasks to transform the manuscript into a book. Some of the tasks include developmental editing (checking the structure and accuracy of the book), copy editing (correcting spelling and grammar), designing (preparing the typography and layout), and production (printing the book).

The book then moves to the distributor, which manages the sale of books to outlets such as retail bookstores, academic institutions, and wholesalers for resale. Distributors often manage logistics as well, such as warehousing and shipping the books, as well as order- and returns-processing. Some larger publishers perform many of the distribution functions in-house.

Wholesalers often sell books through a variety of outlets, such as retail bookstores, libraries, and specialty outlets (like the sale of cookbooks at Williams-Sonoma). Large wholesalers like the Ingram Book Company and Baker & Taylor carry a large number of titles.

Retail bookstores, such as Barnes & Noble, will place orders for books based on their forecast for books and related materials that they believe will sell well. Retailers work with wholesalers (and sometimes directly with distributors) to ensure smooth operations. Books that languish on the shelves for months are not profitable for the bookstore, nor is stocking out of the hottest bestseller.

Of course, the book distribution model is undergoing significant change. Authors can now self-publish their works through avenues like Amazon's CreateSpace instead of working with a traditional publisher. Many self-publishing companies specialize in distribution to online merchants, such as Amazon.com.

The popularity of electronic versions of books (ebooks), such as books encoded for Amazon.com's Kindle format, reduces logistics concerns significantly, because the expense of printing, shipping, and stocking books is essentially driven to zero. If books are printed, it is often now accomplished using print-on-demand (POD) technologies, which makes it economical to print small quantities of books as orders arrive.

Distribution channel members in the traditional publishing process are adapting to the new digital era model. For example, Baker & Taylor now emphasizes its ability to manage digital content, and offers TextStream, a digital print service.

Digital technology has significantly changed the publishing industry. Now, authors can choose to publish with a major publisher, self-publish and arrange for books to be printed on demand, or even distribute their work over their blog.

Paulo Coelho, known for his bestselling novel *The Alchemist,* distributes some of his content via his blog
*Source*: Shutterstock

## Marketing Planning in Action

**Paulo Coelho: Book Distribution by Blog**. Paulo Coelho, the bestselling Brazilian author, looks to the Internet as an alternative distribution channel. The author has sold more than 100 million books, including the novel *The Alchemist*, which has sold over 65 million copies in more than 150 countries. Despite working with major publisher HarperCollins, he still insists on giving away his content free on his blog (http://paulocoelhoblog.com/pirate-coelho/). Some authors choose to make their content available online for free with the intent to increase brand awareness of the author. Other authors publish online for altruistic reasons. Online posting has stirred much debate, with some believing that it increases book sales by accelerating word of mouth and others (especially publishers) believing that the practice will undermine book sales and contracts for foreign rights and distribution.[1]

# Distribution Intensity

In this section, we start by reviewing how to select the appropriate type of distribution intensity for the marketing plan's product or service, based on its intended sales level. Next, we will show how to adapt the intensity level for different stages during the product/service life cycle.

## Distribution Intensity: Overview

**Distribution intensity** refers to the availability and number of locations, called outlets, which make the product or service available for sale. As Figure 9.2 shows, distribution intensity has three levels: **intensive distribution**, **selective distribution**, and **exclusive distribution**.

**Intensive Distribution.** The objective of intensive distribution is to maximize sales by making the product available through a great number of outlets. Because of the wide variety of outlets, it is difficult to maintain brand control and differentiation. It is often used with consumer packaged goods. For example, Frito-Lays maximizes sales of its corn chips by selling them in hundreds of outlets, such as supermarkets, grocery stores, liquor stores, and convenience stores.

**Figure 9.2** Distribution Intensity Overview

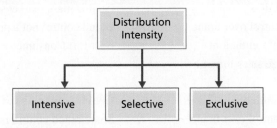

## Key Terms

**Distribution channels**   Means to transfer goods or services from manufacturers (or service providers) to end customers.

**Distribution channel members**   Organizations, like wholesalers and retailers, that transfer products and services from manufacturers to end customers.

**Distribution intensity**   Availability and number of outlets (locations) making the product or service available for sale. Intensity levels are classified as intensive, selective, or exclusive.

**Intensive distribution**   Maximizing outlets (locations) to maximize sales, as for consumer packaged goods items.

**Selective distribution** Intermediate distribution intensity level between intensive and exclusive distribution; provides a measure of brand control while still encouraging sales.

**Exclusive distribution**   Limits access to product or service to only a few selected sales outlets (locations). Often, the outlets are owned by the manufacturer for strong brand control.

**Selective Distribution.** This type of distribution uses a moderate number of outlets, with a level of brand control and differentiation between that of intensive distribution and exclusive distribution. It is often used for goods that, while not luxury goods, want to maintain their distinction in the market. For example, cosmetic manufacturer Kiehl's (www.kiehls.com) sells its line of skin and hair care formulas through only a limited number of luxury-oriented retailers, like Bloomingdales.

**Exclusive Distribution.** In exclusive distribution, access to the product is limited to a few selected outlets. The outlets are often owned by the manufacturer to give the maximum possible control over the brand's equity. This type of distribution highlights the product's differentiation over competing products. It is often used for premium luxury goods, like the Gucci brand.

Figure 9.3 presents a decision chart on distribution intensity.

## Distribution Intensity: Adapting to Life Cycle Stages

Marketers should adjust the findings of the decision chart to the product or service's stage in its life cycle, as shown in Figure 9.4.

**Figure 9.3** Decision Chart: Distribution Intensity Levels: Intensive, Selective, and Exclusive

| Distribution Intensity | Description | Decision Guidelines: Best Used for Following Situations: |
|---|---|---|
| Intensive | Many outlets<br>Little control over brand<br>Little differentiation<br>Maximize sales through channels | Goal is mass market sales<br>Brand control not a priority<br>Best for: Consumer packaged goods |
| Selective | Several outlets<br>Some control over brand<br>Limited differentiation | Goal is a mix of sales & brand focus<br>Some brand control is desired<br>Best for: Nonmass-market goods |
| Exclusive | Number of outlets very limited<br>Tight control over brand<br>Highlights differentiation | Goal is to maximize brand equity<br>Brand control is paramount<br>Best for: Luxury goods & services |

**Figure 9.4** Decision Chart: Distribution Intensity during Life Cycle Stages

| Criteria | Introduction | Growth | Maturity | Decline |
|---|---|---|---|---|
| Distribution Intensity | Selective. Very few channel members exist | Selective–Intensive. Must add desirable new channels before monopolized by competitors | Intense. Firm might enter new channels to boost sales, such as geographic expansion | Exclusive or selective with only a few outlets offered |

**Introduction:** Distribution in this stage is selective (or perhaps exclusive, in the case of a luxury good or service) and scattered as the firm searches for channels that will carry the new product.

**Growth:** Distribution intensifies from selective to intensive. As the adoption rate of its product or service grows, the organization should add new channels to increase its potential distribution reach. Companies must acquire desirable channels at this stage or risk losing them to competitors, shutting the organization out of key markets and hampering future growth.

**Maturity:** Distribution is at its most intense at this stage. Organizations might consider expanding their channels geographically to target new markets. In general, the high volumes and variety of alternative channels available during maturity often justify long-channel (many channel partners) approaches.

**Decline:** The number of channels will be severely curtailed, with only a very few number of outlets making the product or service available for sale. Main channels will be used. Alternative channels will be dropped.

## Marketing Planning in Action

**Gucci: Exclusive Distribution for an Exclusive Brand**. Gucci, long associated with luxury fashion, found its image tarnished by overexposure from licensing and discount stores. To stop the dilution of its brand, Gucci decided to limit distribution to selected retailers and open its own line of Gucci stores. By 2009, it had opened 264 stores, with some in new markets, such as Asia, to take advantage of demand for luxury goods in quickly developing areas. Gucci's premium brand proved to be a double-edged sword. On the one hand, the strength of the brand accounted for high regard for its premium purses, many costing thousands of dollars each. On the other hand, consumers perceived the expensive goods as overly indulgent in the recession-weary period of the late 2000s, resulting in slow sales. Gucci will likely continue to pursue an exclusive distribution strategy, however, to ensure that consumers still covet the brand once economic conditions improve.[3]

# Distribution Channel Levels, Consumer Markets

In this section, we start by reviewing the process of selecting the appropriate number of levels for consumer distribution channels, and then show how the process is adapted to correspond to different stages in the product/service's life cycle. This section covers a fairly typical distribution structure, but many varieties are possible to suit different market situations.

## Consumer Distribution Channel Levels: Overview

Distribution channels are structured into levels, with the manufacturer always being on the top level and the end consumer always being on the bottom level. The number of levels between the two represents the number of intermediary marketing channel members involved and depends on the consumption situation.

**"Short" distribution channels**, those with few intermediaries like zero-level and one-level channels, work well for products and services that are complex (made to order or configured to suit a particular purpose), expensive (often targeted to a niche, discriminating audience), and perishable (not able to withstand the rigors of long channels). Short channels are suited for geographically concentrated markets (not requiring long transportation distances), with companies that can take on some of the duties associated with channels (like processing orders and returns, as well as providing financing).

For example, short channels are suitable to automobile sales, where autos are shipped directly from the manufacturer to dealers' lots, bypassing other intermediaries.

By contrast, **"long" distribution channels**, those with many intermediaries, work well for products and services that are standardized (all customers get the same item), cheap (sold to a mass market), and durable (not susceptible to breakage or spoilage). Long channels are suited for geographically dispersed markets (needing long-distance hauling), with manufacturers that lack the resources to perform channel functions.

For example, long channels are suitable for consumer packaged goods, such as snack foods, where several intermediaries may be involved.

In this section, we cover typical distribution channel levels for consumer markets. Later, we will discuss levels for business markets.[4]

**Zero-Level**. The simplest form of distribution channel is the zero-level distribution structure. At the zero level, sometimes called a "short" channel, no intermediaries are involved, and the product moves directly from the manufacturer to the consumer.

For example, some smaller manufacturers sell directly to customers through the manufacturer's website, such as the sale of Valentine Research's Valentine One automotive radar detectors through the manufacturer's website, www.valentine.com.

**One-Level**. A one-level distribution channel structure includes one intermediary, the retailer. **Retailers** offer **value-added services** to both the manufacturer and the customer. Manufacturer-related services include tasks such as order processing (placement and returns of orders), market research (gathering information from customers), and co-op advertising (creating communications with manufacturers to stimulate demand). Customer-related services include tasks such as consulting (advising customers on products and services), financing (negotiation on final price, as well as loan preparation), and installation (setting up new products and services).

For example, specialty retailer Radar Test (radartest.com) advises customers on automotive radar detectors to select based on individual needs.

**Two-Level**. A two-level distribution channel structure includes two intermediary members, the wholesaler and the retailer.

**Wholesalers** collect goods from multiple manufacturers, hold them until needed, and then transport them to multiple retailers or a single large retail chain. Wholesalers are often used for two categories of goods: large, bulky items like building materials (where wholesalers' central locations help to reduce shipping costs) and standardized, high-volume goods, such as laundry detergent and other consumer packaged goods (CPG), where the same goods are sent to many retailers.

**Distributors** are sometimes used in conjunction with, or instead of wholesalers. Distributors generally distribute goods for manufacturers, and carry a large assortment of items. By comparison, wholesalers carry large quantities of fewer items. Both sell to retailers in the consumer market.

**Three-Level**. A three-level distribution channel structure, sometimes considered a "long" channel, includes three intermediary members: the wholesaler, the retailer, and the jobber.

**Jobbers** are independent contractors who work with bulk goods such as food, fuel, lumber, hardware, and textiles, and deliver an assortment of products to retailers. For example, jobbers are often found stocking convenience store shelves with snack foods from several manufacturers. By contrast, a wholesaler would have a difficult time justifying sending a tractor-trailer full of Hostess Twinkies throughout a busy city to stock gas station convenience stores!

Figure 9.5 presents a decision chart on distribution channel levels for consumer markets.

## Consumer Distribution Channel Levels: Adapting to Life Cycle Stages

Marketers should adjust the findings of the decision chart to the product or service's stage in its life cycle, as shown in Figure 9.6.

**Introduction**: Established companies will generally use their existing channel structure to introduce new products. New companies will generally use shorter channels until demand justifies longer ones, and will initially struggle to find retailers that will carry their new, untested products or services in their stores. Sometimes, the retailers will agree to sell the items, but only for a considerable trade margin (percentage of sales price that goes to distribution channel).

**Growth**: Retailers, always on the lookout for hot new products, become interested in carrying the product in their offerings. As more retailers sell the product, growth accelerates. For example, in the early 2000s, mineral-based cosmetics, such as Bare Escentuals, grew in popularity, which attracted retailers such as Nordstrom and Sephora to carry the products.

### Key Terms

**Short (distribution) channel** Distribution channels with few intermediaries.

**Long (distribution) channel** Distribution channels with many intermediaries. Popular for consumer packaged goods.

**Retailer** Distribution channel member selling goods directly to the consumer, generally in small quantities.

**Value-Added Services** Extra services provided to consumers and manufacturers by retailers and distributors during the sale of a product or service. Some example of consumer-based value-added services include consulting (such as providing advice on applying a special paint) or configuration assistance (such as setting up an email account on a new computer).

**Wholesaler** Distribution channel member selling goods to retailers, generally in large quantities.

**Distributor** Agent that supplies goods to retailers and other businesses that sell to consumers.

**Jobber** Distribution channel member who deals in small lots of goods or "jobs." Jobbers buy merchandise from manufacturers or wholesalers and resells it to retailers.

**Figure 9.5** Decision Chart: Distribution Channel Levels, Consumer Markets

| Distribution Levels | Description | Decision Guidelines: Best Used for Following Situations: |
| --- | --- | --- |
| 0-Level | Manufacturer selling directly to consumer (like online sales)<br>No intermediaries are involved | Complex (made to order) products<br>Expensive (niche market) products<br>Perishable (fragile) products<br>Geographically concentrated market<br>Manufacturer can perform channel duties, like processing orders |
| 1-Level | Manufacturing selling to retailers<br>Retailers (often specialty retailers) dealing directly with manufacturers<br>Consumer buying from retail store | Specialty retailer brings some consulting expertise to sale<br>Manufacturer lacks resources to perform channel duties |
| 2-Level | Manufacturer selling to wholesaler<br>Wholesaler aggregating goods from several manufacturers<br>Retailer dealing with wholesalers<br>Consumer buying from retail store | Standardized products<br>Cheap (mass market) products<br>Durable products<br>Geographically dispersed market<br>Manufacturer lacks resources to perform channel duties |
| 3-Level | Manufacturer selling to wholesaler<br>Wholesaler aggregating goods from several manufacturers<br>Jobber delivering products to local locations like convenience stores<br>Consumer buying from convenience store | Similar to 2-level, but used more for bulk goods like food, fuel, lumber, hardware, and textiles<br>Often used for stocking of small convenience and corner stores |

**Figure 9.6** Decision Chart: Distribution Levels for Consumer Markets during Life Cycle Stages

| Criteria | Introduction | Growth | Maturity | Decline |
| --- | --- | --- | --- | --- |
| Levels, Consumer | Small businesses fight to get channels to accept new, unknown product or service | Consumer channels more receptive to carrying product due to increasing sales | Long channels used; Financial incentives offered to channel members to promote product or service | Short channels used;<br>Alternative channels dropped |

**Maturity**: Sales are at their highest at this point, justifying the use of longer channels. To differentiate their products from those of competitors, manufacturers often encourage retailers to feature their product by providing financial incentives such as sales promotions. For example, consumer packaged goods giant Procter & Gamble might pay Safeway retail stores to feature their products on eye-level shelves or endcap displays to boost sales.

Growth of the Bare Escentuals brand attracted the interest of top cosmetics retailers
like Sephora
*Source*: Alamy

**Decline**:  Channel lengths shorten, with products and services only available through
direct sales from the manufacturer or service provider, or a handful of retailers. For
example, video cassette recorders (VCRs), once popular in the 1980s, were virtual
dinosaurs in the early 2000s with the introduction of digital versatile disc (DVD)
players. The few retailers that still carried them sold only a handful of models,
rarely put them on sale, hid them at the back of the store, and rarely (if ever)
advertised them.

## Marketing Planning in Action

**Honest Tea: Expanding Its Distribution Channels**. Honest Tea, which produces
tea certified by the U.S. Department of Agriculture to be organic, expects to
increase its sales by 70 percent within one year by expanding its distribution
channels within the United States. Honest Tea will keep its existing independent
distributors in the New York and Mid-Atlantic markets (where the brand started)
and leverage the muscle of Coca-Cola Enterprises to expand its distribution
elsewhere. Coca-Cola Enterprises, which owns 40 percent of Honest Tea, has
committed to the expansion, which will include sales to retail giant Walmart and
drugstore chain CVS Caremark Corp.[5]

# Distribution Channel Levels, Business Markets

Just as we did for consumer markets, we will review the process of selecting the appropriate number of levels for distribution channels in business markets, and then show how the process is adapted to correspond to different stages in the product/ service's life cycle. This section covers a fairly typical distribution structure, but many varieties are possible to suit different market situations.

## Business Distribution Channel Levels: Overview

Business market distribution channels are structured like those for consumer markets. Similar to the framework for consumer market channels, business market channels are structured with the manufacturer at the top level and the business customer at the bottom. Instead of wholesalers, jobbers, and retailers, business markets use manufacturer's representatives, manufacturer's sales branches, and industrial distributors to distribute products. Examples are given of the distribution of industrial goods, common for business markets.[6]

**Zero-Level**: The simplest form of business channel distribution is the zero-level distribution structure, where manufacturers sell directly to business customers through their website.

For example, Central Blower (centralblower.com), which manufactures air-handling equipment such as blowers for large industrial plants, features an online submittal form to request a quotation for air-handling equipment.[7]

Industrial distributors stock a dizzying array of items, from motors to mortar, to supply to companies
*Source*: Shutterstock

**One-Level**:  A one-level business distribution channel structure includes one intermediary, the industrial distributor. Industrial distributors collect components from many manufacturers and resell them to business customers. (By contrast, distributors for consumer markets generally only sell goods to retailers, which resell the goods to consumers.)

For example, Grainger (grainger.com) is an industrial products distributor that sells electrical components, material handling equipment, motors, and many other types of products directly to customers. It operates brick-and-mortar stores and an e-commerce website.8

**Two-Level**:  A two-level business distribution channel structure includes two intermediary members: a manufacturer's representative and (sometimes but not always) an industrial distributor. Manufacturer's representatives provide consulting services to assist in the sales of industrial products, which are often complex and benefit from the technical expertise a manufacturer's representative brings. Manufacturer's representatives often specialize in particular areas, such as commercial lighting.

For example, Lumenation (lumenation.net) is a full-service independent manufacturer's representative, providing consulting and sales of lighting products for 40 of the lighting industry's top manufacturers.[9]

**Three-Level**:  A three-level business distribution channel structure includes an industrial distributor and (sometimes but not always) a manufacturer's representative as before, and adds a manufacturer's sales branch. The manufacturer's sales branch facilitates sales through an indexed catalog of products. Products are manufactured by the manufacturer (level one). Sales are coordinated through a manufacturer's sales branch (level two), and sales fulfillment is often executed through an industrial distributor (level three).

For example, Anvil International (anvilintl.com) manufactures piping products and maintains sales branch operations, using print and online catalogs, as well as several physical customer service and distribution centers. Orders are fulfilled using industrial distributors, such as the David Janes Supply Company (janessupply.com), which carries a diverse selection of pipes, valves, and fittings for the oilfield, industrial, and agricultural industries.[10, 11]

Figure 9.7 presents a decision chart on distribution channel levels for business markets.

## Business Distribution Channel Levels: Adapting to Life Cycle Stages

Just as we did for consumer markets, marketers should adjust the findings of the decision chart to the business market's product or service's stage in its life cycle, as shown in Figure 9.8.

**Introduction**:  To save money, some companies might choose to sell their products through independent manufacturers' representatives until sales are strong enough to warrant hiring company salespeople. For example, Cunningham Manufacturers' Representative company (cmreps.com), based in Texas, represents several specialty plumbing manufacturers too small to warrant their own sales force.

**Growth**:  Similar to consumer markets, business market channels will be more receptive to carrying products and services growing in popularity. As a result, trade discounts to persuade business channels to carry the product or service might be reduced.

**Figure 9.7** Decision Chart: Distribution Channel Levels, Business Markets

| Distribution Levels | Description | Decision Guidelines: Best Used for Following Situations: |
|---|---|---|
| 0-Level | Manufacturer selling directly to business customer<br><br>No intermediaries are involved | Straightforward orders, with no consulting required<br><br>Manufacturer able to perform channel activities, such as e-commerce site operation, order processing, and service |
| 1-Level | Manufacturer selling to industrial distributor<br><br>Industrial distributor dealing directly with manufacturers<br><br>Business customer buying from industrial distributor | Fairly straightforward orders, with some consulting desired<br><br>Manufacturer unwilling or unable to perform channel member services<br><br>Industry-specific applications |
| 2-Level | Manufacturer selling through manufacturer's representative<br><br>Manufacturer's representative provides consulting services to assist in sale<br><br>Industrial distributor sometimes, but not always, used to facilitate sale | Complex orders where consulting services are required<br><br>Specialize in specific applications and industries |
| 3-Level | Manufacturer selling through manufacturer's sales branch<br><br>Manufacturer's sales branch maintains indexed catalog of products<br><br>Industrial distributor usually, but not always, used to facilitate sale | Complex orders where assistance is required to select from many (often thousands) of possible products<br><br>Broad product line<br><br>Manufacturer lacks resources to perform channel services |

**Figure 9.8** Decision Chart: Distribution Levels for Business Markets during Life Cycle Stages

| Criteria | Introduction | Growth | Maturity | Decline |
|---|---|---|---|---|
| Levels, Business | Businesses might align themselves with distributors to expand distribution reach | Business channels more receptive to carrying product due to increasing sales | Long channels used; Firm might add industry-specific channels | Short channels used; spare parts made available |

**Maturity**: Similar to consumer market distribution, business market organizations might expand into new markets. Additionally, new product or service variants, such as industry-specific versions, can be introduced to capture additional market share through alternative channels.

**Decline**: Businesses selling to other businesses typically agree to provide spare parts for a period of time after a product is discontinued. The spare parts are often unique to specific models, have no real competition, and are sold at high prices.

## Marketing Planning in Action

**No Free Lunch: Just Say No to Pharmaceutical Manufacturer's Reps**. No Free Lunch (nofreelunch.org) is an organization that asks doctors to pledge not to receive manufacturer's representatives from drug companies. Some in the medical industry believe that the promotions the representatives provide, such as free pens, lunches, and drug samples, can influence doctors to write more prescriptions for that manufacturer's drugs. According to the Pharmaceutical Research and Manufacturers of America (PhRMA), drug companies spent $23 billion in marketing to physicians in 2004, including $15.9 billion in free drug samples. Manufacturers, on the other hand, support the role of their representatives, saying that they provide needed information on the safety and efficacy of their drugs.[12]

# Logistics: Physical Distribution of Goods

In this section, we will review the basic logistics decisions needed to be addressed in the marketing plan, and then show how those decisions can be adapted to correspond to different stages in the life cycle.

## Logistics: Overview

From a marketing context, the field of **logistics** involves planning, delivering, and controlling the flow of goods to markets to fulfill customer demands. Even the finest product will fail if retail stores continually run out of it (called a stock-out), so logistics is essential to marketing plans. Logistics decisions include order processing (how should we handle orders?), warehousing (where should we locate our stock?), inventory (how much stock should we hold?), transportation (how should we ship our products?), and location (where shall we place our retail stores or service centers?). Figure 9.9 shows essential logistics functions.[13]

**Figure 9.9**  Essential Functions in Logistics

**Order Processing and Fulfillment**: Marketing plans should briefly discuss how order processing (accepting, tracking, and managing the order) and fulfillment (executing the order) will be managed to ensure accuracy and reduce time.

For example, chemical giant BASF implemented automated order processing, using electronic data interchange (EDI) to link its order entry system to its enterprise resource planning (ERP) system , reducing order processing time significantly and improving order accuracy. Reverse logistics, incorporated into many order processing systems, manages the return of goods, including the return-to-vendor credit process.

**Warehousing**. For marketing plans covering high-volume products, companies must decide how to manage warehouse operations to rapidly fulfill orders.

For example, online retailer Amazon.com uses a sophisticated network of warehouses at strategic geographical locations to fulfill orders quickly and cost-effectively.

**Inventory**. Marketing plans covering products in high demand (like popular toys) need a section on how inventories will be managed, especially if the topic is not already addressed in a warehouse management plan. Inventory-carrying costs, such as building rental, must be weighed against potential stock-outs.

For example, computer manufacturer Dell holds a smaller amount of inventory than some of its rivals, because its computers are not built until customers configure and order them.

**Transportation**. Marketing plans for products or services with unusual transportation requirements (such as promises of overnight delivery anywhere in the world) should discuss how those requirements will be accomplished.

Although less glamorous than other marketing plan sections, effective logistics is vital to distribution efforts
*Source*: Shutterstock

For example, advances in transportation logistics have improved efficiencies through approaches such as containerization, where standardized containers are used on trucks, trains, and ships, and global positioning systems (GPS), to track the location of goods in transit.

**Location**:  The location of retail stores can have a major impact on logistics, just as it can on sales. Planners should consider several location factors if their plans indicate that a new retail store or service center is required:

- **Types of Products or Services**: The type of products will dictate the type of location.
  - **Convenience products**, such as snacks and beverages, must be easily accessible. Gas station locations, or locations within existing stores, such as Starbucks locations within Safeway supermarkets, work well.
  - **Showroom products**, such as furniture and automobiles, are high priced and purchased infrequently, and demand special settings to stimulate sales. Showroom stores should be located near similar other stores (like other auto dealerships) to attract relevant traffic.
  - **Specialty products**, such as boating supplies or high-end ski rentals, should be near their areas of usage (near docks or ski resorts, in this case).
- **Types of Customers**: Check customer demographics and psychographics indicated for candidate locations before committing to the store location. Be sure that the location will provide sufficient traffic of customers relevant for the product or service. Also be sure the location does not shun the right types of customers because of its adjacent stores. For example, a premium scuba gear rental shop near a resort beach could attract the right type of customers, but not if it is situated near a smelly bait shop.
- **Types of Infrastructure**: Check for any special infrastructure required, such as parking (an issue in urban areas), power (an issue for high power consumption services, such as teaching pottery classes using high-voltage kilns), delivery truck loading (an issue in congested areas where large items like furniture are sold), and zoning (some municipalities disapprove of big-box stores in their neighborhoods, or liquor sales on Sundays).

## Marketing Planning in Action

**Walmart: Lost in Translation?** Walmart is one of the world's largest retailers. It generated over $400 billion in sales in 2010. Yet its plans to open international locations have endured growing pains. While the "Walmart location method" (place big-box, low-price stores just outside major cities) worked well in the United States, the results were so bad in Germany and Korea that the company exited those countries in 2006. International locations have suffered from Walmart's lackluster brand, scaling of its complex supply chain system, and cultural bias against its discount model. Walmart executives are confident, however, that they will achieve the right balance between local knowledge and global scale to make the expansion a success.[14]

## Key Terms

**Logistics**   Planning, delivering, and controlling the flow of goods to markets to fulfill customer demand.

**Figure 9.10** Decision Chart: Logistics during Life Cycle Stages

| Criteria | Introduction | Growth | Maturity | Decline |
|---|---|---|---|---|
| Logistics | In nascent stage; Technical support sometimes done by R&D team | Will need to grow to accommodate rise in orders | Optimized for high volume operations; Flexible logistics to handle channel demands | Order processing and fulfillment, as well as support, cut or outsourced |

## Logistics: Adapting to Life Cycle Stages

Logistics issues will vary according to the product or service's stage in its life cycle, as shown in Figure 9.10.

**Introduction**:  The introduction stage often turns out to be a "shaking-out" period, where organizations must adjust their logistics systems to handle the new product or service. Order processing can pose problems if order volume becomes much higher than forecast, swamping the order processing infrastructure. Support operations are sometimes conducted by the research and development staff, because the customer support system has not yet been finalized.

**Growth**:  The logistics services organization may need to grow due to the rise in orders. Some services might be strained as the organization begins to add more variants to its offering.

**Maturity**:  Logistics is likely to be optimized for high-volume operations at this stage. Logistics must remain flexible to accommodate new and alternative channel demands.

**Decline**:  Order processing and fulfillment, as well as customer support, might be outsourced to save costs.

### Marketing Planning in Action

**Scribd: Social Network-based Logistics**. Remember when book distribution logistics meant printing books and then shipping them to bookstore shelves? Not any more. Scribd introduced a new "send-to device" service that automates the publishing logistics process by sending documents to consumers' e-readers or smartphones. Scribd is a document-sharing social network service that connects over 10 million documents with a social network of readers using e-reading devices like Amazon's Kindle or Apple iPhones. The large selection of titles gives Scribd the ability to provide what they call "the long tail of content," not currently available through traditional publishers.[15]

## Practical Planning

In this section, we continue demonstrating the marketing planning process using our ongoing example, Expedia online travel agent (OTA) services.

**Figure 9.11** Distribution Tactics: Expedia Adventure Vacations (Introduction Stage)

| Criteria | Phase: Introduction | Expedia Adventure Vacation Packages |
| --- | --- | --- |
| Intensity | Selective. Very few channel members exist | Selective, through Expedia websites |
| Distribution Levels, Consumer Markets | Small businesses fight to get channels to accept new, unknown product or service | Short channel; Direct sales through internet channel |
| Distribution Levels, Business Markets | Businesses might align themselves with distributors to expand distribution reach | Not applicable |
| Distribution Logistics | In nascent stage. Technical support sometimes done by R&D team | Expedia must coordinate with travel accommodation providers to ensure high quality and unique experiences |

Because it is a new service, we will consider distribution tactics for the introductory stage of the product/service life cycle.

**Distribution Intensity**: Expedia will use selective distribution, offering Adventure Vacation packages on several of its websites, such as Expedia.com and TripAdvisor.com.

**Distribution Levels**: Expedia emphasizes direct sales through its Internet sites.

**Distribution Logistics**: Expedia must coordinate with the travel accommodation providers, such as the hotels and specialty staff (such as adventure guides), to ensure high quality and unique experiences.

Figure 9.11 presents the example decision chart for Expedia Adventure Vacations distribution tactics for the introduction stage.

## Summary

General Omar Bradley acknowledged the importance of distribution and logistics when he said, "Amateurs talk strategy. Professionals talk logistics."

This chapter covered distribution and logistics tactics in several important areas:

- Distribution Intensity
- Distribution Levels, for Consumer and Business Markets
- Distribution Logistics

Distribution intensity refers to the number of locations, called outlets, which make the product or service available for sale. Distribution intensity has three levels: intensive (maximize sales by offering in many outlets), selective (maintain some degree of brand control by offering in a few outlets), and exclusive (maintain strict brand control by offering the product or service only in a very limited number of outlets).

Distribution levels vary from zero to three for consumer products. At the zero level of distribution, consumers buy directly from the manufacturer. In a one-level distribution structure, consumers buy from retailers, who purchase goods in bulk from the manufacturer. In a two-level distribution system, consumers purchase from retailers, who buy from wholesalers, who in turn buy from manufacturers. In three-level distribution systems, consumers buy from retailers, who are stocked by jobbers, who purchase their goods from wholesalers, who in turn buy from manufacturers.

Business distribution levels are similar, varying from a zero-level structure to a three-level structure. Just as with consumers, businesses buy directly from other businesses at the zero level. In a one-level business distribution structure, businesses buy from industrial distributors, who buy from manufacturers. In a two-level structure, a manufacturer's representative is added between the industrial distributor and the manufacturer. In a three-level structure, a manufacturer's sales branch is added between the manufacturer's representative and the industrial distributor.

Distribution logistics refers to the acquisition, storage, transportation, and delivery of products along the supply chain. From a marketing plan standpoint, four key logistical areas need to be addressed: order processing (how should we handle orders?), warehousing (where should we locate our stock?), inventory (how much stock should we hold?), and transportation (how should we ship our products?).

We concluded the chapter with a Practical Planning section, showing how to apply distribution and logistics tactics, in this case to our planned Expedia travel-related service.

The next chapter covers the fourth, and final, element of the marketing mix, promotion.

## Key Terms

**Distribution channels** Means to transfer goods or services from manufacturers (or service providers) to end customers. (p. 182)

**Distribution channel members** Organizations, like wholesalers and retailers, that transfer products and services from manufacturers to end customers. (p. 182)

**Distribution intensity** Availability and number of outlets (locations) making the product or service available for sale. Intensity levels are classified as intensive, selective, or exclusive. (p. 185)

**Distributor** Agent that supplies goods to retailers and other businesses that sell to consumers. (p. 188)

**Exclusive distribution** Limits access to product or service to only a few selected sales outlets (locations). Often, the outlets are owned by the manufacturer for strong brand control. (p. 185)

**Intensive distribution** Maximizing outlets (locations) to maximize sales, as for consumer packaged goods items. (p. 185)

**Jobber** Distribution channel member who deals in small lots of goods or "jobs." Jobbers buy merchandise from manufacturers or wholesalers and resells it to retailers. (p. 189)

**Logistics** Planning, delivering, and controlling the flow of goods to markets to fulfill customer demand. (195)

**Long (distribution) channel** Distribution channels with many intermediaries. Popular for consumer packaged goods. (p. 188)

**Retailer** Distribution channel member selling goods directly to the consumer, generally in small quantities. (p. 188)

**Selective distribution** Intermediate distribution intensity level between intensive and exclusive distribution; provides a measure of brand control while still encouraging sales. (p. 185)

**Short (distribution) channel** Distribution channels with few intermediaries. (p. 188)

**Value-added services** Extra services provided to consumers and manufacturers by retailers and distributors during the sale of a product or service. Some example of consumer-based value-added services include consulting (such as providing advice on applying a special paint) or configuration assistance (such as setting up an email account on a new computer). (p. 188)

**Wholesaler** Distribution channel member selling goods to retailers, generally in large quantities. (p. 188)

Discussion Questions

1. What messaging would you use to entice channel members, like retailers, to stock your product? If you are marketing your services through a retailer, what message would you give the retailer to emphasize your service to customers? Would the only incentive be a share of revenue, or would the retailer achieve other benefits as well from your product or service?

2. Consumers demand convenience in shopping for goods. To satisfy that demand, many businesses offer their goods over multiple outlets, such as company-owned stores, specialty stores, and the Internet. How do you avoid channel conflict in this type of distribution structure?

3. Some people say that the speed of many Internet transactions have "spoiled" consumers into believing they will receive items instantly after they order them (like the downloading of computer software or a document in electronic format). How does that impact logistics operations for products?

 Exercises

1. Determine how intensive the distribution should be. How many outlets will you employ? How will you avoid channel conflict among them?

2. Prepare a decision table showing the number of levels for your distribution channels. What is the role of each channel member and how will it increase the value to the end consumer?

3. Develop a set of logistics tactics for your product or service. If it is a physical product, how do you plan to fulfill orders? If it is a service, what service providers will you use, where will they be located, and how will you maintain the quality of your services?

## CHAPTER 10

# Promotion

## INTRODUCTION

Promotion is the set of activities to increase the visibility of a product or service, often to encourage sales. Effective promotion is crucial to market success. In this chapter, we start at a high level, defining the top-level promotion tactics appropriate for the product/service's stage in its life cycle. Next, we establish the overall mix of promotion vehicles that satisfy our goals. The final step is to decide on the tacticsj for the individual promotion vehicles.

## CHAPTER CHECKLIST:

We cover the following marketing plan sections in this chapter:

❏ **Promotion Tactics**: Declaring the goals, target markets, and push–pull approach, based on the offering's stage in the product/service life cycle

❏ **Integrated Marketing Communications**: Establishing the overall mix of promotion vehicles

❏ **Promotion Vehicles**: Determining the tactics for individual promotion vehicles

SUBWAY's $5 Footlong promotion grew sales for the franchise
*Source*: Alamy

## Marketing Planning in Action

**SUBWAY: Promoting a $5 Footlong for the Franchise**. Subway generated $3.8 billion in sales from its $5 Footlong sandwiches, catapulting the privately held company among the top 10 fast-food brands in the United States. Stuart Frankel, a New York resident who owned two New York Subway franchise stores, came up with the idea for $5 Footlong sandwiches when he watched sales suffer on the weekends. He created a promotion to sell every Footlong sandwich on Saturday and Sunday for $5, about a dollar less than the usual price.

After sales rose by double digits, he approached Subway management to develop the promotion across the entire chain of stores. Subway's marketing team generated a memorable promotion campaign establishing the $5 Footlong nationwide. Subway brought in advertising agency MMB Boston, who used hand gestures and an "irritatingly addictive jingle" to convey both the price (five fingers) and the product (hands spread about a foot apart). The move resonated with customers, boosting sales in some stores by as much as 35 percent.[1]

## Promotion Tactics

Effective promotion tactics begin by deciding on the goals for the promotion (what we are trying to accomplish), the target markets (the kind of people we wish to reach with our efforts), and our **push–pull marketing** approach.

As Figure 10.1 shows, companies (product manufacturers and service providers) apply push marketing toward distribution channel members, such as wholesalers and retailers, to motivate intermediaries to carry, promote, and sell the company's products and services.

In pull marketing, companies use advertising and other promotion techniques to persuade customers to demand the company's products and services from intermediaries, thus "pulling" the products and services through intermediaries.[2]

As we will see, the tactics will be influenced by the product or service's stage in its life cycle. To demonstrate this life cycle-based approach, we use four example products from the consumer television market at different life stages in the year 2010: advanced three-dimensional (3D) television sets (introductory product life cycle phase), Blu-ray digital versatile disc (DVD) players (growth phase), liquid crystal display (LCD) television sets, and videocassette recorders (VCRs).

## Introductory Phase

In the introductory phase, our promotion tactics must focus on building awareness for the product or service, and developing a market for it. For this phase, we will consider the promotion efforts for an advanced-technology 3D television.

**Promotion Goal.**  Promotion should seek to create product/service awareness and to educate potential customers about the product/service. In addition, marketers should seek to stimulate trial of the new product or service, such as demonstrating the 3D affect in retail stores.

**Target Markets.**  Promotion should be aimed at innovators and early adopters. For example, the person wanting to purchase the 3D set looks for the latest technology, is not very price sensitive, and reads technically oriented home theater content.

**Figure 10.1**  Push and Pull Marketing Approaches

**Push Marketing**
Target Customers via Intermediaries

| Company: Manufactures/ Service Providers | → | Distribution Channel Members | → | Customers (Consumers or Businesses) |

**Pull Marketing**
Target Customers Directly

By contrast, the person wanting to purchase a mass market LCD television shops more on price than on advanced features and likely scans retailer ads to look for promotions.

**Push–Pull Marketing**. Promotions at this stage benefit from both push and pull marketing efforts. Push marketing (targeted at distribution channel members) should center on product or service demonstrations by organizational representatives at consumer retailer stores. Pull marketing should center on educating consumers on the benefits of the new product/service, the new technologies it may leverage, and the new category it might represent.

## Growth Phase

During the growth phase, promotion tactics must consider the impact of competitors in the market. For this phase, we will consider the promotion efforts for Blu-ray DVD players.

**Promotion Goal**. Promotion should seek to build upon the product/service awareness developed in the introductory phase.

**Target Markets**. Once the life cycle reaches the growth phase, marketers should target promotion efforts to the early majority. Sometimes also referred to as the "up-and-comer" segment, this type of individual consider themselves keeping up with current trends, but not quite exhibiting the eager behavior of an early adopter.

For example, the "up and comer" buyer in the consumer television market might not yet be ready to justify the high price tag of 3D TV, but would consider the merits of Blu-ray DVD, because it is a relatively new device which provides a great improvement in DVD playback resolution at a moderate cost.

**Push–Pull Marketing**. In the early part of the growth phase, push and pull efforts will continue to make consumers aware of this new product/service and the unique benefits it brings, relative to indirect competition.

As the growth phase continues, push marketing should shift toward retail channel efforts to show how the organization's product or service is superior to those of competitors, perhaps using an in-store display or demonstration guide. Correspondingly, pull marketing will shift toward comparison advertisements, showing how the organization's product or service is superior to others in the market.

## Maturity Phase

Promotion tactics during the maturity phase should emphasize differentiation of the organization's product or service compared to those of competitors. This phase often incurs the highest promotion budget, due to the intensive amount of promotion required

---

### Key Terms

**Push–Pull Marketing**  Balancing efforts between promotion efforts to distribution channel members (push) and efforts toward end consumers (pull).

to maintain (and build) market share despite competitive pressures. For this stage, we shall consider the promotional efforts for LCD televisions, available on the market for over a decade, and now available at mass market channels such as Costco and Walmart.

**Promotion Goal**. Promotion should seek to differentiate the product or service from those of competitors. Organizations might show that the reliability or quality is higher in their product or service than those of competitors. Companies can introduce new enhancements to keep the product or service "fresh," thereby extending its life cycle. In addition, the organization should strive to build brand loyalty of existing customers.

**Target Markets**. Promotion in the maturity phase of the life cycle should target the late majority type of customer, sometimes also referred to as the mainstream. The people in this stage are not keen to adopt new technologies or services.

For example, mainstream television consumers waited many years before replacing their old cathode ray tube (CRT) TVs with LCD units. In fact, many did not purchase an LCD TV until they were forced to in 2009, when they found their old CRT TVs would not support the changeover from analog to digital television.

**Push–Pull Marketing**. Push marketing is generally intense at this stage, with marketers actively engaging with retailers to differentiate their product or service from the myriad of near-identical products and services provided by competitors. Retailers might use in-store displays, sales promotions, or value-added services (such as consulting or installation assistance) to get consumers to select the organization's product or service over others.

Pull marketing is intense as well, with marketers using multiple media channels to highlight differences that make their product or service unique from the rest.

## Decline Phase

Promotion tactics at this stage will change as sales steadily drop. The organization might decide to continue the product or service (instead of discontinuing it) if it believes that some kind of niche market will continue to buy it. To maintain some level of profitability in this stage of weak sales, costs are aggressively cut by limiting product/service variants and slashing promotion expenditures.

For example, some companies continue to manufacture VCRs and tape cartridges for a niche market that perceives value in them, but promotion costs are kept to an absolute minimum.

**Promotion Goal**. Promotion efforts at this stage are limited to offering the product or service to people who still see value in it.

**Target Markets**. Some products and services continue to live on (even though their popularity has long since waned) because of laggards (the last people to purchase a product or service) or a loyal niche segment still attracted to their value proposition.

For example, some consumers own VCRs and continue to use them, perceiving little benefit from switching to newer technologies, such as DVRs (digital video recorders).

**Figure 10.2** Decision Chart: Promotion Tactics during Life Cycle Stages

| Criteria | Introduction | Growth | Maturity | Decline |
|---|---|---|---|---|
| Goals | Create awareness; Educate customers; Stimulate trial | Build awareness; Build brand; preference | Differentiate from competitors; add features to keep "fresh" in market | Limited to continuing to offer product or service |
| Target Markets | Innovators; Early adopters | Early majority; Up and comers | Late majority; Mainstream | Laggards; Niche markets |
| Push/Pull Marketing | Push: Product/service demonstrations at retailers<br>Pull: Educating consumers on benefits | Push: Shift from education about benefits to competitive comparisons<br>Pull: Similar to push | Push: In-store displays and other techniques to differentiate product.<br>Pull: Competitive comparison ads | Push: Keep product on store shelves (but in back)<br>Pull: Little, if any, advertising |

**Push–Pull Marketing**. Push marketing is limited to paying a minimal fee to retailers to include the product in their store. Little, if any, effort is spent to highlight the product, and it is often stored on the lowest shelf, in the back of the store, to reduce costs. Manufacturers might also make the product available for direct sales on their websites (another low-cost sales method).

Pull marketing is generally eliminated altogether. For example, some stores still carry VCRs and VCR cartridges but spend no efforts on advertising their availability.

Figure 10.2 presents a decision chart recommending sample promotion tactics through the product/service life cycle.

## Marketing Planning in Action

**Panasonic 3D TV: Targeted to Early Adopters**. Panasonic sold out of its first 3D television sets during the first week of their being offered for sale, despite stiff prices—thousands of dollars higher than their non-3D counterparts—and stock-outs. Best Buy's website features the emergence of 3D technology and touts the benefits of the technology. The website is clearly aimed at early adopters who thirst for technical information. Not all people are early adopters, however. In a review of some of the early 3D television sets, one reviewer likens them to the 3D movie fad of the 1950s. At one point the reviewer states, "Before I plunk down a few grand on a 3D TV—which for me is about what I'd pay for a car—I want to be sure that it's not a fad and that there is plenty of product in the pipeline." This person is definitely not in the early adopter market segment.[3]

Panasonic's 3D TV promotion targeted early adopters, emphasizing cutting-edge technology over price and practicality
*Source:* Shutterstock

# Integrated Marketing Communications

Having established our high-level promotion tactics, we turn next to establishing the overall marketing communications mix to achieve our tactics. We must allocate our marketing communications budget over several communications elements—advertising, sales promotions, social media, and so on—to create our specific marketing communications mix.

## Integrated Marketing Communications Goals

Marketers should establish a consistent message throughout each element of the mix to ensure **integrated marketing communications** (IMC). In an effective IMC approach, each element is telling a part of a cohesive story. Maintaining consistent messaging throughout the elements can improve the cost-effectiveness of our marketing communications budget, because each element synergistically supports the other.

## Integrated Marketing Communications Mix

Each communications tool has its own set of strengths that make it appropriate for specific communications objectives (and less suitable for others). In this section, we briefly review the communications tools and summarize with a decision chart showing guidelines of tools to select for various communications objectives, with the objective of selecting an overall mix to achieve our high-level promotion tactics. In the next section, we review the promotion vehicles in more detail to establish individual tactics for each.[4]

**Advertising**. One of the most popular forms of marketing communications is advertising. Advertising is broadly defined as any paid form of nonpersonal promotion by an identified sponsor. Advertising vehicles are generally recommended for situations requiring pervasiveness (advertising reaches a wide audience, with multiple exposures) and credibility (organizations which advertise are perceived as more credible than those that do not, because it shows that the company is serious about developing its market).

**Social Media and Digital Marketing**. **Social media and digital marketing** vehicles actively attempt to engage prospects using "networked conversations" (to borrow a phrase from *The Cluetrain Manifesto*). As Figure 10.3 shows, traditional "conversations" from organizations' websites employ a one-to-many publishing model. The conversations are created by an authority of some sort, and others are expected to come to the website to read about it. Little, if any, convenient means are provided to engage in a conversation about the topic.[5]

Social media and digital marketing techniques, on the other hand, employ a many-to-many model, where content is generated by users, and multiple participants can engage in discussion about a topic. Social media websites promote discussion by providing tools to create content, leave comments, and provide ratings or opinions about products and services.

A few examples of different kinds of social media and digital marketing vehicles include social networking (Facebook, LinkedIn, MySpace), blogs (Blogger, Typepad, WordPress,), video sharing (Flickr, Vimeo, YouTube), and **location-based social networking** tools for mobile devices (Facebook places, Foursquare, Gowalla). Social media has transformed society and business, as chronicled by the socialnomics video at socialnomics.net/video/.[6]

---

**Figure 10.3** Marketing Shift: From Traditional Marketing to Social Media and Digital Marketing

One-to-many "Conversations"                        One-to-many "Conversations"

Company                                            Company

Customer   Customer   Customer      Customer   Customer   Customer

**Traditional Marketing**            **Social Media and Digital Marketing**

---

## Key Terms

**Integrated marketing communications (IMC)** Maintaining consistent messaging across multiple media with the goal of mutual reinforcement.

**Social media and digital marketing** Adopting a "many-to-many" publishing model to encourage user interaction instead of the traditional "one-to-many" promotion style.

**Location-based social networking** Enhancing the social networking experience by incorporating location, such as learning about events occurring nearby, or "checking in" with local merchants. Sample apps include Facebook places, Foursquare, and Gowalla.

Social media and digital marketing has transformed the way marketers engage with customers, using tools such as social media sites, blogs, picture and video sharing, and location-based mobile device marketing
*Source*: Shutterstock

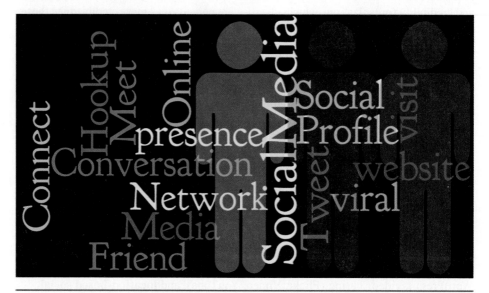

Social media and digital marketing techniques work well in situations where the organization emphasizes its Internet presence as part of its business model (social media can drive traffic to websites), where brand perceptions are based on thought leadership (social media can drive brand associations in a personally meaningful way), when relationships with influencers are vital (many users of social media are active in many areas and can spread the influence of the organization), where credibility should be boosted (users trust opinions of other users), and where information must be timely (networked conversations happen in real time).

**Sales Promotions**. **Sales promotions** are short-term incentives that companies give to entice people to purchase particular products or services. An example of a sales promotion would be a coupon in a newspaper or magazine, or a "promotion code" for discounts on online purchases.

Sales promotions work well for situations requiring a boost in sales in the short term (promotions often include deadlines, forcing people to buy within a certain time) and price-sensitive items (sales promotions target price-conscious shoppers).

**Public Relations (PR)**. **Public relations** is the set of activities that companies use to build and maintain their reputations in the media. Examples include writing press releases, placing stories in print or online magazines, or even surveying blogs for negative postings about the company. A properly run PR initiative can have very positive results for a company.

Public relations activities work well for situations requiring improvement to a company's perceived reputation (to eliminate misconceptions about a company), adding emotion to a product, service, or organization (news stories often emphasize drama and the human element to increase readership and bring the story "alive" to the reader), and managing crises (an extreme version of managing reputation).

**Events and Experiences Sponsorship**. One example of an event is a company-controlled activity, such as Red Bull's Flugtag event. An alternative is sponsoring another organization's event, such as giving money to a racing team to showcase a company logo on a NASCAR racing car.

Event sponsorship works well for developing personal relationships with brands (events and experiences can show how the product or service can play a meaningful role in customers' lives) and for engaging with promotion-weary audiences (the "soft-sell" from events and experiences can be more effective than traditional "hard-sell" approaches).

**Direct Marketing**. In **direct marketing**, marketing messages are targeted to individual consumers. Companies reach out directly to customers using personal contact channels, such as telephone, email, and postal mail. An example of a direct marketing effort would include an email message from clothing retailer Men's Wearhouse.

Direct marketing works well for situations where customers value relevant information (customers can "opt-in" for updates and promotions they find useful), where communications should be timely (messages can be prepared and sent quickly), and where some level of interactivity is desired (customers are encouraged to reply to the messages).

**Personal Selling**. In **personal selling**, a company representative interacts directly with the prospect. The approach is well suited for situations involving expensive complex products (such as automobiles, sold by salespeople at auto dealerships), high involvement products and services (such as homes, sold by realtors), and where longer-term relationships are a goal (such as many service organizations, which emphasize personal selling to facilitate repeat business).

Figure 10.4 presents a decision chart on marketing communications mix elements. The chart suggests sample scenarios where the characteristics of different communications mix elements are well suited. Other scenarios in addition to the ones listed here are, of course, also possible depending on the situation.

## Marketing Planning in Action

**New York City Schools: Multimedia Campaign to Boost Attendance**. NYC schools chief Joel Klein unveiled a new plan to help sell kids on the notion that "school is cool." Working with an advertising agency, he devised a multimedia campaign to "re-brand" academics. In the campaign, 15,000 middle school children from high-poverty neighborhoods would be given free cell phones. The children would hear messages from entertainment and sports celebrities through their new phones, reminding them to do well in class. The phones could also download recorded interviews with successful men and women who discussed how they leveraged school success into financial security. Children who improved their behavior, such as increasing their attendance or getting better grades, would be rewarded with free minutes on their cell phones.[7]

## Key Terms

**Sales promotions** Short-term incentives given by companies to entice people to purchase particular products or services.

**Public relations** Set of activities companies use to build and maintain their reputations in the media.

**Direct marketing** Marketing through a promotion using messages targeted to, and delivered to, individual customers.

**Figure 10.4** Decision Chart: Marketing Communications Mix Elements

| Element | Description | Decision Guidelines: Best used for following situations: |
|---|---|---|
| Advertising | Any paid form of non-personal promotion by an identified sponsor | Pervasiveness<br>Credibility |
| Social Media | Promote "networked conversations" by moving from one-to-many communications model to many-to-many model | Internet-based business model<br>Brands based on thought leadership<br>Relationships with influencers<br>Credibility<br>Timely |
| Sales Promotions | Short-term incentives enticing people to purchase a particular product or service | Short-term sales boost<br>Price-sensitive products/ services |
| Public Relations | Build and maintain organizational reputation in the media | Perceived reputation<br>Connect to users through emotion<br>Crisis management |
| Events & Experiences | Sponsored activity with brand as co-star | Show how brand can enrich life<br>Target "soft-sell" over "hard sell" |
| Direct Marketing | Marketing message targeted to individual customer | Relevant ("opt-in") information<br>Timely<br>Some interactivity |
| Personal Selling | One-on-one interaction to sell a product or service | Complex, expensive products<br>High-involvement products<br>Long-term relationship desired |

## Promotion Vehicles

Now that we have established the overall mix of promotion tools to implement an integrated marketing communications campaign, we dig a little deeper to determine the tactics for the individual promotion vehicles.

### Advertising Programs

Companies often utilize the services of advertising agencies to create campaigns using different types of media, such as television and print advertising.

In this section, we focus on non-digital media. The next section will focus exclusively on social media and digital marketing. Even if advertising agencies are used, some decisions still need to be made by the company's marketing team. In this section, we cover common advertising decisions that marketers must make to maximize cost-effectiveness and include decision charts to aid in preliminary advertising program planning.

- **Advertising Objectives**: What is to be accomplished with the advertising program?
- **Advertising Budget Factors**: What factors influence the amount spent on advertising?
- **External Agency Usage**: Should the program be done in-house, or should an agency be hired?
- **Media Selection**: Which media choices are best suited to certain advertising objectives?

**Advertising Objectives**.  The advertising objective states the goal to be accomplished with a specific audience in a specific period of time. Objectives must be consistent with the overall goals of the organization and its products and services. As shown in Figure 10.5, objectives fall into one of four categories: [8]

- **Informative Advertising**: In **informative advertising**, the organization seeks to acquaint the audience with important facts about the organization's offering. For example, financial services giant Chase featured television and radio commercials informing the public of its new *QuickDeposit* service, where consumers can deposit checks by taking photos of them using their Apple iPhone or Android-powered smartphone. This type of objective works well for building brand awareness (by informing the audience about aspects of the brand they might not have known) and for the introduction of new products and services (by informing the audience about what makes this new offering special).

- **Persuasive Advertising**: The **persuasive advertising** objective attempts to create liking and stimulate purchase of a product or service. Advertisements comparing one brand with another are popular tactics for this type of objective. For example, S.C. Johnson ran print ads comparing its Ziploc brand of resealable plastic bags with those of competitors, demonstrating how the poor seal of the other bags resulted in food spoilage. The objective works well for building brand preference (by making the audience like the brand more than those of competitors) and brand attitudes (by reinforcing positive attitudes toward the brand and eliminating negative ones).

**Figure 10.5** Advertising Objectives: Overview

## Key Terms

**Personal selling**    Sales approach where company representatives interact directly with the prospect.

**Informative Advertising**
Advertising objective, seeking to acquaint the target audience with important facts about the company's product or service.

**Persuasive advertising**
Advertising objective, seeking to create liking and stimulate purchase of the company's product or service by its target market.

- **Reminder Advertising**: In **reminder advertising**, the company seeks to stimulate repeat purchase behavior of products or services already launched in the market. For example, Frontier Airlines sends email messages on a regular basis to customers, reminding them of the low fares the airline has made available to selected destinations. The approach works well for situations involving brand loyalty (by asking customers to stay true to their brand) and long-term sales (by reminding the audience to use the product or service).

- **Reinforcement Advertising**: The **reinforcement advertising** objective attempts to convince current purchasers that they have made the right decision. For example, Bay Alarm security monitoring services provider typically places a sign reading "Bay Alarm/Since 1946" on the front yard of the monitored property, reinforcing the company's long-term commitment to security (and discouraging potential thieves from attempting a break-in!). The objective works well for high-involvement products such as cars (by congratulating them on purchasing such a fine automobile) and products that require significant knowledge to maximize their usefulness (by urging customers to read the manual and learn about the product's dazzling capabilities).

Figure 10.6 presents a decision chart on selecting advertising objectives.

## Marketing Planning in Action

**HP Objective: Target Teens with Tech**. The Teen Vogue store in Short Hills, New Jersey, features some new additions. Amid the prom dresses and vanities, the store now features red and pink Hewlett-Packard (HP) laptop computers. One of HP's marketing objectives is to counter flagging sales by increasing sales to girls and women. Accordingly, HP developed its Vivienne Tam-designed mini laptop and touchscreen-based TouchSmart PCs to court females. Brochures next to the laptops urge girls to "Say hello to computer couture." Girls can use the stylish machines, complete with special HP-designed software, to make believe they are a fashion magazine editor, inserting their photo in a simulated *Teen Vogue* magazine and adding jazzy headlines.[9]

**Figure 10.6** Decision Chart: Advertising Objectives

| Advertising Objective | Description | Decision Guidelines: Best used for following situations: |
|---|---|---|
| Informative Advertising | Acquaints audience with facts about the organization's offerings | Brand awareness<br>New product/service introduction |
| Persuasive Advertising | Seeks to create liking and purchase of an organization's offerings | Brand preference<br>Brand attitudes |
| Reminder Advertising | Stimulates repeat purchase behavior of products and services already launched into the market | Brand loyalty<br>Long-term sales |
| Reinforcement Advertising | Convinces current purchasers they made the right decision | High-involvement products<br>Products requiring skill to operate |

**Figure 10.7** Advertising Budget Factors: Overview

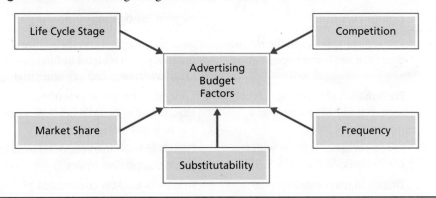

**Advertising Budget Factors**.  The required size of the organization's advertising budget will be influenced by several factors, as shown in Figure 10.7. When deciding upon a budget to cover advertising expenses, those factors can impact the level of spending required to successfully introduce a new product or service and keep it successful throughout its life cycle. Here, we cover a few relevant factors and show how they influence budgets.[10]

- **Life Cycle Stage**: Generally, new products and services require higher budgets, because they require expensive efforts to boost awareness and encourage customer trial. Mature products and services generally require lower amounts of funding as a percentage of sales. Declining products can have high amounts of funding as a percentage of sales (despite lower total expenditures), due to the declining period's lower sales volume.

- **Market Share**: Brands with lower market share generally require higher advertising budgets, as a percentage of sales, than those with high market share, because the sales rate is lower.

- **Competition**: Brands in highly competitive markets must advertise more heavily to remain on customers' consideration lists.

- **Advertising Frequency**: Brands in markets subjected to significant amounts of advertising, such as those of consumer packaged goods, generally must advertise more frequently to reach its audience with a designated number of repetitions. Higher frequency results in higher budgets.

- **Product Substitutability**: Brands in markets where offerings are perceived as nearly identical (such as the market for airline services) require higher budgets to emphasize their differentiation.

Figure 10.8 presents a decision chart on factors influencing advertising budgets.

## Key Terms

**Reminder advertising**
Advertising objective, seeking to stimulate repeat purchase behavior of products or services already launched in the market.

**Reinforcement advertising**
Advertising objective, seeking to convince current purchasers that they have made the right decision.

**Figure 10.8** Decision Chart: Advertising Budget Factors

| Budget Factor | Lower Budgets | Higher Budgets |
|---|---|---|
| Life Cycle Stage | Products or services in the mature phase require lower expenditures as a percentage of sales | New products and service require relatively high budgets to fund brand awareness and customer trial |
| Market Share | High market share brands often require lower expenditure as a percentage of sales | Low market share brands often require higher budgets (as % of sales), due to lower sales level |
| Competition | Brands in niche markets with few competitors | Brands in mass markets, dominated by fierce competitive rivalry |
| Advertising Frequency | Brands in uncrowded markets | Brands in markets confounded by advertising clutter |
| Product Substitutability | Brands in markets where offerings are considered highly differentiated | Brands in markets where offerings are seen as near-substitutes for each other |

## Marketing Planning in Action

**BP's Advertising Budget Spills Over**. In April 2010, the Gulf of Mexico suffered a major oil spill from a leak in a British Petroleum (BP) deep-water oil well. The leak was finally stopped in September of that year, after it had released 206 million gallons of oil into the Gulf. To counter the tide of criticism against the company, BP estimated that it spent nearly $100 million on corporate advertising, which was three times the amount that the company spent on ads during the same period the previous year. The company defended its huge advertising budget for the spill, stating that much of it went to informing Gulf Coast residents about BP's efforts to stop the leak, and also how it would help with the Gulf's recovery.[11]

**External Agency Usage**. We must decide if we plan to develop the advertising within the organization (in-house), or if we want to employ the efforts of an external advertising agency. As Figure 10.9 shows us, several factors can influence our decision to use an external agency. Using an external agency gives us the advantage of potentially greater creativity, objectivity, and expertise, while internal agencies have the potential of saving significant amounts of money, as well as providing greater control of the work.

As a result of tight marketing budgets (and dissatisfaction with previous agency work), some larger companies are moving their advertising work in-house. The decision chart below shows some guidelines on the decision of using an external agency.[12]

- **Account Size**: Smaller accounts are generally not attractive to external advertising agencies, especially top-tier agencies, because they perceive limited revenues from the account.

**Figure 10.9** External Agency Usage: Overview

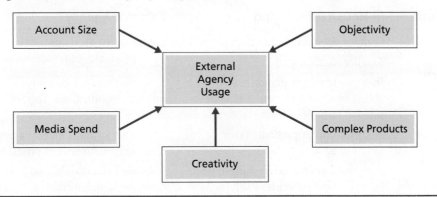

- **Media Spend**: Smaller amounts spent on media (such as television, radio, or print ads) are less economically attractive to external agencies, because many agencies take a commission (often near 15 percent) of the amount spent on media.
- **Objectivity**: External agencies claim to be more objective than in-house advertising efforts, because they can ignore the influences of others in the organization.
- **Complex Products**: External agencies are not as well suited for complex products, because spending the money to train agency members in the nuances of the complex product can be expensive.
- **Creativity**: External agencies claim to show more creative skills than in-house advertising services. Indeed, external agencies can justify expensive training on the latest techniques, such as advanced social media tactics, because the training can be leveraged against multiple accounts.

Figure 10.10 presents a decision chart on factors influencing the decision to use an external advertising agency.

## Marketing Planning in Action

*Mad Men*: **Responsible for Recession**? Advertising agencies, such as the Sterling Cooper agency pictured in the AMC cable television series *Mad Men*, bear at least some of the responsibility for the economic recession of 2007–2010, according to a Harris interactive poll. The poll estimates that 66 percent of Americans believe that agencies are partially to blame for the recession because they "caused people to buy things they could not afford." The study results suggest that the public at large has a general contempt for the advertising profession. Many advertising agencies would likely not be surprised by this finding and often state how difficult it is to cut through the clutter of the hundreds, if not thousands, of ads that people are exposed to every day.[13]

**Figure 10.10** Decision Chart: Factors Influencing the Use of External Advertising Agencies

| Decision Criteria | In-House Advertising | External Agency |
|---|---|---|
| Account Size | Smaller sized accounts | Larger-sized Accounts |
| Media Spend | Smaller media spend | Larger media spend |
| Objectivity | In-house team has demonstrated ability to remain objective, despite internal turmoil | In-house team can be swayed by internal organizational factors |
| Product Complexity | Highly complex products favor in-house advertising approaches | Expensive to train external agency members on nuances of product |
| Creativity | In-house team has advertising-based backgrounds and prides itself on its creativity | In-house team does not include members with advertising background or training |

**Media Selection (Non-digital).** Even if an external agency is used, marketers will often be involved in the selection of non-digital media to carry the advertisement's message. We want to deliver the required number and type of exposures to the target audience in a cost-effective way. To do this, we will consider the reach, frequency, and impact of the media choices, as well as evaluate the characteristics of the medium for its suitability for the advertising objective.[14]

**Media reach** refers to the audience size (number of different people) exposed to a particular message at least once during a specified time period. **Media frequency** is the number of times an average person is exposed to the message within the time period. **Media impact** is the qualitative value of the exposure through a given medium. Multiplied together, they result in a weighted number of exposures, which can be interpreted as the total number of exposures a target audience member sees the ad, weighted by the impact value of the medium.

Reach is generally considered the most important criterion for launching new brands or extensions of existing brands, because we want to expose as many people as possible to the ad. Frequency is considered the most important for markets with strong competitors, because the ad will need repetition if it is to be noticed in a market with so much clutter.

Each medium, such as television, radio, and print advertising, has its own sets of strengths and weaknesses. Accordingly, we present here a brief discussion of typical media and summarize with a decision chart suggesting different types of media to use based on the objective of the advertising program.

- **Television**: TV has the advantages of high reach and the ability to combine sight, sound, and motion but suffers from high cost and clutter. Because of its characteristics, TV is well suited for mass market coverage, product demonstrations, and ability to add drama.

- **Radio**: One of the principal advantages of radio is its excellent segmentation (separate stations for news, classical, country, and so on) within defined geographic areas. As a result, radio is well suited for high selectivity (such as niche markets), advertising requiring moderate to high reach (such as new products and services), and local advertising (such as small business ads).

- **Magazines**: Printed magazines offer excellent psychographic and geographic selectivity. They can give detailed information about a product or service. Printed magazines suffer from long lead times for ads, and generally declining readership. Printed magazines are well suited for programs requiring high selectivity, high-quality color reproduction (such as fashion and food ads), and programs where the medium's long lead times will not pose a problem.

- **Newspapers**: Local newspapers are excellent for nearby events and have short lead times for their ads, but dropping circulation rates make them unattractive. Newspapers are well suited for local coverage, small business ads, and timely events.

- **Yellow Pages**: Ads in telephone directories are good for local coverage and are relatively low in cost. Because most directories are only published once per year, lead times are a big problem. In addition, ads are placed directly next to those from the competition, making it difficult to get noticed among the clutter. Most yellow page publishers also include Internet-based directory listings. The medium is good for small businesses and businesses where geographic proximity plays a strong role, such as restaurants, household repair (such as plumbers), and professional services.

- **Outdoor**: Outdoor advertising, such as billboards and transit ads, have the advantage of a high exposure rate in urban areas. Outdoor ads can help connect the brand to the urban consumer. Its limitations are exposure time (billboards can pass by quickly), clutter, and graffiti. Outdoor ads work well for brands catering to the urban market, such as edgy fashion brands. They also work well when strategically placed, such as giving directions to a nearby store.

- **Product Placement**: In **product placement**, audiences watching movies and television shows see the product in an everyday situation, which helps gain exposure for the product as well as relate to it. Video games reach captive audiences—if they want to play the game, they will be exposed to the ad. Product placement can be selective as well—the choice of film to showcase the product can determine its target market. The limitations include its high cost and growing resentment to overly aggressive product placement in many shows.

- **Point of Purchase**: Point of purchase ads, such as display stands and aisle markers, are often effective because they are there at the "moment of truth"—when the purchase is being decided at the store. On the downside, such ads can be costly,

---

### Key Terms

**Media reach**    Refers to the audience size exposed to a particular message at least once during the specified time period.

**Media frequency**    Number of times an average person is exposed to a particular message within a given time period.

**Media impact**    Qualitative value of a particular medium exposure.

**Product placement**    Marketing technique to increase visibility and demonstrate usage scenarios by embedding goods or services in

content, such as television programs, movies, and video games.

and some consumers complain that the stands block already crowded aisles. Point of purchase advertising works well during push programs targeted at retailers.

Figure 10.11 presents a decision chart suggesting applications well suited to the characteristics for various popular media.

**Figure 10.11** Decision Chart: Non-digital Media Characteristics and Decision Criteria

| Medium | Characteristics | Decision Guidelines: Best used for following situations: |
|---|---|---|
| Television | Advantages: High reach; Combines sight, sound, motion | Mass market coverage<br>Product demonstrations |
| | Limitations: High cost; High clutter; Short exposure time | Drama |
| Radio | Advantages: High selectivity; Mass use; Low cost | High selectivity (niche markets)<br>Good reach within target area |
| | Limitations: Audio only; Lower attention rate; Short exposure time | Local advertising |
| Magazines | Advantages: High psychographic and geographic selectivity; Detailed information possible | High selectivity<br>High-quality photos important<br>Long lead times not a problem |
| | Limitations: Long lead times for ads | |
| Newspapers | Advantages: Local coverage; Short lead times for ads | Emphasis on local coverage<br>Small businesses |
| | Limitations: Poor quality photo reproduction; Dropping circulation | Timely events |
| Yellow Pages | Advantages: Local coverage; Credibility | Small businesses<br>Local businesses |
| | Limitations: Long lead times; Clutter | |
| Outdoor | Advantages: High exposure rate; Can be dramatic | Target urban customers<br>Strategic placement |
| | Limitations: Short exposure time; Clutter; Graffiti | |
| Product Placement | Advantages: High reach; Captive audience; "Soft sell" | Showcase new products<br>Show usage scenarios for brand |
| | Limitations: High cost; Growing resentment on aggressive placement | Target certain buyers (videogames) |
| Point of Purchase | Advantages: Purchase reminder; present at "moment of truth" | Push marketing efforts<br>Decision made in store |
| | Limitations: High cost; Clutter in stores | Reminder advertising |

## Marketing Planning in Action

**Test Drive Unlimited: Product Placement Paradise**: "Test Drive Unlimited," Atari's popular multiplayer video game, showcases many product brands. Players ride around on Ducati SuperSport motorcycles and visit a virtual Lamborghini dealership. Ben Sherman, a men's apparel retailer in London, paid about $500,000 to have its stores featured in the game. Video game product placement targets a huge captive audience—132 million teens and adults in the U.S. play video games. The advertising approach proves effective because it shows the brand in context of its usage situation. For example, Ubisoft's detective game, "CSI: 3 Dimensions of Murder," demonstrates the power of Visa's fraud-protection service by alerting players to a stolen credit card during the game, helping gamers solve a murder case. According to G. Jon Raj, head of advertising and emerging-media platforms at Visa, "We've never before been able to have the consumer really engage with the message."[15]

## Social Media and Digital Marketing

"Digital marketing" is a relatively new term that highlights the significance of the Internet in promotion decisions. As Figure 10.12 shows, marketers can select from many types of social media and digital marketing vehicles.

Marketers should consider the return on investment when using digital marketing techniques. In the early days of digital marketing, companies were satisfied with simple metrics such as "eyeballs" (unique visitors on website pages) and "stickiness" (time spent on website pages). While measurement was simple, the metrics did not

**Figure 10.12** Social Media and Digital Marketing Vehicles

correspond to actual sales. The next step was examining **click-through rates (CTR)** for Internet ads and cost per click (CPC) rates for search engine marketing efforts. CTR and CPC values provide a bit more insight, but still do not tell the whole story. Modern digital marketing focuses more on **conversion rate optimization (CRO)**. CRO seeks to increase customer revenue through improvements in conversion rate, such as increasing conversions from Web surfer to paying customer.

In this section, we cover several areas within digital marketing and give general guidelines in their use for marketing promotion (caveat: given the fast pace of digital marketing, some of the examples might be obsolete or irrelevant by the time you read this book!). We summarize the areas using a decision chart.

**Social Networking**.  Social networks, as first coined by Professor J.A. Barnes in the 1950s, are associations of people drawn together by family, work, or hobby.

**Social networking** can be useful in several situations: for engaging with customers (such as on a company's Facebook wall), for professionals wishing to build a network of business contacts (such as using the LinkedIn Groups feature on business networking site LinkedIn), for small businesses wishing to build their business by sending announcements (informing group members of events, job openings, or vendor recommendations), and for targeted advertising (many social networking sites allow advertisers to choose two of seven criteria to target, including geography, industry, seniority, and company size).[16]

**Blogs**.  Blogs (Weblogs) hold several promising promotion opportunities for companies. Company blogs can be used to engage with customers in an open forum, to demonstrate thought leadership through expert opinion blog posts of relevant topics, to communicate announcements (such as product introductions or new customers), and to clear up misconceptions about the company in the market.

Blogs can also provide consumer feedback, especially blogs with high volumes of user interaction, such as microblog site Twitter. Companies must monitor non-company blogs for critical postings, using tools such as Google's Blog Search product.[17]

**Search Engine Optimization.**  **Search engine optimization (SEO)** improves "organic search" (non-paid search) rankings of search engines (such as Google) by adjusting content on company website pages, editing website HTML (hypertext markup language, the language of Web pages), and making other changes, such as adding links toward the site.

SEO increases company visibility (so prospects know about it), boosts sales to target markets (by using specific keywords relevant to those markets), and enhances company credibility (by associating it with relevant keywords).[18]

**Search Engine Marketing.**  **Search engine marketing (SEM)**, also called pay per click (PPC) advertising (such as Google's SEM offering, AdWords), places ads in search engine results that correspond to a user's search. SEM allows businesses to create advertising using keywords related to their business, which are displayed during user searches.

SEM works well for niche marketing (keywords can be very specific to niche markets), where conversion rates must be increased (businesses can target customers likely to buy by using relevant keywords), and gathering feedback on the relevance of the company's messaging (SEM analytics show the effectiveness of different messaging campaigns).[19]

**Video Sharing**.  According to an eMarketer survey, 86.6 percent of the U.S. Internet population will watch video online in 2011, up from 62.8 percent in 2006. Marketers can upload promotional videos to **video sharing** sites such as YouTube, thus making it available for the world to see.

Video sharing works well for driving website traffic (search engine algorithms rank video highly in search results), for demonstrating products and services, for adding drama to a company's offerings (videos can act as a mini-movie), and for viral marketing (covered next).[20]

**Viral Marketing.  Viral marketing** can generate a tremendous amount of "buzz" (visibility, along with a sense of excitement) for modest budgets by spreading messages quickly using the so-called viral organic and self-replicating nature of the approach. For example, blender manufacturer Blendtec generated publicity through its "Will It Blend?" viral campaign by sharing wild videos of its powerful blenders demolishing items such as mobile phones, rake handles, and Apple iPads.

Viral marketing works best for promotions where the user believes the message will interest others (such as sharing tools that others may find useful), feature outrageous antics (such as the Blendtec campaign), and quickly generate brand awareness (such as building awareness for a new movie release).[21]

**Mobile Marketing.  Mobile marketing** is a promotional activity designed for delivery to mobile phones, usually as part of a multichannel campaign. According to industry analyst firm The Kelsey Group, mobile advertising revenues of the United States will grow to $3.1 billion in 2013, up from $160 million in 2008, representing a compound annual growth rate (CAGR) of 81.2 percent.

Mobile device techniques work well for location-based promotions (mobile phones accompany users wherever they go), mobile search-based promotions (mobile search advertising is quickly outpacing traditional mobile short message advertising), and promotion campaigns using app-vertising (branded mobile phone applications), such as

---

## Key Terms

**Click-through rate (CTR)** Percentage of people clicking on a Web-based promotion compared to the total population viewing the ad.

**Conversion rate optimization (CRO)** CRO seeks to increase customer revenue through improvements in conversion rate, such as increasing conversions from Web surfer to paying customer.

**Social networking** Defined in the 1950s as associations of people drawn together by family, work or hobby. Businesses often use social networking for promotion-based activities such as engaging with customers, linking with other professionals, and advertising to targeted segments.

**Search engine optimization (SEO)** Seeks to improve nonpaid (also called "organic") Internet search results of search engines by various means, such as adjusting website content.

**Search engine marketing (SEM)** Also called **pay per click (PPC),** SEM places ads in Internet search engine results that correspond to keywords in user searches.

**Video Sharing** Posting video clips to websites such as Vimeo and YouTube to share with others online.

**Viral marketing** Marketing technique to encourage the spreading of messages (such as a virus) to increase visibility.

**Mobile marketing** Promotional activity designed for delivery to mobile phones, usually part of a multichannel campaign. Popular uses include location-based promotions, mobile search-based promotions, and app-vertising (branded mobile mobile phone applications). See also Location-based social networking.

Blendtec's "Will It Blend" viral marketing campaign used online videos of outrageous stunts, such as blending mobile phones, to generate visibility for its brand
*Source*: Fotolia

the Adidas Urban Art Guide, a cell phone application giving a walking guide to Berlin street art, while prominently displaying the Adidas logo.[22]

**Internet Advertisements**. According to a Standard & Poor's report, Internet ads (such as banner ads) are still popular, with U.S. online advertising revenues rising 11 percent in 2008 and 3 percent in 2009, and projected to increase by 12 percent in 2010 and 10 percent in 2011. Many ad systems now use **contextual advertising** approaches, which scan the text of recently viewed websites for keywords and delivers ads targeting those keywords.

Internet ads can work well for programs requiring great reach (ads are exposed to many viewers), for ads with compelling offers (such as the giveaway of a desirable item), and for ads promising free samples (product samples or service trial periods).[23]

**Company Websites**. Almost all digital media promotion campaigns utilize the organization's own website. For example, at insurance service company website Geico.com, users can learn more about the insurance services provided and get a free, quick rate quote.

Company website techniques work particularly well in converting customers (from passive viewers into active buyers), delivering complex product or service information (early adopters desire detailed technical information for new products and services), and providing a means of engaging with customers (many company websites feature company blogs).

**Online Newsletters**. Online newsletters continually engage customers through an ongoing series of messages. Some newsletters, such as *Adweek* (advertising), *DailyCandy* (travel), and *Housecall* (health), offer fresh, engaging content, and users "opt-in" to receive them on a regular basis.

The medium is excellent for reminder advertising (users receive them on a regular basis), for small businesses (to differentiate them from other similar businesses), and for introducing new products or services.[24]

Figure 10.13 presents a decision chart on guidelines for different social media and digital marketing elements.

## Marketing Planning in Action

**Beautystat Cosmetics Marketing: Social Media Is More than Skin Deep**. Beauty social marketing consultancy Beautystat's study on the use of social media for cosmetic marketing found several companies not using new media tactics to their full potential, despite the seductive effectiveness promised by social media tools. The Beautystat report remarks that while average U.S. consumers spend 17.8 hours per week on the Internet and 14 hours per week watching television, cosmetics firms still spend much more on traditional advertising approaches than they do on digital marketing.

To track social media effectiveness, Beautystat tracked the degree of engagement the top ten beauty companies had with their customers. Estee Lauder brands showed a wide range, from a high engagement score of 5.3 for its Bobbi Brown brand to an appalling 0.0 percent for its Ojon brand. The top performer was Avon products, which boasted an engagement rate of 6.9 percent, reflecting the commitment the company made to tap into social media websites, consistent with the direct sales approach that originally built the brand.[25]

## Key Terms

**Contextual advertising**
Advertising approach that scans the text of recently viewed websites for keywords and delivers ads targeting those keywords.

**Figure 10.13** Decision Chart: Social Media and Digital Marketing

| Social Media Technique | Examples | Decision Guidelines: Best used for following situations: |
|---|---|---|
| Social Networking | Facebook, LinkedIn, MySpace | Engaging with customers<br>Build network of business contacts<br>Send announcements to network<br>Targeted advertising |
| Blogs | Blogger, Typepad, WordPress | Engage with customers in forum<br>Demonstrate thought leadership<br>Communicate announcements<br>Obtain consumer feedback<br>Monitor blogs with search tool |
| SEO | Optimization for Bing, Google, Yahoo | Build visibility<br>Boost sales in target markets<br>Enhance credibility |
| SEM | Bing adCenter, Google AdWords, Yahoo Sponsored Search | Target niche markets<br>Improve conversion rates<br>Gather feedback on messaging |
| Video Sharing | Flickr, Vimeo, YouTube | Drive website traffic<br>Product/service demonstrations<br>Add drama to offerings<br>Viral marketing |
| Viral Marketing | BlendTec, Cloverfield, Hotmail | Sharing message will benefit others<br>Promotions with outrageous antics<br>Boost brand awareness |
| Mobile Marketing | Facebook, Foursquare, Twitter | Location-based marketing<br>Mobile search-based promotions<br>App-vertising |
| Internet Advertisements | Wells Fargo banner ad on Yahoo page | Wide reach<br>Compelling offer (giveaway)<br>Free product sample or service trial |
| Company Websites | Geico insurance page with rate quote | Enhance conversion rates<br>Complex product information<br>Engage with customers |
| Online Newsletters | *AdWeek, DailyCandy, Housecall* | Reminder advertising<br>Small businesses<br>Introduction of new services |

## Sales Promotions

Whereas advertising offers a reason to buy, sales promotion offers an incentive to buy. The purpose of sales promotion is to stimulate quicker or greater purchase of particular products or services using a collection of incentive tools, mostly short term. Sales promotions are divided into two types: **consumer promotions** (aimed at end customers) and **trade promotions** (aimed at distribution channel members). Consumer promotion includes tools such as samples, coupons, and free trials. Trade promotion includes tools such as advertising and display allowances, as well as free goods.[26]

**Consumer Promotions.** Companies should select the type of promotion based on the marketing objective for the product or service. Figure 10.14 shows an overview of consumer promotions objectives.

- **Customer Trial**: Free samples can be very effective in persuading customers to try a new product or service. For example, H&R Block gives discounts for first-time users of their tax return preparation services to get them to try the service.

- **Enhance Brand Image**: For companies wanting to enhance the brand image of a product or service, it often helps to run a co-op advertisement, an ad showing the product featured at a retailer with high brand equity. For example, shoe manufacturer Ferragamo could run a co-op ad with Nordstrom department stores to showcase its line of stylish footwear.

- **Increase Market Share**: To help companies increase market share, they can offer consumers coupons that target users of competing brands. For example, Bare Escentuals, a brand of mineral-based cosmetics, could run ads in *Vogue* magazine, enticing Maybelline users to switch.

- **Increase Sales**: Organizations can use various techniques to boost sales, such as coupons, prizes, and rebates. While the techniques can boost short-term sales, care must be taken to avoid overuse of these methods, or risk eroding brand equity by

**Figure 10.14** Consumer Promotions Objectives: Overview

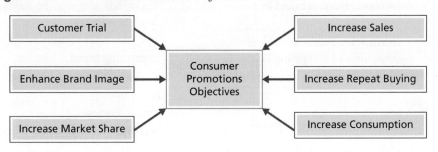

### Key Terms

**Consumer promotions** Sales promotions targeted at consumers; see also trade promotions.

**Trade promotions** Sales promotions targeted at distribution channel members; see also consumer promotions.

lowering the consumer's perception of value for the brand. For example, breakfast cereal manufacturers run frequent sales promotions, causing many consumers to believe "sale" prices are effectively the real prices.

- **Increase Repeat Buying**: Companies can provide an incentive for repeat buying to reduce the cost of sales. For example, Dial soap might include a coupon for a discount on the consumer's next bar of Dial soap.

- **Increase Consumption**: Companies can motivate consumers to increase their consumption through sales targeted to key events (such as back to school sales), or by discounting the purchase of large amounts of product. For example, fast-food restaurants offer "supersize" discounts for consumers who purchase bundled offerings of products, such as hamburgers, French fries, and soft drinks.

Figure 10.15 presents a decision chart on selecting consumer promotions for typical marketing objectives.

**Trade Promotions**. Similar to consumer promotions, companies should select the type of promotion based on the marketing objective for the product or service. Figure 10.16 gives an overview.

- **Increase Distribution**: Manufacturers can increase distribution by persuading the trade to carry their product lines. Persuasion tools typically include trade allowances, payments, or discounts offered in return for the retailer's agreement to feature the manufacturer's products. Manufacturers might also offer free cases of product to the retailer to introduce the brand to the retailer.

**Figure 10.15** Decision Chart: Consumer Promotions to Target Specific Marketing Objectives

| Marketing Objective | Description | Guidelines: Recommended Tactics |
|---|---|---|
| Customer Trial | Persuade consumer to try a new product or service | Free samples of product<br>Free samples of service |
| Enhance Brand Image | Increase regard of brand by consumers | Co-op ads with retailers having high brand equity |
| Increase Market Share | Increase long-term sales by enticing consumers of competing brands to switch | Coupons targeted to users of competing brand |
| Increase Sales | Boost sales (generally more focus) | Coupons targeted to users of same brand<br>Prizes, contests, games<br>Rebates |
| Increase Repeat Buying | Lower costs and increase loyalty by encouraging consumers to repeatedly purchase company's products | In-pack coupon<br>Frequent flyer program |
| Increase Consumption | Motivate consumers to increase their consumption amount per purchase, or total consumption amount | Back-to-school sales<br>Supersize discounts |

**Figure 10.16** Trade Promotions Objectives: Overview

- **Increase Trade Support**: To continue the support of trade members in the carrying of their brand, manufacturers can periodically offer price-offs (discounts from list price) for a certain time period.
- **Liquidate Inventories**: If the manufacturer plans to launch a new type of product, it might decide to eliminate inventories of existing products using a variety of techniques, such as rebates.
- **Increase Goodwill**: Manufacturers who wish to improve relations with distribution channel members can offer goodwill gestures. Some approaches include offering free cases of product for trade members who buy a certain quantity or who feature a certain flavor or size. Manufacturers can also offer sales contests, such as free trips to top-selling channel members.

Figure 10.17 presents a decision chart on selecting trade promotions for typical marketing objectives.

**Figure 10.17** Decision Chart: Trade Promotions to Target Specific Marketing Objectives

| Marketing Objective | Description | Guidelines: Recommended Tactics |
| --- | --- | --- |
| Increase Distribution | Persuade trade to carry product lines | Trade allowance<br>Free cases of product for trial |
| Increase Trade Support | Increase (and continue) support of trade members in carrying a brand | Offer price-off (discount off list price) for certain time period |
| Liquidate Inventories | Eliminate inventories for various reasons, such as making room for new product | Rebates<br>Price-off |
| Increase Goodwill | Improve relations with channel members | Offer free cases of product for trade members who buy a certain quantity or who feature a certain flavor or size<br>Offer contests, such as free trips to top sellers |

## Marketing Planning in Action

**Curacao: 500,000 Reasons to Visit**. The Dutch Caribbean island of Curacao struggled to make itself stand out over other tourist destinations. A prolonged economic recession only worsened matters. So it came up with a bold plan. It advertised the Curacao Treasure Hunt contest, where 10 finalists would be chosen to scramble around the island looking for a treasure chest with $500,000. The campaign could be perceived as an investment, because the increased awareness and tourist revenue generated by the program would be worth far more than the prize money.[27]

## Public Relations

Public relations (PR) is the practice of managing the communications between an organization and its internal stakeholders (such as employees, labor unions, and shareholders) and external stakeholders (such as customers, communities, and the media). According to the Public Relations Society of America (PRSA.org), public relations management encompasses five functions: research, counseling, action, lobbying, and planning and evaluation.[28]

The Curacao Treasure Hunt sales promotion targeted consumer trial of this island paradise near Aruba in the Caribbean Sea
*Source*: Shutterstock

**Figure 10.18** Public Relations' Roles in Achieving Marketing Objectives: Overview

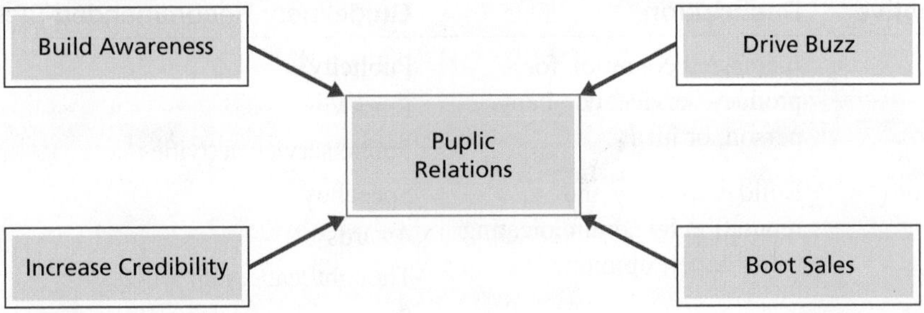

Public relations organizations are versatile and can help organizations achieve several marketing objectives, as shown in Figure 10.18.[29]

**Build Awareness**. Public relations organizations can build awareness for a product or service (or even a company, person, or idea). For example, the Make It Right movement used news articles and press releases to build awareness of the plight of Katrina-ravaged New Orleans. Various PR tactics can be used to build awareness, such as publicity (published articles in news media), press-kit distribution (furnishing packages of information about the company), and public service activities (such as contributing time and money to good causes).[30]

**Increase Credibility**. PR can leverage different tactics to build credibility, such as speeches (such as the CEO speaking at a major conference), awards (winning prestigious industry awards), articles (publishing thought leadership articles), public opinions (conducting opinion polls, monitoring blogs, and reviewing industry analyst reports), and even crisis management (counseling executives during company-related catastrophes).

**Drive Buzz**. Various PR tactics can be used to drive buzz (excitement), such as mentions in influential news outlets (such as company mentions in prominent group-edited technology blog TechCrunch), the gradual release of news using multiple outlets (onlookers will see the company as pervasive, hearing about them through multiple sources), and news announcements (such as winning a new customer or releasing an exciting new service).

**Boost Sales**. Sales-oriented PR tactics include SEO-enabled press releases (press releases with embedded relevant search keywords), creating message platforms (aiding sales through consistent messaging), and company-created content (such as brochures and annual reports). Some public relations agencies also participate in lobbying efforts to influence or change public policy in a way that benefits sales (or at least prevents new legislation that could reduce sales). For example, cellular phone companies actively lobbied Congress not to pass restrictive cell phone legislation for drivers.[31]

Figure 10.19 presents a decision chart on selecting different public relations techniques for typical marketing objectives.

**Figure 10.19** Decision Chart: Public Relations Tactics to Target Specific Marketing Objectives

| Marketing Objective | Description | Guidelines: Recommended Tactics |
|---|---|---|
| Build Awareness | Increase recognition for a product, service, company, person, or idea | Publicity<br>Press kits<br>Public service activities |
| Increase Credibility | Build credibility and reputation by communicating using expert opinion | Speeches<br>Awards<br>Thought leadership articles<br>Public opinion monitoring<br>Crisis management |
| Drive Buzz | Increase excitement leading up to the launch of a new product or service | Mentions in major news outlets<br>Gradual release of information<br>News announcements |
| Boost Sales | Boost sales using tactics generally less expensive than traditional advertising techniques | SEO-enabled press releases<br>Messaging platforms<br>Company-generated content<br>Government lobbying |

## Marketing Planning in Action

**Google: Doing No Evil**? Google, the Internet search giant, is countering negative public opinion with a coordinated PR campaign. Google's market dominance has fueled discontent with many people. Book authors complain of its efforts to digitize millions of books. Advertisers complain that they have no bargaining power because Google commands over 70 percent of Internet search advertising. In response, Google has launched an intensive public relations campaign to change public perception of the brand. To avoid the antitrust problems of Microsoft in the late 1990s, Google company officials are speaking with key stakeholders and thought leaders, such as reporters, academics, and lawmakers, to explain the benefits the company brings and why "Google should be loved, not feared."[32]

## Events and Experiences

Companies can create their own events (such as RedBull's Flugtag) or sponsor-existing events (such as Coca-Cola's sponsoring of NASCAR auto racing) to achieve a number of marketing objectives, as shown in Figure 10.20. Events and experiences should be used in conjunction with integrated marketing campaigns to take advantage of cross-promotion activities. In this section, we cover several common objectives and recommend events tactics for each. [33]

**Build Awareness**. Events tactics can increase brand recognition by displaying the brand at events (such as company logos on NASCAR cars) or giving

**Figure 10.20** Events and Experiences: Objectives

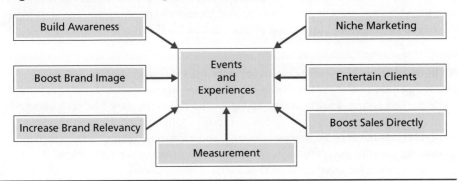

away samples at the event (such as offering bottles of a new sports drink at an outdoor event).

**Boost Brand Image.** Different events tactics can be used to increase brand image, such as corporate image-based events (such as sponsoring a cause-related event such as the American Cancer Society's Relay for Life) and associating the brand with prestige (such as sponsoring the Masters Golf Tournament).

Red Bull's FlugTag event builds brand recognition and associates the brand with zany, high-energy antics
*Source*: Alamy

**Increase Brand Relevancy**. Companies can use events to show how a brand fits into their lives or to evoke feelings for a brand. Tactics include launch parties (such as model year introduction events by automotive manufacturers where consumers can sit behind the wheel) and organized user group events (such as Land Rover owner's club off-road driving events).

**Niche Marketing**. Companies can target niche markets by creating or sponsoring events that cater to that market. For example, Subaru sponsors several outdoors-related niche markets (skiers, snowboarders, and mountain bikers) to show how its four-wheel drive cars are relevant to their adventurous lifestyle. Different events tactics include lifestyle events (such as the Subaru example), geographically related events (such as sponsoring a surfing competition on the coastline), or demographically related events (such as targeting teenaged consumers at a teen-oriented event).

**Entertain Clients**. Events offer the opportunity to entertain important clients or reward key employees. Different tactics can be used, such as special seating (such as skyboxes or VIP rooms), special services before and after the event (such as limousine transportation to the event), and hospitality tents (for clients to meet with key company executives).

**Boost Sales Directly**. In addition to the indirect sales that events can provide through brand awareness and brand image, events can provide direct sales. Typical approaches

**Figure 10.21** Decision Chart: Events Tactics to Target Specific Marketing Objectives

| Marketing Objective | Description | Guidelines: Recommended Tactics |
| --- | --- | --- |
| Build Awareness | Sustained exposure to brand names available at events | Brand displayed at events<br>Give away samples at event |
| Boost Brand Image | Increase public's image of brand through its association with certain events | Cause-related events<br>Prestigious events |
| Increase Brand Relevancy | Show how brand fits into one's life and how it can stir excitement | Launch parties<br>Organized user group events |
| Niche Marketing | Increase relevancy of brand toward market niche by showing relevance | Lifestyle events<br>Geographic events<br>Demographic events |
| Entertain Clients | Entertain important clients or reward key employees | Special seating at events<br>Transportation services<br>Hospitality tents |
| Boost Sales Directly | Increase direct sales of merchandise, in addition to indirect sales from brand awareness | Merchandising<br>Promotion |
| Measurement | Measure marketing effectiveness of events | Supply side<br>Demand side |

include merchandise opportunities (specially branded merchandise recognizing the event, such as Coca-Cola cans with NASCAR sponsorship logos) and promotion options (such as contests associated with the event).

**Measurement**. Marketers have two major tactics they can employ to measure the effectiveness of events. The first is supply-side measurement, which approximates the amount of time or physical space devoted to media coverage of the brand during the event (such as the number of seconds a logo is exposed). The second is demand-side measurement, which focuses on the effects of the exposure on consumers (such as surveying spectators to see how their brand attitudes changed because of the event).

Figure 10.21 presents a decision chart on selecting different events tactics for typical marketing objectives.

## Marketing Planning in Action

**Ambushed: Crying Foul to Sports Sponsorships**. Corporations spent a staggering $43.8 billion to sponsor major sporting events in 2009. Due to the high expense, some of the corporations are angry because of the growing number of companies that bend the rules to get brand exposure at events without paying, referred to as "ambushing." For example, American Express showed television ads in 1992 with scenes of Barcelona, Spain, the host city of the Summer Olympics that year, with the tagline "You don't need a visa" to visit Spain. Visa, an official sponsor of the Olympics, was understandably furious.

Ambush activities are separated into direct activities (such as intentional attacks, such as American Express's alleged tactics), indirect ambushes (such as street-style promotions near an event), and incidental ambushing (such as an announcer mentioning that a swimmer is wearing Speedo swim trunks, when Speedo is not an official sponsor of the event).[34]

## Direct Marketing

Direct marketing targets end users directly, without going through distribution channel intermediaries. Marketers can leverage a database of contacts and a variety of direct contact techniques (such as telephone, print, and email) to contact customers with the offer but should avoid sending excessive unsolicited offers (spam). Marketers can use direct marketing and the market feedback inherent in the approach (examining how sales change with different messaging and offers) to fulfill several marketing objectives, as shown in Figure 10.22.[35]

**Boost Direct Sales**. Direct marketing is one of the most "direct" routes to sales. A well-crafted direct marketing campaign with a popular product/service and a compelling offer that is targeted to relevant individuals can have a substantial impact on sales.

Direct marketing tactics include postal mail (such as sending printed catalogs), telemarketing (such as calling individuals with offers), electronic mail (such as "opt-in" email marketing programs), and text messages to mobile devices.

**Promote Cross-selling**. Customer databases can be analyzed for cross-selling opportunities by examining correlations among products. For example, a person purchasing a *Harry Potter* book would be likely to respond to an offer for another such book.

**Figure 10.22** Direct Marketing: Objectives

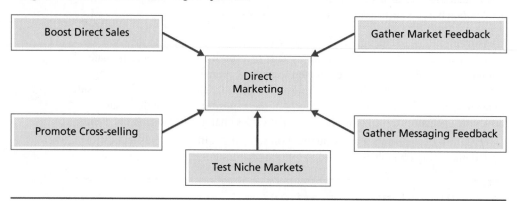

Direct marketing tactics include analyzing databases (checking correlations among products), checking purchase histories (targeting individuals who have purchased one of the highly correlated products), and then developing cross-selling offers (acknowledging the first sale and stating why the individual would be interested in complementary products).

**Gather Market Feedback**. Marketers can gather market feedback on the effectiveness of direct marketing efforts by measuring response rates with different tactics.

Tactics include varying which features get emphasized on offers (some features can be more important to customers than others), alternating the order of the features (if multiple features are offered, change the order in which they are mentioned), and mentioning the number of features (in some offers, mention one or two key features; in others, mention many features).

**Gather Messaging Feedback**. Companies can test the effectiveness of their product or service messaging by developing different offers with different messaging, and then comparing the response rates of each.

Direct marketing tactics include company/product emphasis (such as emphasizing the product in the offer and the company in another), the benefits orientation (some markets, such as that of technical designers, prefer messaging that emphasizes features, not benefits), and the offer itself (such as testing the response rates between a free 30-day trial or 10 percent off the price).

**Test Niche Markets**. Companies with broad offerings can use direct marketing to cater to niche markets. For example, outdoor gear retailer L.L. Bean (llbean.com) uses a variety of catalogs to target different market niches.

Direct marketing tactics include niche market catalogs (print or online catalogs with products and services appealing to niche markets) and unique offers to each niche.

Figure 10.23 presents a decision chart on selecting different direct marketing tactics for typical marketing objectives.

**Figure 10.23** Decision Chart: Direct Marketing Tactics to Target Specific Marketing Objectives

| Marketing Objective | Description | Guidelines: Recommended Tactics |
| --- | --- | --- |
| Boost direct sales | Increase sales substantially by contacting customers directly with offer | Print<br>Telemarketing<br>Email<br>Mobile devices |
| Promote cross-selling | Boost sales by analyzing correlations among products and services, then cross-selling them. | Database analysis<br>Purchase history<br>Cross-selling offers |
| Gather product/service feedback | Vary description of product or service in different offers, then measure differences in response rates | Emphasizing different features<br>Varying order of features<br>Varying number of features |
| Gather messaging feedback | Test effectiveness of messaging by comparing response rates of offers with different messaging | Company vs. product emphasis<br>Benefits vs. features emphasis<br>Offer details |
| Test niche markets | Target individual niches within markets using special offers | Niche market catalogs<br>Niche offers |

## Marketing Planning in Action

**Williams-Sonoma: At Home with Direct Marketing**. Founded in 1956, home-centered Williams-Sonoma originally specialized in selling restaurant-quality kitchenwares for home use, but quickly found that it could expand its market by targeting related market niches. It now targets six market niches with its six brands: Williams-Sonoma (cooking enthusiasts), Pottery Barn (discriminating home furnishing buyers), PB Teen (teens with needs for creative spaces), Pottery Barn Kids (children's furnishings), Williams-Sonoma Home (casual elegance), and West Elm (style-savvy customers who love modern, accessible design). Each niche has its own catalog dedicated to product offerings the niche would find relevant. Williams-Sonoma leverages its database marketing expertise to implement direct marketing tactics to targeted customers.[36, 37]

## Personal Sales

In personal selling, company representatives (or "reps") interact directly with the prospect. The approach is well suited for several situations, such as those involving complex, expensive products (such as automotive salespeople at car dealerships), high-involvement products and services (such as realtors selling homes), and transactions favoring long-term business relationships (such as business to business sales).[38]

**Figure 10.24** Decision Chart: Salesforce Staffing

| Topic | In-house Salespeople | Contractual sales force |
|---|---|---|
| Personal Sales Staffing | Salesforce size constant over time <br> Stable markets <br> Long sales cycles | Introductory life cycle stage <br> Unstable markets <br> Short sales cycles <br> Short-term sales boosts |

In the past, sales management issues were rarely addressed in marketing plans. In today's climate of lean organization management, though, sales staffs are sparse, so we must ensure that sufficient resources exist to sell the new product or service we advocate as part of our marketing plan. Companies have the choice of staffing sales positions using a direct sales force (full- or part-time employees who work exclusively for the company) or a contractual sales force (outside organizations which "lease" sales representative for a contracted period of time, often two years).

**In-house salespeople**. In-house salespeople work well in situations where salesforce sizes stay relatively constant over time (to avoid the cost of hiring, firing, and training employees), for stable markets (constant demand), and long sales cycles (prospects often value doing business with the same person for the entire sales cycle).

**Contractual sales forces**. Alternatively, contractual sales forces work well in situations such as early life cycle stages (many new companies do not have the cash to hire sales employees), unstable markets (contractually based reps are easier to terminate than employees), short sales cycles (less likelihood that turnover of contractual reps will affect sales cycles), and during short-term sales boosts (such as obtaining additional contractual salespeople to help with the holiday sales rush).

Figure 10.24 presents a decision chart on selecting between in-house salespeople and contractual sales members.

## Practical Planning

In this section, we continue demonstrating the marketing planning process using our ongoing example, Expedia online travel agent (OTA) services.

### Promotion Tactics

Because it is a new service, we will consider promotion tactics for the introductory stage of the product/service life cycle. Throughout all the marketing communications, we will maintain consistent messaging of exciting activities, exotic locales, and once-in-a-lifetime adventures.

Figure 10.25 presents the example decision chart for Expedia Adventure Vacations promotion tactics for the introduction stage. As the chart shows, our goals are to create awareness around the new service and to encourage consumers to try them.

**Figure 10.25**  Promotion Tactics: Expedia Adventure Vacations (Introduction Stage)

| Criteria | Phase: Introduction | Expedia Adventure Vacations |
| --- | --- | --- |
| Goals | Create awareness, educate customers, and stimulate trial | Create awareness around service, and encourage consumers to try vacations |
| Target Markets | Early adopters | Adventure enthusiasts |
| Push/Pull Marketing | Push: Product/service demonstrations at retailers; Pull: Educating consumers on benefits | Push efforts through Expedia-owned websites. Pull efforts through Web (including SEO & SEM), mobile devices, and social networking. |

The target markets in this case would be adventure enthusiasts. The push–pull approach includes push efforts (targeting Expedia-owned websites to include information about the vacations) and pull efforts (targeting consumers through digital marketing and other means).

## Marketing Communications Mix

Figure 10.26 shows a summary chart showing our plans for each of the marketing communication mix elements. The following elements are planned.

**Advertising**. Because this is a new service, our objective is informative advertising, to get customers familiar with the new service. Budget factors (new introduction in a crowded market with major competitors), along with a large, unidentified audience will mean a large budget. The large media buys we expect, in addition to the creativity we need, indicate an external agency.

Media will include major media advertising such as television commercials, ads in travel magazines, outdoor advertising, and less traditional advertising routes, such as Smart cars emblazoned with the Expedia logo, Expedia.com Cafes in busy airports, and billing statement inserts accompanying bills from Expedia's Citi Premier Pass World MasterCard.

**Social Media and Digital Marketing**. Social media and digital marketing will be employed extensively to build brand awareness and trust, influence acceptance of Web-based information, generate website traffic, create viral buzz, and add incoming links to improve SEO. Also, creating pathways for educational, empowering, and emotional connections will allow customers to gather travel information, post opinions, and share their adventure travel experiences with others.

Social networking will include content on Expedia's Facebook page (facebook.com/expedia), MySpace page (myspace.com/expedia), and Twitter (twitter.com/expedia). Blogs will include Expedia TripTips, Expedia's WordPress blog (expediatriptips.com). SEO will consist of edits to content on Expedia.com to achieve high organic search results, as well as inbound links from Expedia-related sites, such as social networking pages. SEM will include Google AdWords and other tools to attract customers. Video sharing will include YouTube's Expedia Channel (youtube.com/user/expedia). Viral marketing includes a spoof of the ultimate adventure trip—Flights to Mars.

**Figure 10.26** Marketing Communications Mix Elements: Expedia Adventure Vacations

| Element | Description | Expedia Adventure Vacations |
|---|---|---|
| Advertising | Any paid form of non-personal promotion by an identified sponsor | Objective: Informative advertising<br>Budget Factors: New service; High market share; High competition; Crowded market; Substitutes available<br>In-house vs. External: Large account; High spend levels; Objectivity required; Simple offering; Creativity required<br>Media: TV, Travel magazines, Outdoor, Company logo cars, Branded airport cafes, Billing statement inserts |
| Social Media | Promote "networked conversations" by moving from one-to-many communications model to many-to-many model | Social Networking<br>Blog<br>SEO<br>SEM<br>Video Sharing<br>Viral Marketing<br>Mobile Devices<br>Internet Advertisements<br>Company Website<br>Online Newsletter |
| Sales Promotions | Short-term incentives enticing people to purchase a particular product or service | Standard loyalty program<br>Elite loyalty program<br>Expedia co-branded credit card |
| Public Relations | Build and maintain organizational reputation in the media | Objective: Build awareness<br>SEO-enabled press releases<br>Publicity (articles) |
| Events & Experiences | Sponsored activity with brand as co-star | Objective: Build awareness<br>Sponsor adventure-related events, like extreme sports |
| Direct Marketing | Marketing message targeted to individual customer | Objective: Boost adoption<br>Email campaign to target adventure travel enthusiasts |
| Personal Selling | One-on-one interaction to sell a product or service | Expedia Adventure Travel content given to members of Expedia Travel Agent Affiliate Program |

Mobile device tools include TripAssist, an app for the Apple iPhone. Internet advertisements include usage on travel-related websites and portal sites such as Yahoo! Expedia's website will include dedicated Web pages for adventure travel with a sign-up area for *Expedia Email*, Expedia's online newsletter.

**Sales Promotions**. Expedia Travel Adventures should minimize the use of deep-discount sales promotions to avoid being perceived as emphasizing low cost over the quality of its adventures. In general, promotions will be limited to Expedia's existing rewards programs for all customers, including the Thank You Rewards traveler loyalty program, the Citi PremierPass/Expedia World MasterCard loyalty program, and the Expedia ElitePlus program for its best customers.

**Public Relations**. To publicize the new Adventure Vacations, Expedia will issue SEO-enabled press releases announcing the new alternative to traditional vacations. Weblinks in the press release will take users to Expedia Web pages showing adventure travel choices, as well as travel tips for adventure travelers. In addition, Expedia will work with travel magazines and websites to get articles published showcasing the new Expedia Adventure Vacations.

**Events and Experiences**. Expedia will investigate sponsorship opportunities of adventure-oriented activities, such as extreme sports events to target adventure seekers.

**Direct Marketing.** Expedia will leverage its impressive direct marketing operations to conduct email campaigns to email lists filtered to emphasize adventure travel enthusiasts.

**Personal Selling.** Brochures outlining the highlights of the Expedia Adventure Travel program will be given to members in the Expedia Travel Agents Affiliate Program. Affiliates can then offer their clients the opportunity to embark on an Expedia Adventure Travel trip.

## Summary

As an unknown person once said, "Two-thirds of promotion is motion." Effective promotion tactics (along with masterful execution) are vital to the success of marketing ventures and make up a significant portion of many marketing plans.

The chapter started by examining how promotion goals, target markets, and push–pull approaches can vary during the life cycle of a product or service. For example, the promotion goals during the introduction stage of the life cycle are to create awareness and stimulate trial, whereas the goal at maturity is to differentiate the product or service from that of the competition.

We then quickly reviewed different promotional vehicles, such as advertising and social media, to get an understanding of when they should be used.

Advertising can be broadly defined as any paid form of non-personal promotion by an identified sponsor. To aid in the decisions of advertising tactics, we reviewed a number of decision tables, including advertising objectives, budget factors, the use of external agencies, and media usage.

Social media and digital marketing seek to engage prospects using networked conversations. We can use many tools in our efforts to promote such conversations, including social networking (such as Facebook and LinkedIn), blogs (such as those created using Blogger and WordPress), SEO (search engine optimization), SEM (search engine marketing), video sharing (such as YouTube), viral marketing (such as BlendTec's "Will it Blend?" viral campaign), mobile devices (such as Expedia's iPhone travel apps), Internet advertisements (such as banner ads), company websites (such as community content on Expedia.com), and online newsletters (such as *Expedia Email*).

Sales promotions are incentives, often short-term ones, to stimulate the demand of products and services. Sales promotions are divided into consumer promotions (targeting end users with promotions such as coupons and rebates) and trade promotions (targeting distribution channel members with incentives such as bonuses and discounts to carry new products and services).

The practice of public relations (PR) manages the communication between an organization and its internal stakeholders (such as communicating with employees) and external stakeholders (such as issuing press releases). PR is an effective promotion tactic because it can be viewed as credible while still being cost-effective.

Events and experiences can be an effective way for companies to show consumers how the brand relates to them. For example, bicycle manufacturer Cannondale sponsors bicycle Division 1 road racing teams to engage with bicycle enthusiasts.

Direct marketing promotions target end users directly, leveraging databases of contacts and different contact techniques. Marketers can use campaign feedback to infer the effectiveness of product features, messaging, and tapping into niche markets.

We concluded the chapter with our Practical Planning section, showing how the decision charts could be used to determine promotion tactics for online travel agent Expedia.

The next chapter covers finance measures to help ensure commercial success of the product or service.

 ## Key Terms

**Click-through rate (CTR)** Percentage of people clicking on a Web-based promotion compared to the total population viewing the ad. (p. 223)

**Consumer promotions** Sales promotions targeted at consumers; see also trade promotions. (p. 227)

**Contextual advertising** Advertising approach that scans the text of recently viewed websites for keywords and delivers ads targeting those keywords. (p. 225)

**Conversion rate optimization (CRO)** CRO seeks to increase customer revenue through improvements in conversion rate, such as increasing conversions from Web surfer to paying customer. (p. 223)

**Direct marketing** Marketing through a promotion using messages targeted to, and delivered to, individual customers. (p. 211)

**Informative Advertising** Advertising objective, seeking to acquaint the target audience with important facts about the company's product or service. (p. 211)

**Integrated marketing communications (IMC)** Maintaining consistent messaging across multiple media with the goal of mutual reinforcement. (p. 209)

**Location-based social networking** Enhancing the social networking experience by incorporating location, such as learning about events occurring nearby, or "checking in" with local merchants. Sample apps include Facebook places, Foursquare, and Gowalla. (p. 209)

**Media frequency** Number of times an average person is exposed to a particular message within a given time period. (p. 219)

**Media impact** Qualitative value of a particular medium exposure. (p. 219)

**Media reach** Refers to the audience size exposed to a particular message at least once during the specified time period. (p. 219)

**Mobile marketing** Promotional activity designed for delivery to mobile phones, usually part of a multichannel campaign. Popular uses include location-based promotions, mobile search-based promotions, and app-vertising (branded mobile mobile phone applications). See also Location-based social networking. (p. 223)

**Personal selling** Sales approach where company representatives interact directly with the prospect. (p. 211)

**Persuasive advertising** Advertising objective, seeking to create liking and stimulate purchase of the company's product or service by its target market. (p. 211)

**Product placement** Marketing technique to increase visibility and demonstrate usage scenarios by embedding goods or services in content, such as television programs, movies, and video games. (p. 219)

**Public relations** Set of activities companies use to build and maintain their reputations in the media. (p. 211)

**Push–Pull Marketing** Balancing efforts between promotion efforts to distribution channel members (push) and efforts toward end consumers (pull). (p. 205)

**Reinforcement advertising** Advertising objective, seeking to convince current purchasers that they have made the right decision. (p. 215)

**Reminder advertising** Advertising objective, seeking to stimulate repeat purchase behavior of products or services already launched in the market. (p. 215)

**Sales promotions** Short-term incentives given by companies to entice people to purchase particular products or services. (p. 211)

**Search engine marketing (SEM)** Also called **pay per click (PPC)**, SEM places ads in Internet search engine results that correspond to keywords in user searches. (p. 223)

**Search engine optimization (SEO)** Seeks to improve nonpaid (also called "organic") Internet search results of search engines by various means, such as adjusting website content. (p. 223)

**Social media and digital marketing** Adopting a "many-to-many" publishing model to encourage user interaction instead of the traditional "one-to-many" promotion style. (p. 209)

**Social networking** Defined in the 1950s as associations of people drawn together by family, work or hobby. Businesses often use social networking for promotion-based activities such as engaging with customers, linking with other professionals, and advertising to targeted segments. (p. 223)

**Trade promotions** Sales promotions targeted at distribution channel members; see also consumer promotions. (p. 227)

**Video Sharing** Posting video clips to websites such as Vimeo and YouTube to share with others online. (p. 223)

**Viral marketing** Marketing technique to encourage the spreading of messages (such as a virus) to increase visibility. (p. 223)

 ## Discussion Questions

1. How does the concept of "promotion" change with the introduction of Web 2.0 technologies, such as those supporting social media tools?

2. Given their high cost and the prevalence of social media, why do so many organizations still outsource their creative promotion work to advertising agencies?

3. How can organizations ensure consistent messaging across all forms of promotion, when (especially in large companies) different people—and even different departments—are responsible for different promotion vehicles?

 ## Exercises

1. Identify the promotion goals for your product or service based on its stage in the life cycle.

2. Select the social media and digital marketing vehicles to implement for your product or service using the decision tables presented in this chapter.

3. Develop a summary table of the promotion tactics for your product or service based on the summary table shown in the Practical Planning section.

# 11

# Finance

## INTRODUCTION

Organizations consider financial viability before embarking on a new project. To that end, we cover some basic financial tools that marketers should include as part of the marketing plan.

## CHAPTER CHECKLIST:

Marketing plan sections discussed in this chapter

❏ **Break-even point**: Determining the point when product/service revenue will equal or exceed costs

❏ **Pro forma operating income statement**: Estimating profitability of the proposed new project

❏ **Capital budgeting analysis**: Appraising proposed new projects as long-term financial investments

❏ **Marketing budget**: Allocating organizational funds to translate marketing plan goals into action

Executives are keenly interested in the financial aspects of marketing plans
*Source:* Shutterstock

# Break-even Point

When organizations invest in new products and services, they want to know the point at which the revenue from that product or service will equal or exceed its costs. The point is called the **break-even point**. Break-even points can be described in units (i.e., how many units must we produce before we begin to turn a profit?) or in time (at what time in the future will we begin to make a profit?).[1]

Break-even analysis is best explained by example. Suppose we are the marketing managers for a fictitious company called Acme. Acme designs and manufactures consumer electronics. We discover a market need for a new home theater receiver, which we plan to call the X-1000.

To construct a break-even analysis, we gather the following information: NAICS code, fixed cost, unit cost, the manufacturer's suggested retail price (MSRP) of the unit, and a sales forecast that shows the projected unit sales over time. Figure 11.1 summarizes the data for our analysis.

## Fixed Cost

As we learned in the pricing chapter, fixed costs are costs which stay constant regardless of the number of units made (within limits). Examples include rent, depreciation, and insurance.

**Figure 11.1**  Acme X-1000 Home Theater Receiver Financial Data (Fictitious Example)

| Financial Data | Description |
| --- | --- |
| Fixed Cost | Fixed Cost, Total: $400,000 |
| Unit Cost | Cost Per Unit: $200 |
| Price | Price Per Unit: $400 |
| Sales Forecast | Projected Unit Sales |
| | • Year 1: 1,800 Units |
| | • Year 2: 4,200 Units |
| | • Year 3: 2,500 Units |

## Unit Cost

As we covered earlier, unit cost is the cost to produce each unit, including material and labor as well as any allocated overhead costs. In equation form, we have: Unit cost = Variable cost + Fixed cost/Unit sales. Variable costs are costs which vary according to the number of units made, such as parts and materials per unit, as well as direct production labor per unit. In our simplified example here, we assume no overhead allocations, so our unit costs are the same as our variable costs.

## Price

We use the pricing techniques discussed in the pricing chapter to arrive at a suggested price. For example, we might conduct market research to determine typical competitive pricing for products similar to ours, as well as poll representatives of our target market for indications for what they would expect to pay for such a unit.

## Sales Forecast

Our sales forecast gives us the expected number of units to be sold per year for the next three years. We arrived at the forecast by examining the actual sales history of similar units sold in the past, adjusting those numbers to reflect current situations.

## Break-even Volume Calculation

With our data assembled, we are now ready to calculate the break-even point. The break-even volume (number of units) is calculated according to the following formula:

$$\text{Break-even Volume} = (\text{Fixed Cost})/(\text{Price} - \text{Unit Cost})$$

Inserting our data, we get:

$$\text{Break-even Volume} = (\$400,000)/(\$400 - \$200) = 2,000 \text{ units}$$

**Figure 11.2**  Break-even Chart: Acme X-1000 Home Theater Receiver

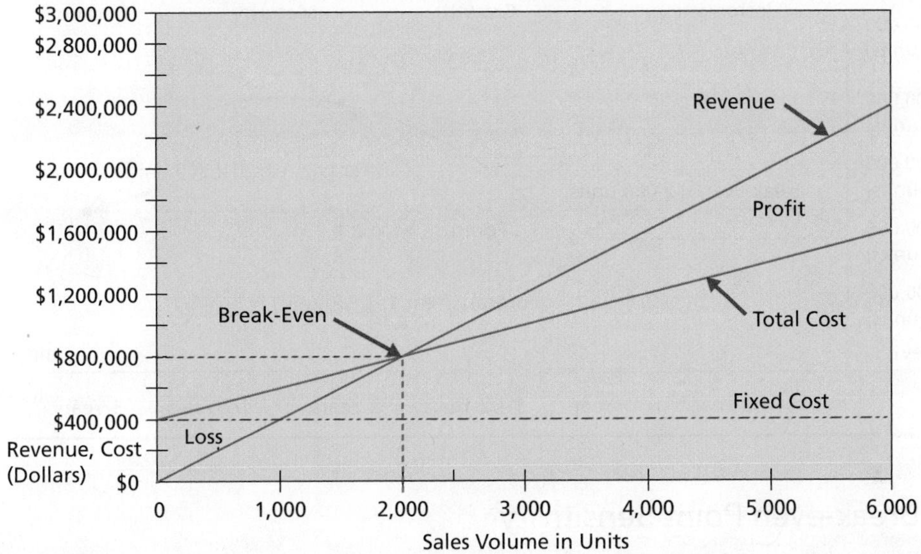

*Source:* Adapted with permission from Braun, Tietz, and Harrison, *Managerial Accounting*, 2nd ed. (Upper Saddle River, NJ: Pearson Prentice-Hall, 2010), Figure 7.4, p. 372.

We can graph the result to get visual insight into the data. Figure 11.2 shows the break-even chart, which includes the lines for total cost and revenue. The lines meet at the break-even point.

The chart agrees with the equation: We break even at 2,000 units.

## Break-even Time Calculation

In order to get the expected time for break-even, we can superimpose our sales forecast for the next three years on a typical S-shaped sales plot. The result is Figure 11.3, which shows the forecasted sales for years one, two, and three, as plotted on a typical sales plot. The sales plot shows the familiar product life cycle: introduction, growth, maturity, and decline. Not surprisingly in the fickle consumer electronics market, our life cycle only lasts about three years. The plot also shows the break-even point. Here, our break-even point occurs at about the one-year mark.

### Key Terms

**Break-even point**   Volume of sales (or calendar date) when sales revenue of a product or service equals its costs.

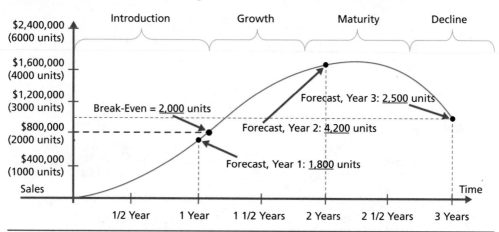

**Figure 11.3** Forecasted Sales Graph: Acme X-1000 Home Theater Receiver

## Break-even Point Sensitivity

We can determine the sensitivity of our break-even point to changes in costs. For example, if we reduce our fixed costs from $400,000 to $350,000, and reduce our variable costs from $200 to $150 (through cost reduction efforts like supplier price negotiations), we decrease our break-even point to only 1,400 units:

$$\text{Break-even Volume} = (\$350,000)/(\$400 - \$150) = 1,400 \text{ units}$$

If our fixed and variable costs rise to $450,000 and $250, respectively, we have a problem on our hands, because our break-even point increases to 3,000 units, delaying payback substantially:

$$\text{Break-even Volume} = (\$450,000)/(\$400 - \$250) = 3,000 \text{ units}$$

Therefore, we can see that changes in fixed and variable costs can have a big impact on the break-even point, as well as profitability, which we cover in the next section.

## Marketing Planning in Action

**X Marks the (Break-even) Spot**. Xmarks, the formerly free bookmark syncing service, plans to start charging for its service. Xmarks had originally proposed to stop the service, but reconsidered after overwhelming user support for a paid version. Xmarks calculated that it needs $4 million to break even each year, which could be a problem. That level of revenue would represent converting 10 percent of their user base to paying for the service. But the conversion rate for free to premium users typically runs at only 1–3 percent. Xmarks hopes to beat the odds by leveraging the enthusiasm of its loyal user base.[2]

# Pro Forma Income Statement

Our next step is to forecast the income that our product or service will generate over the next three years. To do this, we generate a **pro forma operating income statement**. The Latin term *pro forma* means "as a matter of form," and shows expected financial results of a venture in a standard format. Pro formas are widely used for new ventures, because they indicate the anticipated profitability of proposed plans.[3]

## Revenue

Revenue is the total amount of money we make selling our product before any costs are subtracted. To calculate revenue, multiply the number of units forecasted to be sold by the price per unit. For example, in year one, our forecast shows that we expect to sell 1,800 units. At a price of $400.00 per unit, the expected total revenue should be $720,000.

## Cost of Goods Sold (COGS)

**Cost of goods sold (COGS)** represents the direct costs we incur in making the product. In some cases, COGS might be higher than the manufacturing unit costs due to other direct costs, such as shipping. To calculate COGS, multiply the number of units forecasted to be sold by the cost per unit. For example, in year one, our forecast shows we expect to sell 1,800 units. At a cost of $200 per unit, the expected cost of goods sold is $360,000.

## Gross Margin Amount

The **gross margin amount** represents the amount of money we make before any expenses are subtracted. To calculate the gross margin amount, we subtract the full absorption cost from revenue. The full absorption cost is defined as the sum of variable costs (direct labor and materials costs) as well as overhead costs allocated to that product line. In our simplified example, we assumed no overhead, so the gross margin would simply be revenue less the cost of goods sold. Alternatively, we can use the term **contribution margin**, which is computed as revenue less variable costs.

---

### Key Terms

**Pro forma operating income statement**    Financial statement showing expected financial results of a venture in a standard format. Typically includes projected sales, cost of goods sold, expenses, and resulting operating income.

**Cost of goods sold (COGS)** Direct costs related to the production of goods, such as labor and materials and associated costs, such as shipping.

**Gross margin amount**    Gross margin amount is calculated by subtracting full absorption cost from revenue. Full absorption cost is the sum of variable cost and allocated overhead.

**Contribution margin**    Amount of money contributed to the organization from product sales. Calculated by subtracting variable costs from revenue.

To continue with our example, in year one, we would subtract our COGS, $360,000, from our revenue, $720,000, to arrive at our gross margin amount, $360,000.

## Gross Margin Percentage

The **gross margin percentage** represents the contribution margin divided by revenue. We can compare our gross margin with that of other similar products in our industry and determine if we are higher or lower than the industry average (higher is better). To calculate gross margin percentage, use the following formula:

$$\text{Gross Margin Percentage} = (\text{Revenue} - \text{Cost of Goods Sold})/\text{Revenue}$$

For example, in year one, we divide $360,000 by $720,000 to arrive at a 50 percent gross margin percentage.

## Expenses, Total

The total expenses represent all the miscellaneous, nonproduction costs associated with making the product. It includes expenses such as rent, depreciation, insurance, and advertising.

## Operating Income

To calculate operating income in our examples, we subtract total expenses from the gross margin amount. For example, in year one, we would subtract expenses of $390,000 from our gross margin expenses of $360,000 to arrive at – $30,000. The negative income represents a loss, which is not uncommon for new products in their first year of production.

---

### Marketing Planning in Action

**Apple iPad Magazine App Ads: 5 Times the Revenue**. The wide reach of the iPad commands an advertising premium, with companies paying newspaper and magazine publishers up to five times as much to place ads in their iPad applications as similar advertising on standard websites. Although online ads still generate just a fraction of news companies' advertising revenue, early evidence suggests the iPad can help publishers get more money out of advertisers. While challenges exist for the potential new source of ad revenue, publishers are optimistic in the potential of tablet devices for their industry. According to Lou Cona, executive vice-president of Conde Nast Media Group, "I think it will redefine publishing and also redefine how advertisers connect with our audience."[4]

---

Figure 11.4 shows a typical simplified pro forma income statement.

**Figure 11.4**  Pro Forma Income Statement: Acme X-1000 Home Theater Receiver

| Financial Element | Year 1 | Year 2 | Year 3 |
|---|---|---|---|
| Revenue:<br>= (Units × Price/Unit) | $720,000<br>= (1,800 units × $400) | $1,680,000<br>= (4,200 units × $400) | $1,000,000<br>= (2,500 units × $400) |
| Cost of Goods Sold (COGS)<br>= (Units × Cost/Unit) | $360,000<br>= (1,800 units × $200) | $840,000<br>= (4,200 units × $200) | $500,000<br>= (2,500 units × $200) |
| Gross Margin Amount<br>= Revenue − COGS | $360,000<br>= $720,000 − $360,000 | $840,000<br>= $1,680,000 − $840,000 | $500,000<br>= $1,000,000 − $500,000 |
| Gross Margin %<br>= (Revenue − COGS)/Revenue | 50%<br>= $360,000/$720,000 | 50%<br>= $840,000/$1,680,000 | 50%<br>= $500,000/$1,000,000 |
| Expenses, Total | $390,000 | $435,000 | $300,000 |
| Operating Income | −$30,000<br>= $360,000 − $390,000 | $405,000<br>= $840,000 − $435,000 | $200,000<br>= $500,000 − $300,000 |

# Capital Budgeting Analysis

We can decide whether the proposed project is a good use of the company's capital investment funds by conducting a **capital budgeting analysis**. Figure 11.5 shows an example.

As an example of capital budgeting analysis, suppose we must decide between two proposed projects. The cash flow from project 1 begins relatively strongly, but quickly diminishes. By comparison, the cash flow from project 2 starts small, but quickly rises higher than the initial cash flow from project 1. Which one should we choose?

**Figure 11.5**  Capital Budgeting Analysis: Selection of Alternative Projects

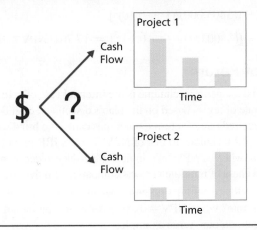

In this section, we discuss two common capital budgeting techniques to guide us in the decision: net present value (NPV) and internal rate of return (IRR).[5]

## Net Present Value (NPV)

**Net present value (NPV)** analysis incorporates the time value of money (acknowledging that a dollar now is worth more than a dollar later) by discounting the cash flows from the proposed project to their present value using the discount rate.

The **discount rate** (the rate by which the cash flows are reduced to reflect the time value of money) is generally the rate of return that the organization could earn on an investment with similar financial risk.

To calculate NPV, we sum up the discounted cash flows from each year of the proposed project. NPVs greater than 0 mean that the proposed plan generates more discounted cash flow than an investment with equivalent financial risk, so it is a wise use of capital. To calculate NPV, we use the following formula:

$$\text{NPV} = [(\text{Cash flow from year 0})/(1 + \text{discount rate})^{t=0}]$$
$$+ [(\text{Cash flow from year 1})/(1 + \text{discount rate})^{t=1}]$$
$$+ [\text{remaining discounted cash flows}]$$

For example, if our Acme project has a discount rate of 10 percent and required a $450,000 initial investment (negative $450,000 cash flow at year 0), and pays out cash flows of –$30,000 at year 1, $405,000 at year 2, and $200,000 at year 3 (actual cash flows can differ from operating incomes due to depreciation, tax considerations, and other factors), then we would calculate its NPV as follows:

$$\text{NPV} = [(-\$450,000)/(1 + 0.10)^0]$$
$$+ [(-\$30,000)/(1 + 0.10)^1]$$
$$+ [(\$405,000)/(1 + 0.10)^2]$$
$$+ [(\$200,000)/(1 + 0.10)^3] = \$7,701: \text{NPV} > 0, \text{ so approve plan}$$

## Internal Rate of Return

Another popular capital budgeting technique is the **internal rate of return (IRR)** analysis, which calculates the rate of return based on the plan's discounted cash flows and compares it to the company's required rate of return (sometimes called the **hurdle rate**). Some companies prefer the IRR technique to that of NPV, because IRR provides the actual expected rate of return, whereas NPV only indicates a go/no-go decision of a single project, or the relative attractiveness of multiple projects compared with their respective NPVs.

To calculate the IRR, we set NPV to zero (because the actual rate of return is the same as the "discount rate" when NPV = 0), then solve for the rate of return. We demonstrate the process on our Acme example:

$$\text{NPV} = 0 = [(-\$450,000)/(1 + \text{IRR})^0]$$
$$+ [(-\$30,000)/(1 + \text{IRR})^1]$$
$$+ [(\$405,000)/(1 + \text{IRR})^2]$$
$$+ [(\$200,000)/(1 + \text{IRR})^3] \rightarrow \text{IRR} = 10.8\%$$

Therefore, if 10.8 percent exceeds the organization's hurdle rate, the project is likely to gain financial approval.

## Marketing Planning in Action

**VC Financing: Clearing the Financial Approval Hurdle**:. Venture capitalists (VCs) and angel investors seek certain minimum return rates (hurdle rates) in their investments in small companies. In addition, they demand minimum market sizes to support sustainably large companies (many VCs look for $500 million + market sizes to enable company sizes of $100 million), moderate financial risk (as risk goes up, so does the VC's hurdle rates), and, of course, a strong understanding of the market.[6]

Venture capitalists and other investors consider projected results, like rates of return, in their investment decision
*Source*: Shutterstock

## Key Terms

**Net present value (NPV)**   Method of discounting future cash flows to calculate future value in today's dollars. Often used in capital budgeting analysis.

**Discount rate**   Rate by which cash flows are reduced to reflect the time value of money.

**Internal rate of return (IRR)**   Rate of return used in **capital budgeting analysis** to measure and compare the profitability of proposed long-term investments.

## Marketing Budget

Budgets offer a mechanism for translating marketing plan goals (like widespread exposure of a marketing message) to action, by allocating amounts that support those goals (like spending on social media). Consequently, budgeting for marketing plan projects should follow the goals and objectives of those marketing plans.

For small businesses, SCORE (Service Corps of Retired Executives, "the Counselors to America's Small Business") and the U.S. SBA (Small Business Administration) advise a total marketing budget of 2 percent–10 percent of sales, noting that budgets will vary according to the market, the product or service, and other factors. In fact, some companies, like those in retail and pharmaceuticals, can exceed 20 percent during their peak brand-building years.[7]

Marketing plan budgets will typically contain some or all of the expenses described below.

### Advertising Expenses

Typical expenses include items such as creative development, media placements (such as television, radio, or print), agency costs, and advertising to distribution channels (for push-oriented campaigns). Advertising is the largest expense category for many companies.

### Social Media and Digital Marketing Expenses

Common expenses include items such as SEO (search engine optimization expenses, often done by external contractors), SEM (search engine marketing expenses, paid to Internet advertising organizations like Google for its AdWords program), webinar hosting expenses (like those for WebEx), and advertising done on websites and mobile devices.

Depending on the organization's accounting standards, the budget might also include labor for creation of content and monitoring of social networking sites, blogs, videos, and online newsletters. This budget category is growing rapidly, with studies finding some companies allocating over 20 percent of their budget toward it.[8]

### Sales Promotions Expenses

Normal expenses include the cost of free samples, co-op ads, coupons, rebates, and contests.

### Public Relations Expenses

Customary expenses include items such as press release wire fees (such as those of *BusinessWire*), subscriptions to industry analyst reports and services, press-kit materials, and press tours. Some organizations also include marketing research expenses in this category.

### Events and Experiences Expenses

Typical consumer market event expenses include items such as the cost of developing, advertising, and holding an event created by the organization. Alternatively, it can include the cost of sponsoring an external event, like a golf championship.

Business market event expenses generally include costs for industry trade shows. Virtually every industry has its own trade show, and sponsoring the show, such as staffing a booth there, can increase exposure within the company's target market.

## Direct Marketing Expenses

Common expenses include items such as purchasing contact lists to target individual prospects (such as fees from contact list provider InfoUSA, infousa.com), email transmission fees based on the quantity of emails sent (such as expenses from email delivery firm Constant Contact, constantcontact.com), printing and mailing expenses (for direct mail campaigns), as well as the cost of the offer that compels targets to respond.

## Personal Selling Expenses

Selling expenses will depend if the sales force is comprised of employees of the organization, or members of a contracted sales force.

Figure 11.6 summarizes a sample marketing plan budget format. The format shows a sample allocation of budget over different types of marketing vehicles, such as advertising and social media. The format also includes space to allocate marketing budget over the months of the year. For example, the Practical Planning section of this chapter shows how Expedia can assign different categories of its budget over the time period of the plan.

In some cases, like industrial products, line item expenditures remain relatively constant month after month. In other cases, like sales of children's toys, marketing expenses increase sharply toward the latter half of the year to accelerate sales in the Holiday season.

**Figure 11.6** Sample Marketing Budget (Simplified)

| Budget Category | Amount % | Jan | Feb | Mar | Apr | May | Jun | Jul | Aug | Sep | Oct | Nov | Dec |
|---|---|---|---|---|---|---|---|---|---|---|---|---|---|
| Advertising | 20 | | | | | | | | | | | | |
| Social Media & Digital Marketing | 20 | | | | | | | | | | | | |
| Sales Promotions | 10 | | | | | | | | | | | | |
| Public Relations | 10 | | | | | | | | | | | | |
| Events | 10 | | | | | | | | | | | | |
| Direct Marketing | 10 | | | | | | | | | | | | |
| Personal Selling | 10 | | | | | | | | | | | | |
| Total | 100 | | | | | | | | | | | | |

**Key Terms**

**Hurdle rate**    Company's required rate of return. Often used in capital budgeting analysis.

Chipotle Mexican Grill keeps the marketing budget lean by avoiding traditional advertising
*Source:* Alamy

## Marketing Planning in Action

**Chipotle: Burrito Buzz on a Budget**. Chipotle Mexican Grill saves its marketing dollars by avoiding traditional advertising, like TV commercials. Chipotle restricts its small amount of advertising to billboards or radio, spending only $4.5 million in 2006 (1 percent of its annual revenue). Indeed, it spends less advertising budget in a year than McDonald's spends in 48 hours. Instead of advertising, Chipotle relies on building sales through word of mouth, an approach many perceive as more credible than paid pitches by major corporations. The approach has worked, with same-store sales increasing by 13.7 percent in 2006, its ninth straight year of double-digit increases. "Chipotle so far has got it nailed," says Dan Buczaczer, senior vice-president of Denuo, a new-media consulting division of Publicis Groupe, "You have people evangelizing the brand because they love it."[9]

# Practical Planning

In this section, we continue demonstrating the marketing planning process using our ongoing example, Expedia online travel agent (OTA) services. To show how the process works we show how the financial analyses would be applied for use with our Expedia example.

In the previous chapters, we decided on the marketing mix tactics for our Expedia adventure travel vacation packages. We now continue the process by executing financial analyses for the new offering.

**Break-even Point**. Figure 11.7 presents the proposed cost structure and sales forecast. Fixed costs cover the funds to develop the packages (such as legal fees for contracts with travel providers). Unit cost represents the average total amount paid to travel providers for the vacations, as well as internal costs to administer the system, on a per-client basis. Price is an average for all vacation packages (actual prices will vary widely, depending on the details of the trip). The sales forecast is based on the strong growth rate anticipated for this segment of travel, while acknowledging that total numbers will be low at first due to the niche nature of this offering. (Fictitious financial data are shown here to preserve confidentiality.)

We calculate our break-even point as follows:

$$\text{Break-even Volume} = (\text{Fixed Cost})/(\text{Price} - \text{Unit Cost})$$

$$\text{Break-even Volume} = (\$20,000)/(\$2,000 - \$1,800) = 100 \text{ trips}$$

Because the break-even volume is the same as the projected number of trips for our first year of operation, we will break even at the end of the first year.

**Pro Forma Operating Income Statement**. We move on now to our pro forma operating income statement, shown in Figure 11.8. The statement shows no operating income in the first year, with net income gains in subsequent years. The statement also shows a consistent 10 percent gross margin percentage. We plan to work with suppliers to reduce costs, thereby increasing the gross margin during actual operations.

---

**Figure 11.7** Expedia Adventure Vacation Packages, Financial Data (Fictitious Data)

| Financial Data | Description |
| --- | --- |
| Fixed Cost | Fixed Cost, Total: $20,000 |
| Unit Cost | Cost Per Unit: $1,800 |
| Price | Average Price/Trip: $2,000 |
| Sales Forecast | Projected Unit Sales<br>• Year 1: 100 trips $\times$ $2,000/trip = $200,000<br>• Year 2: 150 trips $\times$ $2,000/trip = $300,000<br>• Year 3: 200 trips $\times$ $2,000/trip = $400,000 |

**Figure 11.8** Expedia Adventure Vacation Packages, Pro Forma Income Statement (Fictitious Data)

| Financial Element | Year 1 | Year 2 | Year 3 |
|---|---|---|---|
| Revenue: | $200,000 | $300,000 | $400,000 |
| Cost of Goods Sold = (Units × Cost/Unit) | $180,000 = (100 units × $1,800) | $270,000 = (150 units × $1,800) | $360,000 = (200 units × $1,800) |
| Gross Margin Amount = Revenue – COGS | $20,000 = $200,000 – $180,000 | $30,000 = $300,000 – $270,000 | $40,000 = $400,000 – $360,000 |
| Gross Margin % = Gross Margin/Revenue | 10% = $20,000/$200,000 | 10% = $30,000/$300,000 | 10% = $40,000/$400,000 |
| Expenses, Total | $20,000 | $26,000 | $32,000 |
| Operating Income | 0 = $20,000 – $20,000 | $4,000 = $30,000 – $26,000 | $8,000 = $40,000 – $32,000 |

**Capital Budgeting Analysis**. If we assume an $8,000 initial investment, a 10 percent discount rate, and annual cash flows of $0, $4,000, and $8,000, respectively (as we saw earlier, actual cash flows can differ from operating incomes due to a variety of factors), then the NPV for the project can be shown to be positive:

$$NPV = [(-\$8,000)/(1 + 0.10)^0] + (\$0)/(1 + 0.10)^1] + [(\$4,000)/(1 + 0.10)^2]$$

$$+ [(\$8,000)/(1 + 0.10)^3] = \$1,316$$

**Marketing Budget**. Figure 11.9 shows the proposed marketing budget for the project. The budget only includes marketing efforts dedicated toward Expedia Adventure Vacation packages; Expedia will continue to run its general brand-building campaigns in addition to the Adventure Vacation packages effort.

**Figure 11.9** Example Adventure Vacation Packages, Marketing Budget (Fictitious Data)

| Budget Category | Amount % | Jan | Feb | Mar | Apr | May | Jun | Jul | Aug | Sep | Oct | Nov | Dec |
|---|---|---|---|---|---|---|---|---|---|---|---|---|---|
| Advertising | 30 | 1 | 1 | 1 | 1 | 1 | 1 | 5 | 5 | 2 | 2 | 5 | 5 |
| Social Media & Digital Marketing | 40 | 2 | 2 | 2 | 2 | 2 | 2 | 6 | 6 | 2 | 2 | 6 | 6 |
| Sales Promotions | 5 | 0.4 | 0.4 | 0.4 | 0.4 | 0.4 | 0.4 | 0.4 | 0.4 | 0.4 | 0.4 | 0.4 | 0.4 |
| Public Relations | 5 | 0.1 | 0.1 | 0.1 | 0.1 | 0.1 | 0.1 | 1 | 1 | 0.1 | 0.1 | 1 | 1 |
| Events | 10 | 0.2 | 0.2 | 0.2 | 0.2 | 0.2 | 0.2 | 2 | 2 | 0.2 | 0.2 | 2 | 2 |
| Direct Marketing | 5 | 0.1 | 0.1 | 0.1 | 0.1 | 0.1 | 0.1 | 1 | 1 | 0.1 | 0.1 | 1 | 1 |
| Personal Selling | 5 | 1 | 1 | 1 | 1 | 1 | | | | | | | |
| Total | 100 | | | | | | | | | | | | |

The proposed budget level is 6 percent of projected annual sales. Therefore, the first-year budget would be $12,000, the second year would be $18,000, and the fourth year would be $24,000. The budget will be allocated in a varying manner, with increased spending in the summer and end-of-year high-travel periods (values in the figure are approximate due to round-off error). Due to the Web-intensive nature of Expedia, a substantial amount of the budget is spent on social media and digital marketing.

The budget line items break down as follows.

- **Advertising Expenses**: Costs include creative development and media placement for ads in travel magazines, outdoor venues, and other media, using the existing advertising agency. Dedicated television advertisements are not planned.
- **Social Media and Digital Marketing Expenses**: Expenses include costs for SEO contract services, SEM pay-per-click costs, banner ad costs on portal sites, costs to sponsor ads on social media sites like Facebook, costs to create relevant photos and videos to upload onto sites like Flickr and YouTube, and costs for labor to monitor the impact of keywords and to monitor social media conversations.
- **Sales Promotions Expenses**: Costs include funds to continue existing frequent traveler loyalty programs.
- **Public Relations Expenses**: Expenses include wire fees of SEO-enabled press releases.
- **Events and Experiences Expenses**: Expenses include costs to sponsor adventure-related events, such as extreme sports.
- **Direct Marketing Expenses**: This line item includes costs for email campaigns.
- **Personal Selling Expenses**: Here, we include costs for training-affiliated travel agents, to be completed in the first few months.

## Summary

As the Bible says, "A feast is made for laughter, and wine maketh merry: but money answereth all things" (Ecclesiastes, 10.19).

Some of the first questions executives ask when they review a marketing plan are financial in nature:

- "How much will this new venture make for the organization?"
- "How long will it take to get my money back?"
- "How much will it cost to bring it to market?"

To answer those questions, this chapter covered several essential financial tools for marketing planning.

The first tool is the break-even analysis. The break-even analysis identifies how long it will take for the revenue from a new product or service to equal the sum of the fixed cost and the variable cost. It is calculated by the following formula:

$$\text{Break-even Volume} = (\text{Fixed Cost})/(\text{Price} - \text{Unit Cost}).$$

The second tool is the pro forma operating income statement. The pro forma operating income statement shows the expected financial results of the project, including its revenue, the costs of producing the product or service, the gross margin, the expenses, and the expected income.

The third tool we covered was capital budgeting analysis. Often, the company is faced with several attractive projects, and capital budgeting analysis can determine whether the proposed projects are a good use of the company's capital investment funds. We covered two methods for the analysis: using net present value, and using internal rate of return.

The fourth tool is the marketing budget. Marketing budgets are useful for identifying the costs associated with a marketing effort and the way in which funds will be allocated over different vehicles during the time period of the plan (generally one year).

## Key Terms

**Break-even point** Volume of sales (or calendar date) when sales revenue of a product or service equals its costs. (p. 245)

**Capital budgeting analysis** Financial appraisal of proposed company long-term investments. (p. 251)

**Contribution margin** Amount of money contributed to the organization from product sales. Calculated by subtracting variable costs from revenue. (p. 249)

**Cost of goods sold (COGS)** Direct costs related to the production of goods, such as labor and materials and associated costs, such as shipping. (p. 249)

**Discount rate** Rate by which cash flows are reduced to reflect the time value of money. (p. 252)

**Gross margin amount** Gross margin amount is calculated by subtracting full absorption cost from revenue. Full absorption cost is the sum of variable cost and allocated overhead. (p. 249)

**Gross margin percentage** Gross margin amount divided by revenue, expressed as a percentage. (p. 250)

**Hurdle rate** Company's required rate of return. Often used in capital budgeting analysis. (p. 252)

**Internal rate of return (IRR)** Rate of return used in **capital budgeting analysis** to measure and compare the profitability of proposed long-term investments. (p. 252)

**Net present value (NPV)** Method of discounting future cash flows to calculate future value in today's dollars. Often used in capital budgeting analysis. (p. 252)

**Pro forma operating income statement** Financial statement showing expected financial results of a venture in a standard format. Typically includes projected sales, cost of goods sold, expenses, and resulting operating income. (p. 249)

## Discussion Questions

1. What are some measures we can take to accelerate the time to break even?

2. When would it make sense to develop a pro forma income statement looking forward more than three years?

3. How have budget allocations among marketing vehicles (advertising, direct marketing, social marketing, and so on) shifted in your organization during the past year?

 Exercises

 **1.** Prepare a cost summary table showing your product or service's fixed cost, unit cost, proposed price, and sales forecast for three years. Conduct a break-even analysis using the cost data. When will the project break even, in terms of units? When will the project break even, in terms of time?

 **2.** Develop a pro forma income statement for your marketing plan's new product or service. What is the gross margin percentage? What type of expenses do you expect?

 **3.** Create a marketing budget for your plan. What categories would you include? How would you allocate budget among the categories? How would you allocate budget over time?

# 12

# Implementation

## INTRODUCTION

Even the best marketing plans will fail if they are improperly executed. To help ensure success, it is helpful to regard the implementation of the marketing plan as a project management exercise. To that end, this chapter covers three types of project monitoring and control tools specifically tailored for marketing plan implementation.

## CHAPTER CHECKLIST

We cover the following marketing plan sections in this chapter:

❑ **Project Schedules**: Managing the project with a tool to show specific tasks, durations, resources, and milestones

❑ **Control Metrics**: Monitoring the project with marketing metrics to provide insight

❑ **Contingency Plans**: Planning proactively with alternative courses of action to be implemented if things go wrong

Effective controls are important, whether for a marketing project or for a ship
*Source:* Shutterstock

Well-crafted planning and control tools, such as schedules, control metrics, and contingency plans, can assist marketing plan implementations, especially in large, complex organizations. The prudent marketer considers the environment in which the marketing plan is to implemented, especially in the areas of collaboration (working with others and getting buy-in), culture (the norms and values of the organization), and the courses of action (gaining clarity into the hands-on management process).  Figure 12.1. summarizes these three vital implementation factors.

**Collaboration**.  Without buy-in from key stakeholders, even the most carefully developed plan is doomed to failure, as we mentioned in Chapter 1. Which stakeholders must sign off on the plan? What are their expectations? How much involvement do they expect to have with the implementation?

**Figure 12.1** Implementation Factors to Consider, Especially for Large Organizations

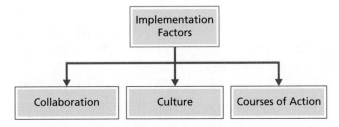

**Culture**. Planning and control tools should reflect the culture of the organization to avoid potential conflict. How are decisions made—autocratically or by consensus? What are the expectations of stakeholders? How is success measured in the organization?

**Courses of Action**. Schedules and other tools should make plans, processes, and personnel responsibilities clear. Who will be in charge—a person or a committee? Which personnel will be involved, and what will they be doing? What are the major milestones of the project?

## Project Schedules

While a full primer on project management is beyond the scope of this book, it is worthwhile to emphasize the importance of a well-developed schedule on the success of a marketing project. Schedules should include the following information:

**Tasks**. Schedules must list the actions to be accomplished, including their name and description.

**Duration**. Schedules must show start and end dates (or start dates and duration) for tasks.

**Resources**. Schedules must indicate the resources required, such as personnel and equipment.

**Milestones**. Schedules must include progress points (milestones) and deliverables.

Figure 12.2 shows an example of a simplified schedule. The schedule shows tasks (including task number and description), duration (start dates and end dates), resources

**Figure 12.2** Example Marketing Plan Project Schedule (Simplified)

| Task | Description | Resources | Status | Jan | Feb | Mar |
|------|-------------|-----------|--------|-----|-----|-----|
| 1 | **Infrastructure Activities** | | | | | |
| 1.1 | Sign distribution agreement with Acme wholesalers | Bob Acme rep. | 100% | Start: 1/3 | End: 2/3 | |
| 1.2 | Obtain trademark registration for new product name | Mary Attorney X | 80% | Start: 1/3 | End: 2/3 | |
| 2 | **Prelaunch Activities** | | | | | |
| 2.1 | Develop creative for ads and schedule ads for placement | Bill Agency Y | 30% | Start: 1/7 | End: 2/7 | |
| 2.2 | Conduct training on new product for retail salespeople | Jane Sales mgr. | 40% | Start: 1/7 | End: 2/7 | |

| Task | Description | Resources | Status | Jan | Feb | Mar |
|------|-------------|-----------|--------|-----|-----|-----|
| 3 | **Launch Activities** | | | | | |
| 3.1 | Update social media sites with announcement of new product | Mary IT | New Task | | Start: 2/10 | End: 3/20 |
| 3.2 | Conduct direct marketing campaign with email and mobile | Bob Mobile rep. | New Task | | Start: 2/10 | End: 3/20 |
| 4 | **Milestones/ Deliverables** | | | | | |
| 4.1 | Decision on new retailer | Jane | Pending | | Event: 2/15 | |
| 4.2 | Reach total sales of 1,000 | Bill | Pending | | | Event: 3/31 |

(personnel and equipment), and milestones (significant events and deliverables). This particular version divides tasks into four categories:

**Infrastructure Activities**: Tasks to support the ongoing success of the project.

**Pre-launch Activities**: Tasks to prepare for the launch of new products, services, or initiatives.

**Launch Activities**: Tasks to support the announcement and initiation of new products or services.

**Milestones and Deliverables**: Major accomplishments toward the success of the plan.

## Marketing Planning in Action

**Delhi Metro: Subway Train Project on Track**. The Delhi Metro subway system, a $2.3 billion project, completed its first phase on budget and three full years ahead of schedule, thanks to the efforts of civil engineer Elattuvalapil Sreedharan. Three aspects led to his success. The first was not being reluctant to obtain loans from a Japanese bank when funds were not available within India. Second, he searched worldwide to find top talent—engineering consulting from Japan, train cars from Korea, and the automatic train control system from France. Third, and most remarkable, he managed to get the various Indian government agencies to all work together. The system is already delivering results—the average bus speed is up to 11 mph from 8 mph, a serious achievement in such a congested city.[1]

The Delhi Metro subway system project completed its first phase on budget and three years ahead of schedule, thanks to effective project management
*Source:* Shutterstock

## Control Metrics

Once the project launches, key performance metrics must be monitored to control it. Control metrics can be measured by tools such as control charts, marketing dashboards, and metrics family tables.

### Control Charts

**Control charts** are graphical tools to monitor and control important marketing metrics. The charts form a graphical record of performance over time and can signal if corrective actions are required. Control charts can be used with many different types of marketing-related variables, such as sales by product/service, sales by distribution channel, sales leads, customer satisfaction, and many others.

For example, the marketing expense to sales control chart is particularly useful because it shows at a glance if the company is overspending to achieve its goals. Figure 12.3 shows an example of such a chart.[2]

Several aspects of the chart are worth noting.

**Vertical Axis.** The vertical axis shows the performance metric we are measuring. In the case of Figure 12.3, it is marketing expense as a percentage of sales.

**Horizontal Axis.** The horizontal axis shows time in months.

**Figure 12.3** Example Control Chart: Marketing Expense as Percentage of Sales

*Source:* Adapted with permission from Philip Kotler and Kevin Keller, *Marketing Management*, 13th ed. (Upper Saddle River, NJ: Pearson Prentice-Hall, 2009). Figure 22.6, p. 652.

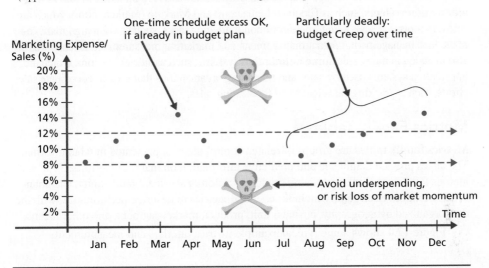

**Target Value**. In this example, we have targeted a 10 percent marketing expense/sales rate. Note that the target value might change over time. For example, companies in the toy industry might increase marketing spending during the Holiday season.

**Tolerance Band**. Many organizations aim to control marketing spending within a tolerance band centered about the target value.

**Upper Control Limit**. The upper control limit represents the maximum spending limit. Spending in excess of the upper control limit could get us in trouble with our finance department.

**Lower Control Limit**. The lower control limit represents the minimum spending limit. Underspending could be just as bad as overspending, because we risk the loss of market momentum by not spending enough to maintain our presence in the market.

**Budget Creep**. While a one-time schedule excess is usually forgivable (such as an unusual large expense), budget creep is not. Budget creep is particularly sinister because it has a tendency to edge up over time. Budget creep can result in excessive spending over multiple months and once started, is difficult to correct.

Control charts can be created to monitor many different types of marketing metrics, such as actual sales, brand awareness, and market share against forecasted amounts.

### Key Terms

**Control charts**    Graphical tools to monitor and control important marketing metrics over time.

## Marketing Dashboards

**Marketing dashboards** help measure the effectiveness of marketing efforts by aggregating key performance indicators in a graphical display. Dashboards are included in **marketing automation systems**, such as Eloqua (eloqua.com) and Marketo (marketo.com), which are software tools that seek to automate common marketing tasks, such as campaign management, lead management, contact management, and marketing measurement. Dashboards are also included in many **salesforce automation systems**, such as salesforce.com, which are information systems used by sales and marketing organizations that seek to coordinate sales efforts, such as tracking sales leads and forecasting sales.

## Metrics Family Tables

**Metrics family tables** are groups of related control metrics, presented in tabular format. The tables provide diagnostic and predictive information on marketing efforts. Typical metrics families include customers, products, customer service, brand equity, and channel distribution. Each family includes essential metrics to describe performance, with the data organized by geography, business unit, product, market segment, and other means.

Figure 12.4 shows some typical example metrics families and measurements.

**Figure 12.4** Example Metrics Family Table

| Metrics Family | Description | Example Metrics |
|---|---|---|
| Lead Generation: Google AdWords | Shows performance of Google AdWords search engine marketing | Leads from Google AdWords<br>Leads by Google Campaign<br>Top 10 keywords<br>Top 10 ad headlines<br>Opportunity stage from AdWords |
| Sales and Pipeline | Shows summary of sales, organized by various means: Product, industry, etc. | Closed sales, year to date, total<br>Closed sales, quarter to date<br>Closed sales by industry<br>Closed sales by product<br>Closed sales by geography<br>Key opportunities (pipeline) |
| Marketing Channels | Shows performance of marketing channel efforts, such as partner recruitment | Partner recruitment by program<br>Partner recruitment by region<br>Partner recruitment status (YTD)<br>Partner segmentation analysis |
| Customer Satisfaction | Shows performance of efforts toward customer satisfaction | Customer referral score<br>Customer satisfaction score<br>Support rep satisfaction score<br>Net promoter score |

## Marketing Planning in Action

**Marketing Metrics: ROI or DOA?** Despite the recent focus on marketing metrics, many chief financial officers (CFOs) believe that marketing departments do a poor job in measuring their returns on marketing investments. According to a study by the Marketing Management Analytics (MMA) organization (mma.com), only 7 percent of finance executives are satisfied with their companies' ability to measure marketing ROI (return on investment), whereas 23 percent of marketing executives believe they measure the returns of their efforts well. According to another study, the consumer packaged goods industry leads other industries, thanks to their pioneering efforts in the 1990s. Other industries are developing metrics-based programs, but the MMA concludes that most are still in the early stages.[3]

# Contingency Plans

**Contingency plans** are alternative courses of action to be implemented if (or when!) things go wrong. Some people refer to them as backup plans. Contingency plans should be prepared as part of the overall marketing planning process, and approved by executive management before the project launches. If disaster strikes, the resulting emotional and turbulent environment will make it difficult to get alternative plans approved then, so it is essential that plans be prepared and approved in advance. As the saying goes, if you don't attack the risks, the risks will attack you.

Disasters lurk nearby. Be prepared for them with an effective contingency plan.
*Source:* Shutterstock

**Figure 12.5**  Example Contingency Plan

| Scenario | Trigger | Actions |
|---|---|---|
| Political Changes | Congress enacts new law | Determine impact of law<br>Examine opportunities |
| Economic Changes | Economy enters boom/recession | Re-estimate sales forecast<br>Investigate new target markets |
| Social Changes | Societal preferences change | Determine impact of change<br>Consider reframing product/service |
| Technology Changes | Market adopts new technology | Determine long-term impact<br>Reposition/pull existing product<br>Design new product |
| Late Entry into Market | Launch delayed 3 months from plan | Adjust first year sales downward |
| New Competitor | Discovery that competitor has entered | Conduct competitive analysis<br>Predict competitor's target market |
| Partner Support | Partner rescinds partnership agreement | Arrange for backup partner |
| Sales Drop | 10% reduction in sales versus forecast | Conduct customer survey<br>Conduct competitive analysis<br>Use feedback for future forecasts |
| Sales Increase | 10% increase in sales versus forecast | Determine competitive advantage<br>Feed data into future designs<br>Use feedback for future forecasts |

Figure 12.5 shows an example contingency plan. As shown in the figure, effective contingency plans include three elements: a description of the scenario, the trigger to initiate the contingency plan, and the specific actions to be taken. Of course, the specific actions taken will vary according to the situation.[4]

While every contingency plan will be different, some useful generic scenarios are listed below. Alternatively, contingency plans can show actions to take if the metrics examined in the metrics family table falls below plan.

**Political Changes**. New laws can cause dramatic effects on organizations. They can benefit the organization (such as solar energy credits helping solar energy companies), or hurt it (such as luxury taxes targeting high-priced automobiles).

**Economic Changes**. The economic climate can affect the success of a new product or service. Marketing in a time of prosperity is often easier than marketing in recessionary periods. For example, prices of used automobiles in the recessionary period of

2007–2010 actually rose, instead of dropping, due in part to people wanting to save money over purchasing a new car.

**Social Changes**. Consumer's choices can change over time. For example, some of the fads of the 2000s endured to become successful new categories (wireless camera phones turned to smartphones) and others did not (LiveSTRONG yellow wristbands, once pervasive, are now essentially gone).

**Technology Changes**. If a company's target market adopts a new type of technology that threatens to make the company's technology obsolete, the consequences can be dire. An example is the rapid boom and bust of e-learning tools in the early 2000s.

**Late Entry into Market**. If the company encounters a delay launching the project represented by the marketing plan, the plan must be modified accordingly. In particular, the projected sales for the first year must be reduced in proportion with the delay.

**New Competitors**. Perhaps a new company enters the market with a compelling product or service. In that case, the marketer should conduct a new competitive analysis, with an emphasis on predicting the target market for that competitor.

**Partner Support**. Many marketing plans count on the support by a key business partner, such as a technology vendor or distribution channel member, for success of their plan. Contingency plans should include sections describing actions to take if those partners fail to provide the assumed level of support.

**Sales Drop**. Drops in actual sales of 10 percent, or even 20 percent, (compared to predicted sales) could be due to an over-optimistic forecast or poorer-than-expected market conditions. In either case, it pays to conduct market research on customers and competitors to determine if the assumptions made in the plan are accurate.

**Sales Increase**. If actual sales are more than predicted sales by 10 percent, or even 20 percent, the organization should find out why. Perhaps the market perceives a fundamental competitive advantage with the product or service that is not readily evident to the company. If that is the case, the offering should be positioned to strengthen that perception.

---

## Key Terms

**Marketing dashboards**
Collection of multiple marketing-oriented measurements often portrayed using a graphical format. Found in many **marketing automation systems**.

**Marketing automation systems**
Software tools to automate common marketing tasks, such as campaign management and lead management.

**Salesforce automation systems**    Software tools to automate and coordinate sales efforts, such as sales lead tracking and sales forecasting.

**Metrics family tables**    Groups of related control metrics, presented in tabular format, intended to offer diagnostic and predictive information on marketing efforts.

**Contingency plans**    Plan describing alternative courses of action to be implemented if specific conditions (called "triggers") occur.

## Marketing Planning in Action

**Woolworths UK: Caught without a Contingency Plan**: Woolworths UK was already in trouble when Robert McDonald was named CFO of the organization in 2008. He knew that the troubled retailer had lost over 100 million Euros in the previous six months. Nevertheless, he had joined an army of new executives, including a new CEO, to bring the brand back to profitability. But apparently none of the new chiefs had prepared a contingency plan. So when its cash crisis worsened, they were left with no alternative but to shut down all the stores. Perhaps metrics-driven market feedback would have alleviated the situation. According to Neil Griffiths, a partner in the restructuring team at UK law firm Denton Wilde Sapte, says, "If you're in distress you want daily [rather than monthly or quarterly] information coming through so you can see how close to the edge you are."[5]

Project leaders must remain vigilant to spot any potential problems that might arise and take swift action before matters worsen. Given that market environments are dynamic, some changes to the marketing plan are inevitable during the course of the project.

# Practical Planning

We now continue the Expedia marketing plan example by creating project monitoring and control tools to ensure successful implementation of the plan.

## Schedule

Figure 12.6 shows an abridged schedule for our new offering. The schedule organizes tasks into four categories:

**Infrastructure Activities**.  Support tasks are listed, like getting a new Facebook page, "Adventure Travel."

**Pre-launch Activities**.  Preparatory tasks are shown, like developing content for social media websites.

**Launch Activities**.  Announcement tasks are given, like sending out email blasts to lists of prospects.

**Milestones and Deliverables**.  Major accomplishments and deliverables are listed, like signing up the 100th customer.

## Metrics Family Table

Figure 12.7 shows the metrics families we will monitor to keep the project on track.

**Sales Channel Traffic**.  We will monitor the traffic each sales channel brings to the Expedia Adventure Travel order page to gauge channel performance. Channels include

**Figure 12.6** Example Marketing Plan Project Schedule (Simplified): Expedia Adventure Vacations

| Task | Description | Resources | Status | Jan | Feb | Mar |
|---|---|---|---|---|---|---|
| 1 | **Infrastructure Activities** | | | | | |
| 1.1 | Obtain trademark registration for Expedia Adventure Vacations | Joe Attorney X | 80% | Start: 1/3 | End: 2/3 | |
| 1.2 | Acquire unique Web pages for social media outlets: Facebook… | Chris | 60% | Start 1/3 | End: 2/3 | |
| 2 | **Pre-Launch Activities** | | | | | |
| 2.1 | Develop creative for ads for selected travel magazines | Maria Agency X | 30% | Start: 1/7 | End: 2/7 | |
| 2.2 | Create content for social media websites | Julio | 40% | Start: 1/7 | End: 2/7 | |
| 2.3 | Prepare training material for Expedia-affiliated travel agents | Lisa | 80% | Start: 1/3 | End: 2/3 | |
| 3 | **Launch Activities** | | | | | |
| 3.1 | Update social media sites with announcement of new service | Chris | New Task | | Start: 2/10 | End: 3/20 |
| 3.2 | Conduct direct marketing campaign with email | Bill. | New Task | | Start: 2/10 | End: 3/20 |
| 3.3 | Send training material packages to affiliated travel agents | Lisa | New Task | | | |
| 4 | **Milestones/ Deliverables** | | | | | |
| 4.1 | Availability of 20 adventure packages in 5 continents | Lisa | Pending | | Event: 2/15 | |
| 4.2 | Sign up 100th customer with new adventure package | Bill | Pending | | | Event: 3/31 |

**Figure 12.7** Metrics Family Table: Expedia Adventure Vacations

| Metrics Family | Description | Example Metrics |
|---|---|---|
| Sales Channel Traffic | Shows performance of sales channels, measured by traffic per channel | % Expedia.com direct (SEO) <br> % Other Expedia sites (TripAdvisor) <br> % SEM Ads (Google AdWords) <br> % Internet banner ads <br> % Direct marketing <br> % Print & other advertising <br> % Social media sites <br> % Travel agent affiliates |
| Community Engagement | Shows performance of social media | Tier 1: Size of community <br> Tier 2: Level of engagement <br> Tier 3: Word of mouth |
| Web Experience | Shows performance of web experience | Conversion rate per channel <br> Average order size per channel <br> Cart abandonment rate |
| Travel Portfolio | Shows performance of trip selection | Bookings sales, by time of year <br> Bookings sales, by activity type <br> Bookings sales, by location |
| Customer Satisfaction | Shows performance of efforts toward customer satisfaction | Customer Satisfaction Score <br> Customer Repeat Purchases <br> Customer Referral Score |

direct traffic to the Expedia.com Adventure Travel Web page (from search engines), traffic from other Expedia sites (like TripAdvisor.com), traffic from SEM-based ads, traffic from Internet banner ads, traffic from social media sites, traffic from direct marketing, traffic from other advertising (such as magazine ads with offer codes), and traffic from travel agent affiliates.

**Community Engagement**. We will monitor the performance of our social media and digital marketing efforts, as measured through a three-tier hierarchy of metrics. In the first set of metrics, we gauge the overall size of the online community (such as registered number of users). In the second set of metrics, we gauge the engagement level (such as number of posts, number of words per post, number of replies to each post). In the third and highest set of metrics, we gauge the word of mouth by the community (such as re-tweets to users outside the immediate community).

**Web Experience**. We will monitor the performance of the Expedia Adventure Travel website, as measured by its ability to convert browsers into buyers. At a minimum, we will measure conversion rate by sales channel, average order size by channel, and cart abandonment rate.

**Travel Portfolio**. We will monitor the performance of our travel portfolio, as measured by the trips that customers select. We will measure bookings by time of year (to find popular travel times), by activity type (to identify the most popular activities), and by location (to gather feedback on preferred destinations).

**Customer Satisfaction**. We will monitor the performance of the quality of the Expedia Adventure Travel trips experience. Performance will be measured using customer satisfaction metrics (such as surveys and monitoring of online posts), by customer repeat purchases, and by customer referral scores (traveler recommendations).

## Contingency Plan

Figure 12.8 presents a contingency plan for Expedia Adventure Vacations. The plan includes scenarios to address poor performance in the control metrics families.

**Low Sales Channel Traffic**. If traffic per channel varies by more than 50 percent (such as 90 percent of traffic coming from one channel, and only 10 percent from another), we will assess the performance of each channel and its contribution to total channel traffic, and improve messaging on low-performing channels. If, after improvements on low-performing channels, the problems persist, we will consider eliminating that channel.

**Low Community Engagement**. If the growth of Expedia-controlled social Web communities is under 10 percent per year, we will examine actual community growth

**Figure 12.8** Example Contingency Plan: Expedia Adventure Vacations

| Scenario | Trigger | Actions |
|---|---|---|
| Low Sales Channel Traffic | Traffic per channel varies by more than 50% | Assess Expedia-based channels<br>Examine traffic from print & ads<br>Determine traffic from social media<br>Measure traffic from agent affiliates |
| Low Community Engagement | Growth of social media sites under 10% | Examine community growth<br>Assess mentions per day<br>Measure re-tweets |
| Low Web Experience | Conversion rate under 1% | Assess conversion rate per channel<br>Examine cart abandonment rate |
| Low Travel Portfolio Interest | Adventure trip selection (vs. other Expedia trips) less than 1% | Examine types of activities<br>Assess types of locations |
| Low Customer Satisfaction | Below 90% in customer satisfaction | Assess blog post customer stories<br>Social media: sentiment trends<br>Customer satisfaction questionnaires |

rate (to gauge level of interest), mentions per day (to assess engagement), and re-tweets (to consider word-of-mouse recommendations) to determine necessary corrective actions.

**Low Web Experience**. If conversion rate on the Expedia website is under 1 percent, we will assess the conversion rate per channel and examine the cart abandonment rate to determine improvements to be done in this area.

**Low Travel Portfolio Interest**. While Expedia Adventure Vacations are not for everyone, we would be concerned if less than 1 percent of all trips took advantage of this new offering. If so, we will examine the types of activities and locations and determine if they resonate with our target audience, adventure travelers.

**Low Customer Satisfaction**. If Expedia Adventure Vacations score less than 90 percent in customer satisfaction, we will assess customer stories written on Expedia's blogs for clues of their disenchantment with the new service. In addition, we will examine sentiment trends (positive or negative) on social media sites and will conduct customer satisfaction studies using questionnaires.

## Summary

Walt Disney, founder of the Walt Disney Company, understood the importance of implementation in his ambitious ventures, when he said, "Of all the things I've done, the most vital is coordinating the talents of those who work for us and pointing them towards a certain goal."

The marketing plan must indicate how the project will be properly controlled and implemented once the project is launched. To that end, we covered three essential implementation tools.

The first tool is the schedule, which should address four aspects of the project. The first aspect is a list of the tasks, including their name and description. Second, the schedule should include the duration of the tasks, as well as their start and end dates. Third, the resources assigned to do the work should be specified. And fourth, the milestones (major accomplishments) and deliverables expected from the project should be stated.

The second tool is the control plan, based on one or more control mechanisms. This chapter covered three control mechanisms. The first mechanism is the use of control charts, which are graphical tools to monitor and control marketing metrics, such as expenses. The second mechanism is the use of marketing dashboards, which provide vital information on marketing performance at a glance. Marketing dashboard functionality is available with some popular salesforce automation and marketing automation systems. The third mechanism is the use of metrics family tables, which show a group of related control metrics to monitor during the course of the project.

The third essential implementation tool is the contingency plan. Contingency plans are alternative courses of action to be implemented if (or when!) things go wrong. Effective contingency plans identify different scenarios, the specific trigger to spark action, and the actions to perform in the event of that scenario occurring.

Key Terms

**Contingency plans** Plan describing alternative courses of action to be implemented if specific conditions (called "triggers") occur. (p. 269)

**Control charts** Graphical tools to monitor and control important marketing metrics over time. (p. 266)

**Marketing automation systems** Software tools to automate common marketing tasks, such as campaign management and lead management. (p. 268)

**Marketing dashboards** Collection of multiple marketing-oriented measurements often portrayed using a graphical format. Found in many **marketing automation systems**. (p. 268)

**Metrics family tables** Groups of related control metrics, presented in tabular format, intended to offer diagnostic and predictive information on marketing efforts. (p. 268)

**Salesforce automation systems** Software tools to automate and coordinate sales efforts, such as sales lead tracking and sales forecasting. (p. 268)

 Discussion Questions

1. Who would be responsible for implementing the project management of the new product or service discussed in the marketing plan? What departments would be involved in the project's execution?

2. How would automated tools (such as salesforce automation or marketing automation) assist with the ongoing implementation of a project?

3. How would you go about identifying all the things that could go wrong (or right) with a project, in order to develop contingency plans? What if you missed something?

 Exercises

1. Develop a schedule for the project your marketing plan recommends. Identify the description of the tasks, their duration, the person(s) responsible for them, and major milestones of the project.

2. Create a list of metric families you plan to use to keep your project on track. What categories of metrics will you use? How do you plan to monitor them?

3. Build a contingency plan for your project. How could foreseeable events on the horizon hurt your project? How could they help it? After completing the table, what changes would you make to the product or service, or to the marketing mix, to avoid the potential problems listed in the contingency plan?

## CHAPTER 13

# Sample Marketing Plan

## INTRODUCTION

In this chapter, we demonstrate the concepts discussed in the book with two versions of a product-based marketing plan (we covered service-based marketing plans with the Expedia Practical Planning sections throughout the book).

The first marketing plan version uses the traditional **report-based marketing plan format**. This format presents the marketing plan as a report, with explanatory text and figures. Some organizational cultures appreciate the depth of information the longer, traditional plan provides. Other organizations demand brevity, so we introduce a shorter format as well. The second version is the abbreviated **ten slide marketing plan format**, which uses only ten presentation slides (like those of Microsoft PowerPoint) to summarize essential aspects of the plan.

## CHAPTER CHECKLIST

We cover two versions of a sample marketing plan:

❑ **Report-based marketing plan format**: Using the tried-and-true report-like structure, this version utilizes supporting text and figures to describe the plan in detail

❑ **Ten slide marketing plan format**: Using only ten presentation slides to cover the entire plan, this version is becoming the standard in many organizations

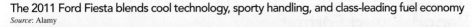

The 2011 Ford Fiesta blends cool technology, sporty handling, and class-leading fuel economy
*Source*: Alamy

Our sample marketing plan addresses the introduction of the 2011 Ford Fiesta subcompact automobile into the U.S. market. The plan uses publicly available data to avoid confidentiality issues.

## Marketing Planning in Action

**Ford Fiesta: Frugal, Frisky, Fun-to-Drive**. The 2011 Ford Fiesta could very well be the reincarnation of the Ford Model T, according to *Car and Driver* magazine. The Model T leveraged a standardized design and economies of scale to offer lower pricing and increased market share. It was one of the world's most successful automobiles, selling over 15 million units. Similarly, Ford developed the Fiesta as a global car, offering the same general design in multiple geographic markets to reduce costs and increase market share. Early reviews of the Ford Fiesta have been favorable, citing superlatives like "frisky handling, precise steering, respectable snort, and all-day comfort quotient"—all while delivering basic dependability and 40 miles per gallon. Henry Ford would have been proud.[1]

---

### Key Terms

**Report-based marketing plan format**    Traditional report-based marketing plan format, providing explanatory text for each section of the plan.

**Ten slide marketing plan format**    Abbreviated marketing plan format using only ten presentation slides to summarize essential aspects of the plan.

# Sample Marketing Plan: 2011 Ford Fiesta: Report-Based Format

## Executive Summary

Ford has an opportunity to capture market share within the subcompact automotive market in the United States. Due to increasing fuel prices, the market for large vehicles such as sport utility vehicles (SUVs) is shrinking. Meanwhile, the market for subcompact cars, like the 2011 Ford Fiesta, is poised to grow.

This marketing plan explores Ford's opportunities in the subcompact car market and discusses marketing tactics to introduce the new 2011 Ford Fiesta. Figure 13.1 summarizes the highlights of the plan. The data for the figure are from the respective marketing plan sections.

## Objectives

**Mission**. The Ford mission, displayed on its website as the ONE Ford, encompasses three principles: One Team (everyone working together as a lean, global enterprise), One Plan (accelerating new product development), and One Goal (profitable growth).[2]

**Competitive advantage**. Ford's competitive advantages are its strong brand, its worldwide distribution channels, and its global manufacturing strategy. Ford's flexible

**Figure 13.1** Executive Summary: 2011 Ford Fiesta Marketing Plan

| Criteria | Metric | Comments |
|---|---|---|
| Objective | 10% Share by 2012 | Increase market share of subcompact cars sold in United States |
| Market Overview | Size: 460K units/year | Market trends point to continued growth |
| Market Segments | Primary buyer: Millennial (14–29 years): | Millennials: 80 million people, 20% of buying market |
| Competitive Landscape | Market leader: Honda Fit: 14.6% share | Market is crowded with major competitors, all with strong-selling, contemporary products |
| Product | Number 1 in fuel economy | Strong value proposition; differentiation through premium features typically only found in larger luxury cars |
| Pricing | $13,320–$17,120 MSRP | Premium pricing to support premium product positioning |
| Distribution | 3,800 U.S. Ford dealers | Exclusive distribution through dealer network. Dealers to emphasize differentiation, not discounts. |
| Promotion | 25% of budget: digital and social media | Promotions to target Web-savvy Millennials demographic through emphasis on use of digital and social media |
| Finance & Implementation | 3 primary metrics: awareness, market share, and satisfaction | Focus on three metrics to deliver results. Execute contingency plan if metric goals are not met. |

manufacturing plants give it the capability to respond quickly to changing market needs, while improving quality and efficiency.[3]

To support Ford's mission of profitable growth through new products and its competitive advantage of global manufacturing prowess, we declare the following objective:

**Objective**. Increase market share of subcompact cars sold in the U.S. market to 10 percent by the end of 2012, leveraging global automotive assets. The objective follows the S.M.A.R.T. guidelines, in that it is specific (10%), measurable (10% of the subcompact market equates to about 46,000 units, as we shall discover in the Market Overview section), achievable (we will leverage Ford's core competencies in manufacturing and distribution), realistic (the unit volume is consistent with non-U.S. sales of the new generation of Ford Fiestas to date) and time-based (end of 2012).

## Market Overview

We start this portion of the plan with a summary of the small car market, summarized in Figure 13.2.

**Market Description**. We describe the market using the following data.

- **Industry**: Automobile manufacturing. The category is small (subcompact) cars.
- **NAICS/ SIC Code**: The NAICS code for automobile manufacturing is 336111. The SIC code is 3711.[4]
- **Customer Needs**. Direct customer needs include basic transportation. Indirect customer needs include satisfying feelings of freedom, self-expression, and self-esteem.[5]

**Market Sizing**. We size the market and its growth rate using the following data.

- **Market Size**: Figure 13.5 displays U.S. subcompact car sales for leading manufacturers, totaling 459,802 units sold in 2009, the latest available data.
- **Market Growth Rate**: Edmunds estimates that light vehicle sales, including subcompacts, will increase by about 11 percent in 2010.[6]

---

**Figure 13.2** Market Overview: Subcompact Cars

| Market Factor | Description |
|---|---|
| Industry | Automobile manufacturing. Category: Small (subcompact) cars |
| NAICS/ SIC code | NAICS 336111: Automobile manufacturing<br>SIC 3711: Automobile manufacturing |
| Customer Needs | Direct needs: Transportation<br>Indirect needs: freedom, self-expression, self-esteem |
| Size | About 459,802 subcompacts sold in U.S. market in 2009 |
| Growth Rate | About 11% growth rate for light vehicle sales in U.S. market for 2010 |
| Political Trends | NHTSA CAFÉ standard: 35.7 MPG in 2015 |
| Economic Trends | Continuing high gasoline prices favor subcompact cars |
| Social Trends | Small cars seen as fashionable; negative perception of large SUVs |
| Technological Trends | Increased usage of safety technologies, like ABS and ESC, in smaller cars |

---

**Market Trends**. We have identified the following trends in the market.

- **Political Trends**: The National High Traffic Safety Administration's (NHTSA) Corporate Average Fuel Economy (CAFE) fleet-wide fuel economy standard will increase to 35.7 miles per gallon (MPG) by 2015, which will benefit the subcompact car category.[7]

- **Economic Trends**: As gasoline prices increased, sales of fuel-hungry SUVs decreased by more than 25 percent, while sales of small cars increased. Because gasoline prices are unlikely to return to their historic lows, small car sales should continue to stay strong.[8]

- **Social Trends**: Small cars suffered from a negative stigma in the United States in the past, with a prevailing notion that large, powerful cars symbolized success. But this perception is changing as society finds small cars more appealing. Society has even come to eschew SUVs, which symbolize greed and wastefulness to some people. Population aging is also contributing to the trend toward smaller cars. As the baby boomer generation reaches into their retirement years, it is predicted that many will downsize to smaller, more practical vehicles.[9]

- **Technological Trends**: Automotive safety technologies, such as antilock braking systems (ABS) and electronic stability control (ESC) systems, will improve safety in small cars.[10]

## Market Segments

In this section, we discuss the planned market segmentation, targeting, and positioning for the 2011 Ford Fiesta in the United States.

**Segmentation: B2C**. For the consumer market, we propose to focus on the millennial demographic segment. The millennial demographic segment (also called generation Y or echo boomers), are those people born between 1982 and 1995. The targeting section below cites reasons for this selection.

**Segmentation: B2B**. In addition to sales to consumer markets, we considered sales to business markets, like commercial and governmental organizations. These so-called fleet sales make up 80 percent of vehicle sales for some vehicles, such as large vans and sedans. It is not currently anticipated that the 2011 Ford Fiesta will be attractive to fleet-based organizations, but we will conduct ongoing reviews of market data for signs of business demand.[11]

**Targeting**. As summarized in Figure 13.3, several aspects make the consumer segment worthwhile to target:

- **Potential**: Millennials account for 80 million people, making it a large market segment. Population forecasts show that the segment will comprise 20 percent of the automotive car buying market at the time of the vehicle's proposed launch in

**Figure 13.3** Targeting Chart, Millennial Segment: 2011 Ford Fiesta

| Market Segment | Potential | Alignment | Marketability |
|---|---|---|---|
| Millennials | 80 million people | Ford's new technologies a good fit for technology-savvy market | Accessible via digital media |

**Figure 13.4** Positioning Chart, Millennial Segment: 2011 Ford Fiesta

| Market Segment | Positioning Approach | Points of Difference | Points of Parity |
|---|---|---|---|
| Millennials | Benefits: "All of the benefits of a larger car in a smaller package." | Premium elements in a subcompact car: Bluetooth; SYNC; Satellite Navigation; Leather | Ford reputation; quality; wide availability of dealers |

the United States. In addition, many millennials are waiting longer to get married and raise children, delaying the need for large, child-carrying vehicles, which makes small cars like the Fiesta more attractive.[12, 13]

- **Alignment**: Ford's new technologies, such as its new Ford SYNC system, which features hands-free calling, audible text messages, voice-activated music, and turn-by-turn directions, will appeal to the technology-savvy millennial generation.[14]

- **Marketability**: Millennials, sometimes called "digital natives," were born into the digital millennium and as such are accessible via digital media (like blogs and social networking sites).

**Positioning**. The 2011 Ford Fiesta will be positioned using a benefits-oriented approach to target the millennial market, as shown in Figure 13.4. Older consumers have positioned previous small cars in the United States as cheap "econoboxes" due to their unattractive, boxy styling, cheap feeling interiors, and lack of creature comforts. By contrast, the Fiesta will be positioned as a "premium" vehicle with significant benefits over traditional small cars. Consumers will be able to trade in their premium vehicle, such as the Audi A4, for the Fiesta and not give up Bluetooth connectivity, satellite navigation systems, and heated leather seats. At the same time, they will be reassured with Ford's quality, reputation, and vast dealer network.[15]

## Competitive Landscape

The competitive landscape for subcompact cars is crowded, but a market whitespace appears to exist for a premium, reasonably priced new entry.

**Market Structure**. Figure 13.5 displays U.S. sales of subcompact cars for major manufacturers. Due to the many competitors in the automotive market, we focus on our direct competitors, leaders in the premium subcompact car category.

**Direct Competitors**. We will compare the Honda Fit (rated number 1 in the premium subcompact car category by *Consumer Reports*), the Toyota Yaris (Honda's rival), and the BMW MINI, which essentially defined the premium subcompact category when it launched in 2001.[16]

Data for the figure come from company press releases announcing U.S. sales for 2009, the latest available data.[17, 18, 19, 20, 21, 22, 23, 24, 25, 26, 27]

**Indirect Competitors**. Non-premium subcompact cars (like the Kia Rio), public transportation (which meets the need for basic transportation on a budget), and used cars (which also meet the need for budget transportation) could be considered indirect competitors. None appears to be an immediate threat, so they will not be addressed further in this plan.

**Figure 13.5** Market Structure: U.S. Sales of Subcompact Cars for Major Manufacturers

| Manufacturer | Subcompact Model | U.S. Sales (Units), 2009 | Market Share |
|---|---|---|---|
| BMW | MINI | 45,225 | 9.8% |
| Chevrolet | Aveo | 38,516 | 8.4% |
| Honda | Fit | 67,315 | 14.6% |
| Hyundai | Accent | 68,086 | 14.8% |
| Kia | Rio | 36,532 | 7.9% |
| Mercedes/Smart | ForTwo | 14,595 | 3.2% |
| Nissan | Versa | 82,906 | 18.0% |
| Scion | xD | 14,499 | 3.2% |
| Suzuki | SX4 | 20,704 | 4.5% |
| Toyota | Yaris | 63,743 | 13.9% |
| Volkswagen | Rabbit/Golf | 7,681 | 1.7% |
| TOTAL | | 459,802 | 100% |

**Competitive Comparison Framework**. Data for primary competitors are shown in Figure 13.6.

- **Market Share**: Figure 13.5 displays the market share for each vehicle.
- **Messaging**: External messaging was obtained from competitor websites.
- **Competitive Advantages**: The table shows areas of particular strength, beyond the expected competencies in manufacturing, quality, and distribution networks. For example, the BMW MINI used its competitive advantage in innovative marketing to help it become a style and performance leader in the subcompact market.
- **Strengths**: Ford's turnaround from its problems in the early 2000s shows its new "can-do" culture of optimism.[28]
- **Weaknesses**: Ford does not have a strong reputation for technological innovation. For example, its new hybrid models suffered software problems.[29]
- **Product**: Ford leads the pack in fuel economy, a vital attribute in the subcompact car category.
- **Pricing**: The Ford Fiesta is premium-priced, to support its "premium" positioning and amenities. Manufacturer's suggested retail pricing (MSRP) is from manufacturer's websites and reflects similarly appointed models. Prices in the group range from the super-premium pricing for the BMW MINI to the relatively low pricing for the Toyota Yaris.
- **Distribution**: Each competitor boasts a worldwide network of dealers, as well as Internet-enabled sales.
- **Promotion**: Ford will emphasize social media and digital marketing techniques to attract its millennial audience.

**Figure 13.6** Competitive Comparison Framework Chart: 2011 Ford Fiesta

| Criteria | Ford Fiesta | BMW MINI | Honda Fit | Toyota Yaris |
|---|---|---|---|---|
| Market Share (units) | New model to United States | 8.4% | 14.6% | 13.9% |
| Messaging | Premium features and technologies of a larger car in a subcompact format for millennials | European luxury and performance for style-conscious drivers | Quality and design, with cargo capacity of a small SUV for practical drivers | Quality and reliability of Toyota, for budget-minded drivers |
| Competitive Advantage | Operations (global manufacturing operations) and infrastructure (considerable company assets) | Edgy marketing and sales | Technological development (great design) | Operations and procurement (such as advanced inventory systems) |
| Strengths | Optimistic, can-do culture; large dealer network | Reputation for precision engineering and racing heritage | Reputation for well-designed, well-built, quality cars | Reputation for quality and manufacturing innovation |
| Weaknesses | Not a strong reputation for innovation | Reputation for high service costs | Customers might seek something more innovative | Massive product recalls damaged reputation for quality |
| Product | MPG: 30 city/40 highway | MPG: 32 city 37 highway | MPG: 27 city/33 highway | MPG: 29 city/36 highway |
| Pricing | Premium; $17,120 (5-door hatchback) | Premium to super-premium; $19,500 (hardtop) | Moderate; $18,260 (5-door hatchback) | Low; $13,705 (5-door hatch-back) |
| Distribution | Worldwide dealer network; Internet-enabled sales | Worldwide dealer network; Internet-enabled sales | Worldwide dealer network; Internet-enabled sales | Worldwide dealer network; Internet-enabled sales |
| Promotion | Strong focus on social media and digital marketing | Traditional, as well as social, media | Traditional, as well as social, media | Traditional, as well as social, media |

The BMW MINI is considered a primary competitor due to its European styling and performance, plus its edgy marketing campaigns
*Source*: Shutterstock

The Honda Fit is considered a primary competitor due to its reputation for quality and design, plus its roomy cargo space rivaling small SUVs.
*Source:* Alamy

# Strategy

We select our strategy to meet our plan objective, while taking advantage of market opportunities. Figure 13.7 summarizes the market opportunity and corresponding strategy.

**Market Opportunity**.  Based on the competitive comparison framework, there appears to be a potentially profitable opportunity not already dominated by competitors. We identify the opportunity as premium subcompact cars targeted to millennials, with differentiating functionality including high technology features and luxury appointments, at a price lower than the super-premium BMW MINI.

**Strategy Selection**.  Our market opportunity involves product development using differentiating functionality. Therefore, we will select a product development strategy, developing and launching a U.S. version of the Ford Fiesta into the market. We plan to take advantage of the Fiesta's global design platform to keep development costs reasonable.

To leverage our competitive advantages in global manufacturing capability and quality, we will employ a product development strategy that targets quality attributes. By targeting quality attributes, we can deliver a high-quality, near luxury car in a subcompact size. The strategy thus addresses our market opportunity for delivering premium subcompact cars to our target market.

The Toyota Yaris is considered a primary competitor due to its reputation for quality and reliability, plus its budget-friendly price.
*Source:* Alamy

## Marketing Mix: Product

We begin our plan for the marketing mix for the 2011 Ford Fiesta with product tactics.

**Product Tactics.** Figure 13.8 summarizes product tactics, acknowledging that the 2011 Ford Fiesta is in the introduction stage in the U.S. subcompact market.

- **Customers to Target**: We will target early adopters within the millennial demographic, who will appreciate the digital technologies that the Fiesta has to offer.
- **Features**: The 2011 Ford Fiesta's features can be placed into four categories: Blockbuster features (class-leading miles per gallon, or MPG), technology features

**Figure 13.7** Market Opportunity and Strategy: 2011 Ford Fiesta

| Objective | Market Opportunity | Strategy |
|---|---|---|
| Increase market share of subcompact cars in United States to 10% by end of 2012 | Premium subcompact cars for millennials | Launch 2011 Ford Fiesta in United States<br>Market goal: target millennials<br>Design goal: leverage global design<br>Volume goal: 46,000 units/year |

**Figure 13.8** Product Tactics: 2011 Ford Fiesta

| Product Criteria | 2011 Ford Fiesta |
| --- | --- |
| Targeted Customer Segment | Early adopters within millennial demographic |
| Features | Blockbuster feature: Class-leading MPG<br>Technology features: SYNC, Bluetooth, Sat-Nav (desired by millennials)<br>Premium features: Leather seats, high-quality feel of interior<br>Parity features: Meets expectations for cargo volume, etc. |
| Quality | Leverage Ford's reputation for quality |
| Packaging | Offer 5 different models to suit different tastes and applications |
| Brand | Emphasize innovation and new technologies to change brand perception |

(SYNC, Bluetooth connectivity, satellite navigation), premium features (leather seats, premium interior materials), and parity features (features subcompact buyers expect, like sufficient cargo volume and at least average reliability).

- **Quality**: The Fiesta will leverage Ford's traditional focus on quality to ensure reliable, trouble-free operation for its buyers.
- **Packaging**: Ford will offer the Fiesta in five different variants (S sedan, SE sedan, SE hatchback, SEL sedan, and SEL hatchback) to suit different tastes and applications.
- **Brand**: Promotions will highlight innovation and new technologies to change brand perception from "traditional" to "innovative" (while still maintaining associations of quality and solid reputation).

**Value Proposition**. The value proposition should entice technology-savvy millennials to purchase a new 2011 Ford Fiesta. Figure 13.9 summarizes the value proposition elements.

- **Targeted Customer Segment**: We plan to target millennials who appreciate luxury amenities in a subcompact package.
- **Customer Purchase Motivation and Use Cases**: Several use cases could be envisioned. First, consumers might purchase the vehicle for themselves as economical transportation. The class-leading MPG is a strong message for this use case. Second, consumers might purchase the vehicle for themselves as a performance-oriented car to quickly maneuver around traffic. The Fiesta's tight handling will address this use. Third, parents might purchase the Fiesta to give to their children for use once they leave home, such as to attend a university. Ford's excellent reputation for quality and safety will help in this regard.
- **Name of Product or Service**: The name "Fiesta" is festive (!), but could remind older consumers of previous Fiesta automobiles, which were slower and not as well styled. The new 2011 Ford Fiesta will use the number "2011" in front of its name, as well as distinctive styling, to set it apart from previous models.

**Figure 13.9** Value Proposition Elements: 2011 Ford Fiesta

| Element | 2011 Ford Fiesta |
|---|---|
| Targeted Customer Segment | Millennials who appreciate luxury amenities in a subcompact package |
| Customer Purchase Motivation and Use Cases | Budget-minded consumers; performance-oriented consumers; family-minded parents to give vehicle to children |
| Name of Product or Service | "Fiesta" name could remind older people of previous lackluster models; must use distinctive styling to set it apart |
| Category of Product or Service | Premium subcompact automobiles |
| Benefits | Head: class-leading MPG; Ford quality. Heart: sexy styling; zippy performance; latest technology |
| Competitors | Direct competitors: other subcompacts. Indirect competitors: public transportation; used cars |
| Differentiation | Primary: features—premium features normally found only in larger luxury cars; Secondary: form—distinctive shape |

- **Category of Product or Service**: The category is premium subcompact automobiles
- **Benefits**: "Head," or rational, benefits include class-leading MPG and Ford's reputation for quality. "Heart," or emotional, benefits include sexy styling, zippy performance, and availability of the latest technology.
- **Competitors**: Direct competitors include other premium subcompacts. Indirect competitors include public transportation and used cars.
- **Differentiation**: The service will be differentiated primarily through premium features (offering features normally only available in larger luxury cars like leather seats, satellite navigation, and Bluetooth connectivity) and secondarily through form (its distinctive styling sets it apart from econoboxes of the past).

The resulting value proposition is:

To (millennials who appreciate luxury amenities in a subcompact package) who (want economy, performance, and safety), the (2011 Ford Fiesta) is a (premium subcompact car) that (offers class-leading MPG and Ford quality with sexy styling, zippy performance, and the latest technology). Unlike (other subcompacts), the Fiesta (doesn't make you give up larger car comfort to take advantage of smaller car virtues).

## Marketing Mix: Pricing

Our use of premium pricing will affirm the car's membership in the premium subcompact category. Figure 13.10 summarizes the pricing tactics.

**Pricing Objectives**. The pricing objective will be product-quality leadership. The relatively high price will help position the 2011 Ford Fiesta as an "affordable luxury."

**Pricing Approach**. To execute on our product-quality leadership objective, we will employ a perceived value pricing approach, setting price relatively high to suggest high value to consumers. We will minimize the use of price discounts and incentives.

**Figure 13.10** Pricing Tactics: 2011 Ford Fiesta

| Pricing Criteria | 2011 Ford Fiesta |
| --- | --- |
| Objective | Product-quality leadership |
| Approach | Perceived value; premium price for a premium product |
| Competitor Impact | Direct competitors: Fiesta includes premium features not included by others<br>Indirect competitors: No used car offers such advanced technology |
| Channel Impact | Ford network of dealers expected to welcome bold new entry to the market |
| Costs | Costs include development costs to tailor the vehicle to the U.S. market, as well as marketing costs |
| Environment | Slow economic recovery and high gasoline prices will favor subcompacts over expensive luxury autos |

**Competitor Impact.** Ford can justify relatively high pricing by emphasizing its luxury car-grade amenities, which addresses both direct competitors (other manufacturers do not include premium items such as push-button start and ambient lighting in their subcompacts) and indirect competitors (no used car offers such advanced technology).

**Channel Impact.** Ford's network of dealers will welcome such a bold, new entry into the market, which could invigorate sales for the Ford brand in general.

**Costs.** Costs are expected to be moderate, including developmental costs for special safety and emissions equipment required for the U.S. market, as well as marketing costs.

**Environment.** The tepid economic recovery after the 2007–2010 recession, as well as continued increase in gasoline prices, will favor lower-priced vehicle categories like subcompacts. The Fiesta is particularly attractive because consumers will not have to sacrifice the luxury features usually only found in larger, more expensive cars.

## Marketing Mix: Distribution

Our distribution tactics reflect the introductory stage of this vehicle in the U.S. market. Figure 13.11 summarizes the distribution tactics.

**Figure 13.11** Distribution Tactics: 2011 Ford Fiesta

| Criteria | 2011 Ford Fiesta |
| --- | --- |
| Intensity | Exclusive: Ford dealers only |
| Distribution Levels, Consumer Markets | Leverage existing Ford dealerships |
| Distribution Levels, Business Markets | Fleet sales not planned for initial launch; will reevaluate as demand grows |
| Distribution Logistics | Inventory levels; sales training; service training; print and online written materials |

**Distribution Intensity**. New 2011 Ford Fiestas will be sold using exclusive distribution outlets, limiting sales only to authorized Ford dealerships to maintain brand control. With Ford's wide network of over 3,800 dealers in the United States, exclusive distribution is not expected to hamper sales. Web-enabled sales will be made available (like preordering over the Internet), but the vehicle will still be picked up at a Ford dealer.[30]

**Distribution Levels**. For consumer markets, new 2011 Ford Fiestas will use the traditional one-level distribution channel, where manufacturers sell automobiles to automotive dealers, who in turn sell them directly to the end consumer.

Sales to business markets (fleet sales) are not planned as part of the original launch plan, but business sales will be re-evaluated as demand grows.

**Distribution Logistics**. We will monitor inventory levels to ensure we do not stock out of what we believe will be a popular car. We will equip Ford dealerships with three essential tools to ensure a smooth launch: sales training (to demonstrate the value of the Fiesta's unique offerings), service training (to educate service personnel on the unique service requirements of the Fiesta), and written materials (print and online versions of brochures, service manuals, and other tools).

## Marketing Mix: Promotion

We have clear promotion goals, as well as a detailed list of proposed communications mix elements. While several elements will be used, social media and digital marketing will play prominently in our promotion plans, due to the high usage of digital media by our target market.

**Promotion Tactics Overview**. As Figure 13.12 shows, our promotion goals are to create awareness about the 2011 Ford Fiesta, to educate consumers into what makes it special, and to get them to test-drive the vehicle at their local Ford dealer. As we indicated earlier, our target market will be millennials, especially early adopters in that group. We will use push efforts (targeting auto dealers with sales training and collateral) and pull efforts (targeting consumers through digital marketing and other means).

**Figure 13.12** Promotion Tactics: 2011 Ford Fiesta

| Criteria | Introduction Phase (General) | 2011 Ford Fiesta |
| --- | --- | --- |
| Goals | Create awareness, educate customers, and stimulate trial | Create awareness, educate customers, and stimulate trial |
| Target Markets | Early adopters | Millennials, especially early adopters |
| Push/Pull Marketing | Push: Product/service demonstrations at retailers; Pull: Educating consumers on benefits | Push: Targeting Ford dealers with sales training and collateral. Pull: Targeting consumers through digital marketing and other means |

**Integrated Marketing Communications**. Throughout all the marketing communications, we will maintain consistent messaging of class-leading fuel economy, zippy performance, and premium features not usually found in subcompact cars. Our goal is to have each element tell a part of a cohesive story. Figure 13.13 shows a summary chart showing our plans for each of the promotion vehicles.

**Advertising**. Because the 2011 Ford Fiesta is new to the U.S. market, our objective is informative advertising, to get customers familiar with the new product. Budget factors suggest a significant budget, due to advertising a new product in a crowded market. We will use an external agency because of the large size of the account, the significant media spending, and our desire for highly creative ads. Non-digital media will include television commercials, radio spots, magazine ads, outdoor advertising, product placement opportunities, as well as displays and supporting material for use at Ford dealers.[31]

**Social Media and Digital Marketing**. During the launch of the 2011 Ford Fiesta extensive use of social media and digital marketing will be made through the Fiesta

**Figure 13.13** Marketing Communications Mix Elements: 2011 Ford Fiesta

| Element | 2011 Ford Fiesta |
| --- | --- |
| Advertising | Objective: Informative advertising<br>Budget Factors: Higher budget due to new product in crowded market<br>In-house vs. External: External due to large account, high media spend, and high creativity desired<br>Media: TV, radio, magazine, outdoor, product placement, dealer point-of-purchase displays |
| Social Media | Ford Fiesta Movement<br>Social networking<br>SEO, SEM<br>Photo sharing<br>Video Sharing<br>Viral Marketing: 100 Agents<br>Fiesta community app |
| Sales Promotions | Fiesta Reservations Program<br>No price-offs or rebates |
| Public Relations | Objective: Drive buzz<br>SEO-enabled press releases<br>Automotive and other media outlets |
| Events & Experiences | Objective: Build awareness<br>Sponsor millennial-based events<br>Race competition version of Fiesta |
| Personal Selling | Leverage Ford dealer network<br>Provide sales training and collateral<br>Fiesta competitive comparison chart |

Movement Campaign, which will build brand awareness and trust, influence acceptance of Web-based information, generate website traffic, create viral buzz, and add incoming links to improve SEO. This important promotion vehicle will also create pathways for educational, empowering, and emotional connections, which will allow customers to gather vehicle information, post opinions, and share their Fiesta brand experiences with others.[32]

Social networking will include content on the Ford Fiesta's Facebook page (facebook.com/fordfiesta), Twitter (twitter.com/fordfiesta), and the Fiesta Movement Facebook page (facebook.com/fiestamovement). Search engine optimization (SEO) will consist of edits to content on Ford.com pages to achieve high organic search results, as well as inbound links from Ford Fiesta Movement sites, such as social networking pages.

Search engine marketing (SEM) will include the use of Google AdWords and other tools to attract customers when searching for such terms as "subcompact cars." Photo and video sharing will include the Ford Fiesta Movement's flickr page (flickr.com/photos/fiestamovement) and YouTube page (youtube.com/fiestamovement). In addition, new owners will be given a USB flash drive with information about the model from which they can download a Fiesta Community app that will help them keep in touch with Ford, their local Ford dealer, and other Fiesta owners.[33]

Viral marketing will be aided by loaning 100 Fiestas to 100 agents (people selected for the span and influence of their networks) for six months in exchange for completing monthly "missions" with different themes (like "Playing Favorites," where agents have five minutes to recreate a favorite film, incorporating their Fiesta). They will record their experiences on Facebook, Twitter, Flicker, and YouTube pages created for the campaign.[34]

**Sales Promotions**. Traditional sales promotions, such as price-offs and rebates, will not be used to avoid price erosion. Instead, sales promotions will be limited to the Fiesta Reservations Program, which will let consumers build, price, and reserve 2011 Ford Fiestas before they become available to dealers. The program will create buzz about the Fiesta's introduction, provide early sales; and capture valuable market feedback on consumer preferences of styles, options, and colors.[35]

**Public Relations**. To publicize the 2011 Ford Fiesta, we will distribute SEO-enabled press releases which will emphasize exciting aspects about the Fiesta, such as early sales successes, unique advertising methods, and the social networking behind it. We will also work with automotive journalists and other important media outlets to place relevant articles.[36]

**Events and Experiences**. In addition to the Ford Fiesta Movement, which will bring intimate experiences to 100 agents, we will feature the Fiesta in events. For example, we plan to provide Ford Fiesta Ride-Alongs at X-Games events and race competition-prepared Fiestas at the Pike's Peak hill climb. We will maintain a "buzz" page on the Ford website to publicize Fiesta-related events.[37]

**Personal Selling**. We will provide sales training and collateral to prepare Ford dealers on the unique attributes of the 2011 Ford Fiesta. In addition, we will include a competitive comparison chart on the Fiesta website so that consumers can get information before visiting dealers. The chart will compare the Fiesta against similar models, showing detailed feature lists, side-by-side photo galleries, and Ford advantages.[38]

**Figure 13.14** Financial Data: 2011 Ford Fiesta (Fictitious Data)

| Financial Data | Description |
| --- | --- |
| Fixed Cost | Fixed cost, Total: $500 million |
| Unit Cost | Cost per unit: $8,000 |
| Price | Average price: $16,000 |
| Sales Forecast | Projected unit sales |
| | Year 1: 40,000 units $\times$ $16,000/unit = $640 million |
| | Year 2: 50,000 units $\times$ $16,000/unit = $800 million |
| | Year 3: 50,000 units $\times$ $16,000/unit = $800 million |

## Finance

The financial aspects of this plan appear feasible, with a break-even point shortly after the first year of production.

**Cost Structure and Sales Forecast**. Figure 13.14 presents the proposed cost structure and sales forecast.

Fixed costs cover automotive design and development, and are staggering for new models. Costs to develop a new vehicle start around $1 billion and can rise to $6 billion for an all-new car on an all-new platform. We estimate the fixed costs to be $500 million, because substantial development on the vehicle was already done for the European model on which the U.S. model is based.

Unit cost represents material and labor costs to produce each vehicle. Sales forecasts are based on a quick ramp-up in sales, propelled by successful social media campaigns (actual financial data are not shown here to preserve confidentiality).[39]

**Break-even**. The cost data result in a break-even volume of 62,500 units, to be achieved after the first year.

Break-even Volume = ($500 million) / ($16,000−$8,000) = 62,500 units

**Pro forma operating income statement**. Figure 13.15 presents the pro forma income statement. The statement shows a loss in the first year of operations, with net income gains in subsequent years.

**Marketing budget**. Figure 13.16 shows the proposed marketing budget for the launch of the 2011 Ford Fiesta. The proposed budget level is 6 percent of projected annual sales, for $38.4 million in the first year. The budget emphasizes spending in the spring and summer seasons, the peak automotive buying seasons. Due to the intensive Internet use of our target market, millennials, 25 percent of the budget will be allocated toward social media and digital marketing. The budget line items break down as follows: [40]

- **Advertising**: This category includes costs for creative development and media placement for ads in television, radio, magazines, outdoor venues, product placement, and other media, using Ford's existing advertising agency.

**Figure 13.15** Pro Forma Income Statement: 2011 Ford Fiesta (Fictitious Data)

| Financial Element | Year 1 | Year 2 | Year 3 |
|---|---|---|---|
| Revenue: | $640 million | $800 million | $800 million |
| Cost of Goods Sold<br>= (Units × Cost/Unit) | $320 million<br>= 40K units × $8K/unit | $400 million<br>= 50K units × $8K/unit | $400 million<br>= 50K units × $8K/unit |
| Gross Margin Amount<br>= Revenue–COGS | $320 million<br>= $640M−$320M | $400 million<br>= $800M−$400M | $400 million<br>= $800M−$400M |
| Gross Margin %<br>= Gross Margin/<br>Revenue | 50%<br>= $320M/$640M | 50%<br>= $400M/$800M | 50%<br>= $400M/$800M |
| Expenses, Total | $480 million | $300 million | $250 million |
| Operating Income | −$160 million<br>= $320M−$480M | $100 million<br>= $400M−$300M | $150 million<br>= $400M−$250M |

- **Social Media and Digital Marketing**: Payments include expenses for SEO contract services, SEM pay-per-click costs, banner ad costs on portal sites, costs to sponsor ads on social media sites like Facebook, costs to create relevant photos and videos to upload onto sites like Flickr and YouTube, and costs for labor to monitor the impact of keywords and social media conversations.
- **Sales Promotions**: Charges include costs to fund Fiesta Reservations Program, to be completed in the first few months after launch.
- **Public Relations**: This category includes expenditures for SEO-enabled press release wire fees and article submissions.

**Figure 13.16** Proposed Marketing Budget: 2011 Ford Fiesta (Fictitious Data)

| Budget Category | Amount (%) | Jan | Feb | Mar | Apr | May | Jun | Jul | Aug | Sep | Oct | Nov | Dec |
|---|---|---|---|---|---|---|---|---|---|---|---|---|---|
| Advertising | 35 | 1 | 1 | 4 | 4 | 4 | 4 | 4 | 4 | 4 | 2 | 1 | 2 |
| Social Media & Digital Marketing | 25 | 1 | 1 | 2 | 3 | 3 | 3 | 3 | 3 | 3 | 1 | 1 | 1 |
| Sales Promotions | 5 | 1 | 1 | 1 | 1 | 1 | | | | | | | |
| Public Relations | 5 | 0.2 | 0.3 | 0.5 | 0.5 | 0.5 | 0.5 | 0.5 | 0.5 | 0.5 | 0.5 | 0.3 | 0.2 |
| Events | 20 | 1 | 1 | 2 | 2 | 2 | 2 | 2 | 2 | 2 | 2 | 1 | 1 |
| Personal Selling | 5 | 1 | 1 | 1 | 1 | 1 | | | | | | | |
| Other Items | 5 | 1 | 1 | 1 | 1 | 1 | | | | | | | |
| Total | 100 | | | | | | | | | | | | |

- **Events**: The events section includes costs to sponsor events popular with the target market, such as the X-Games, as well as racing events.
- **Personal Selling**: This category includes training costs for Ford dealer salespeople, to be completed in the first few months after launch.
- **Other Items**: Other costs are also expected, such as expenses for providing 100 cars for six months to support the Fiesta Movement viral campaign, to be completed in the first few months after launch.

## Implementation

We plan to leverage several planning and control tools to ensure a smooth implementation.

**Schedule**. Figure 13.17 shows a partial launch schedule for the 2011 Ford Fiesta. The schedule organizes tasks into four categories:

- **Infrastructure Activities**: This category addresses tasks to support all ongoing operations, such as registering for a new Fiesta Movement Facebook page to implement the Fiesta Movement plans.

**Figure 13.17** Launch Schedule: 2011 Ford Fiesta (Partial)

| Task | Description | Resources | Status | Jan | Feb | Mar |
|---|---|---|---|---|---|---|
| 1 | **Infrastructure Activities** | | | | | |
| 1.1 | Acquire cars for Fiesta Movement | Joe | 100% | Start: 1/3 | End: 2/3 | |
| 1.2 | Acquire social media pages | Chris | 80% | Start 1/3 | End: 2/3 | |
| 2 | **Pre-Launch Activities** | | | | | |
| 2.1 | Develop creative content for ads | Bill | 30% | Start: 1/7 | End: 2/7 | |
| 2.2 | Develop social media website content | Chris | 40% | Start: 1/7 | End: 2/7 | |
| 2.3 | Prepare dealer sales training material | Maria Sales mgr. | | | | |
| 3 | **Launch Activities** | | | | | |
| 3.1 | Update Fiesta Movement social media | Chris | New Task | | Start: 2/10 | End: 3/20 |
| 3.2 | Launch advertising campaign | Bill Agency X | New Task | | Start: 2/10 | End: 3/20 |
| 3.3 | Conduct dealer sales training | Sales mgr. | | | | |
| 4 | **Milestones/ Deliverables** | | | | | |
| 4.1 | 1,000th Friend on Fiesta Facebook page | Joe | Pending | | Goal: 2/15 | |
| 4.2 | 10,000th Ford Fiesta Customer | Bill | Pending | | | Goal: 3/31 |

- **Pre-launch Activities**: Here we include preparatory tasks, such as developing content for social media websites.
- **Launch Activities**: Launch activities include tasks such as announcements and campaign initiations, such as launching advertising campaigns.
- **Milestones and Deliverables**: We will track major accomplishments, such as recognizing our 10,000th customer.

**Control Metrics**. We will track the values of a metrics family table during the project to ensure the project stays on track. We plan to measure three sets of metrics. Figure 13.18 presents the metrics family table.

- **Awareness**: We will drive positive knowledge for the brand through social media and other channels to build awareness. A Microsoft study found that 70 percent of millennials will be driving in 2010 (the launch date of the car) and that 77 percent of them use a social networking site like Facebook daily (hopefully not while driving!). We will use social media to enable the metrics, like online straw polls to measure brand recognition and recall, and Web analytics to obtain metrics like mentions per day and brand-specific searches.[41]
- **Market Share**: We will monitor Fiesta sales along with those of competitors to calculate relative market share and ensure we are on track to meet our objective. We will also monitor automotive journals to capture their reaction on the Fiesta's relatively high price and assess the price's impact on sales.[42]
- **Satisfaction**: Once customers are aware of the product, they must be satisfied with it to ensure strong word-of-mouth advertising. We will monitor third-party organizations (like ratings from J.D. Powers) and social media (like sentiment trends) to gauge satisfaction, as well as traditional customer satisfaction questionnaires.[43]

**Figure 13.18** Metrics Family Table: 2011 Ford Fiesta

| Metric Family | Description | Example Metrics |
|---|---|---|
| Awareness | Shows performance of efforts toward brand recognition and recall | Brand recognition<br>Brand recall<br>Potential reach (number of fans)<br>Mentions per day<br>Brand-specific searches |
| Market Share | Shows performance of sales efforts | Ford Fiesta sales by month<br>Ford Fiesta sales by geography<br>Competitor sales |
| Customer Satisfaction | Shows performance of efforts toward customer satisfaction | Third party ratings (J.D. Powers)<br>Social media: sentiment trends<br>Customer satisfaction questionnaires |

**Figure 13.19**  Contingency Plan: 2011 Ford Fiesta

| Contingency Scenario | Contingency Plan Trigger | Contingency Plan Actions |
| --- | --- | --- |
| Low Awareness | Awareness below 50% in target market | Gather market research<br>Assess communications vehicles<br>Reevaluate advertising |
| Low Market Share | Market share 20% below forecast | Affirm value of car<br>Provide incentives<br>Reprice |
| Low Satisfaction | Below top 3 in quality rankings | Assess perceptions of quality<br>Target areas for improvement<br>Advertise path to quality |

**Contingency planning**.  The proposed contingency plans provide specific courses of action if the actual marketing metrics fall below their expected values. Figure 13.19 shows a contingency plan that addresses three possible scenarios.

- **Low Awareness**: The first scenario covers the possibility that awareness of the brand falls below 50 percent of the target market. If that occurs, Ford should consider speaking with representatives of the target market to determine what new channels to use. In addition, they should assess if the messaging used is appropriate for the audience, and if the communications vehicles are effective.
- **Low Market Share**: If the market share falls below forecast by 20 percent, Ford will need to investigate why. To address the situation, Ford should take three steps. First, it should convey value-based messaging, affirming that a premium car deserves a premium price. Second, it might consider short-term incentives to dealers to boost car sales. Third, if all else fails, it might need to consider repricing the vehicle more in line with its competitors—this step is taken only as a last resort.
- **Low Satisfaction**: If the 2011 Ford Fiesta falls below the top rankings of independent rankings by J.D. Power and other rating agencies (such as dropping below the top three ranked vehicles), Ford will need to take action. For example, it will need to understand how quality is perceived and target the areas for improvement. It will also need to advertise its efforts to improve quality to ensure that the public understand the importance that quality plays with Ford.

# Sample Marketing Plan: 2011 Ford Fiesta: Ten Slide Format

Many organizations have adopted a ten slide rule, where presenters must limit their presentations to only ten slides. To accommodate this trend, we show here an abbreviated format that condenses the marketing plan content into ten slides. Different organizations use different formats and they can vary from the model shown here. Some formats dictate that the last slide be a call to action. Other formats specify that the last slide be a schedule and list of next steps. Readers should adapt the format to suit their organization's style.[44]

## Marketing Plan: 2011 Ford Fiesta

Figures 13.20 through 13.29 present the marketing plan for the 2011 Ford Fiesta in the ten slide format.

---

**Figure 13.20** Ten Slide Format: Executive Summary

### MARKETING PLAN: 2011 FORD FIESTA
### Executive Summary

| | |
|---|---|
| Objective | Increase market of subcompact cars sold in U.S. market<br>Goal: 10% by end of 2012 |
| Market Overview | U.S. Subcompact car market poised for growth<br>Size: 460K units/year<br>Market trends support sustained growth |
| Market Segments | Primary buyer: Millennial (14 – 29 years)<br>80 million people; 20% of automotive buying market |
| Competitive Landscape | Market leader to date: Honda Fit, 14.6% share<br>Market crowded with major competitors |
| Marketing Mix | Product: #1 in fuel economy; premium features<br>Pricing: Premium pricing to support positioning<br>Distribution: Leverage 3,800 U.S. Ford dealers<br>Promotion: 25% of budget to social media |

---

**Figure 13.21** Ten Slide Format: Market

### MARKETING PLAN: 2011 FORD FIESTA
### Market

| | |
|---|---|
| Size | About 460K units/year |
| Growth | Projected 11% CAGR |
| Market Trends | Political: NHTSA CAFÉ Standard: 35.7 MPG in 2015<br>Economic: Continuing high gasoline prices<br>Social: Small cars seen as fashionable now<br>Technological: ABS and ESC make small cars safer |
| Competitive Landscape | Market leader to date: Honda Fit, 14.6% share<br>Market crowded with major competitors |
| Target Segment | Millennials: Born 1982–1985: "Digital Generation"<br>High potential: 80 million people<br>Strong alignment: New Ford technologies: SYNC<br>Clear marketability: 77% use social media actively<br>Positioning: "Premium features in a subcompact" |

**Figure 13.22** Ten Slide Format: Competitive Landscape

### MARKETING PLAN: 2011 FORD FIESTA
#### Competitive Landscape

| Criteria | Ford Fiesta | BMW MINI | Honda Fit | Toyota Yaris |
|---|---|---|---|---|
| Market Share | New to USA | 8.4% | 14.6% | 13.9% |
| Messaging | Subcompact with big car luxuries | European luxury and performance | Quality & design with cargo size of a small SUV | Quality and reliability of Toyota |
| Strength | Manufacturing | Marketing | Design | Operations |
| Weakness | "Old" brand | Service costs | Launched 2001 | Recalls |
| MPG | 30 city/40 hwy | 32 city/37 hwy | 27 city/33 hwy | 29 city/36 hwy |
| Pricing | Premium | Superpremium | Moderate | Low/moderate |

**Figure 13.23** Ten Slide Format: Product

### MARKETING PLAN: 2011 FORD FIESTA
#### Product

| | |
|---|---|
| Features | Blockbuster feature: Class-leading MPG<br>Technology features: SYNC, Bluetooth (for Millennial market)<br>Premium features: Leather seats, Satellite navigation<br>Parity features: Meets expectations for cargo volume, etc. |
| Quality | Leverage Ford's reputation for quality |
| Packaging | Offer 5 different models to suit different tastes & applications |
| Brand | Emphasize innovation and new technologies<br>Change brand perception: "Old" → "Innovative" |
| Value Proposition | To millennials, who appreciate luxury amenities in a subcompact package, and demand economy, performance, and safety, the 2011 is a premium subcompact car that offers class-leading MPG and Ford quality with sexy styling.<br>Unlike other subcompacts, the Fiesta doesn't make you give up comfort to take advantage of smaller car virtues |

**Figure 13.24** Ten Slide Format: Pricing

## MARKETING PLAN: 2011 FORD FIESTA
### Pricing

| | |
|---|---|
| Objective | Product-quality leadership |
| Approach | Perceived value |
| | Premium pricing to signal premium positioning |
| Management | Minimize price discounts and incentives |
| Competitor Impact | Direct competitors: Fiesta includes premium features not found in competitive models |
| | Indirect competitors: No used car offers such technology |
| Channel Impact | Ford dealer network expected to welcome bold new entry |
| Environment Impact | Slow economic recovery and high gasoline prices favor frugal cars like subcompacts over luxury cars |

As one can see, the ten slide format contains most of the data found in the traditional report-based version, albeit in a shorter form. It is recommended that the marketer prepare the traditional format first in any event and then summarize the content into the ten slide format as needed. In that way, background information is available if needed.

**Figure 13.25** Ten Slide Format: Distribution

## MARKETING PLAN: 2011 FORD FIESTA
### Distribution

| | |
|---|---|
| Intensity | Exclusive; Ford dealers only |
| Levels: Consumer | Leverage existing Ford dealerships |
| | Network: 3,800 U.S. dealers → sample number of outlets |
| Levels: Business | Fleet sales not planned for initial launch |
| | Will reevaluate as demand grows |
| Logistics | Manage inventory levels |
| | Sales training |
| | Service training |
| | Print and online written materials |

**Figure 13.26** Ten Slide Format: Promotion

**MARKETING PLAN: 2011 FORD FIESTA**
**Promotion**

| | |
|---|---|
| Social Media | Strong emphasis; Target to millennial market<br>Social networking: Facebook, Twitter, photo & video Sharing<br>Ford Fiesta movement: Viral marketing via 100 Agents<br>Fiesta Community App |
| Advertising | Leverage existing external agency<br>Pull: TV, radio, magazine, outdoor, product placement<br>Push: Dealer point-of-purchase displays |
| Sales Promotions | Limited to Fiesta reservations program; no rebates |
| Public Relations | Drive buzz through SEO-enabled press releases and articles |
| Events & Experiences | Build awareness by sponsoring millennial events<br>Race competition version of Fiesta |
| Personal Selling | Train Ford dealer salespeople on unique aspects of car<br>Ford Fiesta competitive comparison chart |

**Figure 13.27** Ten Slide Format: Finance

**MARKETING PLAN: 2011 FORD FIESTA**
**Finance**

| | | | |
|---|---|---|---|
| Costs | Fixed cost: $500M;  Unit cost: $8K | | |
| Break-Even | ($500M)/($16K $-$ $8K) = 62,500 units | | |
| Pro-Forma Income | Year 1 | Year 2 | Year 3 |
| Revenue | $640M | $800M | $800M |
| Cost of Goods Sold | $320M | $400M | $400M |
| Gross Margin Amount | $320M | $400M | $400M |
| Gross Margin Percentage | 50% | 50% | 50% |
| Expenses | $480M | $300M | $250M |
| Operating Income | ($160M) | $100M | $150M |

**Figure 13.28** Ten Slide Format: Schedule

**MARKETING PLAN: 2011 FORD FIESTA**
**Schedule**

| Tasks | Description | Person | Jan | Feb | Mar | Apr |
|---|---|---|---|---|---|---|
| 1 | Infrastructure | | | | | |
| 1.1 | Acquire cars for campaign | Joe | Start: 1/5 | | End: 3/1 | |
| 1.2 | Acquire social media pages | Chris | Start: 1/6 | | | End: 4/1 |
| 2 | Pre-launch Activities | | | | | |
| 2.1 | Develop creative content for ads | Bill | Start: 1/9 | | End:3/3 | |
| 2.2 | Build social media website content | Chris | Start: 2/2 | | End:4/2 | |
| 3 | Launch activities | | | | | |
| 3.1 | Update Fiesta movement media | Chris | | | Start:3/1 | End:4/1 |
| 3.2 | Launch advertising campaign | Bill | | | Start:3/1 | End:4/1 |
| 4 | Milestones/deliverables | | | | | |
| 4.1 | 1,000th Friend on Facebook page | Chris | | | | Goal: 6/1 |
| 4.2 | 10,000th Ford Fiesta customer | Joe | | | | Goal: 6/1 |

**Figure 13.29** Ten Slide Format: Control Metrics

**MARKETING PLAN: 2011 FORD FIESTA**
**Control Metrics**

| Metrics Family | Description | Metrics to Track |
|---|---|---|
| Awareness | Brand recognition and recall | Potential reach<br>Mentions per day<br>Brand-specific searches |
| Market Share | Sales performance | Sales by month<br>Sales by geography<br>Sales by competitors |
| Customer Satisfaction | Likelihood to recommend | Third party ratings<br>Social media sentiment<br>Satisfaction questionnaires |

## Summary

Benjamin Franklin understood the power of creating effective plans and executing them faithfully, when he said, "Resolve to perform what you ought; perform without fail what you resolve."

In this final chapter, we examined two examples of a typical marketing plan. The first example used the traditional report-based format for marketing plans.

Much like a typical report, the traditional approach uses explanatory text and footnotes, along with tables and charts to summarize results. The second example showed the use of the alternative format, which uses just ten presentation slides to summarize the entire marketing plan.

The report-based and ten slide formats both have their strengths and weaknesses. The report-based format is quite thorough, but is often longer than desired by time-starved managers. The alternative ten slide version is compact and concise, but fails to give all the detail one sometimes needs.

It is recommended that the marketer first prepare the marketing plan using the report-based format and then summarize it using the ten slide format. In that way, one can document all his or her research in the longer report-style format and be prepared to answer any questions that may arise in the future.

## Key Terms

**Ten slide marketing plan format** Abbreviated marketing plan format using only ten presentation slides to summarize essential aspects of the plan. (p. 278)

**Report-based marketing plan format** Traditional report-based marketing plan format, providing explanatory text for each section of the plan. (p. 278)

## Discussion Questions

1. What types of organizations would best be suited for the report-style marketing plan format? What types of organizations would the ten slide format suit?

2. One criticism levied at the ten slide format is that it does not have enough detail to serve as a stand-alone document to someone unfamiliar with the product/service and/or market. How could the ten slide format be modified to improve its understanding by people not close to the project, while keeping it brief?

## Exercises

1. Convert the marketing plan created thus far into the ten slide format.

2. Test the popularity of the different formats in your organization by circulating both of them to willing senior management participants and ask them which one they prefer.

# ENDNOTES

## CHAPTER 1

1. Donald R. Lehmann and Russell S. Winer, *Analysis for Marketing Planning*, 7th ed. (Burr Ridge, IL: Irwin/McGraw Hill, 2008), 1.
2. "Will Nintendo's Wii Strategy Score?" *BusinessWeek*, September 20, 2006, http://www.businessweek.com/globalbiz/content/sep2006/gb20060920_163780.htm
3. Lehmann and Winer, *Analysis for Marketing Planning*, 5.
4. "Nintendo Does Not Console Microsoft," *Forbes*, January 28, 2009, http://www.forbes.com/2009/01/28/wii-playstation-xbox-personal-finance-investing-ideas_0128_videogames.html
5. "Nintendo Wii Marketing to Exceed $200 Million," *Joystiq Video Console Blog*, November 12, 2006, http://www.joystiq.com/2006/11/12/nintendo-wii-marketing-to-exceed-200-million/
6. "Wii's Future in Motion," *Forbes*, December 1, 2008, http://www.forbes.com/2008/11/28/nintendo-wii-wii2-tech-personal-cz-cs-1201wii.html
7. Tim Calkins, *Breakthrough Marketing Plans* (New York: Palgrave MacMillan, 2008), 28.
8. "Nintendo Hopes Wii Spells Wiiner," *USA Today*, August 15, 2006, http://www.usatoday.com/tech/gaming/2006-08-14-nintendo-qa_x.htm
9. *Joystiq Video Console Blog,* http://www.joystiq.com/2006/11/12/nintendo-wii-marketing-to-exceed-200-million/
10. Evelyn Jerome McCarthy and William D. Perreault, *Basic Marketing: A Global-Managerial Approach*, 14th ed. (Homewood, IL: McGraw-Hill Irwin, 2002).
11. "Revolution Renamed Wii," *Gamespot*, August 27, 2006, http://www.gamespot.com/news/6148462.html
12. "Is a Nintendo Wii Price Drop Finally on the Horizon?" *The Tech Herald*, August 28, 2009, http://www.thetechherald.com/article.php/200935/4326/Is-a-Nintendo-Wii-price-drop-finally-on-the-horizon
13. "Nintendo Launches WiiWare," *CBS News*, May 14, 2008, http://www.cbsnews.com/stories/2008/05/13/paidcontent/main4094460.shtml?source=related_story

## CHAPTER 2

1. "Hilton Expands, Wyndham's Cautious Note," *Forbes.com*, March 4, 2008.
2. Philip Kotler and Kevin Lane Keller, *Marketing Management*, 13th ed. (Upper Saddle River, NJ: Pearson Prentice-Hall, 2009), 42.
3. Hampton website, part of Hilton organization, http://www.hamptonfranchise.com
4. Kotler and Keller, *Marketing Management,* 36.
5. "Hilton Family of Hotels to Utilize Enterprise-Wide Technology at Check-In for Better Guest Recognition and Enhanced Service," *Hilton Press Release,* May 8, 2003.
6. Michael Porter, *Competitive Advantage* (New York: Free Press, 1985).
7. Hilton 2006 Annual Report.
8. Peter F. Drucker, *The Practice of Management* (New York and Evanston: Harper & Row, 1954).
9. Expedia website, Company overview page.
10. Expedia website, Investor relations page.
11. Expedia Annual Report, 2009.

## CHAPTER 3

1. Philip Kotler and Kevin Lane Keller, *Marketing Management*, 13th ed. (Upper Saddle River, NJ: Prentice-Hall, 2009), 9.
2. "An Wang: The Core of the Computer Era," *BusinessWeek*, July 14, 2004.
3. "The Laptop in 2015: Not Your Daddy's Notebook," *PC World*, July 15, 2009.
4. "Report from the NPD Group Shows 45 Percent of Heavy Video Gamers are in the Six- to 17-Year Old Age Group," *NPD Press Release,* September 19, 2006.
5. "Gartner Says Worldwide Mobile Phone Sales Declined 6 Per Cent and Smartphones Grew 27 Per Cent in Second Quarter of 2009," *Gartner*, August 12, 2009.
6. "Combo PET-CT Scans Can Spot Hidden Cancers," *BusinessWeek*, January 12, 2010.
7. Kotler and Keller, *Marketing Management*, 72–86.
8. "New Luxury Tax Trimming Boat Sales," *New York Times*, July 21, 1991.
9. "EU Ponders Carbon Tariff on Imports," *BusinessWeek*, January 8, 2008.
10. "Cash for Clunkers' Lasting Impact," *Newsweek*, August 25, 2009.
11. "Rate Rise Clouds Recovery," *Wall Street Journal*, June 11, 2009.
12. "McDonald's Global Same-Store Sales Rise 5.1% in May," *MarketWatch*, June 8, 2009.
13. "Report: Small Business Credit Card Use Creates Jobs," *Inc.*, July 16, 2010.
14. "Hilton Hotels Corporation Announces Global Sustainability Goals" *Hilton Hotels Press Release*, June 4, 2008.
15. "Marketers Watching Baby Boomer Eating Trends," *(San Francisco) Examiner*, August 10, 2009.
16. "The Decline of the English Divorce," *Economist*, July 16, 2009.
17. "The End of Excess: Is This Crisis Good for America?" *Time*, May 26, 2009.
18. "Notebook Sales Outpace Desktop Sales," *eWeek*, December 24, 2008.
19. "VMworld 2009: Virtualization, Controversy and Eating Your Own Dog Food," *CIO*, September 3, 2009.
20. Michael Porter, *Competitive Strategy* (New York: The Free Press, 1980), 3–28.
21. "Global Brands," *BusinessWeek*, August 1, 2005.
22. Home Depot website: Kids Workshops.
23. "Corn Sugar vs. HFCS: Which Would You Buy?" *Advertising Age*, September 14, 2010.
24. "Chile Plans to Open Up Lithium Mining, Minister Says," *BusinessWeek*, April 30, 2010.
25. "Radiohead's Web Venture Spooks Wall Street," *Cnet*, November 7, 2007.
26. "Global Online Travel Overview: Comparing Three Major Regions: U.S., Europe and Asia Pacific," *PhoCusWright*, February 2010.
27. "Online Travel Growth Expected to Slow Substantially," *Travel Weekly* (Travel industry newspaper), January 27, 2010.

28. "The H1N1 Virus: Varied Local Responses to a Global Spread," *YaleGlobal Online*, September 1, 2009.

29. "Destination 2010: Top Travel Trends to Watch," *Scene Advisor*, November 4, 2009.

30. "Travel Facts and Statistics," U.S. Travel Association (www.ustravel.org).

31. "Great No-Cost Software," *Inc.*, September 1, 2009.

32. "Google May Face U.S. Antitrust Suit over ITA Purchase," *BusinessWeek*, January 14, 2011.

## CHAPTER 4

1. Philip Kotler and Kevin Lane Keller, *Marketing Management*, 13th ed. (Upper Saddle River, NJ: Pearson Prentice-Hall, 2009), 213–226.

2. "Latest Census Data Shows Winners and Losers," *BusinessWeek*, December 10, 2009.

3. U.S. Census Bureau, Metropolitan and Micropolitan Statistical Areas Web page, www.census.gov

4. Claritas PRIZM website, www.claritas.com

5. "You've Been Yelped," *Inc.*, February 1, 2010.

6. Strategic Business Insights VALS website: www.strategicbusinessinsights.com/vals

7. "Marketing: Sell It to the Psyche," *Time*, September 15, 2003.

8. "Shoot the Focus Group," *BusinessWeek*, November 14, 2005.

9. "Intuit's Small Business Maven," *BusinessWeek*, May 12, 2004.

10. "Case Study: Bank of America: How It Learned that What Customers Really Want Is to Keep the Change," *BusinessWeek*, June 19, 2006.

11. "Why Women Secretly Enjoy Business Travel," *Inc*, March 9, 2010.

12. Kotler and Keller, *Marketing Management*, 182–185.

13. "Timken Plots a Rust Belt Resurgence," *BusinessWeek*, October 15, 2009.

14. Kotler and Keller, *Marketing Management*, 226–227.

15. Chicago Nut and Bolt website, www.chicagonutandbolt.com

16. LOD Consulting Group website, www.lod.com

17. Caterpillar website, www.cat.com

18. Aisle-Master website, www.aisle-master.com

19. DM Solar website, www.dmsolar.com

20. Donald Lehmann and Russell Winer, *Analysis for Marketing Planning*, 7th ed. (New York: McGraw-Hill, 2008), 96–106.

21. Kotler and Keller, *Marketing Management*, 228.

22. "Nightlife: No More Dirty Dancing," *Newsweek*, April 18, 2009. 23. "The Top 10 Everything in 2009: Canon EOS-1D Mark IV," *Time*, December 8, 2009.

23. "The Top 10 Everything in 2009: Canon EOS-1D Mark IV," *Time*, December 8, 2009.

24. "Campfire Questions: Like Any Major Organization Catering to Kids, the Boy Scouts of America Need to Attract Young Latinos in Order to Survive," *Newsweek*, January 17, 2009.

25. Kotler and Keller, *Marketing Management*, 228

26. E-A-R website, www.e-a-r.com

27. EnGarde website, www.engardebodyarmor.com

28. "A Look that's Bulletproof," *New York Times*, January 20, 2010.

29. JIMS USA website, www.jimsusa.com/tools

30. Ries and Trout, *Positioning—The Battle for Your Mind* (New York: McGraw Hill, 1981), 43–60.

31. Kevin Keller, *Strategic Brand Management*, 3rd ed. (Upper Saddle River, NJ: Pearson Publishing, 2009), 107–110.

32. Select Comfort website, www.selectcomfort.com

33. "Friendster 2.0: This Isn't Going to End Well," *Newsweek*, December 7, 2009.

34. Al Ries and Jack Trout, *Positioning—The Battle for Your Mind*, 43–60.

35. Komatsu website, www.komatsuforkliftusa.com

36. Crown website, www.crown.com

37. Hyster website, www.hyster.com

38. Toyota website, www.toyota8series.com

39. Aisle-Master website, www.aisle-master.com

40. Marine Lift Systems website, www.marineliftsystems.com

41. Caterpillar website, www.cat.com

42. Keller, *Strategic Brand Management,* 107–110.

43. Caterpillar website, www.cat.com

44. Komatsu website, www.komatsuforkliftusa.com

45. Travel Market Report, "Adventure Travel Put at $89 billion Global Market." August 9, 2010.

46. "Travel Sites Lack Competitive Edge." *The Motley Fool*, August 20, 2001.

## CHAPTER 5

1. Philip Kotler and Kevin Lane Keller, *Marketing Management*, 13th ed. (Upper Saddle River, NJ: Pearson Prentice-Hall, 2009), 301.

2. Ronald D. Michman, *The Food Industry Wars* (West Port, CT: Praeger Publishing, 1998), 111.

3. Donald Lehmann and Russell Winer, *Analysis for Marketing Planning*, 5th ed. (New York: McGraw Hill, 2000), 33.

4. "Nokia Fights to Hold on to Smartphone Dominance," *CNET*, March 11, 2009.

5. Kotler and Keller, *Marketing Management,* 47–50

6. "How Apple Got Everything Right by Doing Everything Wrong," *Wired*, April 2, 2008.

7. "Is Optimism a Competitive Advantage?" *BusinessWeek*, August 13, 2009.

8. "Amazon.com's Reputation Is Well-Deserved," *ComputerWeekly.com*.

9. "Faithful, Sometimes Fanatical. Apple Customers Continue to Push the Boundaries of Loyalty," *San Francisco Chronicle*, March 26, 2006.

10. "Does It Pay to Buy Organic?" *BusinessWeek*, September 6, 2004.

11. "Gartner Says Worldwide Mobile Phone Sales Declined 6 Per Cent and Smartphones Grew 27 Per Cent in Second Quarter of 2009," *Gartner Press Release*, August 12, 2009.

12. Donald Lehmann and Russell Winer, *Analysis for Marketing Planning*, 7th ed. (New York: McGraw-Hill, 2008), 96–106.

13. "Loose Lips Sink You," *Inc.*, June 1, 1999.

14. "Hotel Reservations Keep OTAs Alive, For Now," *HotelMarketing.com*, July 21, 2009.

15. "Priceline, Travelocity, and Expedia Compete with iPhone Apps," *BNET.com*, November 5, 2009.

16. "CEO-Generated Content: Expedia Leader Says No IPO in Store for TripAdvisor," *Tnooz.com* (travel technology website), February 11, 2010.

17. "Travel Sites Lack Competitive Edge," *Fool.com*, August 20, 2001.

18. Ibid.

19. "Priceline.com Retools, Relaunches Itself as a One-Stop Internet Travel Service for Bargain Hunters," *Priceline.com Press Release*, April 11, 2005.

## CHAPTER 6

1. "Malcolm Gladwell on Spaghetti Sauce," *Ted2004 Conference,* ted.com, February 2004.
2. "Fashionably Connected," *Newsweek,* February 19, 2007.
3. BoostMobile website, www.boostmobile.com
4. "Dial D for Diagnosis," *Newsweek,* August 11, 2009.
5. David Aaker, *Strategic Market Management,* 5th ed. (New York: Wiley, 1998), 203–220.
6. Michael Porter, *Competitive Strategy: Techniques for Analyzing Industries and Competitors* (New York: Free Press, 1980), Chapter 2.
7. "P&G's Olay Looks to Exploit New Wrinkle in the Market," *Brandweek,* January 10, 2009.
8. Google website, Google Apps for Business, google.com
9. "Capturing the Niche: Travelers Are Seeking Focused, Meaningful Trips—And Tour Operators Are Happy to Comply," *Newsweek,* May 5, 2007.
10. Igor Ansoff, "Strategies for Diversification," *Harvard Business Review* 35, no. 5 (1957): 113–124.
11. "Zara Looks to Asia for Growth: The Clothing Retailer's Focus on Asian Expansion amid the West's Economic Slump Has Investors Buying Up Shares of Spanish-based Parent Inditex," *BusinessWeek,* August 26, 2009.
12. "FarmVille Surpasses 80 Million Users," *Mashable,* February 20, 2010.
13. "The Race to Build Really Cheap Cars," *BusinessWeek,* April 23, 2007.
14. "At 3M, A Struggle between Efficiency and Creativity," *BusinessWeek,* June 11, 2007.
15. David Aaker, *Managing Brand Equity* (New York: The Free Press, 1991), 17, 270.
16. "The Case for Sustainable Differentiation," *BusinessWeek,* May 14, 2010.
17. Don Peppers and Martha Rogers, *Managing Customer Relationships: A Strategic Framework* (Hoboken, NJ: John Wiley & Sons, 2004), 17–19.
18. Schwab website, www.schwabadvisorcenter.com
19. "Geek Squad: Best Buy's Secret Sauce?" *ZDNet.com,* June 23, 2008.
20. "How Ritz-Carlton Maintains Its Mystique," *BusinessWeek,* February 13, 2007.
21. "Large Brokers Continue to Dominate Market for Serving Affluent, Despite Poor Client Satisfaction," *Phoenix Marketing International,* February 2005.
22. "Online Boutiques," *Newsweek,* March 28, 2008.
23. Philip Kotler and Kevin Lane Keller, *Marketing Management,* 13th ed. (Upper Saddle River, NJ: Pearson Prentice-Hall, 2009), 316–495.

## CHAPTER 7

1. Philip Kotler and Kevin Lane Keller, *Marketing Management,* 13th ed. (Upper Saddle River, NJ: Pearson Prentice-Hall, 2009), 316–495.
2. "Fred Smith on the Birth of FedEx," *BusinessWeek,* September 20, 2004.
3. "The Worst Products of the Year," *Fox News,* November 28, 2005.
4. Kotler, Philip, *Marketing Management,* 6th ed. (Upper Saddle River, NJ: Prentice-Hall, 1988), 349
5. Everest Rogers, *Diffusion of Innovations,* 3rd ed. (New York: Free Press. 1963), 247.

6. "Report from the NPD Group Shows 45 Percent of Heavy Video Gamers Are in the Six- to 17-Year Old Age Group," *NPD Press Release,* September 19, 2006.
7. "It's True: The Zune Is Incompatible with Vista," *ZDNet.com,* November 14, 2006.
8. "Consumer Vigilantes," *BusinessWeek,* February 21, 2008.
9. "Meet the Apple Pack Rats," *Wired,* September 15, 2005.
10. "Expand Your Personal Brand a la Perez Hilton," *BusinessWeek,* September 5, 2009.
11. Kotler and Keller, *Marketing Management,* 278–279.
12. Geoffrey Moore, *Crossing the Chasm* (New York: HarperBusiness, 1991), 161.
13. "Owners of Digital Music Players Represent an Attractive Audience for Consumer Electronics Advertisers," *ComScore Press Release,* November 15, 2006.
14. Tune Hotel website, tunehotels.com
15. Kotler and Keller, *Marketing Management,* 321–325.
16. "Red, White and Bold: Forget Taciturn Toyota. The Carmaker's Got a New American Attitude: It's Taking Risks, Adding US Factories and Wearing Its Ambitions on Its Sleeve," *Newsweek,* April 25, 2005.
17. Kotler and Keller, *Marketing Management,* 326.
18. "Solar Power's New Style," *Time Magazine,* June 12, 2008.
19. Bernard H. Booms, and Mary J. Bitner, "Marketing Strategies and Organization Structure for Service Firms," in *Marketing of Services,* eds., James H. Donnelly and William R. George (Chicago, IL: American Marketing Association, 1981), 47–51
20. Kotler and Keller, *Marketing Management,* 349–352.
21. "Flying Like an Eagle?" *Newsweek,* October 5, 2009.
22. "Quality Service Makes Happy Customers and Greater Profits," *Entrepreneur,* Winter 1998.
23. From the Peppers and Rogers Group, "Inside the Ritz-Carlton's Revolutionary Service," *1to1 Magazine,* February 27, 2007.
24. "Taiwan's Hotel Rating System: A Service Quality Perspective," *Entrepreneur,* November 2007.
25. Westin website, westin.com

## CHAPTER 8

1. "Charlie Rose Talks to Wal-Mart's Mike Duke," *BusinessWeek,* December 1, 2010.
2. Philip Kotler and Kevin Lane Keller, *Marketing Management,* 13th ed. (Upper Saddle River, NJ: Pearson Prentice-Hall, 2009), 383–388.
3. "Why Apple Leaves Low-End Computers to the Competition," *BusinessWeek,* November 11, 2009.
4. "LCD Fights Plasma for Giant TV Market," *BusinessWeek,* August 25, 2006.
5. "Buy-Bye, Wireless Guys: How Silicon Valley Conquered the Carriers," *Newsweek,* February 3, 2010.
6. "Samsung SDI Says Its AMOLED Production to Reach Economies of Scale in 2009," *DigiTimes.com,* April 22, 2008.
7. "Expedia, Priceline and Orbitz Rejoice at Hotel Tax Rollback," *BNET.com,* February 2, 2010.
8. Kotler and Keller, *Marketing Management,* 278–287.
9. "Vinyl Gets Its Groove Back," *Time Magazine,* January 10, 2008.
10. Kotler and Keller, *Marketing Management,* 383–385.
11. "Semiconductor Report: Pricing Free-Fall Ends," *Purchasing.com,* March 13, 2008.
12. Kotler and Keller, *Marketing Management,* 390–395.

13. "Newsweek Plans Makeover to Fit a Smaller Audience," *New York Times*, February 8, 2009.
14. "Extra Fees Add to Travelers' Disdain for Bigger Airlines," *USA Today*, September 15, 2010.
15. Gary Lilien and Arvind Rangaswamy, *Marketing Engineering*, Revised 2nd ed. (Victoria, BC: Trafford Publishing, 2004).
16. "China Car Dealers Cut Prices as Vehicle Demand Cools," *BusinessWeek*, July 22, 2010.
17. "The Price is Wrong; Matching Your Competitors' Prices Could Be Illegal," *Entrepreneur*, May 1996.
18. "Low Prices and Booze Put Brunch on the Rise," *Time Magazine*, November 21, 2009.
19. "Playstation Strikes Back," *MSNBC*, November 20, 2006.
20. Kotler and Keller, *Marketing Management*, 399.
21. "Adventure Travel Put at $89 billion Global Market," *Travel Market Report*, August 9, 2010.

**CHAPTER 9**

1. "Free Speech: Literary Lion Paul Coelho Reveals a Passion for Promoting the Online Piracy of His Own Books. He Thinks Publishers Should Follow Suit," *Newsweek*, February 6.
2. Philip Kotler and Kevin Lane Keller, *Marketing Management*, 13th ed. (Upper Saddle River, NJ: Pearson Prentice-Hall, 2009), 421.
3. "Gucci Renews GG-Logo Purses Priced Below $3,000 under New Chief," *Bloomberg.com*, June 1, 2009.
4. Kotler and Keller, *Marketing Management*, 416.
5. "Coca-Cola to Expand Honest Tea Distribution in U.S," *BusinessWeek*, April 23, 2010.
6. Kotler and Keller, *Marketing Management*, 416.
7. Central Blower website, centralblower.com
8. Grainger website, grainger.com
9. Lumenation website, lumenation.net
10. Anvil International website, anvilintl.com
11. David Janes Company website, janessupply.com
12. "Thanks, But No Thanks: Why More Doctors, Medical Schools and Hospitals Are Just Saying No to Drug Company Promotions," *Newsweek*, October 29, 2007.
13. Kotler and Keller, *Marketing Management*, 464–466.
14. "Wal-Mart's Painful Lessons," *BusinessWeek*, October 13, 2009.
15. "Scribd Pushes Content to Smartphones," *Wired*, February 24, 2010.

**CHAPTER 10**

1. "$5 Footlongs Turbocharge Subway," *MSNBC.com*, November 6, 2009.
2. Philip Kotler and Kevin Lane Keller, *Marketing Management*, 13th ed. (Upper Saddle River, NJ: Prentice-Hall, 2009), 476–491.
3. "3-D House of Horrors: Everything Old Is New Again, Even Generations-Old Technology," *Newsweek*, March 19, 2010.
4. Kotler and Keller, *Marketing Management*, 486–491.
5. Rick Levine, Christopher Locke, Doc Searls, and David Weinberger, *The Cluetrain Manifesto* (New York: Basic Books, 2000).
6. "Social Media—A Definition," *Amy Campbell's Web Log*, blogs.law.harvard.edu, January 21, 2010.
7. "New! Improved! It's School!" *Newsweek*, November 26, 2007.
8. Kotler and Keller, *Marketing Management*, 498–514.
9. "PC Marketing Gets Some Jazzing Up," *BusinessWeek*, April 13, 2009.

10. Kotler and Keller, *Marketing Management*, 498–514.
11. "Update: BP's Advertising Budget during the Spill Neared $100 Million," *Fortune*, September 1, 2010.
12. Kenneth Clow and Donald Baack, *Integrated Advertising, Promotion and Marketing Communications* (Upper Saddle River, NJ: Prentice Hall, 2002), 225–226.
13. "Consumers Blame Mad Men for Recession," *BusinessWeek*, April 22, 2009.
14. Clow and Baack, *Integrated Advertising, Promotion and Marketing Communications*, 266–281.
15. "Product Placement on the Rise in Video Games: Marketers Desperate to Engage Well-to-do Market of 132 Million Gamers," *Forbes*, July 21, 2006.
16. "How to Use Social Networking Sites for Marketing and PR," *New York Times*, December 24, 2008.
17. Google Blog Search website, blogsearch.google.com
18. Google Webmaster Central website, Search Engine Optimization page.
19. Google AdWords Overview page, adwords.google.com
20. "Online Video: Making Content Pay," *eMarketer.com*, August 2007.
21. "47 Outrageous Viral Marketing Examples over the Last Decade," *Ignitesocialmedia.com*, June 28, 2009.
22. "BIA's the Kelsey Group Forecasts U.S. Mobile Local Search Advertising Revenues to Reach $1.3B in 2013," *Kelsey Group press release*, February 24, 2009.
23. "Pricing Improvements? Taking Pulse of the Internet Space," *Investment News*, October 1, 2010.
24. "What Sells Online? Unsexy Newsletters," *BusinessWeek*, February 25, 2009.
25. "Social Media Is a Crucial Marketing Tool but Few Companies Are Ready—Study," *CosmeticsDesign.com*, September 20, 2010.
26. Kotler and Keller, *Marketing Management*, 514–518.
27. "Promotion Commotion," *Newsweek*, May 2, 2009.
28. Public Relations Society of America website, prsa.org
29. Kotler and Keller, *Marketing Management*, 527–528.
30. Make It Right website, makeitrightnola.org
31. "A Car, A Call, and A Terrible Crash," *Newsweek*, May 14, 2001.
32. "Google's PR Campaign: The Search Giant Hopes to Counter Charges of Monopoly Abuse with a Charm Offensive," *BusinessWeek*, April 29, 2009.
33. Kotler and Keller, *Marketing Management*, 527–528.
34. "Ambushed!" *Wall Street Journal*, January 25, 2010.
35. Clow and Baack, *Integrated Advertising, Promotion and Marketing Communications*, 524–537.
36. "Williams-Sonoma's Multi-Channel Marketing Leads to Niche Dominance," *AllBusiness, a Dun & Bradstreet Company*, March 1, 1999.
37. Williams-Sonoma, Inc. website, williams-sonomainc.com.
38. Kotler and Keller, *Marketing Management*, 551–562.

**CHAPTER 11**

1. Karen Braun, Wendy M. Tietz, and Walter T. Harrison, *Managerial Accounting*, 2nd ed. (Upper Saddle River, NJ: Prentice-Hall, 2010), 368–373.
2. "Xmarks Mulls Switch to Premium Service," *Wired*, September 30, 2010.
3. Braun, Tietz, and Harrison, *Managerial Accounting*, 320–333.

4. "In iPad, Publishers See Hope for Ad Revenue," *CBS News*, June 3, 2010.
5. Braun, Tietz, and Harrison, *Managerial Accounting*, 686–693.
6. "The Definition of Success," *Inc.*, February 1, 2007.
7. "Setting a Marketing Budget," *Image Works Studio*, March 19, 2010.
8. "2010 Online Marketing Study," *The Financial Brand*, August 23, 2010.
9. "Burrito Buzz—And So Few Ads," *BusinessWeek*, March 17, 2007.

**CHAPTER 12**

1. "The Miracle-Worker of the Delhi Metro," *BusinessWeek*, March 19, 2007.
2. Philip Kotler and Kevin Lane Keller, *Marketing Management*, 13th ed. (Prentice-Hall, 2009), 651–652.
3. "Finance vs. Marketing: Why They Still Don't See Eye to Eye on Measures of Return," *CFO Magazine*, May 1, 2007.
4. Kotler and Keller, *Marketing Management*, 62.
5. "Ready for the Worst: If Your Company Hits a Wall, Do You Have What It Takes to Make the Best of a Bad Situation?" *CFO Magazine*, February 2, 2009.

**CHAPTER 13**

1. "2011 Ford Fiesta—Road Test," *Car and Driver*, January 2010.
2. Ford website, One Ford Mission, ford.com
3. "Global Manufacturing Strategy Gives Ford Competitive Advantage," *Ford Press Release*, November 5, 2002.
4. NAICS 336111/ SIC 3711, census.gov, Automobile Manufacturing.
5. "Self Esteem: Do You Care What Kind of Car You Drive (I'm Afraid of Minivans)?" *Glamour*, May 1, 2009.
6. "Edmunds.com Looks Back at 2009 and Forecasts 2010 Automotive Trends," *Edmunds.com*, December 22, 2009.
7. National Highway Traffic Safety Administration website, nhtsa.gov, CAFÉ Overview.
8. "As Gas Costs Soar, Buyers Flock to Small Cars," *New York Times*, May 2, 2008.
9. Ibid.
10. "Crash Avoidance Publications," *National Highway Traffic Safety Administration*, nhtsa.gov, April 20, 2006.
11. "Ford's 2011 Fleet Vehicle Lineup Launches with 100 Percent Sustainable Powertrain Technology," *Ford Press Release*, April 22, 2010.
12. "2010 Ford Fiesta and Refreshed 2009 Focus to Satisfy U.S. Craving for Small Cars?" *Car and Driver*, May 2008.
13. "Suddenly Revved about Small Cars," *BusinessWeek*, January 10, 2006.
14. "First Drive: 2011 Ford Fiesta Aims to the New Subcompact King," *Autoblog.com*, April 28, 2010.
15. "2011: #1 in Affordable Small Cars," *US News and World Report*, March 26, 2010.
16. "Subcompact Cars: The Redesigned Honda Fit Tops Other Cars in this Group," *ConsumerReports.org*, March 2009.

17. "BMW Group U.S. Reports December 2009 Sales," *BMW Press Release*, January 5, 2010.
18. "GM Car Deliveries, United States, December 2009," gm.com, *General Motors investor information.*
19. "American Honda December Sales up 15.6 Percent," *Honda Press Release*, January 5, 2010.
20. "Hyundai Motor America Reports December and Full-Year 2009 Sales," *Hyundai Press Release*, January 5, 2010.
21. "Kia Motors America Announces December Sales," *Kia Press Release*, January 5, 2010.
22. "Mercedes-Benz USA Sales Jump 8.2% in December 2009," *Mercedes Press Release*, January 7, 2010.
23. "Nissan North America Announces December Sales," *Nissa Press Release*, January 5, 2010.
24. "Toyota Reports December and 2009 Sales," *Toyota Press Release*, January 5, 2010.
25. "American Suzuki Announces December Sales," *Suzuki Press Release*, January 1, 2010.
26. "Toyota Reports December and 2009 Sales," *Toyota Press Release* January 5, 2010.
27. "Volkswagen of America Announces December 2009 Sales," *Volkswagen Press Release*, January 5, 2010.
28. "Ford's Turnaround on Track, But Not Complete," *BusinessWeek*, July 22, 2009.
29. "Ford to Fix Brake Problem on Two Hybrid Models," *MSNBC*, February 4, 2010.
30. "Driving; My Life, My F-150 Pickup," *New York Times*, November 5, 2004.
31. "Ford Fiesta in Viewer-Controlled Reality Web Show," *Media Post Marketing Daily*, mediapost.com, September 7, 2010.
32. "Ford Bets the Fiesta on Social Networking," *Wired*, April 17, 2009.
33. "Ford's Fiesta Movement Keeps Moving after You've Moved On," *SocialCarNews.com*, June 24, 2010.
34. Ford Fiesta Movement "Chapter 1" website, chapter1. fiestamovement.com/
35. "Ford Fiesta Continues to Turn Heads; More than 6,000 Reservations Booked before Ordering Begins Monday" *Ford Press Release*, February 11, 2010.
36. "2011 Ford Fiesta: It's a Pretty Big Deal," *Ford Press Release*, May 17, 2010.
37. Ford Fiesta Buzz website, fordvehicles.com/cars/fiesta/buzz/
38. Ford Fiesta Comparison Table, www.fordvehicles.com
39. "Why Does It Cost so Much for Automakers to Develop New Models?" *Translogic*, translogic.aolautos.com, July 27, 2010.
40. "Ford Spending 25% of Marketing on Digital and Social Media," *BusinessWeek*, October 16, 2009.
41. "Ford Bets the Fiesta on Social Networking," *Wired*, April 17, 2009.
42. "First Test: 2011 Ford Fiesta SES," *Motor Trend*, April 30, 2010.
43. "Ford Now Has Industry's Highest Customer Satisfaction with Quality, New Survey Shows," *Ford Press Release*, April 19, 2010.
44. "The 10/20/30 Rule of PowerPoint," *Guy Kawasaki Blog*, blog.guykawasaki.com, December 30, 2005.

# INDEX